CITY TOWN & VILLAGE TRIVIA

Paperback edition first published 2020
ISBN: 9781838198329

For Sammy and Jethro, Arron and Ellie, Alicia and Kevin
May all your travels be happy ones. xxx

Backcover photo: Stepcote Hill, Exeter by Brian Highley

Introduction
Why Town Trivia?

In 2018 two Russians visited Salisbury and were later named as suspects in the attempted assassination of former spy Sergei Scripal and his daughter Yulia. Their chosen weapon was the nerve agent novichok.

When CCTV coverage of their visit was discovered and shown internationally on television the two men gained the support of Vladimir Putin who seemed to accept that their alibi was sufficiently watertight to fool the rest of the world. They claimed to have visited the Wiltshire city to admire the cathedral and view its famed 123-metre-tall spire, the tallest in Britain and second in Europe only to Strasbourg. Just the sort of thing all young Russian men do on a day-trip from London. If they'd carried out a bit more research they might have noted that, despite multiple buttresses, arches and ties, the spire tilts to the southeast by 27 inches making it fractionally shorter than its advertised height above ground level.

Every city, town and village in Great Britain has its one or two points of interest that can be found in every guide book and on every website. I have tried to search out the less obvious attractions.

I do apologise if I have failed to notice your favourite trivial titbit about your home location or even missed out your location entirely but I'm sure you'll find somewhere nearby that's entertaining.

The cities, towns and villages are listed in three sections - England, Scotland and Wales. Each section is in alphabetical order so it is easy to find your way around and this has enabled me to save a few trees by not including an index.

A note about Trivia. Trivia is plural, the singular is trivium. The word comes from the Latin for a place where a road splits into a fork forming three (tri) roads (viae). Some maintain that a notice board was often displayed at such locations for people to catch up on the latest news, others say that the point where the roads converged became a public meeting place where gossip was exchanged. Such a meeting point being a common place, 'commonplace' becoming yet another definition for trivial. The truth of the matter is we really don't know and you can't get more trivial than that.

ENGLAND

There are many locations and businesses in this book where I mention they have been 'on-going' or have never closed since some point in distant history. Sadly, at the time of writing, almost all of these have been temporarily closed due to Coronavirus, Covid 19

A

Abbotsbury, Dorset.
Abbotsbury is close to Chesil Beach, an 18-mile bank of pebbles graded from one end of the bank to the other by millions of years of tidal action from tiny to grapefruit-size. Those who have spent most of their lives in the village claim to be able to tell precisely where they are on the beach, if cast ashore blindfolded, just by picking up a pebble.

Abbotsbury Swannery is over 600 years old, now a protected breeding ground for all kinds of waterbirds, it was originally owned by the abbots who used decoys to attract swans that were not being tempted here for protection but to be killed and cooked for the table.

Abingdon-on-Thames, Oxfordshire.
From 1974 to 2012 this historic market town was known just by the name Abingdon but then 'on-Thames' was added to make it sound more up-market..

MG cars were manufactured here from 1929 to 1980 but the town is now probably better known for the

Morland Brewery which produces the excellent Old Speckled Hen ale. Workers at the MG plant had an elderly car they used for trips into town and this car was splattered with paint so was dubbed 'The Old Speckled 'Un'. An ale was brewed to celebrate the vehicle and when the drink became popular nationwide its name was adapted to make it more comprehensible to those who don't know about the spotty car.

Rock band Radiohead formed here when studying at Abingdon School in 1985.

Accrington, Lancashire
Accrington's Haworth Art Gallery boasts Europe's largest collection of Tiffany Glass.

Once they have name-dropped the famed Accrington Stanley Football Club, visitors must be sure to mention that this town produces the world's densest building bricks. The Accrington NORI, IRON backwards, was used in the construction of the Empire State Building and for the building that serves as the base for Blackpool Tower

Acton, Middlesex
Acton is in West London and its name means 'Oak Farm'. More than one third of the food consumed in London is produced on the Park Royal Industrial Estate which was once famed for the Guinness Brewery. Just as Guinness has returned to its native Ireland, Renault has returned to France but from 1926 to 1960 the 4CV and Dauphine were manufactured in Acton.

Acton boasted the UK's first Waitrose store.

The Who came from Acton which explains why Pete Townshend's solo album, 'All the Best Cowboys Have Chinese Eyes', includes the track 'Stardom in Acton'.

Albrighton, Shropshire

Albrighton is the most easterly settlement in Shropshire and is close to the M54 motorway. David Austin grows his acclaimed roses here and tourists are welcomed at the Plant Centre.

The Albrighton Moat Project is a fishing pond created for disabled people in 1992 by the 'Challenge Anneka' TV series featuring Anneka Rice.

The village has four pubs at the time of writing. Charles Dickens was staying at the pub now known as The Harp when he wrote about nearby Tong Church for his book 'The Old Curiosity Shop'. (See Holborn)

Alcester, Warwickshire

The ancient Alcester Abbey was largely demolished during Henry VIII's Dissolution of the Monasteries with the stone from the building being given to the Greville family who used it to construct Beauchamp Court, their family home. For the uninitiated, Beauchamp is pronounced Beecham.

Those interested in the quirky attributes of ecclesiastical buildings should note the unusual positioning of the clock on the tower of St Nicholas Church. This old timepiece looks to be awkwardly placed on the south-west corner of the 14th-century tower. This placement was intentional to make the clock visible from the High Street.

Aldeburgh, Suffolk
Aldeburgh is best known as the home of composer Benjamin Britten who founded the Snape Maltings, the location for the annual Aldeburgh Festival.

As well as music and poetry, discerning tourists visit here for two award-winning fish and chip shops.

103 Martello Towers were built along the southern British coast between 1808 and 1812 to withstand a speculated Napoleonic invasion. The largest and northernmost of these towers stands on the isthmus. It is the only remaining building from the fishing village of Slaughden which was washed into the sea in 1936. The tower is available to rent as a unique holiday apartment.

Alford, Lincolnshire
Pronounced 'Olford' and situated in an Area of Outstanding Natural Beauty at the foot of the Lincolnshire Wolds. The town's last bank closed in 2018 but at the time of writing there were still three supermarkets.

Holes Mill is the tallest, five-sailed windmill still operating to grind grain, the Mill also boasts a busy tearoom.

Alton, Hampshire
Alton is famed for its Jane Austin connections but everybody knows about this so it hardly counts as trivia.

In the 21st century the F in 'Sweet F.A.' is a swearword. 'Sweet F.A.' originated from Sweet Fanny Adams. Eight-year-old Fanny was brutally murdered in Alton during the summer of 1867 by a solicitor's clerk, Frederick Baker. Baker abducted her, dragged her to a hop garden where he killed her and then cut the body into pieces, some parts were never recovered. 5,000 attended Baker's execution on Christmas Eve of that same year.

In 1869 tinned mutton was introduced to British sailors and they claimed it was so disgusting it could be the missing remains of Fanny Adams. Naval slang adopted 'Sweet F.A.' to mean something worthless. The large cans in which the mutton was supplied were recycled for use as mess tins or cooking pots which are still known as Fannies. The grave of Fanny Adams can be visited in Alton cemetery.

Alton, Staffordshire
This Alton village had a population of only 1,266 at the last count but attracts approximately two million visitors each year thanks to the theme park built around the local mansion house, Alton Towers.

True tourists, as opposed to roller coaster riders, might be interested in a visit to the village to view the Chained Oak. Legend tells us that the Earl of Shrewsbury was returning home to Alton Towers when an old woman begged for a coin. The Earl refused to help her so she placed a curse on him saying that every time a branch fell from the oak tree a member of his family would die. That same night an unexpected storm took a branch from the tree and a member of the Earl's family died for no apparent reason. The Earl sent out his servants with orders to chain up every branch of the tree so none could fall. The chains remain to this day and the legend is the subject of the Hex attraction at the theme park.

Altrincham, Greater Manchester
Altrincham is the home of Cotton Traders who

supply vast quantities of leisurewear online. In a very unscientific survey I found that 100% of the people I asked (two guys in the pub) thought Cotton Traders took its name because it supplied clothing made from cotton. The company takes its name because it was co-founded by former England rugby captain Fran Cotton.

Alveston, South Gloucestershire

Few of the thousands of people who pass through here every day actually realise they have been anywhere close to Alveston. Alveston stands at the English end of the first Severn Bridge.

Many local people consider Alveston Parade shopping area to be the centre of the village but others relocate the centre to the late 16th-century Ship Inn.

There are two St Helens churches here. One still used as a church, the other converted for use as a corporate events venue.

Ambleside, Cumbria

Everyone knows that Ambleside stands in the Lake District National Park on the shores of Windermere, England's largest lake.

William Wordsworth wrote 'Daffodils' which was voted Britain's favourite poem in a 1995 BBC poll. Despite what anyone might tell you the setting for the poem was Ullswater, not Ambleside or anywhere else on the shores of Windermere.

Wordsworth's connection with Ambleside is that he worked here at the Old Stamp House for thirty years (1813 to 1843) when he was Distributor of Stamps for Westmoreland. He lived at nearby Rydal Mount throughout this period and until his death in 1850. (See Grasmere)

A poetry lover's visit to Ambleside must take in the Salutation Inn. Alfred Lord Tennyson worked on 'Morte d'Arthur' here and others who stayed included John Keats and Edward Fitzgerald.

Amersham, Buckinghamshire
Several episodes of 'Midsomer Murders' were filmed here but trivia enthusiasts will be far more impressed to learn that the Chuckle Brothers came to Amersham to record one of the 292 episodes of their 'Chucklevision'.

Amersham is divided into two distinct halves. The old town is down by the River Misbourne, the newer half developed around the railway station in the early 20th century. The Misbourne is sometimes reduced to such a low flow rate it almost disappears.

Ruth Ellis, the last woman to be hanged in Britain, was originally buried, according to custom, within the walls of Holloway Prison where she had been executed. When the prison was rebuilt in the 1970s the bodies of all the executed women were exhumed and Ellis was reburied in the churchyard of St Mary's Church in Amersham. The headstone, carrying her maiden name Ruth Hornby, was destroyed by her son Andy shortly before he committed suicide in 1982. (See Rhyl)

Amesbury Wiltshire
The Stonehenge World Heritage Site is seven and a half times larger than New York's Central Park. The first guidebook includes the 'fact' that Stonehenge survived Noah's flood. 7,500 copies of

the current Stonehenge Guide are sold each year. (See Marlborough). Many visitors cannot understand why the bluestones aren't blue. In the Westcountry bluestone meant holy stone. (See Clynderwen)

Andover, Hampshire
The Ministry of Defence is the town's largest employer but far more trivial than that is the fact that this is the home of Kelly's Directory listing businesses and tradespeople in particular towns.

Of course anyone who is genuinely English will already have recognised Andover as the home of Twinings Tea. If it comes as a shock that the tea is packed not grown here you might be surprised to learn that Yorkshire Tea has never been grown in Yorkshire!

'Love Is All Around', a mega hit for Wet Wet Wet was written by Reg Presley who performed the original hit version of the song with his band the Troggs. The Troggs; Presley, Ronnie Bond and Pete Staples were all born in Andover. After Wet Wet Wet spent fifteen weeks at the top of the UK charts Presley spent his unexpected royalty windfall on research into crop circles. James Blount was born here in 1974 and became a top pop performer after leaving the Army and dropping the letter O from his name.

Appleby Magna, Leicestershire
For such a tiny village, (the population at the last count was 1,084 and that includes four outlying hamlets and villages) Appleby Magna boasts a huge church, St Michael's and All Angels'. The size of the church reflects the fact that this was one of Leicestershire's wealthiest parishes throughout the 14th century.

Martyr Joyce de Appleby was burnt at the stake at the orders of Bloody Mary after refusing to convert to Catholicism. Joyce had been a resident at Moat House. Only the gatehouse survives from the original building.

Appleby-in-Westmorland, Cumbria

Until the 1974 local government changes this town was known simply as Appleby.

A good time to sneak into Appleby without being noticed is during the first week of June when the four-day annual Horse Fair takes place. This event is thought to go back even further than the 12th century when it became official, having been granted a charter by Henry II. Today the Fair attracts an estimated 10,000 Gypsies and Irish Travellers along with an additional 30,000 tourists from all over Britain.

George Washington's father and two of his half brothers were educated at Appleby Grammar School. Founding Father and future President Washington was set to follow them but in 1743 his father died suddenly and young George was spared the Atlantic crossing and classical education. TV reporter Helen Skelton and her footballing brother Gavin did make it to the Grammar School.

Arundel, West Sussex

Everyone knows about the fairytale castle but a lesser known fact is that people born in Arundel are known as Mullets. This has nothing at all to do with their hairstyles but because mullet, the fish, were regularly caught in the Arun river.

Arundel had one of the world's first Scout groups,

formed in 1908 within weeks of the birth of the Scouting movement.

Local tradition has it that if you shake yourself on the Arun Bridge on March 1st you will be free of fleas for the rest of the year. It is claimed that secret tunnels lead out of the castle grounds but, as with secret tunnels throughout the kingdom, nobody was able to show me any of these. There are, however, a few known tunnels connecting the cellars of buildings in the High Street.

Ascot, Berkshire

I'm sure most people think of Ascot as a town built to service a racecourse. The course is owned by the Crown with the royal family turning up in droves for the main annual race meeting in June which screws up the traffic for miles around.

John Lennon and Yoko Ono lived at Tittenhurst Park for two years. The country house, in its 72 acre estate, then became the home of Ringo Starr who sold it to Sheikh Zayed bin Sultan Al Nahyan, President of the United Arab Emirates, in 1988.

Lennon originally purchased the property from Peter Cadbury for £145,000 (more than £2.million in 2020) and then spent twice this amount on renovations including hand-woven rugs and a man-made lake, without planning permission, to be viewed from their bedroom window. It is here that Lennon and Ono recorded 'Imagine' which reminds us all to 'Imagine no possessions!'. The 'Hey Jude' album cover photos, the last of the four Beatles together, were taken at Tittenhurst Park.

Not quite as impressive as assorted Beatles but Girls

Aloud singer Sarah Harding was born in Ascot and, at the time of writing, the town is the home of Wet Wet Wet's Marti Pellow (See Andover) and radio/TV presenter Chris Evans.

Ashbourne, Derbyshire

Due to its location, Ashbourne gives itself the dual titles of Gateway to Dovedale and Gateway to the Peak District. At the time of writing the population of 7,112 had a choice of eleven pubs.

Until 2003 this was the home of Carnation Condensed Milk. As the name suggests Ashbourne Mineral Water came from here although for many years the water was taken to Buxton by tanker for bottling.

If you require evidence to convince Vladimir Putin and the rest of the world you have visited here it is worth noting that the church spire rises to a height of 215-feet (66m).

The Royal Shrovetide Football Match takes place at Ashbourne over two days each year with one half of the population playing the other half on a pitch consisting of the entire town with goals three miles apart. It is claimed the noun 'Derby', meaning a sporting contest between two local teams, originated from the Royal Shrovetide Football Match. (See Derby)

Prior to England's win in the 1966 World Cup the German team trained on the town's actual football pitch.

Roy Wood, leader of numerous bands including Wizard whose 'I Wish It Could Be Christmas Every Day' is an essential part of the festive season, is a resident.

Ashburton, Devon
Devonians once enjoyed a drink known as Ashburton Pop, remembered as a strong sparkling beer, that disappeared in 1765 when the brewer died without ever writing down his recipe.

Ashburton was the first place in Britain to elect a Monster Raving Loony into public office when, in 1989, pub landlord Alan Hope made it unopposed onto the Town Council. Hope went on to become Deputy Mayor and then Mayor of the town.

Ashby-de-la-Zouch, Leicestershire
Formerly known simply as Ashby the latter part of the name was added after the Norman Conquest when the town became the property of the La Zouch family during the reign of Henry III.

The brick frontages of many buildings in Market Street are late additions concealing attractive timber structures.

Ivanhoe College takes its name from Sir Walter Scott's novel which is set around Ashby-de-la-Zouch Castle and includes the famous, but purely fictional, occasion when Prince John arranged an archery tournament won by Robin Hood.

Legendary American jazz bassist Charles Mingus wrote and recorded a piece titled 'Ashby-de-la-Zouch', thought to be a joke aimed at Irving Ashby who played guitar on the recording.

Ashford, Kent
Ashford station opened in the mid 19th century on the

London to Dover line and was closed in 1982 due to lack of use. In 1994 the railway returned to Ashford with the opening of Ashford International, serving Eurostar trains. There was a temporary closure of the station from 2007 to 2009 when Ebsfleet International opened but it came back into service following a petition.

The Ashford section of the M20 is part of Operation Stack where HGVs park up when queuing for the Tunnel.

The National Cycle Track has two routes through Ashford and if you fall off your bike the town boasts the oldest surviving St John Ambulance unit.

Askrigg, North Yorkshire

Situated in Wensleydale, Askrigg has a population of less than 600 and they all seem to run cafes serving tourists. This is one of those rare places where surveys regularly show the population to be precisely split, 50% male - 50% female.

Most of the visitors to those many cafes then head straight out of the village for the gentle walk to Mill Gill Force. This waterfall doesn't make a spectacularly long drop but it is undoubtedly very photogenic.

Atherstone, Warwickshire

Watling Street, the old Roman road, runs through Atherstone. This stretch of the road is best known for the Shrove Tuesday football game which celebrated its 800th anniversary in 1999. The only rule is that players are not permitted to kill one another.

Axbridge, Somerset
Television viewers will remember the early 1990s commercials for the NatWest Bank in which Axbridge Town Hall stood in for the bank. Ironically, shortly after the commercial was filmed the NatWest's branch in the town was closed down. More recently Axbridge featured in the hot air balloon commercial for Thatchers Cider which is produced in nearby Sandford.

Axminster, Devon
In the days when I wrote the questions for Trivial Pursuit games Axminster Carpets were one of the few organisations or individuals to sue me, we settled out of court rather than waste the time.

The question was on the lines of: 'In what town has your carpet been made if it was made on the original Axminster looms?' and I stick by the answer which was 'Wilton'. Following a fire in 1828 the remaining looms from Axminster were sold to Blackmores of Wilton, near Salisbury. (See Wilton)

Until 1844 part of Axminster was over the county border in Dorset.

Aylesbury, Buckinghamshire
What have developed into the Paralympic Games began here, at Stoke Mandeville Hospital, the town is also famed for the Roald Dahl Children's Gallery and the Waterside Theatre.

The wonderfully eccentric, singer-songwriter John Otway is from Aylesbury.
Although the tasty Aylesbury Duck is named after the town and features on the coat- of-arms it is not certain that the breed originated here. All types of white duck

were bred in Aylesbury during the 18th century, not for their meat but for the feathers which were used as quill pens.

Aylsham, Norfolk

Edward III's third son John of Gaunt is pictured on the town sign and was Lord of the Manor here from 1372 although it is doubtful he ever visited the town.

In 2008 Aylsham became a plastic-free town but there were problems policing this due to lack of public support. The Aylsham branch of Tesco's supermarket was constructed from wood and recyclable plastics and claims to be the greenest in the world.

B

Badminton, Gloucestershire
This village is divided into two halves, Great Badminton and Little Badminton.

The Duke of Beaufort's residence, Badminton House, is here and it is this seat of the Somerset family that gave its name to the racket sport. During the Second World War the Dowager Queen Mary was evacuated from London to Badminton House.

Badminton doesn't have its own railway station but it does have a small airfield.

Bagshot, Surrey
Bagshot hit the headlines in 2009 when hundreds of protestors demonstrated against the closure of the local branch of the Nationwide Building Society, the village's last remaining bank.

Shortly after Michael Gove gave his support to the protest the bank closed down to be replaced by an ATM outside the Co-op.

The England rugby squad train at Pennyhill Park Hotel and Prince Edward lives at Bagshot Park.

The former Jolly Farmer pub is now a golf supplies shop and, you can probably guess from the clues above, Bagshot has had a Conservative council for many, many years.

Bakewell, Derbyshire
The Peak District National Park Authority is based

here. This is one of many UK towns that has tried, but failed, to keep out Costa Coffee.

An ongoing debate questions the difference between the Bakewell Tart and the Bakewell Pudding.

The nationally known Bakewell Tart is a shortcrust pastry case with jam at the bottom, the case filled with sponge and, optionally, a few toasted almonds scattered on top. A Bakewell Pudding requires a similar pastry case with jam but the jam should rise to the top through a filling of almond paste when baked. Mr Kipling's Cherry Bakewells are also available but a baker I talked to in Bakewell claimed these bear no resemblance to either the proper puddings or the traditional tarts.

In 1974 a 17-year-old council worker, Stephen Downing, was jailed for the murder of a legal secretary in Bakewell Cemetery. In 2002 the conviction was overturned after Downing had served 27 years in prison. This is considered to be the longest miscarriage of justice in British legal history.

Baldersdale, County Durham
Traditionally in the North Riding of Yorkshire but in 1974 Baldersdale was moved into County Durham.

There is a busy YHA Youth Hostel but the village is probably best known as the home of Hannah Hauxwell (1926-2018) who gained fame in the 1970s thanks to a TV documentary showing how she battled to operate a farm in very frugal conditions.

Baldock, Hertfordshire
Baldock stands on the Great North Road and Icknield Way crossroads making it a stopping point for

travellers throughout the ages. Charles I came by on his way to London following his arrest. Methodist preacher John Wesley was a visitor and Dick Turpin is on the list of those who passed through. Daniel Defoe mentions Baldock in his 'A Tour Through the Whole Island of Great Britain' but that accolade applies to just about anywhere you care to visit.

Kayser Bondor stockings came from here, manufactured in a factory that turned out parachutes during World War Two.

In his 'Green Man' Kingsley Amis has Baldock as the closest town to the pub run by his main character whilst Monica Dickens' autobiography refers to her frequent visits to the George and Dragon. (Now The George)

Baldock hosts an annual music festival, the Charter Fair, and a beer festival. The legendary 14th century giant Jack o'Legs who, like Robin Hood, is said to have robbed the rich to feed the poor is associated with the town.

Bamburgh, Northumberland
Dunes and beaches attract tourists here with most of them failing to realise this was the birthplace of Grace Horsley Darling.

Grace was the seventh of nine children. She was born in her grandfather's cottage at Bamburgh. International celebrity came her way after her participation in the rescue of nine crew members from the shipwrecked Forfarshire in 1838.

Financial gifts and marriage proposals flooded in, even a £50 reward from Queen Victoria, In October

1842, four years after her heroic rescue, at the age of 26, Grace died of tuberculosis in Bamburg. She is buried with her parents at St Aidan's Church. Bamburgh's museum, dedicated to local seafarers, includes important tributes to Grace's achievement. Grace was such a huge national attraction memorials to her are to be found all over the country with the most distant from Bamburgh I have found to be seen in a churchyard in Devon. (See Exeter)

Bampton, Devon
The Bampton Pony Fair began selling Exmoor Ponies as recently as 1856 but the cattle market, of which it became a part, has been an annual event since the 13th century. With an eye to pulling in the punters Bampton Fair always takes place during the October schools' half-term holiday.

Bampton, Oxfordshire
Strangers here can gain extra kudos by knowing that many locals call the place Bampton-in-the-Bush.

Bampton Castle is now a private home. The Arts Centre and post office are housed in what was the Market House, which later served as the Town Hall.

The Morris dancing group was founded some 600 years ago and the Bampton Classical Opera has been around for quite some time but to prove your knowledge of this place you need to know about the Society for the Preservation of Ancient Junketing. Members, known as Spajers, organise the annual Bampton Shirt Race. Rules for the race vary from time to time but there used to be 14 pubs in the village and racers participated in teams of two wearing night-shirts with one competitor pushing the other in a pram or 'borrowed' supermarket trolley. A drink having to be taken in each of the 14 hostelries.

Banbury, Oxfordshire
The only difference I can see between Banbury Cakes and the more famous Eccles Cakes is that the former are oval and the latter circular. (See Chorley and Eccles)

There's a castle and a canal but you will not find the original cross from the famous 'Banbury Cross' rhyme. At one time Banbury had several crosses but these were destroyed in 1600 by the Puritans leaving the town crossless until 1859. The current stone cross was erected to commemorate the marriage of Queen Victoria's eldest child, also called Victoria although the Queen's first name was Alexandrina, to Frederick Prince of Prussia.

The bronze statue of the 'Fine Lady Upon a White Horse' is even more modern than the cross, it was unveiled by horse-loving Princess Anne in 2005.

Benjamin Franklin's grandfather, Thomas, is buried here and the inventive Founding Father came to visit the grave in 1758.

Camp comedian Larry Grayson was born in Banbury as was disgraced pop performing paedophile Paul (Gary Glitter,) Gadd. TV cook Gordon Ramsay moved here when he was 16.

Bardon Mill, Northumberland
The village's annual activities include a leek growing competition and the Bardon Mill and Roman Empire Conkers Championships.

Ridley Hall stands just outside the village, it was the

ancestral home of the late Queen Mother's Bowes-Lyons family.

Barking, London

Barking was once famous for its codbangers. Fish brought to the town were kept alive in underwater tanks prior to being killed by a knock on the head from a codbanger. This fish fetched a premium price at Billingsgate thanks to its freshness.

Two tracks on Neil Young's 'Harvest' album, 'A Man Needs a Maid' and 'There's a World', were recorded in Barking Assembly Hall with the London Symphony Orchestra.

Billy Bragg was born here as was David Howell Evans, better known as The Edge, from Irish rock band U2, his parents were Welsh. (See Chinnor)

Barnard Castle, County Durham

The main tourist attraction here is the Bowes Museum with art works including paintings by Goya and El Greco but the one item many come to see is the fish-catching Silver Swan automaton which regularly turns up on TV antiques shows.

Walter Scott was a regular visitor to Rokeby Hall, the home of his friend John Sawrey Morritt. Scott's epic poem 'Rokeby' begins with a guard standing at the top of the tower of the Castle.

Charles Dickens came here, staying with his illustrator Hablot (Phiz) Browne at the King's Head whilst researching 'Nicholas Nickleby'. Dickens popped in to William Humphrey's clock-making shop opposite the hotel to enquire about an exceptional clock he had seen. William explained the clock had been made by his son Humphrey. Dickens chose the title 'Master Humphrey's Clock' for the magazine in which he serialised 'Barnaby Rudge' and 'The Old Curiosity Shop.' (See Holborn)

William Wordsworth, Daniel Defoe, J M W Turner and Dominic Cummings are among others who have visited the town, although there is no evidence to suggest the first three came here to check their eyesight prior to a long drive home

Barnet, Outer London

Also known as High Barnet or Chipping Barnet, the borough is within the Metropolitan Green Belt and boasts sixty-seven Sites of Importance for Nature Conservation and eight Local Nature Reserves.

The A5 forms most of the western border and the North Circular crosses the borough, add to this several tube stations, national rail services and plenty of buses and this becomes a very easy place to get into, and out of.

Charles Dickens is said to have been a regular at the Red Lion on Barnet Hill, Oliver Twist first meets the Artful Dodger in Barnet High Street.

Scottish Congregationalist and explorer Dr David Livingstone lived in Barnet. He can be found at number 44 on the list of 71 people who appear on the 'Sgt Pepper' album sleeve. (See Denbigh)

On the evening before they won the World Cup in 1966 the England football team went to watch 'Those Magnificent Men in Their Flying Machines' at the Hendon cinema in the Borough of Barnet.

Barnsley, South Yorkshire

Even on southern pub menus a double lamb loin chop, cut right across the saddle, is known as a Barnsley Chop. The town's Kings Head pub and Brooklands Hotel both claim to have originated this culinary delight.

Barnsley residents are said to be Britain's biggest sniffers of snuff which might be explained by the proximity of the town to snuff makers Wilsons & Company (Sharrow) Ltd.

In his 'The Road to Wigan Pier' George Orwell makes strong criticism of Barnsley council's waste of money on a new Town Hall rather than improving the living conditions of miners. (See Coatbridge)

I have family in villages not far from Barnsley who all insist the flat cap is no longer a fashion statement and none of them own a pet ferret or whippet. I have been to several weddings here and never witnessed what some claim is the local custom of attaching potato chips to the bridal gown.

Two of the Arctic Monkeys and members of Darkness studied music at Barnsley College. Folk singer Kate Rusby has lived here since birth. Heavy metal band Saxon, part inspiration for the hilarious rockumentary 'This Is Spinal Tap', includes members from Barnsley.

Arthur Scargill, leader of the National Union of Mineworkers and founder/leader of the Socialist Labour Party was born in Barnsley in 1938, three years after Michael Parkinson and five years after cricket umpire Dickie Bird.

Barnstaple, North Devon
Barnstaple claims to be the oldest borough in the United Kingdom. People here will tell you that the town stands on Barnstaple Bay but this is known as Bideford Bay to residents of the nearby town.

Visitors to Barnstaple regularly head for the Pannier Market. Originally known as the Vegetable Market, local farmers brought their produce here in large pannier baskets. Butcher's Row runs the length of the outside of the Pannier Market, ten shops with attractive stone pilasters, only one was operating as a butcher when I last visited.

Barnstaple claims to have the largest crematorium chapel in England, Wales or Northern Ireland with seating for 250 mourners.

Barnstaple rose to international fame in the 1970s as the home of Norman Scott, a male model who blackmailed Liberal Party leader and local MP Jeremy Thorpe over an alleged homosexual relationship. Thorpe's colleagues are said to have phoned an accomplice, former airline pilot Andrew Newton, with instructions to go to Barnstaple and intimidate Scott but, due to a poor phone connection, Newton went to Dunstable in Bedfordshire.

Barrow-in-Furness, Cumbria
Furness was once an outpost of Lancashire, it now promotes itself as a holiday area thanks to its location between Morecambe Bay and the Lake District. Natives are called Barovians. Early in the 20th century this was known as the English Chicago, not due to a gangster problem but thanks to its rapid growth, in more recent years Barrow has become dubbed as the capital of blue-collar Britain because of

its solid working class identity.

Barrow was the setting for Victoria Wood's 'Housewife, 49', based on the World War Two diary of local housewife, Nella Last.

The borough council was the first public body in Britain to face corporate manslaughter charges when a badly maintained air conditioning unit at Forum 28, the arts centre, resulted in seven deaths amongst 172 cases of Legionnaire's Disease. The council was cleared of manslaughter charges but was fined £125,000. The contractor in charge of the air conditioning settled a £1.5 million claim by the Council for damages.

Basildon, Essex
Created as a New Town in 1948 Basildon was an overspill area for London. Basildon town is now one of the most densely populated places in Great Britain.

1980s glam rockers Depeche Mode formed here and Basildon was the home of Keith Chapman, best known as the creator of 'Bob the Builder'.

Bassenthwaite, Cumbria
There are sixteen lakes in the Lake District but the only one actually called a lake is Bassenthwaite Lake.

Basingstoke, Hampshire
Apart from to its residents, Basingstoke is probably best known as a place you cannot quite see from the M3 when travelling from the South West to either Heathrow or Gatwick Airports.

Lancashire comedian George Formby came here in 1944 to film parts of 'She Snoops to Conquer' and

Channel 4's comedy 'Green Wing' is partly set in the town's North Hampshire Hospital.

Basingstoke is often dubbed Doughnut City due to its many roundabouts. A competition was held in the early 2000s to find the town's worst roundabout and shortly after that there were sponsored theatre and ballet performances staged on roundabouts to keep traffic-jammed motorists entertained.

Bath, Somerset

Ask people what converts a town to a city and most will say a cathedral. This is not correct. There are numerous towns in Great Britain with cathedrals just as there are several city's, like Bath, with no cathedral. A Royal Charter makes the difference between a town and a city.

All tourists to this stunning city know about the Royal Crescent and the Roman Baths with afternoon tea in the Pump Room an essential ritual. In 'The Pickwick Papers,' Charles Dickens describes taking the waters, which can be sampled in the Pump Room. Pickwick's servant, Sam Weller, describes the water with its supposed medicinal properties as tasting like 'warm flat irons.' Never having tasted a flat iron I cannot concur with this description but let's just say I can see where Sam Weller was coming from as this is certainly not a beverage you would pay for in a pub.

Emperor Haile Selassie spent four of his exile years at Fairfield House.

Bath almost lost its UNESCO World Heritage Site status in 2009 due to plans for redevelopment of the Riverside area. The City retained its status but UNESCO has requested to be consulted on future developments and demanded that Bath should do more to attract world-class architects for future projects.

Sir Thomas Gainsborough lived and painted in Bath. Jane Austen and her family spent five years here at four different addresses. The city honours her with the Jane Austen Centre, a City Walk, and is the setting for much of 'Northanger Abbey' and 'Persuasion'. The author however was never a lover of the city and wrote to her sister; 'It will be two years tomorrow since we left Bath for Clifton with what happy feelings of escape.'

Batley, West Yorkshire

Rocky, Crunch Creams and multi-coloured Party Rings are just a few of the biscuit varieties produced by Fox's who began baking at a terraced house in Batley in 1853. The town is still the home of the company's head office and main factory. Production Manager for several years was James Montgomerie whose son, Colin, is a world renowned golfer.

The town is still best-remembered for Batley Variety Club where, from 1966 to 1977, the world's greatest entertainers were lured to perform in front of Chicken in a Basket devouring Yorkshire punters. Louis Armstrong, Shirley Bassey, Johnny Mathis, Roy Orbison and the Hollies all performed here. The venue became The Frontier, offering a mix of variety, boxing, snooker and darts. In 2017 entertainment came to an end when the club was turned into a gym.

Joseph Priestley, discoverer of oxygen, lived in neighbouring Birstall. Priestley's invention of soda water leads some to worship him as 'the father of the soft drink' and others to condemn him as 'the man who ruined a billion tots of whisky.'

Battle, East Sussex
It was from Telham Hill that William the Conqueror sighted the English army gathering on Senlac Hill some 1.5km away in the build-up to the Battle of Hastings.

Some claim the battle took place around the abbey but the abbey wasn't built until some time later to commemorate the battle. The location of the high altar is said to have been chosen because it was the spot where Harold died. The town grew up around the abbey with the abbey gateway dominating the southern end of the main street. Most of the abbey has disappeared with the remaining cloisters being occupied by Battle Abbey School.

The most famous record of the Battle of Hastings, which did not take place in Hastings, is the Bayeux Tapestry, which is not a tapestry, it's an embroidery. It is also very unlikely that Harold was killed by an arrow in the eye, he was more probably clubbed to death. The famed embroidery's image of Harold, apparently with an arrow in his eye, is almost certainly due to overzealous restoration. Sketches made prior to restoration show a long dotted line of stitch marks without fletching (feathers at the end) indicating that Harold was in fact holding a spear.

Historic records show that both sides in the battle took a lunch break.

Beaconsfield, Buckinghamshire
When the Beaconsfield Service Station opened on the M40 in 2009 it caused local controversy by becoming an attraction for young, late-night revellers who could find little to do in the town. Planned as Britain's biggest service area with the biggest filling station it was overtaken on both counts by Cobham in 2012.

Beaconsfield is probably more famous for those buried here than for its nightlife. G K Chesterton,

Edmund Burke and poet Edmund Waller all lie here.

Future Prime Minister Tony Blair contested the seat in 1982 and lost to Tim Smith. Smith was later involved with Neil Hamilton in the cash-for-questions scandal.

Bekonscot Model Village, which opened in 1929, was the first such village in the world.

In 2008 the Daily Telegraph named Beaconsfield as Britain's Richest Town based on its average house price of £684,474.

Several scenes in the classic 'Brief Encounter' were filmed here. Beaconsfield was the birthplace of author Terry Pratchett, other famous residents have included 'Play in a Day' guitarist Bert Weedon, Bee Gee Barry Gibb, Benjamin Disraeli, Enid Blyton and Zoe Ball.

Beccles, Suffolk
You know a place doesn't have a lot to offer when it lists one of its main attractions as the Annual Duck race. Beccles boasts two duck races. Race One involves individual ducks, Race Two brings out the big guns in the form of corporate sponsored ducks.

Bedale, North Yorkshire
This area was once known as Hangshire because of the many gallows that once stood on the appropriately-named Hang Bank in the village of Finghall. These were kept busy executing marauding Scots,

Bedale was famed for horse racing in the 18th century. Three-year-old races were first run in England here.

Big Sheep Little Cow petting zoo can be found down by Bedale Beck.

The classic 1945 war film 'The Way to the Stars,' starring Sir John Mills and Sir Michael Redgrave, is set in the Midlands but most of it was filmed in and around Bedale.

Bedford, Bedfordshire

Bedford claims to have one of the largest Italian communities outside Italy. Most Bedfordians have Italians somewhere in the family. Bedford also boasts Britain's largest Sikh temple outside London.

During World War Two the BBC was viewed as a probable target so the music department was moved to here.

Each May Bedford hosts Britain's largest one-day river rowing event which is the second-largest regular outdoor event after Notting Hill Carnival?

Bedford by the Sea is a celebration involving the dumping of tons of sand in the centre of the landlocked town.

'Some Mothers Do 'Ave 'Em' was mostly filmed in Bedford, scenes in 'Batman Begins' and its follow-up 'The Dark Knight' were made in nearby Cardington Sheds with many local people employed as extras. Sportsmen from the town include boxer Joe Bugner, rugby player Martin Bayfield and Olympic ski jumper Eddie (The Eagle) Edwards.

Beer, Devon

This has to be one of the most attractively named towns on the planet but sadly, it is not named after the beverage. Beer takes its name from the Old English word 'bearu' meaning 'grove'.

What look like mats are actually old rubber conveyor

belts, laid along the steep pebble beach to give walkers' shoes a better grip.

Many visitors to the town head for the genuinely fascinating Beer Quarry Caves which are a great choice on a damp day. Take a sweater as the caves can be chilly even in the heat of the summer. One of the local residents is your guide for the hour-long tour and kids love having to wear a miner's helmet while spotting the rare bats.

Few visitors discover anything about the cliffs at Beer from where bacteria were taken in 2008 and then flown to the International Space Station still residing in the bits of rock in which they had been extracted. This became an interesting news story as many of the bacteria were still alive after 553 days in space and continued to be studied in laboratories back on earth. The ability of bacteria to survive on the cliffs at Beer made them important in the investigation of survival in extreme conditions and possibly enabling them to break down rocks and produce oxygen on some future Lunar or Martian manned colony.

Belford, Northumberland

To the east of Belford stands an 18th century, cylindrical stone tower tapering up to its conical Welsh slate roof. Some sources claim this to have been a dovecote, others say it was a windmill. I can find no evidence for it ever having been used as either.

Belford was a coaching stop on the A1 from London to Edinburgh (why do they never say Edinburgh to London?). A by-pass opened in 1983 so the town can once again stage events in the High Street and Market Street.

Belper, Derbyshire
Samuel Slater was born in Belper in 1768. He was fully aware of America's desire to develop cotton spinning machines like those pioneered in England but there was a law against exporting designs so he memorised as much as he could.

In 1789, at the age of 21, Slater set sail for New York to pass on his remembered information and become the founder of the USA's Industrial Revolution. Back home in Belper he will forever be remembered as Slater the Traitor.

Belton, Leicestershire
I found very little of excitement here other than one of the country's few remaining free-standing maypoles if that's your kind of thing.

Belton, Lincolnshire
Cromwell's cavalry met up with Royalists near Belton Park resulting in three soldiers who died during the skirmish being buried at Belton Church. Apart from that not much at this Belton either.

Berkhamsted, Hertfordshire
A large part of this area in the Chiltern Hills is designated an Area of Outstanding Natural Beauty.

After the Battle of Hastings in 1066 King Harold's beaten leaders surrendered to the Normans in Berkhamsted.

A major local employer is the British Film Institute's National Archive, most local industries have declined with an increase in the numbers commuting from here to London.

During his exile General de Gaulle lived in a country villa close to Berkhamsted and, with his wife Yvonne, he attended the Church of the Sacred Heart which has now been relocated to larger premises in Park Street.

Local resident John of Gadsden was the inspiration for Chaucer's Doctor of Phisick in 'The Canterbury Tales', Chaucer was clerk of works at Berkhamsted Castle. The Davies boys (also known by the double surname Llewelyn Davies although the family didn't use this) gave J M Barrie the idea for 'Peter Pan' in which several characters are named after them. Novelist Graham Greene was born here.

The art deco Rex has been named the most beautiful cinema in Britain by the Daily Telegraph. At the time of writing the owner/manager, James Hannaway, still frequently steps out to introduce films.

Berrow, Somerset
Berrow is a small coastal village. The Blue Flag beach is known for the wreck of the SS Norman, a ship that ran aground in 1897. The wreck made news in 2003 when the Council suggested it would have to be removed to save them from possible compensation claims if jet-skiers hit the wreck while it was submerged at high tide.

A golf course on Berrow Dunes is a Site of Special Scientific Interest thanks to the existence of the rare lizard orchid which is a flower not a reptile.

Berrow, Worcestershire
The parish church, dedicated to St Faith, displays a plaque commemorating an 18th century murder. Edward Gummery, his wife Elizabeth, nine-year-old daughter Anne and a visiting relative, Thomas Sheen,

were all murdered in Berrow and the killer(s) never found.

Berwick-upon-Tweed, Northumberland
Once a Scottish burgh, known as South Berwick to avoid confusion with North Berwick in East Lothian, there are still those who dispute Berwick being located in England. As recently as 2008 an SNP MP called for Berwick to become part of Scotland. Berwick Rangers Football Club play in the Scottish league and the Berwick Rugby Union FC play in the Scottish Rugby Union.

There were claims that Berwick was at war with Russia. An edition of the Guardian in December 1966 claimed the London correspondent of Pravda had visited the Mayor of Berwick and brokered a declaration of peace. Robert Knox, the Mayor, told the journalist, 'Please tell the Russian people through your newspaper that they can sleep peacefully in their beds.' This apocryphal story was quickly picked up by the Press Association and reported across the USA.

The Berwick at war with Russia theory began with the town's doubtful location, England? or Scotland?, leading to Queen Victoria signing the declaration of the Crimean War as, 'Victoria, Queen of Great Britain, Ireland, Berwick-upon-Tweed and all British Dominions.' When the Treaty of Paris brought an end to the war Berwick-upon-Tweed was missed out leaving it still at war with Russia. The truth of the situation is that the 1746 Wales and Berwick Act made it clear that any reference to England included Berwick.

Beverley, East Riding of Yorkshire
With a floor area of 3,489 square metres - 37,555

square feet Beverley Minster claims to be England's largest Parish Church. (See Boston. See Hull)

Bexley, Greater London
Formerly in Kent, Bexley has a church spire worthy of note to casual visitors and prospective Russian assassins.

St Mary the Virgin has a fairly standard square tower faced with local pebbles. Atop this tower is an octagonal cone inexplicably balanced on a truncated pyramid.

Described by Edward Burne-Jones as 'the beautifulest place on Earth', Red House was commissioned, designed and lived in by Arts and Crafts Movement founder William Morris. The house is now a National Trust property and is open to the public.

Kate Bush was born in Bexleyheath Maternity Hospital, Led Zeppelin bassist John Paul Jones was born in nearby Sidcup.

Bicester, Oxfordshire
As the crow flies Bicester is equidistant from London and Birmingham, being 51 miles from each. Bicester Village is a shopping outlet with a purpose-built high street claimed by some to be the same length as the Champs-Elysee and by others to be the same length as Oxford Street. (All three are 1.2 miles long so both claims are correct). Few British people from outside the immediate area have ever heard of Bicester Village but in 2017 it attracted 6.6 million tourists, more than the National Gallery or Tate Modern, and the majority of these shoppers were holidaymakers from China. The only place in Britain to attract more Chinese tourists is Buckingham Palace. Bicester railway station actually makes

announcements in Mandarin. China's main online tourist information sites describe the Village as a 'must-go place for visitors to London.'

Not only do the nouveau riche Chinese appreciate cut-price designer products and the facility to claim back VAT, their culture demands they return home from travels with gifts for family and friends so shopping takes precedence over having a good time.

Bicknoller, Somerset

St George's Church has a magnificent mediaeval carved wooden screen, originally made for St Peter's at Huish Champflower and transferred to here in 1726. The churchyard is shadowed by a massive elm tree said to be more than 1,000 years old. The church has a memorial to Archbishop of Canterbury, William Temple, whose only known connection to the place is that he came here a few times on holiday.

The Bicknoller Inn, known locally as 'The Bic', is what I would call a 'proper pub' offering fine ales, a good quality Sunday carvery and I can personally recommend their Fish and Chips.

Biddenden, Kent

In 1100 conjoined twins, Mary and Eliza Chulkhurst, known as the Biddenden Maids, were born here, they survived together for 34 years.

The village is in the Weald of Kent, All Saints Church is mostly 13th century probably on the site of an earlier Saxon church.

Wines, cider and juices are produced from the orchards and vineyards.

Bideford, Devon

Everyone visiting Bideford takes a selfie by the bridge

but how many of them notice that the 24 arches of the bridge are all of different sizes. Although I cannot find a definitive source to support the theory, to me it seems logical that, as was the custom at the time, the building of the bridge was sponsored by local guilds, each contributing a different sum of money, hence the differing sizes of the arches they purchased.

Not quite up to the fame of the Salem Witch Trials, Bideford did have its own witch trials in 1682 involving a trio of local women. All three were hanged after one had claimed to have met the devil. A memorial plaque claims these were the last people to be executed in England for witchcraft but there is evidence of later executions that failed to gain Bideford's notoriety.

Just outside Bideford you will find The Big Sheep. A family theme park with rides, a brewery and a gin distillery but mainly sheep and kids love it.

Bilbrook, Stafordshire

Bilbrook takes the first part of its name from 'billers', an old word for watercress, so just a short step from that to working out that this peppery salad leaf was grown in the local brook.

James Whild Lea (Jim Lea), bass guitarist with glam rock popsters Slade, was brought up here at his parents' pub, The Grange. The Grange closed to become an Indian restaurant which, at the time of writing, is also closed.

Bingley, West Yorkshire

Best known as half of the name of a building society that became a bank that was sold to Abbey National which was owned by Santander, Bingley is now a

Mecca for canal boat enthusiasts who go up and down the Five Rise and Three Rise Locks.

Peter Sutcliffe, the Yorkshire Ripper who killed at least 13 women, came from here. Due to the timing Sutcliffe was at one stage blamed for the killing of four people in the town whose murders were eventually pinned down to Mark Rowntree. Sutcliffe has also been targeted as the possible murderer of local bookie Fred Craven. Craven was quite a character mostly due to his height, he was only 4ft 7in tall. He is thought to have lost his life for the £200 he was carrying. (See Dewsbury)

Birkenhead, Merseyside

Birkenhead Park was the first publicly funded park in Britain. Parts of the town are laid out in a Manhattan-style gridiron pattern.

Birkenhead features in Paul O'Grady's memoir, ''At My Mother's Knee ... And Other Low Joints.'

When the Queensway Tunnel was closed for repair film makers took the opportunity to shoot the scene here from 'Harry Potter and the Deathly Hallows, Pt1' where Harry and Hagrid make their escape on a flying motorcycle.

Birkenhead is on the Wirral Peninsula. (See Wirral)

Birmingham, Warwickshire, Staffordshire, Worcestershire

In the early days of my writing the questions for Trivial Pursuit it was customary to slip an occasional incorrect question/answer into each edition. This was before the days of the internet so people took almost anything they saw in print as being fact and it was possible to pick out the quiz books and TV shows that had robbed questions if they came up with my spurious bit of information. I once asked 'Which British city has 22 more miles of canals than Venice?' and my answer was 'Birmingham'. Although Birmingham does have more miles of canals than Venice, I selected the 22 because this is my birthday. Since then my 22-miles 'fact' has appeared in almost every quiz book, pub and TV quiz and even in an official guide to Birmingham,

There seems to be more misinformation about England's Second City than actual fact.

No matter what the locals tell you Adil's Restaurant in Birmingham's Sparkbrook area did not invent the balti curry. Baltis are named after the iron pot in which they are cooked and served, balti being Bengali for 'bucket'. Baltis are common across Pakistan and India except they don't display menus under a sheet of tabletop glass like they do in Birmingham's Balti Triangle which attracts an estimated 20,000 curry enthusiasts each week.

Local author J R R Tolkien took inspiration from people and places in and around Birmingham for 'The Hobbit' and 'Lord of the Rings.'

Birmingham has the highest concentration of jewellery business anywhere in Europe with approximately 40% of the UK's jewellery production taking place here. TV antique experts regularly refer to an anchor hallmark as indicating that an item has been made in Birmingham. It doesn't, the anchor shows that the item was tested for silver purity at the Birmingham Assay Office.

Although Liverpool prides itself as Britain's rock and roll city few would dispute the importance of Birmingham in the nation's musical history. Bands and solo artists from here include; Led Zeppelin, Black Sabbath, Duran Duran, Jeff Lynne, The Moody Blues, UB40, Roy Wood and many, many more.

Bishop Aukland, County Durham
A hunting lodge here became the main home of the Bishops of Durham, hence the first part of the name. Aukland comes from an Old Norse name for 'additional land.'

Bishop Aukland was once split straight through the middle by Dere Street. The Roman road led to nearby Winchester Roman Fort, Vinovia, which has one of Britain's best preserved Roman military bath houses. Confusion has arisen by the naming of part of Dere Street as Watling Road. The Roman Watling Street was based on an ancient trackway running from Canterbury to St Albans.

In 1909 West Aukland staged what has become known as the debut World Cup when the town took part in the first international football matches. In the final they beat Swiss side FC Winterthur 2-0. Two years later West Aukland once again collected the Sir Thomas Lipton Trophy by beating Juventus 6-1 in the final. (See Glasgow)

Bishop Aukland's amateur football squad loaned three players to Manchester United after the 1958 Munich disaster. In 1996 Manchester United returned the favour by playing a friendly against Bishop Aukland who were in financial difficulties and in 2007 the Premiership team donated floodlights for Bishop Aukland's new ground.

Stan Laurel, of Laurel and Hardy fame, lived here and went to the town's King James Grammar School.

In the mid 18th century a border dispute erupted between Maryland, Pennsylvania and Delaware. This was solved when surveyors Charles Mason and Jeremiah Dixon devised what is still known as the Mason-Dixon Line and is now the acknowledged border between the Northern and Southern United States. Jeremiah Dixon came from Bishop Aukland where he was also famed as an astronomer.

Bishop's Castle, Shropshire
Less than two miles from Wales this was once England's smallest borough.

The Three Tuns Brewery was established in 1642 and is the oldest licensed brewery in Britain. The Victorian gravity-flow tower brewery was built in 1888. The town also boasts two micro breweries. (See Faversham)

The popular Bishop's Castle Arts Festival takes place annually, currently towards the end of February but check the date before travelling there.

Bishop's Nympton, Devon
St Mary's Church is a landmark visible from some distance around and it attracts visitors to view its Norman baptismal font and carved Easter Sepulchre. Easter Sepulchres are found in England and Wales but I couldn't find any in Scotland. They usually consists of a recess where a crucifix and other sacred items are displayed from Good Friday to Easter Sunday. (See Queen's Nympton)

Bishops Stortford, Essex
This is the closest town to Stansted Airport. Essential information for Bishops Stortford residents includes the freephone Stansted Airport Noise Complaint Line. At the time of writing Stop Stansted Expansion is the main local protest group campaigning against a second runway at the airport.

Racist diamond dealer Cecil Rhodes was born in the house that is now the Bishops Stortford Museum standing within the grounds of the Rhodes Arts Complex.

In 2011 the Council cancelled twinning arrangements with Villiers-sur-Marne in France and Friedberg in der Wetterau, Germany. Although no official reason was given for this it is thought that Tory supporters vented their anti-EU feelings on their twins.

Comedy actor Russell Brand was born in Bishops Stortford in 1975.

Blackburn, Lancashire
Yes, we all know, the Beatles read in the news that there are 4,000 holes in Blackburn, Lancashire.

Thwaites Brewery was founded here in 1807 with part of its business being sold to Marston's in 2015. Marston's now brew the popular Lancaster Bomber ale. Thwaites beers can still be found in its own pubs and, after a period specialising in keg beers, a new craft brewery named Crafty Dan was opened in 2011.

Following the murder of three-year-old June Anne Devaney in 1948, Blackburn became the first town to undergo mass fingerprinting with every male, 46,500 of them, over the age of 16 being fingerprinted after prints had been found on a bottle underneath the hospital cot from which the child had been taken. The prints matched those of 22-year-old Peter Griffiths who confessed to his crime but tried to prove he was insane. The jury declared him to be sane and he was hanged in Liverpool. All the fingerprints were later destroyed. (See Polperro)

Blackfriars, London
The priory close to the Thames was once used for state occasions such as meetings of Parliament. Charles V, Holy Roman Emperor, Archduke of Austria and King of Spain, was welcomed here on his 1522 State Visit and it was the location for Henry VIII and Catherine of Aragon's divorce hearing. Henry VIII's final wife, Katherine Parr was born here.

Blackfriars serves as a filming location for dramas set in the Victorian era including the BBC's two-part adaptation of 'David Copperfield' and the 2009 movie 'Sherlock Holmes'.

Blackpool, Lancashire
Many years ago I worked as a mobile DJ and one of my occasional venues was the Casino on Blackpool Pleasure Beach. Now known as the Casino Building it wasn't a place for gambling but for mass entertainment including themed dinners, variety shows and disco parties. When I worked there the Casino was controlled by an elderly woman who lived on a hill somewhere above the Ribble Valley and was legendary for the conscientious care she took with money. A spotlight on top of the Casino tower was pointed directly at her house and by watching, allegedly from her bed, when this light was turned off she knew at what time the last person had checked out

of the building.

Blackpool Tower installed a laser as part of the 2007 Illuminations and this was slammed by 'Sky at Night' astronomer Sir Patrick Moore as 'Light pollution'.

The Tower hasn't changed massively since I was a kid. There is still an aquarium, (originally known as Dr Cocker's Menagerie it predates the tower by 19 years) and there is still a circus (which hadn't missed a season since 1894 until the 2020 Coronavirus pandemic) and there is still the ballroom (Now familiar to all viewers of 'Strictly Come Dancing'). Where you once boarded a lift to visit the top of the Tower the new owners, Merlin Entertainments, have rebranded the top of the Tower as Blackpool Tower Eye and, prior to heading for the lift, visitors enjoy, or, depending on their taste suffer, a film about the resort and the tower accompanied by Kylie Minogue's song 'All the Lovers' which has become an unofficial anthem for Blackpool. (See Accrington)

Tim Burton's 2016 film, 'Miss Peregrine's Home for Peculiar Children' ends with scenes filmed around Blackpool Tower.
(See Scunthorpe and Bradford)

Blakeney, Norfolk

Tripadvisor's Top Things to Do in Blakeney includes four boat trips, a dome and a duck pond.

Blakeney Chapel has been relocated out of Blakeney to Cley Next the Sea and to confuse things further it isn't and never has been a chapel. The four-storey Grade II-listed Blakeney Windmill appears on a mid-18th-century map, this map obviously does not depict the static caravan park which now surrounds the mill.

Blandford Forum, Dorset
The Hall and Woodhouse Brewery promotes a 90-minute tour which ends with a sample pint of Badger Ale at the Brewery Tap. The Sunny Republic Brewery was closed at the time of writing with the suggestion that a new company would soon be taking over the operation.

Bloxwich, West Midlands
CAMRA describes the Turf Tavern in Bloxwich as 'The last truly unspoilt terraced pub left in the country.'

Bodmin, Cornwall
The 90-minute railway journey from Exeter St David's to Bodmin Parkway has to be one of the most beautiful in Britain but if you're heading for Bodmin town centre and don't fancy a long walk you need to preplan your onward journey. Bodmin Parkway is 3.5 miles from the town centre. It is claimed that regular buses run from the station to Bodmin, Padstow and Wadebridge but I tried to shelter from driving rain in the tiny shelter with no sign of busses, I couldn't get a phone signal to call a taxi and I was eventually rescued by a friendly local who took me half a mile in the wrong direction then dumped me in the rain outside his house but at least he did have a wifi link so I could phone for a cab.

The Beast of Bodmin was first spotted on the nearby Moor in 1978. It was claimed that Mary Chipperfield, of the famed circus family, released three pumas when her Plymouth zoo closed in 1978 but there was never any verification to support this.

A week after the release of a 1995 report determining that there was 'no verifiable evidence for exotic cats roaming wild in Britain' the media became excited when a boy discovered what was described as a 'large cat skull' by the River Fowey. The media gave far less coverage some time later when the Natural History Museum reported that they'd checked the skull which was indeed from a male leopard but it had not died in Britain, it had been imported into the country as part of a leopard-skin rug.

Bognor Regis, West Sussex

No matter what you have read in other books, George V's final words were not 'Bugger Bognor', and it is very doubtful his last utterance was the much reported alternative, 'How is the Empire?'. According to his personal physician, the last thing the monarch said was 'God damn you', to a nurse as she injected him with a sedative.

George was a heavy smoker who visited Bognor to recuperate in 1928 following a chest infection. As he was leaving the town on his return journey to London it was suggested he rename the town Bognor Regis and it is reportedly then when he made the legendary, 'Bugger Bognor' declaration.

Billy Butlin opened a holiday camp here in 1960, rechristened Butlin's Bognor Regis Resort, the camp now features three hotels. The Butlin's Bognor Reception Hall and Sun Lounge gained cult infamy when their images appeared in a book of Britain's most boring postcards. My personal history as a worker at Butlin's Bognor can be found in my memoir, 'In Pursuit of Trivia'.

Cynthia Payne, the Streatham brothel keeper who accepted Luncheon Vouchers and became a parliamentary candidate for the Payne and Pleasure

Party, was born in Bognor in 1932. Despite being one of the town's best known progeny I can find no record of the Council erecting a blue plaque to commemorate her childhood home.

Bolsover, Derbyshire

Britain's only known Palaeolithic cave art is to be found at Creswell Crags.

The 1980s miners' strike started in Bolsover.

Bolton, Greater Manchester

Think of designer labels and trendy sports equipment and you think of London, Paris, Rome, Milan and maybe New York so it might come as something of a shock to hear that Reebok was established in 1958 by Joe and Jeff Foster in Bolton which was then in Lancashire.

No matter what Americans try to tell you, the ice cream wafer sandwich was invented in Bolton.

In recent years Bolton has been named Britain's largest town that isn't a city, which it isn't, (See Reading) Britain's Friendliest Town upon which I dare not possibly comment having seen the anger generated amongst the friendly local populace in 2016 when this was named Britain's Most Struggling Town. There are no mountains in Bolton but the town has been credited with having the country's top mountain rescue team.

The BBC seems to visit Bolton to find DJs, the town having spawned Sara Cox, Vernon Kay and Mark Radcliffe. The wonderful Peter Kay and his 'Phoenix Nights' co-star David Spikey came from here and Sir

Ian McKellen is a former pupil of Bolton School.

Warburton's bread comes from Bolton as do most of those disposable bedpans found in hospitals but not from the same factory.

Borehamwood, Hertfordshire

I once suffered a night in a Borehamwood hotel room so small that the end of the bed had to be lifted to open the door to get out, getting in involved squeezing through a partially opened door and climbing over the bed. According to a local councillor, who was revealed to be stealing money from charities, told me this was the only room available in the town that night and it hardly supported the claim by Borehamwood and neighbouring Elstree to be the Hollywood of England.

'Dr Zhivago,' 2001: A Space Odyssey,' 'The Shining' and 'Star Wars' were all filmed here in a studio that was later partly demolished to make space for a Tesco Extra.

This is Soap Central, 'Eastenders' exterior shots are filmed at Borehamwood and the 'Holby City' hospital is here. (See Elstree)

Borrowdale, Cumbria

Known as Cumberland Borrowdale to avoid confusion with the Borrowdale Valley in Westmorland. Author and journalist, Simon Jenkins, claims the view of Borrowdale from Castle Craig is the best view anywhere in Europe.

England's highest mountain, Scafell Pike (978 m - 3,209-feet), is part of the Borrowdale Volcanic Group at the head of Borrowdale.

Boscatle, Cornwall
Boscastle was washed into national headlines in 2004 when extensive damage was caused by flooding which trapped people on their roofs and in their cars. There was further flooding in 2007 but thankfully not as severe.

The South West Coast Path passes through the village which is within the Cornwall Area of Outstanding National Beauty.

Boston, Lincolnshire
St Botolph's Church claims to be the largest parish church in England (20,070 square feet), its 266-feet 9-inch tower was a landmark for sailors and, on a clear day, can be seen as far away as Norfolk. (See Beverley. See Hull) The spire is the famous Boston Stump. (See Hunstanton)

The town gave its name to the city in Massachusetts, famous for its so-called Tea Party.

Coningsby's 16.5-feet diameter clock is the largest single-handed clock in the world whilst nearby Appleby church claims the world's smallest as its clock has no face at all, it lets you know the time by striking the hour on a bell.

Bournemouth, Dorset
A request for obscure facts about Bournemouth produced some interesting statistics. I was told Bournemouth has 13,868 guest beds with visitors consuming 30,000 ice creams (that's more than two each) on a busy weekend. There are 3,000 deckchairs for hire and the beaches are smoothed out by a tractor-pulled rake every morning.

Bournemouth has three cliff railways, the Fisherman's Walk Cliff Railway with a length of just 128-feet found inclusion in the 'Guinness Book of World Records' as the shortest funicular railway on the planet.

In 1998 the Waterfront Complex was built with a 62-foot tower intended to hold an IMAX screen. It blocked residents' views of the sea and the Isle of Purbeck and was voted Britain's Most Hated Building following a poll of 10,000 people organised by Channel 4. It was finally demolished in 2013.

In 2012 Bournemouth failed in its attempt to achieve city status to commemorate Elizabeth II's Diamond Jubilee in a contest won in England by Chelmsford.

Bovey Tracey, Devon
Hyping itself as 'The Gateway to the Moor' Bovey Tracey is an attractive small town on the edge of Dartmoor.

Talk to people on holiday in Devon with kids and most will deny all knowledge of ever visiting Bovey Tracey, yet most of them have at some time been here to experience House of Marbles without realising which town they were in. Based in a historic pottery this tourist draw has a glassworks but the main attraction for youngsters, and many adults, myself included, is the selection of Heath Robinson-style marble runs. Of course you exit through the gift shop with its pick-and-mix selection of marbles.

Bowness-on-Solway, Cumbria
The several locations named 'Bowness' in this area were originally called Bulnes, meaning a headland where bulls graze.

Bowness's tourist attractions include a distillery, a blacksmith's shop and the opportunity to pop over the border to Gretna Green, which takes two and a half hours by bus or twenty minutes by taxi. (See Gretna Green)

Bowness-on-Solway stands at the western end of Hadrian's Wall which is marked by a pavilion on a cliff. The second-largest fort on the Wall, Maia, was here with a civilian settlement outside its southern gate. St Michael's Church is said to have been built over the Roman fort's granary.

Bowness-on-Windermere, Cumbria
A very busy tourist centre Bowness has merged with the town of Windermere but I have listed them separately as they do have two distinct town centres.

Bowness-on-Windermere's big attraction for the young and young-at-heart is the World of Beatrix Potter. After a short film presentation visitors spend an hour or so wandering through Peter Rabbit's Garden, Mr McGregor's Greenhouse which I am reliably informed smells of tomatoes, along with other attractions from the ever-popular children's books to the inevitable gift shop and tea room.

Bowness doubles as the town of Rio in Arthur Ransome's 'Swallows and Amazons'.

Of course boat trips on the lake and visits to some of Britain's most attractive villages will always be the main crowd-pleaser.

Brackley, Northamptonshire
Being just seven miles from the Silverstone motor

racing circuit, this historic market town is the home of the Mercedes AMG Patronas Formula One Team.

Anyone having difficulty locating the remaining earthworks of Brackley Castle would be advised to begin their search at the Tesco supermarket.

H Bronnley and Co produced soap here for the Queen and Prince Charles prior to relocating to Milton Keynes (H Bronnley relocated to Milton Keynes, not the Queen and her son!)

If the thought that Prince Charles once got his soap from here isn't enough excitement for one location, this is also the home of the Brackley Morris Men, the only surviving traditional Cotswold morris dancing side left in Northamptonshire.

Bracknell, Berkshire
The Prime Minister's official residence at 10 Downing Street is constructed from bricks made in Bracknell, although since Tony Blair and his family moved into the larger flat at 11 Downing Street, (also built from Bracknell brick) this has been the home of Prime Ministers.

Local residents all know that at 10am each Monday morning nearby Broadmoor tests its alarm system for two minutes, this is followed by a two-minute all-clear signal to let them know that no-one has escaped. (See Crowthorne)

Bracknell has featured in several; movies including, 'Harry Potter and the Philosopher's Stone' and 'Time Bandits'.

The Wilde Theatre took its name from Oscar Wilde

thanks to him creating Lady Bracknell in 'The Importance of Being Earnest, A Trivial Play for Serious People'. The only Wilde connection I can find with Bracknell is somewhat obscure! His lover, Lord Alfred Douglas's mother, lived here.

Bradford, West Yorkshire

In 2009 Bradford became the first UNESCO City of Film, the city is home to the UK's longest-running animation festival. The former National Museum of Photography, Film and Television, now the National Science and Media Museum, is Britain's most-visited museum outside London, it contains the UK's first IMAX theatre.

Lister Park features in 'Monty Python's Meaning of Life',

Bradford regularly fights off opposition from Glasgow and Wolverhampton to be crowned Curry Capital of Britain and, having tried all three, Bradford gets my vote.

Musicians from here include singer/songwriter Tasmin Archer and Kiki Dee. Kiki joined Elton John on 'Don't Go Breaking My Heart' and was the first white, British singer signed to the Motown label. Rock bands from Bradford include New Model Army, Smokie, Terrorvision and The Cult.

The hit song 'All the Way from Memphis', by glam-rockers Mott the Hoople includes the line: 'Now it's a mighty long way down rock 'n' roll, though the Bradford Cities and the Orioles.' No I don't know what it means but the song still sounds just as great as it did in 1973.

(See Blackpool and Scunthorpe)

Bradford-on-Avon, Wiltshire
Bradford-on-Avon post office, now closed, is one of only two in the UK with a contemporary inscription to Edward VIII. (See Builth Wells)

Braintree, Essex
There are several reasons given for the name of this town but it is almost certain they never grew brains here. Some sources have this as Branoc's Tree and others claim this was the town on the River Braint but the closest river I can find with that name is in Anglesey.

Celebrating Braintree's historic connection with woolens and silk the museum has the UK's second-biggest publicly owned collection of textiles after the Victoria and Albert.

The world's oldest timber-framed barn is at Cressing Temple, near Braintree, it was built by the Knights Templar in 1206.

Famous people who have lived here include Keith Flint, leader of rock band The Prodigy and actress Charlotte Rampling, but not together.

Brampton, Cambridgeshire
Golfers have rated the 4th hole at Brampton Park as England's most difficult par-3, the green is almost completely surrounded by water.

Geoff Capes, shot-put champion, World's Strongest Man and budgerigar breeder was the local Brampton policeman in the 1970s.

Brampton, Cumbria
Brampton's Tourist Information Centre is to be found in the town's octagonal Moot Hall which was built in 1817. St Martin's is the only church designed by Pre-Raphelite architect Phillip Webb who commissioned the stunning stained glass windows, designed by Sir Edward Burne-Jones and produced in William Morris's studio.

The Young Pretender, Charles Edward Stuart, known to his supporters as Bonnie Prince Charlie, spent one night here during the Jacobite Rising in 1745. His visit is commemorated by a plaque on the wall of what is now an antique shop. The year after Charles' visit six Jacobite soldiers were hanged from the branches of the Capon Tree, commemorated by the Capon Tree Monument. The original tree died more than a century ago. Local school children planted an oak sapling in its place in 2013 to celebrate the peace between England and Scotland since the Uprising.

Bridgnorth, Shropshire
Split into High Town and Low Town by the River Severn, the higher and lower parts of High Town are linked by a funicular railway. If that sounds complicated go take a look and it will all make sense. Although it makes little sense that my Spell Check insists 'funicular' should be 'vernacular'.

Bridgnorth's Reel Cinema, known as the Majestic, was opened in 1937 and continues to operate today. The main screen can be viewed by 330 and what was once the balcony now houses two screens each with approximately 80 seats.

Bridgwater, Somerset
Millions drive straight past this large town on the

M5, the closest they ever get is the 39-feet tall Willow Man who has been dubbed the Angel of the South. Reportedly the world's largest statue made from willow which is grown locally. At the time of writing an appeal had been launched to raise funds to reconstruct the Willow Man who was falling apart.

Bridgwater is the home of the Somerset Brick and Tile Museum, housed in an old brick kiln the museum commemorates the town's history manufacturing bricks from clay deposits found in the River Parrett.

Traditionally held on the closest Saturday to November 5th, the Bridgwater Carnival attracts an estimated 150,000 people each year and consists of a parade of spectacular illuminated floats moving slowly along a 2.5-mile route. The parade is followed by the letting off of fireworks outside the Town Hall. There is also an annual funfair, second only to Nottingham Goose Fair in size so far as English fairs are concerned.

A word of warning for canal boat enthusiasts. I once met a very pleasant and apparently intelligent young couple who had come here hoping to take a boat trip along the ancient Bridgewater Canal that they'd heard so much about. They should have noticed the slight difference in spelling. The canal was named after the third Earl of Bridgewater and is 200 miles away in Manchester.

Bridlington, East Riding of Yorkshire
King Henry V came here in 1415 but he didn't come for a dip in the sea, fish and chips or a game of bingo. Henry visited the Priory, dedicated to St John of Bridlington, to whom he attributed his victory at the Battle of Agincourt.

Bridlington Spa is a music venue and conference centre. The likes of David Bowie performed here prior to the 2006-08 refurbishment, since then Madness, Kaiser Chiefs and Kasabian have taken to the stage and it is here Oasis played what they said would be their final outdoor concert in 2009.

Bridport, Dorset

Bridport High Street was once an almost constant traffic jam, especially on Wednesdays and Saturdays when the market spills out along the street. Then in 1987 they opened a by-pass, part of the A35, around the town centre. Locals and motorists alike were jubilant but the resultant lack of through traffic is blamed for the closure of many shops, although online shopping could be just as much to blame and the market is still worth a visit.

Bridport Harbour, known to most as West Bay, has seen a boost in trade thanks to being the location for the TV series 'Broadchurch,' it was also seen in the series 'Harbour Lights' and is where Leonard Rossiter is seen running into the sea at the start of each episode of 'The Fall and Rise of Reginald Perrin.'

Probably Bridport's greatest claim to fame is that its ancient rope making industry led to the goal nets for the legendary 1966 World Cup Final (England 4, West Germany 2) being made here.

Brierley Hill, West Midlands

Brierley Hill promotes its main attraction as being the Merry Hill Shopping Centre, built in the late 1980s on what was once the last remaining urban farm in the West Midlands. A steelworks overlooking the site of the shopping centre employed 3,000 people but this was more than halved when the works closed during the Thatcher Era.

The Devon company, Dartington Crystal, now owns Royal Brierley Crystal, one of the oldest glass manufacturers in the country. (See Great Torrington)

Brigg, North Lincolnshire
Brigg enjoys an annual burst of glory on the first Saturday of August when travellers from all across England visit the Horse Fair, second only in size to the one at Appleby, this is the subject of the popular folk song 'Brigg Fair.'

Lord Lawrence Olivier's wife, Joan Plowright, was born in Brigg.

Brigham, Cumbria
Bounty mutineer Fletcher Christian was born in Eaglesfield in Brigham parish. According to historic records Christian was buried on Pitcairn Island but local residents will tell you his body was secretly brought back to Britain and is interred at St Bridget's, the church where he was christened and where members of his family lie in the churchyard.

Brighstone, Isle of Wight
Strictly speaking Great Britain is the one large island consisting of England, Scotland and Wales. I have carefully weighed up both sides of the argument and have decided several islands should also be classed as parts of Great Britain, including the Isle of Wight.

Brighstone attracts camera clickers to its pretty thatched cottages and anyone still around in December should not miss the Christmas Tree Festival. The Brighstone Scout Hut serves as a Youth

Hostel for a few weeks in the summer.

Brighstone Bay is a 4.3-mile shingle beach suffering from coastal erosion.

Brighton and Hove, East Sussex

Although still thought of as two separate towns, Brighton and Hove were jointly granted city status in 2001. (See Wolverhampton)

In July 1911 the world's first recorded cargo flight left Shoreham to land on Hove Lawns. It was delivering light bulbs for the Osram company and it was said that not a single bulb was broken.

Brighton boasts the world's oldest aquarium, Britain's first casino, Britain's first naturist beach and Britain's oldest, purpose-built cinema.

It is general knowledge that Brighton is recognised as the Gay Capital of the UK but few people realise Hitler gave instructions for his bombers to avoid Brighton Pavilion as he'd selected this as his holiday home after World War Two. (See Oxford)

In 1972 Pink Floyd gave the first live performance of 'Dark Side of the Moon' at Brighton Dome and two years later ABBA came to the same venue to win the Eurovision Song Contest with 'Waterloo.'

In 1899 'The Kiss in the Tunnel' became one of the first ever movies, it was filmed in Hove.

Brighton has been voted Foodie Capital of Britain. Brighton and Hove claim to have more restaurants per head of population than anywhere else in the country with one for every 250 people. With 1,400 licensed premises the city has one drinking establishment for every 320 of the populace.

St Bartholomew's is Europe's tallest brick church, it was built to the same dimensions describing Noah's Ark in the Bible.

Bristol, Bristol

Bristol has been administered by Gloucestershire and Somerset and was, for a time, in the county of Avon. Bristol is now a county in its own right with the official title, the City and County of Bristol.

Fans of 'Only Fools and Horses' visit Peckham, South London, in search of locations seen in the classic TV comedy series. With a bit of research or a copy of this book they'd realise that Nelson Mandela House is behind Bristol City's Ashton Gate ground and the side-splitting Batman and Robin scene was filmed in Broadmead.

In 1979 Clifton Suspension Bridge was the take-off point for the world's first bungee jump and legend has it that a Victorian lady jumped from the bridge in a suicide attempt but floated safely down to the mud beneath with her crinoline acting as a parachute.

Bristol's streets have more than their fair share of Banksy's works and many other street artists have been attracted to decorate walls here with their stencils and paints attempting to emulate Banksy.

My personal favourite non-Banksy is 'Rapunzel' on the wall of Highbury Vaults pub. The top of St Michael's Hill is a long, uphill walk from the city centre to see a Banksy-that-isn't-a-Banksy but it's worth it for a great pub. The Highbury Vaults used to be where condemned prisoners were served their final meal. It is a proper pub serving proper pub food and proper ales. Popular with students and with a very pleasant yard at the back when the weather is fine.

The phrase 'cash on the nail', meaning immediate payment, allegedly comes from the days when business was conducted over four bronze pillars, that look like nails, in Corn Street.

Until it was pulled down and dumped in the harbour by Black Lives Matter protesters in 2020, Bristol displayed a bronze statue of Edward Colston. Colston is one of Bristol's most celebrated sons with the city centre Colston Hall theatre, a street
and tower block, named after him until recent changes. Colston gave schools to the city, almshouses, churches and hospitals, mostly paid for by his sale of slaves. At the time of writing the Colston statue has been rescued from its temporary watery grave and is due to be exhibited in a museum.

Bristol is also proud of its Cabot Circus shopping centre, a statue of the Italian, Giovanni Caboto, known here as John Cabot, stands, or rather sits, outside the Arnolfini Gallery. Despite supporters claiming, he was 'just an explorer'; historical records prove that Cabot was a slave trader. Cabot's son, Bristol-born Sebastian, shipped enslaved Africans to Brazil and owned his own slaves in Spain.

Brixham, Devon

Brixham is one of Britain's busiest commercial fishing ports with plenty to keep tourists interested. The old fish market is the venue for Pirate Thursdays during the spring and summer offering local and visiting children the opportunity to take part in fun activities including Soak the Pirate.

A full-size replica of Francis Drake's Golden Hind is moored in the inner harbour although the ship had nothing whatsoever to do with Brixham. In 2018 The Golden Hind failed to sell at auction but a local businessman paid £195,000 for the boat so he could hold his son's 6th-birthday party on board.

Broadstairs, Kent

Charles Dickens was a regular visitor to Broadstairs, he wrote 'David Copperfield' while staying at Bleak House. It is here he met Mary Pearson Strong who inspired the character Betsey Trotwood. The Broadstairs Dickens Festival takes place each June featuring, talks, plays, beach events and local people wandering the streets in period costume.

John Buchan began writing 'The 39 Steps' in the town and Edward Heath, organist, yachtsman and Prime Minister, was born here in 1916.

Charles Hamilton, who wrote the 'Greyfriars School' stories under the pseudonym Frank Richards, lived in Broadstairs from 1926 until his death in 1961. The 'Guinness Book of World Records' lists Hamilton as the world's most prolific author. It is estimated his published works include some 100 million words, equivalent to 1,200 average-length novels written under at least 25 assumed names. It has to be said that he did take regular time off from writing to visit the Casino in Monte Carlo and during his absences over a twenty-year period some 35 writers assumed his many names to maintain his contracted output in magazines and comic books.

Broadway, Somerset
It would be an easy mistake to make but if someone offers a Broadway launch for your latest theatrical production this is NOT the Broadway you should be aiming for, although occasional productions are performed by local song and drama societies at the Village Hall.

Broadway, Worcestershire
Another Broadway without the glitz and glamour of Manhattan but on a clear day Broadway Tower offers a view of a record 16 counties, Buckinghamshire, Gloucestershire, Herefordshire, Monmouthshire, Powys, Shropshire, West Midlands, Warwickshire, Staffordshire, Leicestershire, Northamptonshire, Oxfordshire, Wiltshire, Gwent, Dyfed and, obviously even on a foggy day, Worcestershire.

Brockenhurst, Hampshire
By population (3,552 at the last count) Brockenhurst is the largest village within the New Forest.

Meerut Road takes its name in memory of Indian troops from Meerut and Lahore who were treated here at the Lady Hardinge Hospital for Wounded Indian Soldiers during World War One. The hospital was handed over to New Zealand in 1916 and was renamed No 1 New Zealand General Hospital.

During World War Two Montgomery and Eisenhower held frequent meetings at what is now the Balmer Lawn Hotel in Brockenhurst to plan the D-Day Landings.

Bromborough, Merseyside
It is claimed the Battle of Brunanburh was fought here in 937, said to have been the most important

battle ever fought on British soil leading directly to the establishment of English nationalism. Anglo Saxon remains have been found in the area but some forty other locations in England and Scotland profess to be the site of this battle.

Bromborough residents can enjoy great views of planes taking off from, and landing at, Liverpool's John Lennon Airport just across the Mersey Estuary but they have a 12-mile road trip to actually get there.

Bromley, Greater London

Formerly a small market town in Kent, Bromley is now very much a part of the Big City despite having its own BR postcode. Comedian Frankie Boyle described Bromley as a 'lobotomy made out of bricks'.

Bromley was the butt of several Monty Python sketches. The Pythons claimed all seven continents could be seen from the top of the Kentish Times building and the 'Spam Sketch' was located at the fictional Green Midget Cafe in Bromley.

H G Well's was born here, his father founded the Bromley Cricket Club. Wells was offered, but turned down, freedom of the town.

Rock stars who have resided in Bromley include David Bowie, Pixie Lott, Peter Frampton, Siouxsie Sioux and Billy Idol.

Bromsgrove, Worcestershire

Until the 1890s nails by the million were made here by hand. Most nailmakers were paid in tokens that could only be spent at shops that purchased and sold their nails.

The Avoncroft Museum of Historic Buildings houses the National Telephone Kiosk Collection.

Bromyard, Herefordshire

Each July Bromyard plays host to Nozstock: The Hidden Valley. This three-day arts and music extravaganza might not offer the international headliners expected at Glastonbury but with ten stages and a total of 5,000 visitors it is said to be more like a private party than a mega-fest. The town also hosts a folk festival in September.

The Time Museum of Science Fiction displays props from some of the best-loved cinema and TV sc-fi productions including 'Doctor Who,' 'Star Wars,' and 'Red Dwarf'.

Buckfastleigh, Devon

Buckfastleigh is equal with two villages both named Buslingthorpe as one of the longest place names in England with no repeated letters. All three locations have 13-letters, or half the letters in the alphabet.

Trinity Churchyard is famous for the tomb of Squire Richard (Dirty Dick) Cabell. Cabell is the subject of a legend that on the night of his death in 1677 black hounds, breathing fire, came across Dartmoor to surround his home, Brook House. Sir Arthur Conan Doyle based the plot of his 'The Hound of the Baskervilles' on this legend. (See Cromer)

The South Devon Railway, an otter sanctuary and a butterfly farm all attract tourists to Buckfastleigh.

The monks at Buckfast Abbey originated a caffeinated, fortified wine based on a traditional French recipe. Now produced under licence, the wine was marketed by the monks as a tonic but in Scotland it became a staple, high-alcohol tipple of choice for drunken yobs. It was claimed that during the 2020 Coronavirus scare people in England and Wales were bulk buying toilet rolls whilst Buckfast Tonic Wine was being shipped to Scotland in tankers.

Buckland, Gloucestershire
The Church of St Michael has stained glass that so impressed William Morris when he visited here that he paid for its re-leading.

Close to the church is Buckland Manor, a country hotel with a classy modern menu. Buckland Rectory, next to the Manor, is claimed to be the oldest in England.

Buckland, Oxfordshire
The River Thames forms the northern border of this parish.

George III's Poet Laureate, Henry James Pye, wrote a poem titled 'Farringdon Hall' which includes the line: 'See Buckland here her lovely scenes display.'

Buckland Abbey, Devon
(See Zeal Monachorum)

Bude, Cornwall
The most easterly town in north Cornwall, Bude is the first place over the border from Devon where tourists are fed Cornish Pasties, such pasties were first recorded in Devon, as were cream teas. (See Tavistock)

From Compass Cove to Furze Cove, Bude's coast is a Site of Special Scientific Interest.

A perspex tunnel at Sainsbury's supermarket in Bude gained unexpected publicity for the town when it was listed as a top tourist attraction on TripAdvisor. Even more admirers and TV crews flocked to the tunnel when it was fitted with thousands of flashing lights to celebrate Christmas 2018.

Budleigh Salterton, Devon

'Unspoilt' is often, correctly, used to describe Budleigh Salterton. For 'unspoilt' read there's not much for kids to do in the town, other than the beach, although there are plenty of juvenile attractions nearby.

Budleigh (as it is always known locally) features as Budleigh Babberton in 'Harry Potter,' the town stands on the Jurassic Coast and one of its main tourist attractions is a bit of wall at the town end of the beach where Sir John Everett Millais set his most famous painting, 'The Boyhood of Raleigh.' I say he 'set' the painting here because it is unlikely he actually did any painting at this spot, more likely he made sketches and completed the painting in his London studio. A blue plaque on the octagonal house close to the wall does claim that Millais painted the picture here. The two boys are Millais' sons Everett and George. The sailor was a professional model. Sit on the wall while looking at a print of the painting and you will realise the sailor is pointing to the south, probably towards the Spanish Main. (See East Budleigh)

Ships once sailed inland into East Devon villages from here but the River Otter silted up putting an end to this important access to trade.

Nearby Bicton Park offers a day out for young and old alike with a world-renowned plant and tree collection, fun mini train journey plus indoor and outdoor kids' play areas. For a short time Bicton was the location for the terribly tacky 'Gotchaland,' aka 'Crinkly Bottom,' so-called theme park launched by Noel Edmonds. People went expecting to see Mr Blobby (I know because I took the kids and talked to other disappointed visitors) but instead they got a green rubber frog called Phibber who nobody had ever heard of.

Bures, Suffolk

Bures boasts a railway station on the Gainsborough Line. A self-service ticket machine was installed at the unstaffed station in 2017 and, at about the same time, the station became a request stop at weekends and during off-peak periods.

Burford, Oxfordshire

In 2009, Forbes, the American business magazine, named this tiny village, known as the Gateway to the Cotswolds, as the sixth most-Idyllic place to live in Europe. The five more desirable locations on the Forbes list were Gaiole in Chianti, Italy, Saint-Remy-de-Provence, France, Copenhagen, Denmark, Kefalonia, Greece and Ljubljana, Slovenia.

Delicious Oxford Blue cheese is produced here to a recipe devised in 1995 by French baron Robert Pouget.

Burnham, Buckinghamshire

Residents of Burnham will remind you that their houses are more expensive than those in neighbouring towns so please don't upset them with a reminder that Burnham railway station is actually in Slough and boundary changes have moved the station out of Buckinghamshire into Berkshire.

Burnham Beeches is a National Nature Reserve, open to the public and well worth a visit. Thanks to Pinewood Studios being close by, Burnham Beeches is a popular filming location having appeared in several Harry Potter movies, 'The Crying Game', 'Goldfinger' and 'Robin Hood Prince of Thieves.'

Burnham Market, Norfolk
Dubbed Chelsea-on-Sea due to its attractiveness to second-home owners from the capital, Burnham self-styled itself Norfolk's Most Beautiful Village.

The influx of affluent part-time residents is probably to blame for village pubs now relying more on food than on ale and banter.

Burnham-on-Sea, Somerset
In 2008 Burnham's concrete pier was rated among the top five in Britain by the Daily Express. Built between 1911 and 1914 it is probably the shortest pier in Britain with a length of 900-feet - 270m.

Following serious flooding a protective sea wall was built along the Esplanade in 1988. The wall has become an attraction thanks to its use as a canvas by street artists.

Burnley, Lancashire
In 2013 Burnley received an Enterprising Britain award for being recognised by the government as the Most Enterprising Area in the UK.

Two miles away in the Pennines can be found the Singing Ringing Tree. This is an architect-designed sculpture, not unlike a tree in shape, that makes strange noises when the wind blows.

Burnley Miners' Social Club claims to sell more Benedictine than any other bar in the world. Locals mix the French liqueur with hot water after being introduced to this by soldiers returning from Normandy after World War One. The club gets through 1,000 bottles per year and even youngsters are taking to the drink with the introduction of the Bene Bomb, Benedictine mixed with Red Bull.

Burton-on-Trent
Also known as Burton upon Trent or, by the locals, simply as Burton.

Burton-on-Trent is famed as Britain's brewing capital being the home of eight breweries. Coors, the British arm of Molson (Canada) Coors (USA) now operate what was the Bass Brewery and other historic breweries have similarly been taken over by massive corporations.

All of these breweries result in an excess of yeast which accounts for the local production of Marmite. The lack of brewing when pubs were closed during the 2020 Coronavirus pandemic resulted in a temporary national scarcity of Marmite.

Bury, Greater Manchester
I am originally from Yorkshire and have been brought up with an unnatural distaste for anything from Lancashire, the county in which Bury formerly stood. However, I have to acknowledge that Bury Market gifted the world with a black pudding that has never been equalled and certainly not bettered anywhere else on the planet.

Locally born Prime Minister Sir Robert Peel founded

the Metropolitan Police, it's his name that resulted in policemen being called Bobbies. Peel was also a founder of the Conservative Party.

Rock band Elbow are from Bury.

Bury St Edmunds, Suffolk
St Edmund has long been favoured to be returned to his rank as Patron Saint of England. In 2015 The Darkness released the song 'Barbarian' telling the story of the ninth century Viking invasion that resulted in the death of Edmund.

Bury St Edmunds attracts tourists to St Edmundsbury Cathedral and the Abbey of St Edmund but the Saint's remains were lost at the time of the desecration of the monasteries by Henry VIII.

At the time of writing, permission has been granted to dig up an old tennis court under which it is claimed will be found an iron chest containing the bones of St Edmund. The excavation is on hold because nobody can be found to fund it.

Buslingthorpe, Lincolnshire
(See Buckfastleigh)

Buslingthorpe, West Yorkshire
(See Buckfastleigh)

Buxton, Derbyshire
At 1,000-feet above sea level Buxton is England's highest market town and uses this distinction to advertise other attractions such as Buxton Opera House being hyped as the country's highest opera house. (See Brynmawr)

Former Goodie, Tim Brooke-Taylor was born here as were disc jockey Dave Lee Travis and leader of the Commotions, Lloyd Cole.

C

Camberley, Surrey

In the movie adaptation of William Golding's 'Lord of the Flies' Hugh Edwards, in his role as Piggy, explains how Camberley got its name. Edwards had been filmed talking, unscripted, to other young cast members and although he did go to Camberley Primary School (now demolished) his explanation of the origin of the name is mostly incorrect. (See Salisbury)

Camberley was originally called Cambridge Town, to avoid confusion with the University City the name was changed to Camberley in 1877. The name is a combination of Cam, the river, and Amber from Amber Hill with 'ley' stuck on the end. Ley is a traditional end to town names meaning a clearing or pasture. (See Cambridge)

Although the Royal Military Academy is located in Sandhurst, Berkshire, its ceremonial entrance is in Camberley, Surrey. (See Sandhurst)

The world's first motorcycle scrambling event took place on Camberley Heath in 1924.

The approach to Camberley on the A30 is famed for the White Elephant. A pipe company created this from its products and when they moved away it was written into future leases that tenants must maintain the upkeep of the landmark.

'Neighbours From Hell,' featuring boy band 5ive was filmed while the boys were residents in Camberley

Cambridge, Cambridgeshire
Millions of words have been written about Cambridge and its university. The city's fame and proximity to London (100 miles) makes it popular with UK and foreign visitors.

Poet Rupert Brooke claimed Cambridge people rarely smile, 'Being urban, squat and packed with guile.'

Hundreds of British towns and cities take at least a part of their name from a river. Cambridge was originally Grantabrycge, or Bridge over the Granta. After the city was renamed Cambridge the river Granta was renamed the Cam so here is a rare example of a river named after the city rather than the other way round.

The Mathematical Bridge over the River Cam is based on an extremely efficient wooden structure that is rigid and self-supporting. Locals like to impress visitors with the 'fact' that the bridge was designed and built by Sir Isaac Newton. Newton died in 1727, 22-years before the bridge was built by James Essex to a design by William Etheridge. The bridge has been rebuilt on two occasions and there is also a copy in Oxford. Although Mathematical Bridges look like an arch every piece of timber is in fact straight. (See Oxford)

Hundreds of the famous and infamous attended Cambridge University. When George Gordon Byron, known as Lord Byron, came to Trinity College in 1805 he was appalled by the draconian rules forbidding him to keep his pet dog, Boatswain, in his room. The rules were not specific when it came to other animals so the poet purchased a bear as a roommate.

At the time of writing affiliates of Cambridge University have been awarded 89 Nobel Prizes in all six disciplines, 29 of these for Physics. At the time of writing the UK has had 55 Prime Ministers. 28 of these went to Oxford and 14 to Cambridge.

In 2019 Cambridge entered record books after registering the hottest temperature ever recorded in Britain, 38.7C but, with global warming, don't hold your breath for Cambridge retaining this record.(See Faversham)

(See Sandford on Thames)

Camden, Greater London
Also called Camden Town, thousands of visitors come here for the markets. Originating in 1973 at Camden Lock the markets have grown to become London's fourth-most popular tourist attraction. Traditionally the markets only traded on Sundays and this is still the busiest day, although some traders operate from permanent premises and are open seven days a week.

Writers Charles Dickens, Beryl Bainbridge, Dylan Thomas, Bernard Levin and Alan Bennett have all lived here.

Two-tone ska survivors, the marvellous Madness, from Camden, still perform with six of their original seven members.

Bon Scott, lead singer of Aussie rockers AC/DC, died here in 1980 following a heavy drinking session. (See Forfar). Amy Winehouse lived and died here, with her death being blamed on alcohol poisoning, a bronze statue of Amy stands in Stables Market.

Canning Town, London
Some sources claim Canning Town took its name because a cannery was located here, others say it was named after George Canning who had a brief spell as Prime Minister in 1827, then there are those who say George Canning's son, Charles, first Viceroy of India is commemorated by the name.

In 2018 Canning Town was listed among the 5 per cent most deprived areas of the UK despite its proximity to the affluent Docklands developments. A £3.7 billion regeneration project is in the planning stages.

The Royal Oak pub (now an estate agents) had a first-floor boxing ring where Frank Bruno trained and the Bridge House pub played host to some of the top rock bands of the 1970s and 80s.

Canterbury, Kent
Canterbury became a place of pilgrimage after the murder of Thomas a Becket in 1170. Chaucer's 'Canterbury Tales' tells the story of pilgrims making their journey to the city. There is no evidence to suggest Chaucer ever actually visited Canterbury.

In the equestrian world 'canter' means to trot or run. The word comes from pilgrims riding their horses faster in order to reach Canterbury prior to curfew.

Nine of the first ten Archbishops of Canterbury became saints. The tenth, Wighard, died of the plague before he could officially take up the post.

Modern visitors are often attracted to the unusual

conical mound in Dane John Gardens. Some say this is a Roman burial mound and others will assure you it is part of a mediaeval defence system. The park itself dates back to 1551 but the mound is much older, being recorded as early as the first century AD when this area was indeed a Roman burial ground. The monument on top of the mound commemorates Alderman James Simmons who gifted the gardens to the city.

Canterbury has two railway stations with names it is hard to explain. Canterbury West is to the north of the city and Canterbury East is to the south.

Cardington, Bedfordshire

The story of the world's first air disaster begins at Cardington when a vast R101 airship took flight in October 1930. Lord Thomson, the Air Minister, rushed through the launch of the R101 despite the required technology still being in its infancy. He wanted to make a spectacular arrival in India for the first Imperial Conference. Some 3,000 people witnessed the largest flying object ever built in Britain as it departed from Cardington and thousands more waved and cheered as she passed overhead.

54 passengers were on board including Lord Thomson. During the afternoon of the following day the weather suddenly deteriorated and the last call from the airship was an enquiry about her location. The lost dirigible hit a hillside in France and immediately burst into flames. Only eight people survived the crash with two of these dying shortly afterwards.

Carlisle, Cumbria
Carlisle is the largest city in Cumbria and also the smallest city in Cumbria, it is the oldest city in Cumbria, the newest city in Cumbria and the highest city above sea level in Cumbria. You might have gathered from these facts that Carlisle is the only city in Cumbria.

Carr's of Carlisle, now part of United Biscuits and marketed in the USA by Kellogg's, is still a name known for Water Biscuits to be served with cheese.

The annual Carlisle Food Fair takes place each August and is renowned for Cumberland Sausage.

Carlisle fell within the North West England constituency for the European Parliament and in 2014 elected three Labour, two Conservative and three UKIP MEPs. The UKIPers included former Tory Paul Nuttall who demonstrated his intelligence by denying climate change and left UKIP in 2018 to join the equally ludicrous Brexit Party. Nuttall was an unsuccessful UKIP candidate in no less than six parliamentary elections.

Cartmel, Cumbria
Cartmel claims to be the home of Sticky Toffee Pudding, a similar claim is made by the Sharrow Bay Hotel in the Lake District with their recipe allegedly having been traced back to a woman from Lancashire who said she'd been given it by two Canadians.

Castle Ashby, Northamptonshire
The village is named after a country house which was castellated in 1306.

Castle Ashby House has grounds open to the

public but the house itself can only be visited if an appointment has been arranged. A Christian music festival was staged in the grounds during the late 1980s and early 1990s.

One source claims Jane Austen based 'Mansfield Park' on Castle Ashby House.

Castle Combe, Wiltshire
Best known for the eponymous motor racing circuit on the site of the RAF Castle Combe airfield.

Castle Combe was the location for the musical movie 'Doctor Dolittle' (1967) and this resulted in the village becoming one of the very rare locations to be seen in 'The Simpsons'. 'Cue Detective' (2016) sees Principal Skinner making his students watch 'Doctor Dolittle,' Castle Combe appears in the clip shown during what is usually an entirely animated TV show.

In addition to 'Doctor Dolittle', the village appears in the movies 'Stardust' and 'Wolfman' and, more recently it was a location for Steven Spielberg's 'War Horse.'

Castle Donington, Leicestershire
Ayrton Senna won the European Grand Prix here in 1993 and Donington Park was contracted to stage the British Formula One Grand Prix for ten years from 2010 but could not raise the funds to upgrade the track.

Donington Park is best known for music festivals. Monsters of Rock took place here in the 1980s and 90s and the Download Festival since 2003.

Norton Motorcycles and British Midland airline

(BMI) have their headquarters at Donington Hall.

Castleton, Derbyshire
Many tourists visit Castleton for its four showcaves, by far the most famous being the Blue John Cavern. Small quantities of the semi-precious stone are still mined at the cavern outside the tourist season and your summer tour guide is likely to be one of the winter miners.

Although Blue John can include blue veins it is often seen in shades of yellow which is thought to account for its name: 'bleau-jaune' being French for blue-yellow.

Catford, Greater London
There are those who claim Catford took its name because it was where black cats, associated with witchcraft, were drowned in the river. It is more likely that the name comes from this being where cattle crossed the ford, an abbreviation of Cattleford.

Despite there probably being no link with cats, a large model of a black cat is a landmark above the entrance to Catford Shopping Centre and the Black Cat pub is popular.

Comedian, script-writer and author Ben Elton was born in Catford in 1959.

Cattistock, Dorset
The Church of St Peter and St Paul had England's first carillon, a musical device consisting of 35 bells, which drew tourists here until it was destroyed by fire in 1940. This church has been recognised as 'the masterpiece amongst Dorset churches.'

Until 2017 Cattistock was the home of the Dorset Knob Throwing Competition. Dorset Knobs are a bread-like biscuit which to my personal taste are better used for throwing than for eating. At the time of writing the record for Knob Throwing is 96-feet.

Chard, Somerset

The USA showered the Wright Brothers with awards for inventing powered flight and tourists are still attracted to Kitty Hawk where they made their debut flight in 1903.

John Stringfellow, a Yorkshireman, came to Chard and it was here in 1842 he patented the Aerial Steam Carriage along with William Samuel Henson, this proved to be impractical due to the weight of the steam engine, in 1843 they incorporated the Aerial Transit Company. In 1848 Stringfellow achieved the world's first powered flight using an unmanned aircraft with a ten-feet wingspan.

So it might be correct to say the Wright Brothers were first to put a man on a plane but powered flight had taken off in Chard 55-years prior to the US venture.

Charlbury, Oxfordshire

Charlbury stands at the edge of Wychwood Forest where can be found early long barrows and later round barrows, demonstrating that the area has been settled for at least 5,000 years. (See Shipton-under-Wychwood)

The annual Charlbury Beer Festival incorporates the World Aunt Sally Open Singles Championship which involves throwing sticks at a model of an old woman's head.

Charmouth, Dorset
(See Lyme Regis)

Chatham, Kent
Chatham developed around the dockyard with a number of Army barracks providing defence around the facility. This is still the base for the Corps of Royal Engineers. The dockyard closed in 1984.

An online slang dictionary informs readers that the word 'chav' is derived from 'Chatham average', this is not correct, 'chav' actually comes from a Romany word meaning 'youngster.'

This is yet another place that once boasted Charles Dickens as a resident. Fashion designer Zandra Rhodes was born in Chatham as was Victorian painter Richard Dadd who stabbed his father to death and spent his final 20 years in mental institutions.

Cheadle, Greater Manchester
It could be easy to mix up your Cheadles as the village of Cheadle borders Cheadle Hulme and Cheadle Heath while Cheadle Bulkeley and Cheadle Moseley were once separate parishes that were joined to form Cheadle in 1879.

Cheadle, Staffordshire
St Giles' Catholic Church, known as Pugin's Gem, has a 200-feet spire and is considered by many to be the closest Augustus Pugin got to achieving his ideal.

One of England's most important water vole breeding sites can be found at the Cecilly Brook Nature Reserve.

Cheddar, Somerset
The Cheddar Gorge is to the north of the village and the area has long been a centre for strawberry growing but, obviously, the name of the village is known internationally thanks to the cheese that originated here in the 12th century, although only one cheese maker remains in the village. Attempts to imitate Cheddar Cheese are made worldwide with varying degrees or lack of success, by far the worst 'Cheddar' I ever tasted was in the USA but even some British factories come up with pretty bad ones.

In the centre of Cheddar is the 15th century Market Cross which was enclosed in its hexagonal structure in the 17th century. The cross is a Scheduled Ancient Monument but this did not guarantee its safety. In 2000 the building suffered severe damage in a traffic accident, it was rebuilt in 2002 but badly damaged again in 2012 when two sides were demolished by a taxi. Steel posts with wooden cladding have now been erected to keep traffic at bay. The actual cross is missing.

Chelmsford, Essex
There is evidence to support the claim that Robert the Bruce, King of Scots, was born at Montpeliers Farm, Chelmsford in 1274.

Australian opera diva Dame Nellie Melba is probably best remembered as the inspiration for a peach and ice cream dessert but she made Britain's first public audio broadcast from Chelmsford in 1920. Marconi opened the world's first wireless factory here in 1899.

Chelmsford was temporarily the Capital of England when the seat of government was moved to here some 600-years ago. Chelmsford was granted city status to celebrate the Diamond Jubilee of Elizabeth II in 2012. (See Bournemouth)

In a letter to clergyman Thomas Beard, Charles Dickens expressed the viewpoint; 'If anyone were to ask me what in my opinion was the dullest and most stupid spot on the face of the Earth, I should decidedly say Chelmsford.' (See Yarmouth)

Chelsea, London

Chelsea's affluence is reflected in the term Sloane Ranger to describe its residents, Sloane Square being one of the most expensive locations in Britain. The Square saw the landing of a Dalek spaceship in the film 'Daleks - Invasion Earth 2150 A.D.'

The King's Road is dedicated to Charles II but is now a major shopping street and was a rainbow of colour during 1967 at the height of the Swinging London phenomenon.

In the 19th century Chelsea was looked upon as something of a bohemian quarter, major artists including Dante Gabriel Rossetti, James McNeill Whistler, John Singer Sargent, J M W Turner and William Holman Hunt all lived and worked here.

In 1999 Chelsea FC, based at Stamford Bridge in Fulham, became the first English club to field a completely foreign lineup. (See Fulham)

Cheltenham, Gloucestershire

Cheltenham's town crest depicts three pigeons in honour of the day in 1715 when someone noticed an extremely healthy looking flock of the birds in a field at the edge of the village. When the ground was inspected a mineral spring was discovered and it was the salts in this water that attracted the birds. This was the birth of Cheltenham as a spa town.

Cheltenham is now famous for its annual racing festival that takes place either to include or very close to St Patrick's Day. Thousands of Irish horse lovers congregate at this event and, at the time of writing, theirs and their fellow racegoers record for sinking pints of Guinness during the four-days was 265,000, this might have been much higher if they hadn't also downed 120,000 bottles of wine and 20,000 bottles of champagne.

In 2015 the Cheltenham Festival awarded a world record prize pot for a jumps festival with winners and placed horses collecting £4,150,000. £150 million is bet on the festival each day and the local economy is boosted by an annual £100 million.

The Cheltenham Festival went ahead, with Government blessing, during the 2020 Coronavirus epidemic, resulting in the Cheltenham area having the highest spike of hospital cases suffering from the disease following the festival.

Cheshunt, Hertfordshire
Elizabeth I lived in Cheshunt for a while and Cardinal Wolsey was given land here by Henry VIII. Richard Cromwell died here.

Victoria Beckham, also known as Posh Spice, went to the rather posh St Mary's High School.

Cheshunt had the world's first passenger-carrying monorail, not quite to the standard of the high-speed monorails of the 21st century, the Cheshunt monorail was horse-drawn and only about three-quarters of a mile long.

Chester, Cheshire
The Roodee, named because of its 'rood' or raised mound, is Britain's oldest, still operating, racecourse having staged races since the early 16th century.

Bond actor Daniel Craig was born here and in a 2013 poll Chester was the only UK city on a list of Europe's Prettiest Cities as voted for by American tourists. Chester is undoubtedly attractive but the US tourists obviously hadn't visited many other beautiful British cities.

Chester claims to be the only place on the planet with a double-deck shopping street, Chester Rows.

The Chester branch of Spud-U-Like closed down in 2018 after gaining fame as the world's only fast-food outlet where you could visit a Roman hypocaust in the basement.

Chesterfield, Derbyshire
The whole world must surely know about the crooked spire, which twists 45 degrees and leans 9 feet 6 inches, but not so many realise Chesterfield has Britain's oldest civic theatre, The Pomegranate, and one of the nation's largest outdoor markets.

Chief Guide Olave Baden-Powell lived here from 1918 to 1977, other local residents have included Princess Diana's butler Paul Burrell, MP Barbara Castle and author Peter Wright whose 'Spycatcher' went on record as the least-read bestseller of all time until Dan Brown came along.

Chichester, West Sussex
According to the Met Office, Chichester is Britain's Sunniest City with an average 1920.8 hours of sun per year.

The Fishbourne Roman Palace is nearby and the oval bank in the park at the site of East Gate is what's left of a Roman amphitheatre.

Chichester Cathedral is unusual in having a bell tower , campanile, separate from the main building. The Cathedral contains the shrine of Saint Richard of Chichester and a memorial to local MP William Huskisson whose only entry in most history books is due to him being the first person to be run over by a railway train, suffering injuries from which he died, when he was in collision with Stephenson's Rocket at the opening of the Liverpool and Manchester Railway.

Britain's first official astronaut, Tim Peake, was born in Chichester in 1972.

Chiddingly, East Sussex
Burgh, Gun, Holmes, Pick, Scrappers, Stone and Thunders are the seven hills of Chiddingly. (See Morley)

Chinnor, Oxfordshire
U2 are renowned worldwide as an Irish rock band and claim to be Ireland's second-biggest export after Guinness. Adam Clayton, the band's drummer is from Chinnor, 350 miles by car and ferry from Dublin. (See Barking)

Chinnor's main landmark for many years was the chimney of the cement works which was demolished in 2008.

The village once had seven pubs but at the time of writing only three of these remain open with four having closed between 2000 and 2013..

Chippenham, Wiltshire
The annual Chippenham Folk Festival usually takes place during the Whitsuntide weekend but it is a rock and roll tragedy that attracts many music lovers to the town.

On 17th April 1960 singer/songwriter Eddie Cochran died when a taxi in which he was travelling blew a tyre at high speed on the A4 in Chippenham. Cochran's fiancee, Sharon Sheeley, rock and roller Gene Vincent, tour manager Pat Tompkins and the taxi driver survived the crash. There is no truth in the regularly repeated myth that Dave Dee, who became leader of the group Dave Dee, Dozy, Beaky, Mick and Titch, was one of the police officers called to the accident. Dee was a police cadet at the time and his only connection is that Eddie Cochran's belongings were impounded at Chippenham police station until after the inquest and Dee is said to have taken the opportunity to play a few chords on Cochran's iconic Gretsch guitar.

Chipping Campden, Gloucestershire
The official Olympic torch passed through Campden (as it is known to the locals) in 2012 but since 1612 the town has staged its own Olimpicks (sic). The Cotswold Olympic Games are claimed to be the

forerunner of the Modern Olympics. Sports seen in these games but inexplicably missing from the official Olympics have included shin-kicking and dwile flonking which involves throwing beer-soaked rags at the opposition. (See Much Wenlock)

Chipping Norton, Oxfordshire

Chipping Norton is the highest town in Oxfordshire. The former Bliss Tweed Mill is now apartments but it retains its unusual chimney standing on a dome.

A blue plaque commemorates the discovery here by the Rev Edward Stone of the active ingredient in aspirin.

Between 1972 and 1999 just some of the records produced at Chipping Norton Recording Studios include such classics as Gerry Rafferty's 'Baker Street,' Status Quo's 'In the Army Now.' Fairground Attraction's 'Perfect' and 'I Just Died in Your Arms Tonight' by Cutting Crew.

Chiswick, Greater London

There is a marvellous smell in Chiswick thanks to Fuller's Brewery producing beer here since the 17th century. The brewery and the nearby narrow island, Chiswick Eyot, are guaranteed an annual name check in the University Boat Race TV commentary.

The Chiswick flyover was opened in 1959 by Hollywood actress Jayne Mansfield. The Kray gangsters are said to have disposed of the body of Ginger Marks in the foundations of the flyover.

Chiswick Pier is the home of one of London's two RNLI lifeboat stations.

Hugh Grant grew up here and the recording studios in the High Road have been used by Rihanna and Beyonce. The walls of Chiswick are peppered with blue plaques commemorating those who were born, lived or worked here.

Chorley, Lancashire

The main difference between a Chorley Cake and an Eccles Cake is that the former is dried fruit encased in shortcrust pastry while the latter encloses its fruit in puff pastry. Chorley Cakes are less sweet than Eccles Cakes and are traditionally served spread with butter, a hunk of crumbly Lancashire Cheese on the side, and ideally washed down by a pint of good ale. (See Banbury and Eccles)

Christchurch, Dorset

For such a small place Christchurch has lots to offer holidaymakers with not one, not two but six beaches.

Bournemouth Aviation Museum is in Christchurch as is Bournemouth Airport, still known locally as Hurn. From 1945 until Heathrow opened a year later, Hurn was Britain's transatlantic airport with scheduled flights to La Guardia, New York, taking 17 hours 40 minutes. England's first land-landing service to Australia took off from here in the 1940s, the journey lasting three-days.

Church Stretton, Shropshire

Church Stretton is the only town in the Shropshire Hills Area of Outstanding Natural Beauty. The hilly surrounding landscape found this dubbed Little Switzerland in the Victorian era resulting in the town becoming a health resort.

Mineral water is extracted and bottled at what the

locals know as the 'Pop Works'. A tap outside the factory enables passers-by to fill their bottles for free but this facility is only available from Monday to Friday as the pump delivering water from an underground aquifer is turned off when the factory is closed.

Cirencester, Gloucestershire

An 1892 Cirencester by-election could have been the first ever to be settled by the toss of a coin following a draw. A re-run of the election was called for and this time the Liberals beat the Conservatives into second place.

Many buildings in Cirencester were constructed from stone reclaimed from the Abbey. Henry VIII ordered the destruction of the Abbey which was 400-years old, he kept the ornate jewels, silver plate and even the lead from the roof.

Cirencester was Britain's second-largest Roman town after London, it boasts a Roman amphitheatre which later became a fortress and then a rabbit warren.

City of London, City of London

The City is the oldest part of London however few truly ancient building remain due its having been destroyed in the Great Fire of 1666 and heavily bombed during World War Two. About 25% of the city's buildings are replaced every 25 years.

Until 1980 all banks operating in the City had to have an office within a ten-minute walk of the Bank of England so that, in the event of a crisis, the Governor of the Bank of England had the CEO of every bank close to hand.

The City of London has more American banks than Manhattan and more Japanese banks than Tokyo yet it is the UK's smallest city by area. (See St Davids)

More international business telephone calls are made from the City of London than anywhere else in the world. Geographical location has a lot to do with this as the City's business day, either in the morning or in late afternoon, overlaps with all the world's major financial centres.

Clacton-on-Sea, Essex

Known to London day-trippers as Clackers and easy to find without resorting to satnav as it's at the eastern end of the A133.

One of the first German airmen to bail out at the start of World War Two landed in Clacton. The populace had no idea what to do with him so they treated him like a VIP celebrity prior to handing him over to the military.

Mods and Rockers battled here in the 1960s when Bultin's Holiday Camp was at its peak of popularity. With the increase in overseas package holidays Clacton saw a considerable slump and what was once an extremely busy bus station is now a car park.

Despite the town's working-class holiday image, the residents of Clacton-on-Sea lean far to the right politically with its former Tory Council being taken over by UKIP and its MP from 2005-17, Douglas Carswell, making a similar change from Tory to UKIP and then to Independent.

Clapham, Greater London

Being so close to central London there is little that

most people don't know about Clapham and its famous Common but Clapham South is one of the very few places named after an Underground station rather than the other way round.

Cleckheaton, West Yorkshire

Charles Roger Hargreaves, author of the 'Mr Men' and 'Little Miss' series of children's books was born here and there is a blue plaque at his childhood home in Halifax Road. His books have sold in excess off 85 million copies in 20 languages. (See Gomersal)

Cleethorpes, Lincolnshire

Despite Cleethorpes being referred to as a 'seaside resort' and treated as such by thousands of visitors each year the town is actually situated on the Humber Estuary, not the coast.

Grimsby FC play home matches in Cleethorpes.

Clerkenwell, Greater London

You have to peer in through a window of Well Court in Farringdon Lane to see what remains of the Clerk's Well from which Clerkenwell takes its name.

In the 17th century this was a trendy place to live with even Oliver Cromwell owning a house here.

London's original Little Italy was in Clerkenwell after some 2,000 Italians settled here in the 1850s.

There were once three prisons in Clerkenwell. In 1867 a group of Fenians, an organisation working to establish an independent Irish Republic, attempted to break one of their members out of Clerkenwell House of Detention by blowing up part of the prison wall. They succeeded in killing 12 local people and injuring a further 120. They did not succeed in releasing their associate.

(See Farringdon)

Clifton-Without, North Yorkshire
A flying circus visited here in 1933 giving the Council the idea to open an airport for the nearby city of York. York Municipal Aerodrome opened its runway in 1936 offering a flying club and air taxi but not a single scheduled flight. Following wartime use by military aircraft the proposed airport fell into disuse and is now mostly covered by a retail park. The closest airport to York is Leeds/Bradford.

Clitheroe, Lancashire
What was once the courtyard of the Swan and Royal Hotel is now an open-air shopping arcade with plans afoot to keep out the weather with a roof. The Swan and Royal was the venue for wartime meetings between Rolls-Royce and Rover, planning the development of the jet engine. Jet engine inventor Frank Whittle is celebrated in the name of the town's Whittle Close residential area which was built on the site of the former test beds. (See Haltwhistle)

Clovelly, Devon
Loved by tourists from around the world Clovely consists of a collection of thatched houses and shops, most of them listed buildings, down the sides of a very steep street descending to the sea. Deliveries have to be made by sledge or donkey. Disabled visitors can be taken to the beach from the hilltop car park by Land Rover to admire the view from the bottom of the street.

J M W Turner and Rex Whistler painted here with

Whistler's cameos appearing on Wedgwood pottery. Charles Dickens describes Clovely in his 'A Message from the Sea.'

Clovelly is undoubtedly very beautiful but if you don't like crowds I would suggest visiting outside any holiday season and preferably when the sun isn't shining. I did once take photographs for a magazine here with not a person to be seen but this was at 8am on a very cold and damp November morning.

Clun, Shropshire
In 'A Shropshire Lad' A E Housman claims, 'Clunton and Clunbury, Clungford and Clun are the quietest places under the sun.'

Clun is close to the Welsh border with Offa's Dyke nearby. The Dyke is an earthwork running approximately along the border between England and Wales. It is claimed the Dyke, which reached a height of 65-feet in some places, was constructed at the instructions of Offa, an Anglo-Saxon king of Mercia. Other sources have this as a Roman construction with its name deriving from 'Ofer' an Old English word for a border or edge. You're reading this book so make your choice. (See Johnstown, Wrexham)

Clyst St Mary, Devon
The village is now split into two by the busy A3052 leading to Dorset via the Westpoint Exhibition Centre but Clyst St Mary was the scene for one of the bloodiest incidents in the Prayer Book Rebellion (See Sampford Courtenay). Lord John Russel brought an army estimated at 8,600 men into the area killing and taking prisoners as they went. Russell set up camp at Clyst Heath where he had 900 prisoners bound, gagged and their throats slit. Chronicler John

Hayward recorded that all 900 died within a ten minute period.

The village is close to the M5 at the Exeter Services turn-off and the quality of Neil's home-baked pasties at the Londis store will save you the bother of driving all the way down to Cornwall.

Coalville, Leicestershire
It doesn't take a genius to work out from the name that this small town was once the location for several collieries.

Coalville is the home of Action Man, Tiny Tears, Pippa, Strawberry Shortcake and the Care Bears thanks to Politoy being a major employer here from 1937 to 1985.

Cobham, Surrey
Cobham is an ancient village but is now best known for the massive service station between junctions 9 and 10 on the M25. (See Beaconsfield)

Cockermouth, Cumbria
Don't snigger at the back. This town is so named because it is situated at the point (mouth) where the River Cocker flows into the River Derwent. 'Cocker' comes from an ancient word 'kukra' meaning 'the crooked one.'

One of the favoured walking places is the main cemetery which includes streams, bridges and spectacular views.

William Wordsworth was born at what is now known as Wordsworth House. (See Ambleside, See Grasmere, See Hawkshead)

Colchester, Essex
There is absolutely no truth in the myth that Colchester is named after a lung infection.

Colchester is one of several that claim to be the oldest town in England. In 77AD the Roman writer Pliny the Elder says that Anglesey was 200 miles from Camulodunum (Camulodunum being the Roman name for Colchester) so we know the town was established by then, coins minted here have been dated back to 20-19 BC and, even further back to the Palaeolithic period flints were worked in the area.

In his 'Nineteen Eighty-Four' George Orwell mentions that many cities across the world were destroyed as a result of nuclear attack but the only town actually named as a target is Colchester.

Colchester claims to have been the seat of King Cole making this the birthplace of the rhyme 'Old King Cole,' During the siege of Colchester, in the Civil War, One-Eyed Thompson, a Royalist sniper, sat in the church belfry, thanks to his excessive weight he was given the nickname Humpty Dumpty, He had a great fall when he was shot down and it is claimed this is the birth of the 'Humpty Dumpty' rhyme although there are those who claim Humpty Dumpty was a large cannon sited at the top of the church.

Jane Taylor who wrote 'Twinkle Twinkle Little Star' lived in Colchester making this the possible home of three of the nations best-known nursery rhymes.

Coleshill, Warwickshire
The town's main tourist attractions include the restored whipping post and pillory in the Market Square and a rare post box with the seal of Edward

VIII erected prior to his abdication.

Colyford, Devon
Motorists driving through Colyford, are often surprised to see the old fashioned petrol pumps standing outside a garage. This was a motor museum, closed at the time of writing.

T E Lawrence, Lawrence of Arabia, was a customer at the filling station and it is claimed that on the day he died in a tragic accident his last act was to fill up his motorcycle with petrol before heading up the hill towards his home in Dorset. In those days your tank was filled by a young chap who made polite conversation so Lawrence's last words were spoken to a lad at this garage. The boy didn't recognise him until some days later when Lawrence's photograph appeared in a press report about the accident, he had forgotten what conversation passed between himself and the hero so Lawrence's final words were never recorded.

Combe Martin, Devon
The Crown Jewels include items that include silver from Combe Martin, evidence of mining tunnels can still be seen.

Locals will tell you that Combe Martin has England's longest village High Street but this is disputed. Confusion began in 2002 when Combe Martin held the world's longest street party to celebrate the Queen's Golden Jubilee. So it had the longest street party but not necessarily held in the longest High Street. Combe Martin High Street has a length of 2 miles (3 km) but this is not populated for its entire length. (See Stewkley)

There is a very nice beach at Combe Martin but there are no dinosaurs at the Combe Martin Wildlife and Dinosaur Park.

Damien Hirst, reportedly the world's richest, living artist, owns a house here valued at £3.5 million at the time of writing.

The village has several pubs but the most interesting is The Pack o'Cards. Built as a private house in 1690 by a local squire to celebrate his gambling success. The building celebrates all things connected with cards. It is built on a site 52-feet x 53-feet, there being 52 cards in a pack or 53 if you include the joker. There are four floors representing the four suits, each floor has 13 doors and 13 fireplaces to equal the number of cards in each suit and there are 52 stairs in the building. At one time the pains of glass in the windows equalled the number of points in a pack of cards but the window tax resulted in many of these being bricked up.

Commondale, North Yorkshire

Commondale is one of those very rare places that had precisely the same number of residents, 129, in the 2001 census as it had in the 2011 census. In fact it's the only one I can find but if I give it exclusivity I can guarantee someone will come up with another location with the same claim to fame.

The village pub is the Cleveland Inn. One of the posts on the pub's own Facebook page is from someone who walked for two hours to get there to find it closed.

Compton, Surrey

Compton is the home of the Watts Gallery. George

Frederic Watts (1817 - 1904) was acclaimed as 'The English Michelangelo'.

Congleton, Cheshire
Legend has it that, in the 17th century, the people of Congleton held a collection to purchase a new Bible for the town then spent the cash on a dancing bear to replace one who had died.

Coniston, Cumbria
Coniston is situated between the third longest lake in the Lake District, Coniston Water, and a hill known as the Old Man of Coniston or Coniston Old Man.

The history of Coniston is the subject of the Ruskin Museum, named after Victorian art critic John Ruskin who also gave his name to the village primary school.

Corby, Northamptonshire
Corby steel works once employed so many Scots that the town was known as Little Scotland. The people of Corby allegedly drink more Irn-Bru than any other town outside Scotland with the local Asda supermarket claiming to sell 17-times more bottles of the soft drink than any other Asda store in England. The title track of rock band Big Country's 'Steeltown' album tells the story of Scottish steelworkers in Corby.

In June 1969 the Apollo 11 astronauts listened to a news bulletin that included the information that in Corby an Irishman named John Coyle had won the World Porridge Eating Championship by eating 23 bowls of instant oatmeal in 10 minutes. This explains why, in 1970, a crater on Mars was named Corby.

Corfe Castle, Dorset
The name gives a heavy hint that Corfe Castle is

obviously a castle but it doesn't explain that it is also the name of the surrounding village.

The castle belonged to the crown until Elizabeth I sold it in 1635, only fragments of the building remain but these are picturesque hilltop ruins that attract artists, photographers and tourists.

A model village situated in the village square shows what the place would have looked like in the mid-17th century.

Enid Blyton based some of the castles in her children's books on Corfe. 'Five on a Treasurer Island' was filmed here and Corfe also features in Disney's 'Bedknobs and Broomsticks.'

Cornhill-on-Tweed, Northumberland
Cornhill sits within yards of the Scottish border. Campfield Kettle Hole and Barelees Pond are included here because they are local Sites of Special Scientific Interest not just for their unconventional names. Both are kettle holes. When a piece broke off a glacier and then sank into a bog it eventually melted leaving a void in which the kettle hole formed.

Coton in the Elms, Derbyshire
This is the most distant point from the sea in the UK with at least 70 miles to travel for a paddle in the waves.

Cottingley, West Yorkshire
Elsie Wright and Frances Griffiths took five photographs in Cottingley in 1917 claiming these showed fairies. Sir Arthur Conan Doyle said the photos were clear evidence that fairies existed and he used them to illustrate a book. In the 1980s Elsie

and Frances finally confessed their photographs were faked using cardboard cutouts.

Coulsdon, Greater London
In 1782 businessman Thomas Byron bought estates taking in half of Coulsdon. The manor house and its surrounding parkland are now a luxury hotel and golf course.

Cane Hill Psychiatric Hospital opened as an asylum in 1882, holding 3,500 patients at its peak. All but the secure unit closed in 1991 with demolition beginning in 2008.The hospital's administration building features in a cartoon illustration on David Bowie's 1971 album 'The Man Who Sold the World'. (This album has had several different covers but the 1971 US cover depicting a man in red jacket and cowboy hat with a rifle under his arm, is now considered to be the definitive one.) Bowie's half-brother, Terry Burns, was a patient here, he committed suicide at Coulsdon South station in 1985..

Covent Garden, Greater London
Covent Garden owes its name to a spelling mistake. This was once the garden of a convent.

There was a market here from the 1600s but the current neoclassical building was constructed in the 1830s and was London's main fruit and vegetable market.

Tourists, and some 44 million come here each year, compared with 39 million visiting Manhattan's Times Square, 32 million for Niagara Falls and !8 million going to DisneyWorld, Orlando, think of Covent Garden as being the Piazza area with shops, restaurants and bars on the site of the old market but

Covent Garden is actually an entire neighbourhood.

Property prices here are sky-high with only multimillionaires able to afford to live in what were formerly brothels.

Eliza Doolittle from 'Pygmalion' which became 'My Fair Lady' met Professor Higgins in Covent Garden (See Tottenham Court Road) and Alfred Hitchcock, whose father was a greengrocer here, made the 1972 movie 'Frenzy' about a Covent Garden fruit seller who became a serial killer.

The Royal Opera House is known as 'Covent Garden'

Coventry, West Midlands
There's not a lot most people don't know about Coventry, its cathedral and Lady Godiva, but the locals will tell you 'facts' that, to be kind, at the very best, should be described as disputable.

Saint George was a Roman soldier of Greek origin but you don't have to spend too long in a Coventry pub before someone tells you that the dragon-slaying Patron Saint was a local lad. This probably has equal veracity to the 'fact' that 18-year-old William Shakespeare was about to marry a Coventry lass then unceremoniously dumped her on the eve of their wedding to go back to Stratford to marry 26-year-old Anne Hathaway who just happened to be pregnant at the time.

Chuck Berry really did record his only UK number-one hit, 'My Ding-a-Ling' at Coventry's Locarno ballroom even though it comes from an album titled 'The London Chuck Berry Sessions.'

'True Blue' was a Madonna album and single title but the phrase originated in Coventry in the 14th century when fabric dyed Coventry Blue was expensive and fashionable. Being 'Sent to Coventry' originated in the Civil War when Royalists were imprisoned in this pro-Parliament city and given a difficult time by local guards.

George Orwell intended using Coventry as his model for a study of 1930s poverty in England but he discovered the place was actually quite affluent so, as a last minute substitute, he went on 'The Road to Wigan Pier.'

At the time of writing Coventry has been named the UK City of Culture 2021. (See Paisley)

Cowes, Isle of Wight

Cowes, the home of international yacht racing, is just across the Medina estuary from East Cowes, both locations taking their names from their likeness to cows when they were just a couple of sandbanks.

Cowes Week is the world's oldest regular regatta, it began in 1826, and it is also the largest regular regatta with over 8,000 competitors taking part in 350 races. The R.Y.S. £100 Cup was a trophy, worth £100, contested for by yachts in a round-the-island race during the regatta. First competed for in 1851 when it was won by a US sailing boat named 'America'. The US contestants didn't understand the British monetary system and had the trophy engraved '100 Guinea Cup'. A guinea being one pound and one shilling. This is now the prestigious America's Cup.

Crackington Haven, Cornwall

Middle Crackington and Higher Crackington are

located on the hill to the southeast of Crackington Haven.

Geologists and tourists come here to view the folded strata in the surrounding cliffs. Nearby High Cliff, as its name suggests, is Cornwall's highest cliff and southern Britain's highest sheer-drop with a height of 735-feet.

Crackington Haven suffered badly during the 2004 floods which caused severe damage to the bridge, several houses and the Coombe Barton Inn.

Crawley, West Sussex
Crawley is the home of the world's busiest, single-runway airport, Gatwick.

Yorkshireman and former choirboy John George Haigh, the Acid Bath Murderer, killed and dissolved three of his victims in Crawley.

Sheila Snelling lived here until her death in 1995. Ms Shelling was instantly recognisable by her filthy raincoat and floppy hat, she shouted and snarled at anyone who came near and because of this trait and her eccentric clothing everyone knew her as Mad Mary. In 2012 a beer was created in her memory and there is talk of a statue.

Crawley Down, West Sussex
Thanks to its proximity to London and the lenience of the local law enforcement officers Crawley Down was once a centre for bareknuckle prizefighting. Huge crowds gathered for a spectacle that provided valuable revenue for the village.

Crewe, Cheshire
From 1946 to 2002 Rolls-Royce cars were produced here but it's railways that still attract the train-spotters. Trains are inspected and maintained here. Crewe Heritage Centre is a railway museum displaying full-size trains, miniature trains and three signal boxes, two from Crewe and one from Exeter.

In the 1984 apocalyptic TV war movie 'Threads' Crewe is destroyed by a Soviet nuclear device.

Crewekerne, Somerset
Crewkerne is close to the Dorset border and I actually found one website that relocated the town to Devon. Back in the 18th and 19th centuries much of the webbing and sailcloth used by the Royal Navy was produced here and this is reflected in the collection of the Crewkerne and District Museum with its emphasis on the flax and linen industry.

This is the home of the Ariel Motor Company which produces the Ariel Atom, the world's first exoskeletal road car. This has no bodywork or roof being built entirely around a tube chassis.

Cricklewood, Greater London
The 1997 movie 'Titanic' collected eleven Oscars including one for Visual Effects. Those Visual Effects include the engine room scenes which were filmed in the Cricklewood Pumping Station.

From Gladstone Park, where Mark Twain used to hang out, on a clear day you can see Wembley Stadium, the Shard and the London Eye.

Former residents have included serial killer Dennis Nilson, London Mayor Ken Livingstone and Andrew

Sachs, better known as Manuel in 'Fawlty Towers.'

Cromer, Norfolk

Local myth claims that Sir Arthur Conan Doyle gained inspiration for his 'The Hound of the Baskervilles' while on a golfing holiday in Cromer. He stayed at Cromer Hall and, it is said, here he heard a local legend about a ghostly dog. This myth conveniently manages to ignore the fact that the novel is set on Dartmoor at the opposite side of the country. (See Buckfastleigh)

Just 600 years ago what is now the seaside resort of Cromer was inland and what was then the coastal town, Shipden, disappeared beneath the waves.

Fifty boats once fished for the justifiably revered Cromer crabs. I would not dispute the boast that Cromer crabs are the sweetest in the UK but most modern young people show little interest in the hard work involved in catching them and only a few vessels continue with the trade.

Norfolk has no motorways.

Crooklands, Cumbria

Crooklands is the home of the Westmorland County Agricultural Show, the show has been held since 1799, moving to its current site in the 20th century.

Cropredy, Oxfordshire

Cropredy was the temporary resting place of Saint Fremund (See Southam) but is best known for the annual music festival staged by folk-rock band Fairport Convention.

Crosthwaite, Cumbria

Crosthwaite is the home of the Lake District

Sheepdog Experience where you get to do things with a border collie they did on the TV series 'One Man and His Dog' .

Crowthorne, Berkshire
Once a tiny hamlet, Crowthorne's population had grown to almost 7,000 at the last count thanks to the siting here of Wellington College and Broadmoor maximum security psychiatric hospital, home of Peter Sutcliffe, the Yorkshire Ripper, at the time of writing. (See Bracknell. See Bingley. See Dewsbury)

Croyde, Devon
Farming has been replaced as Croyde's main money earner by surfing. There are two holiday parks and you might be forgiven for thinking that every VW camper van on the planet is to be found here. Although surfable waves are in short supply there is a strong rip current so injuries are frequent.

Croyde hosts an annual surf and music festival, Goldcoast Oceanfest, on the closest weekend to the Summer Solstice.

Croydon, Greater London
Croydon was the first place outside central London to have postcodes and if it was a city it would be the 8th-largest in Britain.

The UK's first international airport was at Croydon which boasts the world's oldest air traffic control tower.

Six Archbishops of Canterbury adopted St Mary's the Blessed church as their second home, renaming it Addington Palace. All six of them are buried here.

Henry VIII lived in Croydon, on and off, while wooing local resident Catherine of Aragon. Henry considered the town to be 'rheumatic'.

In more recent times Croydon became the birthplace of dubstep.

Cuckfield, West Sussex

Claims of financial chicanery in national politics are often denied but in Cuckfield it seems money is more important than anything if you wish to become mayor. Mayoral votes can be purchased for one penny each and there is no limit as to how many each voter is permitted to purchase. The pennies go to charity and, once he's bought it, the title of Mayor is purely ceremonial.

D

Danby, North Yorkshire
The Duke of Wellington retains its pubiness with good ale and real fires in the winter. The inn advertises comfortable rooms and British food from local produce. Sounds like a good place to stay along the Esk Valley Walk which runs through the village.

Darlington, County Durham
The world's first steam-powered passenger train journey set out from here on 27th September 1825. It travelled to Stockton on Tees at a speed of 6mph. The railway was originally intended just for horse-drawn wagons to haul coal but George Stephenson strengthened the track to take his new steam-driven locomotive, Locomotion No 1, which pulled 600 passengers on that first journey.

Darlo, as the locals call it, is the largest settlement in County Durham.

Dartford, Kent
The locals call it Dirtford but they get very cross when they hear visitors using the same derogatory description. Henry VIII held Privy Council meetings in Dartford in 1545 and his fourth wife, Anne of Cleeves, lived here for her final four years.

The Mick Jagger Centre is a performing arts venue in the grounds of Dartford Grammar School, it is named after the Rolling Stones' singer who attended the school.

Margaret Thatcher was unsuccessful when she ran as

MP for Dartford in 1950 and again in 1951.

Dartington, Devon
Darlington Hall has been the venue of an annual International Summer School since 1953. This is a music school and festival combining the talents of amateurs and professionals.

I have met people who travelled here hoping to see the production of Dartington Crystal but they had come to the wrong end of Devon. (See Great Torrington)

Dartmouth, Devon
Geoffrey Chaucer visited here in 1373 and 'The Shipman's Tale' in his 'Canterbury Tales' features a traveller from Dartmouth, or 'Dertemouth' as Chaucer knew it.

Thomas Newcomen, inventor of the steam-powered pumping engine, was born in Dartmouth in 1663.

Sir Humphrey Gilbert and his half-brother Sir Walter Raleigh lived on the Greenway Estate which was later the home of Agatha Christie.

This is the location of the Britannia Royal Naval College for Naval Officers. The Dartmouth Regatta is a major event taking place at the end of August each year.

Daventry, Northamptonshire
In 1935 the world's first RADAR demonstration took place in Daventry. Robert Watson-Watt set up his equipment in an old Morris van in a field at nearby Weedon from where he detected an RAF Handley Page bomber flying in the area.

Dawlish, Devon
Dawlish stands on what has to be one of Britain's most beautifully situated railway lines. The line's coastal location sees waves breaking over trains when the sea is rough, resulting in temporary closure for the strengthening of its foundations which were washed away during a violent storm in 2014 leaving the railway lines hanging in mid-air. (See Okehampton)

Dawlish Water, the town centre outlet to the sea of a small river, is an attraction thanks to its black swans.

Dawlish Warren, Devon
Dawlish Warren consists mainly of holiday accommodation, some in old railway carriages, slot machines and a nature reserve on an easily accessed spit of sand with a profusion of birdlife.

In 1983 Britain in Bloom judges claimed a combination of heat and a very long, hard day could have been to blame for the slight error of judgement when they awarded the certificate for Second Prize to a slot machine arcade at Dawlish Warren only to be told by the arcade's jubilant owner, that every item in his magnificent floral display was made from plastic.

Deal, Kent
Over the years Deal has been winner of the Daily Telegraph High Street of the Year award and the same newspaper voted it into its Top Ten Places to Lay Your Beach Towel.

Henry VIII built one of three castles here to defend this bit of coastline from possible invasion by European Catholics.

The pier has gone through its ups and downs, the

current version of Deal Pier was opened by the Duke of Edinburgh in 1957, it reopened in 2018 after a period of closure to install new gas mains, there's a cafe and people come here to fish.

The big attraction for the many thousands who celebrate New Year's Eve in Times Square, Manhattan, is the anticlimactic, midnight dropping of the Time Ball. Deal has a Time Ball Tower Museum celebrating the era when ships relied for an accurate time check on seeing a ball dropped at 1pm each afternoon from the Time Ball Tower. When the Deal Time Ball Museum is open visitors can thrill to the sight of a ball being dropped every hour.

Deddington, Oxfordshire
After the 1066 Norman Conquest William the Conqueror handed the Manor of Deddington to his step-brother Odo, the Bishop of Bayeux. The outer bailey, built by Odo, at Deddington Castle can still be seen at the eastern end of the town.

Dedham, Essex
John Constable's link with the village at the heart of what is now promoted as Constable Country brings in many tourists. Constable attended the town's grammar school. Constable is hailed as a painter of the Suffolk countryside. Dedham Vale, the subject of most of Constable's best known works, is on the Essex-Suffolk border, so some of those iconic images were painted in Essex, not Suffolk.

Deeping St James, Lincolnshire
(See Market Deeping)

Denton, Greater Manchester
From the 18th century Denton was dependent on hat

making and coal mining but in 1865 Joseph Oldham came here and opened his factory which became internationals-known for the Oldham Battery, named after the man, not after the nearby town.

A grave at St Lawrence's Church is pointed out to visitors because the tombstone includes a skull and crossbones which some locals will tell you is evidence that a pirate is buried here. In reality Samuel Bromley, a deceased soldier, is interred beneath what is a masonic symbol.

Derby, Derbyshire
The Arboretum Park in Derby opened in 1840 to become England's first public park. Frederick Law Olmsted visited the park in 1859 and incorporated elements from it in his design for New York's Central Park.

Derby Silk Mill has a good claim to being the first factory in the world but its silk-throwing machines were the result of what is thought to have been the world's first example of industrial espionage after John Lombe visited Piedmont in 1717 and returned to Derby with details of machines used by Italian craftsmen.

Bonnie Prince Charlie lodged at Exeter House, Full Street, in 1745 on his journey south to seize the British crown.

Although nearby Ashbourne claims to be the source for the noun 'Derby', meaning a sporting contest between two local teams, it is far more likely that the word comes from the Derby horse race, named after the Earl of Derby in 1780 and meaning any sporting contest. None of this has anything to do with Derby as the Earl who founded the horse race and future Earls of Derby through to the present day lived near Liverpool. (See Ashbourne. See Wallasey.)

Dereham, Norfolk
Also known as East Dereham, the village almost became a spa town after a building was erected over a spring that sprang at the site of the tomb of Saint Withburga after her body had been stolen and taken to Ely. The building was deemed to be extremely ugly and was demolished in 1880.

The car park at the Dereham branch of Tesco has been calculated as the geographical centre of Norfolk.

Devizes, Wiltshire
6X and Bishop's Tipple are the two best known beers from Wadsworth of Devizes. The brewery tour is listed at the top of things to do here.

The Wiltshire Museum with its collection, designated as being of National Significance, is well worth a visit especially with children on a rainy day.

The Crammer, a pond near the town, played an essential part in concealing smuggled goods when contraband was brought through Devizes on its way to customers in the Midlands. Barrels of French brandy were submerged in the pond and when customs officers caught locals trying to retrieve the barrels using rakes the men told the officers they were raking for the big cheese, this being a reflection of the moon on the surface of the water. The customs officers let them go free believing them to be simple yokels and this is said to be why people from Wiltshire are still known as Moonrakers. (See Middleton)

Dewsbury, West Yorkshire
Wallace Hartley, bandmaster on the Titanic, moved to Dewsbury from Huddersfield. In 2013 more than 600 people queued to see Hartley's violin when it was displayed in Dewsbury prior to going to auction in Wiltshire. The guide price was £300,000 but after just ten minutes the instrument was knocked down for £900,000.

In recent years this has been called 'The town that dare not speak its name' due to links with horrific crimes. Amongst several notable crime connections the leader of the gang responsible for the 2005 London bombings lived nearby and the Yorkshire Ripper, Peter Sutcliffe, was brought to Dewsbury after his arrest. (See Bingley)

In 2015 Princess Anne came to Dewsbury and made a speech that lasted little longer than one minute about the restoration of justice. The council enforced a ban on media coverage of the visit and her speech, claiming this was a ruling from the Royal Household, a claim denied by Buckingham Palace.

Didcot, Oxfordshire
When Isambard Kingdom Brunel engineered his Great Western Railway from London to the West Country the planned route to Bristol was through Abingdon but Lord Wantage, the landowner, refused permission for the line to cross his estate so it was moved further south to Didcot. The town then became a junction on the Newbury and Southampton Railway making it of immense military importance during the two World Wars.

Didcot station was renamed Didcot Parkway and is now more carpark than railway station but a subway beneath the station gives access to the Didcot Railway

Centre. Housed in an old engine shed the Centre has a collection of Great Western locomotives and rolling stock. It often appears in movies and TV shows requiring period rail themes and can be seen in 'The Elephant Man,' 'Anna Karenina,' and 'Sherlock Holmes: A Game of Shadows.'

Diss, Norfolk
This small market town is probably best known for its 6-acre lake, Diss Mere. The lake is the source of a major mystery that scientists have been unable to solve. Some say the lake was the result of glacial activity in the Ice Age but the flat landscape at one side of the lake, it includes a cricket pitch, suggests this theory must be wrong and also casts doubt on the volcanic crater theory. Others question where the water originally came from but there is evidence a spring once flowed through.

The lake is very similar in size and shape to Il-Maqluba in Malta and current research suggests this is a crater caused by a meteorite strike.

Ditchling, East Sussex
The order confirming the establishment of the South Downs was signed in Ditching which is surrounded by the National Park.

Wartime singer Dame Vera Lynn, actor Sir Donald Sinden and illustrator Raymond Briggs have all lived here.

Docklands, Greater London
First known as London Docklands in a 1971 report on redevelopment plans. The riverfront and docks were once the world's largest port.

With accommodation here improving from near slum conditions in the 1960s to luxury apartments at the end of the 20th century the population has more than doubled in that period. Canary Wharf now challenges the City of London as the nation's financial capital with more skyscrapers than anywhere of a similar size in Europe.

Doddiscombseleigh, Devon
A Dartmoor village with a pub well worth making a diversion for. The Nobody Inn apparently takes its name from the occasion when a landlord died and his coffin was carried back to the pub for his wake. When the pallbearers and mourners arrived back at the pub there was, quite obviously, nobody in, and the name has stuck. The pub has the largest selection of whiskies I have seen anywhere. I'm not sure if the offer still stands but a former landlord once told me if I could name a Scotch whisky he couldn't serve he'd buy me a bottle.

Doncaster, South Yorkshire
William Bradford and William Brewster, two of the Pilgrim Fathers, were born in Doncaster.

The St Leger, staged in Doncaster each year, is the world's oldest 'classic' horse race. In 1909 the racecourse hosted Britain's first Aviation Meeting.

David Bowie's father was born in Doncaster but this town must surely win a trivia award for claiming to be the home of the world's oldest goldfish. Tish was awarded as a funfair prize in 1956 and was buried in his owner's garden in 1999.

The Mallard, built in Doncaster in 1938, still retains the world speed record, 126 mph, for a steam locomotive.

Dorchester, Dorset
Everyone knows about Thomas Hardy's connection with Dorchester and this is, of course, the site for Prince Charles' experimental town of Poundsbury but how many people know about the Dorset Teddy Bear Museum?

There are vintage teddy bears, modern teddy bears, even human-sized teddies living in Teddy Bear House where they collect, you've guessed it, teddy bears. You can even meet Pooh, Paddington, Yogi and Sooty

Dorchester-on-Thames, Oxfordshire
Strictly speaking the River Thames is only known as the Thames downstream from this village, upstream from here it is the Isis.

Steeped in history and often featured in 'Midsomer Murders' (Oxfordshire is a hotbed of locations for TV murders) Dorchester-on-Thames is a quaint, scenic village, a short drive from the centre of Oxford.

Douglas, Isle of Man
The Isle of Man is not part of Great Britain, it is a possession of the Crown so, it belongs to the Queen who holds the title Lord of Mann. Strictly speaking the island has no place in this book but I thought its inclusion might generate a few extra sales.

The Isle of Man has three legs as its arms.

Douglas is home of the Manx Parliament, Tynwald, which has allegedly met since 979 without a break making it the oldest continuous parliament in the world. In 1881 Tynwald became the world's first national legislative body to give women a vote in general elections.

Although most people think of the Bee Gees as Australian, the Gibb brothers, Barry, Maurice and Robin were born in Douglas.

Dover, Kent

One of Britain's most patriotic songs, 'The White Cliffs of Dover,' was a hit for Vera Lynn in World War Two. The song was written by two Americans who clearly did no research on native British birds as bluebirds have never been known to fly over the White Cliffs.

The White Cliffs of Dover conceal tunnels carved out by prisoners during the Napoleonic Wars, the tunnels were enlarged to house artillery in the Second World War.

St Edmund's Chapel in Dover claims to be the smallest church in Britain. (See Peebles)

Matthew Webb began what is credited as the first successful cross-Channel swim from Dover in 1875. Webb died attempting to swim the rapids below Niagara Falls.

Dover Sole does not necessarily come from Dover, this is the port where it was traditionally brought into the country.

Downham Market, Norfolk

Once home to a weekly butter market and an annual horse fair, a heritage centre called Discover Downham is to be found in the former fire station.

Charles I hid here in 1646 following the defeat of his Royalists at the Battle of Naseby. The only two things he is said to have done while here were to have his hair cut and then buy a new hat which doesn't say a lot for the local barber.

Droitwich Spa, Worcestershire
Droitwich stands on massive salt deposits, salt has been produced here for thousands of years, Brine from Droitwich contains 2.5 pounds of salt per imperial gallon which makes it ten-times saltier than sea water. You can swim in this water in the pool at Droitwich Spa Lido.

Among the Luxembourgs and Hilversums on old radio dials you can find Droitwich. The high salt content in the ground was excellent earthing for more powerful radio signals so the BBC located its MW/LW transmitter here.

Dudley, West Midlands
Dudley is often referred to as the Capital of the Black Country. The Black Country took its name because coal could be found at the surface here.

Dudley Zoo is a major tourist attraction. A few weeks following the opening of the zoo, a bear escaped and after it bit someone it was hit on the head by a policeman wielding his truncheon. Three days later the bear broke out again and this time it was shot dead. A snow leopard escaped from its enclosure in 2018 when a keeper failed to lock it. The leopard was shot and the zoo announced that its killing was 'euthanasia'.

The far-right, Islamophobic,English Defence League has held several protests in the town.

Dukinfield, Greater Manchester
Coal and cotton resulted in the development of

Duckinfield during the Industrial Revolution.

Actress Kathy Staff, better known as Nora Batty, was born here.

Dulverton, Somerset
In 2009 Dulverton was dubbed Britain's Most Unfriendly Town after someone there took a pot shot with a rifle at a journalist and a restaurateur had his pet stags killed and dumped on his doorstep. I have to say I gave the town's Bridge Inn a try and found the staff and locals to be very friendly and worth a visit for the ale and pie.

The Exmoor National Park Authority has its headquarters here and the village is known as the Gateway to Exmoor.

Dumbleton, Gloucestershire
In St Peter's Church can be found a painted statue of Sir Charles Percy and his wife, Dorothy Cocks, kneeling over the body of their dead child.

The Rev Charles Cocks is the subject of a trompe-l'oeil painting on a blocked window at the back of the Old Rectory.

Dummer, Hampshire
Within earshot of traffic on the M3, Dummer attracted tourists in 1986 when a local lass, Sarah Ferguson, married Prince Andrew. Socialite Tara Palmer-Tomkinson also came from the village.

Dunsop Bridge, Lancashire
Dunsop Bridge claims to be the exact geographical centre of Britain. (See Haltwhistle)

Dunstable, Bedfordshire
The first play performed in Britain was written and staged in Dunstable by Geoffrey de Gotham in the 12th century.

Henry VIII's marriage to Catherine of Aragon came to an end here in 1533 when Thomas Cranmer declared their union illegal because Catherine had previously been married to Henry's brother, Arthur.

Dunstable is the closest town to Whipsnade Zoo.

Dunster, Somerset
Dunster is situated on the Bristol Channel, just within the boundary of the Exmoor National Park.

Grabbist Hill is the 'Purple-headed mountain' in the popular hymn 'All Things Bright and Beautiful.' Cecil Alexander wrote the hymn while staying in Dunster. At the time of Alexander's visit the hill was topped by purple heather but this has long disappeared beneath hill-topping trees.

Although the north coast of Somerset might be considered one of the unlikeliest of spots for the Germans to invade Britain, pillboxes and other World War Two defences can still be seen on and around Dunster Beach.

Durham, County Durham
Sorry to disappoint the millions of tourists who have taken photographs of the Sanctuary Knocker on the main door of Durham Cathedral but it is a replica. The original lion-headed knocker can be seen in the Cathedral Treasures exhibition. Fugitives who managed to grasp the knocker were granted 37 days of sanctuary before either facing their accusers or

being given safe passage to the coast.

The Cathedral was constructed over the shrine of St Cuthbert whose body reportedly remained intact when examined on several occasions from shortly after his death in 687 through to the early 19th century. Someone who actually viewed St Cuthbert's remains in 1899 reported seeing, 'just bones with some skin and ligaments attached.'

The annual Durham Miners' Gala is the largest regular Socialist trade union event on the planet.

Although Norwich claims to be the home of English mustard, the condiment was actually invented in Durham by a Mrs Clements, her first name is lost in the mists of time. (See Norwich. See Tewkesbury)

Causey Arch, built in 1725/26 is the world's oldest railway bridge, with a length of 102-feet it was the longest single-span bridge in Britain. Stonemason Ralph Wood was so convinced his arch, which still stands, would soon collapse that he committed suicide.

Duxford, Cambridgeshire
RAF Duxford was important in World War Two, it was later used by the USA Army Airforce as a base for their P-47 Thunderbolt aircraft, it is now the home of the Imperial War Museum, Duxford.

The Duxford Imperial War Museum's collection includes a restored Concorde, donated to the museum in 1977.

Dymchurch, Kent
In the 16th century a courtroom here was controlled

by a magistrate known as the Leveller of the Marsh Scotts. The so-called Scot Tax (yes just one letter 't') was introduced to fund maintenance of the sea walls which have existed since Roman times. Those outside the boundary did not have to pay the tax so they got off 'Scott Free' (with two letter 't's). This is said to be the origin of 'Scot-free' but some sources claim the phrase originated due to the mythical Scottish tightness with money.

Russell Thorndyke set his novels about smuggler Rev Dr Syn in and around Dymchurch.

E

Ealing, Greater London
London's largest Sikh community is in Ealing, as is the world's oldest, still operating, film studio.

The 1970/80s kids' TV comedy series 'Rentaghost' was filmed in Ealing as were many 'Doctor Who' episodes.

Rolling Stones Mick Jagger and Keith Richards first met Brian Jones at the 1962 Ealing Jazz Festival.

I couldn't find anyone able to explain the reason for the statue known as the Ealing Horse but it is amazing to discover how many local residents admit to trying to mount it after a drinking session. The horse has its own Facebook page and a plaque indicates it was unveiled by Her Majesty the Queen on March 7th 1985.

Earls Court, Greater London
Diana Spencer, the future Princess Diana, was gifted a house in Earls Court by her parents as an 18th birthday present. She boosted her finances by renting out spare rooms to friends.

It is hard to walk more than 100 yards in Earls Court without passing a blue plaque to a greater or lesser-celebrated former resident.

Polish immigrants settled here after World War Two giving Earls Court the title the 'Polish Corridor,' In the 60s cheap property attracted large numbers of Australians and New Zealanders and this became 'Kangaroo Valley.'

Easington, County Durham
Billy Elliot is set in the fictional town of Everington and the film was mostly shot in Easington.

Easingwold, North Yorkshire
At the foot of the Howardian Hills, an Area of Outstanding Natural Beauty where you will find Castle Howard, between the North York Moors National Park and the Vale of York, the town developed from an amalgamation of two communities, Lessimers and Uppleby.

East Budleigh, Devon
In the very attractive church, you can see the Ralegh (sic) Family Pew. Raleigh's parents are buried here. Sir Walter was born at the house called Hayes Barton close to East Budleigh. Raleigh's birthplace is not open to the public but it is claimed tobacco grows wild around the house. I've got to say I live close by and I've never seen any.

The bronze statue of Raleigh at the top of the village cost £30,000 which was funded by British American Tobacco. This was unveiled in 2006 by the Duke of Kent, I'm sure purely coincidentally, in the same week tougher anti-smoking laws were introduced to the UK.

After his execution Raleigh's body is said to have been buried in St Margaret's Church, Westminster. It is claimed his head was preserved at the orders of his wife who kept it in a leather case which she carried in a bag. In 2018 a silk bag was discovered at West Horsley Place, near Guildford, former home of Lady Raleigh, and this is thought to have been the bag in which she carried her husband's head.

East Grinstead, West Sussex
Sackville College, the Jacobean almshouses, was built in 1609, it is here, in 1853, that John Mason Neale wrote the words of the Christmas carol 'Good King Wenceslas' which was set to the melody of a 13th-century spring song. The statue outside the almshouses is in honour of Sir Archibald McIndoe a pioneering plastic surgeon from New Zealand.

The Town Council building sits on the Prime, or Greenwich, Meridian, giving staff the opportunity to work with their body in two different hemispheres.

East Horsley, Surrey
Deemed Britain's Richest Village by the Daily Telegraph in 2011 and again in 2015. In the 2011 census East Horsley had 1,343 detached houses and only 183 of any other home types.

The hotel and conference centre, Horsley Towers, originally called East Horsley Park, is on the list of the Ten Most-Haunted Places in Europe.

East Molesey, Surrey
Although many people only know of East Molesey this, along with West Molesey, is half of the suburban district of Molesey. East and West have a shared high street. East Molesey receives the plaudits being the location for most of the large and expensive properties.

Hampton Court Palace is in East Molesey but, due its importance, I have given this its own entry.

Eastbourne, East Sussex
During World War Two Eastbourne was England's most-bombed seaside town with almost 4,000 bombs being dropped here.

A skeleton found in Eastbourne in 2014 was dated to approximately 425AD. This was the remains of a woman aged about 30, she had the skeletal structure of an African and, tests suggested, almost certainly black skin, further tests have placed her home location as being south of the Sahara at a time when the Roman Empire extended no further to the south than North Africa.

In the same year as the skeleton discovery much of the pier was destroyed by fire. The government promised the town £2 million for the loss of trade and tourism.
Beachy Head is to the west of the town and the Eastbourne Downland can be seen from most places in Eastbourne.

Lewis Carroll spent holidays here, as did Karl Marx and Frederick Engels. At his own request Engels' ashes were scattered from Beachy Head.

Claude Debussy completed 'La mer' while staying at the Grand Hotel and in the song 'The Laughing Gnome' David Bowie gives his gnome 'roasted toadstools and a glass of dandelion wine' before putting him on 'a train to Eastbourne.'

Eastleigh, Hampshire
Richard Block and David Quayle formed a DIY company originally called Block and Quayle which has been abbreviated to B&Q. B&Q's headquarters are in Eastleigh. Mr Kipling Cakes were baked here until 2005. There never was anyone connected with these cakes called Mr Kipling.

Prior to international fame as a comedian, Benny Hill worked at Eastleigh Railway Works.

Eccles, Greater Manchester
Just about anywhere from Land's End to John o'Groats you'll find a shop selling Eccles Cakes. (See Banbury and Chorley)

Manchester City Airport is in Eccles. This was the UK's first purpose-built municipal airport.

Eddystone Lighthouse, Devon
The Eddystone Lighthouse stands on rocks south of Rame Head. Rame Head is in Cornwall but the rocks on which the lighthouse stands are in Devon. (See Dalbeattie)

Edenbridge, Kent
Many towns have their own special November 5th celebrations but Edenbridge Bonfire Society arrange celebrations that have become known worldwide. The big event is the burning of 10-metre effigies including an annual Celebrity Guy.

Hever Castle, close to Edenbridge, was the childhood home of Anne Boleyn.

Egham, Surrey
Egham is in the Runnymede Borough, close to the water-meadow, Runnymede, where just about everyone will tell you King John signed Magna Carta, except that he didn't. It is unlikely John could even write, he placed his seal on Magna Carta which includes the information that this took place at 'Ronimed, inter Windlesoram et Stanes,' (Runnymede, between Windsor and Staines.)

Many people visit the John F Kennedy memorial at Runnymede thinking this is just a simple block of stone. Read what is carved on that stone and you realise that the surrounding acre of beautiful and historic Runnymede was given by the people of Britain to the people of the USA in memory of the assassinated President. So this is an acre of the USA in the heart of the English countryside and you do not require a passport to visit.

Ellesmere Port, Cheshire

Ellesmere Port was established at the side of the River Mersey to serve the Ellesmere Canal linking Liverpool to the West Midlands. The canal was never completed but the town prospered and is the home to a major oil refinery and a Vauxhall Motors plant employing 1,100 staff. producing the second generation Opel/Vauxhall Astra at the time of writing.

As with many towns the old town centre is suffering at the hands of online shopping and a large shopping and leisure development, the Cheshire Oaks.

Ellington, Various Counties

There is an Ellington in Cambridgeshire, another in Northumberland and Ellingtons High and Low in North Yorkshire. All are small villages with not a lot to write about.

Elstree, Hertfordshire

Elstree Film and TV studios are actually in Borehamwood. (See Borehamwood)

Ely, Cambridgeshire

Oliver Cromwell lived in Ely for ten years prior to heading out to take over the country. His former home is now a museum in which the bedroom is reputedly haunted.

In 1944 the University Boat Race was staged on the Ouse at Ely, rather than on the Thames, due to the war. (See Sanford)

In 1974 Ely received its Royal Charter to become a city.

In 1986 Ely Cathedral, known as the Ship of the Fens, became the first in Britain to start charging an entry fee. At the time of writing the charge is £8 for the Cathedral, £12.50 for the Cathedral and the glass museum and £16.50 for a tour of the Cathedral and its tower. Ely Cathedral stood in for Westminster Abbey in several movies including, 'The King's Speech', 'Revolution' and 'The Crown'.

Enfield, Greater London
The world's first cash machine (now known as an ATM) was installed at the Enfield branch of Barclays Bank and officially opened on 27th June 1967 by local resident Reg Varney, best remembered as Stan Butler in the TV comedy series 'On The Buses' but, at the time, already a household name thanks to roles in 'The Rag Trade' and 'Beggar My Neighbour'.

The town boasts a gold-painted post box to celebrate the gold medal won by Enfield sportswoman Charlotte Dujardin who was one-third of the GB equestrian team at the 2012 Olympics

Epping, Essex
Known to tourists for its forest and for being the last station at the top end of the Underground's Central Line. Winston Churchill was MP for Epping from 1924 to 1945.

In the 12th century Henry II declared Epping Forest to be a Royal Forest where local people could graze their animals but only the King was allowed to hunt. Elizabeth I had a hunting lodge in the forest from which royal parties could look through the windows for deer and sportingly shoot them with a crossbow. Victoria made this a People's Forest.

Dick Turpin had a hideout here and Dickens begins 'Barnaby Rudge' with a description of Epping Forest.

Epsom, Surrey

Epsom Salt has no connection with normal salt. It is named after a bitter spring in Epsom where it occurs naturally. Epsom salt is said to be good for the body, the mind and some plants in the garden but no science-based tests have ever proved these claims.

The Epsom Derby was named after Edward Smith-Stanley the 12th Earl of Derby. It is said that the Earl and his co-founder of the race Sir Charles Bunbury tossed a coin at a dinner after the first running of the Oaks to decide after which of them the new race would be named. Legend has it that Bunbury won the toss but deferred to his host at the dinner. (See Wallasey. See Ashbourne)

'Derby' is now used as a generic name for all kinds of sporting occasions. The Derby Stakes was first run at Epsom in 1780. Suffragette Emily Wilding Davidson stepped out in front of the King's horse at the 1913 Derby. It is claimed she hadn't left home intending to kill herself as she had a return train ticket in her pocket, however her 8s 6d ticket was for a Derby Day excursion so probably cheaper than a normal single ticket.

Esher, Surrey

Esher is the home of Sandown Park racecourse. (See Sandown)

Eskdale, Cumbria
Listed as a proposed nuclear waste facility Eskdale was not actually named in the report but scientists knew exactly where they were talking about when they referred to the 'granitic rocks forming part of the Lake District Batholith.' This could only mean the Eskdale granite as similar granite at Ennerdale had already been named in the report along with the Solway Plain.

A Scottish glen is called Eskdale and there is an Eskdale valley in North Yorkshire.

Euston, Suffolk
I can find no record of the number of people who have come here hoping to catch a train.

Euston's parish church, dedicated to St Genevieve, is the only 17th century church in Suffolk.

Eversely, Hampshire
Charles Kingsley lived at the Rectory. (See Wokingham)

Evesham, Worcestershire
Eoves (or Eof), gave his name to Evesham. He was a swineherd who once saw a vision of the Virgin Mary. Eoves told his story to Egwin, Bishop of Winchester, who had an abbey built on the site of the apparition. In 2008 a bronze statue of Eoves with a couple of pigs was erected in the town centre.

Exeter, Devon
The Royal Clarence Hotel on Cathedral Green was the oldest building in Britain to be known as an hotel until it burnt down in 2016. At the time of writing (2020) the Royal Clarence was said to be being

restored but a visit by the author showed little actual activity taking place and the site had just been sold.

Exeter Guildhall is is the oldest, still used, civic building in Britain with parts dating back to 1160. Exeter ship canal, opened in 1566, is the oldest pound-lock canal in Britain. (See Lincoln)

Parliament Street, in Exeter, is Britain's narrowest street. (See Whitstable)

A memorial to Grace Darling can be seen outside St Thomas Church, in Cowick Street. (See Bamburgh)

On average people in Exeter are paid 20% more than those in Plymouth some 40 miles down the road.

Some websites claim J K Rowling was born in Exeter, she wasn't but she did go to Exeter University. (See Chepstow) Coldplay singer/songwriter Chris Martin was born in Exeter and was brought up on the family farm in nearby Whitestone (pronounced whit-stone). Martin's great-great-grandfather was William Willett whose campaigning made daylight-saving time an international practice.

Exmouth, Devon
Exmouth stands on the Exe Estuary, just to the south east of Exeter, and has a level, two-mile esplanade leading from the Marina past sand dunes, to Orcombe Point at the most westerly end of the Jurassic Coast with its ever-changing cliff colours, here in Exmouth the rocks are red. (See Studland. See Weymouth)

At the time of writing Exmouth seafront is being redeveloped. The old Fun Park has gone and is being replaced by a Jurassic-themed play area, theatre events, screenings and a food village. There have been protests including funereal flowers being left on the site of the Fun Park when it closed but it needs to be said that the area was looking very tired and there was little there to attract local children or modern holidaymakers.

Eyam, Derbyshire.

In 1665 a local taylor, Alexander Hadfield, brought a bundle of clothes to Eyam from London. The cloth was infested with fleas and brought the plague to the village. It was decided to quarantine the entire village with families required to bury their own dead. 273 died out of a population of 350.

Fakenham, Norfolk
If you've never been here your perspective of Fakenham might well be coloured by your choice of reading material. In the 1990s the online 'Nowhere Guide' listed Fakenham as 'the most boring place on Earth', more recently Fakenham was voted the seventh best place to live in Britain in a 'Country Life' poll.

Kinnerton Confectionery employs 700 people here.

Falmouth, Cornwall
Falmouth has the world's third-deepest harbour after Sydney, Australia and Mahon, Minorca,

If you like to work up a thirst before visiting a pub the Jacobs Ladder Inn is for you with 111 stone steps connecting the Moor, in the town centre, to the pub at the top of the hill.

Kenneth Graham was staying at the Greenbank Hotel in 1907 when he went on a boat trip along the River Fowey. This inspired him to start writing 'The Wind in the Willows,' which originated as a series of letters to his son.

Farringdon, London
Farringdon is the collective name for Farringdon Within and Farringdon Without, Within and Without denoting whether that part of Farringdon was inside or outside the London Wall.

The appropriately named Cock Lane in Farringdon

was once the only street in London where prostitution was legal.

Farringdon Station links the Underground to the National Rail service, the station is not in Farringdon but in Clerkenwell. (See Clerkenwell)

Farnborough, Hampshire
Say 'Farnborough' and the whole world thinks 'Airshow'. American Wild West showman Colonel Sam Cody claimed to be the son of Buffalo Bill but wasn't, his real surname was Cowdery, Cody/Cowdery made the first manned powered flight in the UK on Farnborough Common in 1908 and the rest, as they say, is history.

Farnham, Surrey
The ruined Waverley Abbey was the first monastery built in Britain by Cistercian monks.

Bird World boasts all kinds of flying creatures but also animals and an underwater section featuring Godfrey the Grumpy Turtle.'

The Shepherd and Flock pub's claim to fame is that it stands on 'probably Britain's largest inhabited roundabout.'

Faversham, Kent
There are many declarations from towns claiming to have recorded the highest temperature in Britain but the highest officially accepted until 2019 was the 38.5C recorded in Faversham on 10th August 2003. (See Cambridge)

Shepherd Neame was founded in 1698 and claims to be Britain's oldest brewery. (See Bishop's Castle)

Faversham hosts an annual Hop Festival and, since 2014, a Hat Festival.

Fawkham, Kent
Fawkham Station became Longfield Station in 1961.

Most of the things to do in Fawkham are centred around Brands Hatch motor racing circuit. In addition to motor racing there's a hotel and spa and you can book an Experience Day during which enthusiasts can drive around the track where the likes of Stirling Moss, Ayrton Senna and Jackie Stewart once raced.

Felixstowe, Suffolk
Felixstowe had the smallest Marks and Spencer high street store in Britain. In 2019 this was closed and, at the time of writing, plans were afoot to turn the building into 16 flats.

The Port of Felixstowe is Britain's largest container port with 42% of the nation's containers passing through here in an average year.

The pier was built in 1906 then pulled down early in the Second World War when it was considered to be an easy landing point for enemy troops. It was rebuilt and reopened in 2018 but not to its original length.

Wallis Simpson spent time here while waiting for Edward VIII to abdicate and T E Lawrence (Lawrence of Arabia) was calling himself T E Shaw when he worked at the Felixstowe Marine Craft Section.

Ferndown, Dorset
Ferndown is one of those places that doesn't seem to quite make it into first place in any category.

Ferndown's population of 26,559 at the most recent count makes it the second-largest inland town in Dorset after Dorchester. The town is close to Bournemouth Airport but Christchurch is closer.

Finchley, Greater London
Finchley comes high on the list of British places featured in literature, music and other forms of entertainment.

Mr Garland, a principle character in Dickens' 'The Old Curiosity Shop' (See Holborn) resides at Abel Cottage, Finchley. In Steinbeck's 'Once There Was a War' a woman is described as wearing a costume that 'would have done her honour and protected her from scandal in Finchley.'

Pop music lovers who remember the Swinging 60s will probably sing along immediately they see the first lines to The New Vaudeville Band's top-20 hit, 'Finchley Central.' 'Finchley Central, is two and sixpence, from Golders Green on the Northern Line, and on the platform, by the kiosk, that's where you said you'd be mine,' they don't write them like that now!

Even further back in time Bluebottle from 'The Goon Show' came from Finchley, his creator, Peter Sellers, was living there at the time. Sellers' fellow-Goon Spike Milligan lived in Finchley from 1955 to 1974, he was President of the Finchley Society, a post he is said to have taken very seriously, and his bronze statue sits on a bench in the town.

In Disney's 'The Chronicles of Narnia' the Pevensie children are from Finchley and 'Monty Python's' 'Funniest Joke in the World' sketch is set here.

Fleet, Hampshire
Fleet is the main town in the Hart District of Hampshire. This is one of the richest and least deprived areas of England. Every year from 2011 to 2015, then again in 2017, Hart was voted the Best Place to Live in the UK in a survey run by the Lloyds Banking Group. Before you ask, Winchester temporarily sneaked in at the top spot in 2016.

During their lifetime most people's only sojourn into the area of Fleet will be a motorway stop at Fleet Services, one of the few places in Britain where you will find KFC, McDonalds, Harry Ramsden's, Starbucks and Burger King all serving up their nutritious delicacies around a shared block of toilets.

Folkestone, Kent
The world's highest brick viaduct was built in Folkestone in 1843 to link the South Eastern Railway with ferries in Folkestone Harbour. The ferries no longer run and the viaduct is silent.

Victorian builders found a lead container hidden in an alcove at St Eanswythe's (pronounced Ayns-wyth's) Church in which were the remains of a young woman. Tests on the bones in 2020 confirmed that these are those of the Saint for whom this, England's oldest nunnery, was created. The bones are England's oldest verified bones of a saint.

A clifftop promenade called the Leas claims to be one of the most photogenic walks in Britain but rather spoils this claim by adding that, on a clear day, you can spot Dungeness power station in the distance.

Samuel Plimsoll is buried at St Martin's Church. The

Plimsoll Line, which he devised to show the safe limit to which a ship could be loaded, is engraved on his tombstone.

Fordingbridge, Hampshire
Known as the Northern Gateway to the New Forest Fordingbridge suggests it can offer competition to Dublin and Prague when it comes to hen and stag parties. Activities in the Forest include longbow and crossbow shooting with outrageous costumes encouraged.

Fordwich, Kent
With a population of 381 in the 2011 census Fordwich is the smallest town in England. (See Manningtree and Llanwrtyd Wells))

Forest Row, East Sussex
The forest from which this village takes its name is the nearby Ashdown Forest. In 1963 John F Kennedy attended a service at Our Lady of the Forest Church whilst holding discussions with PM Harold Macmillan who resided at nearby Birch Grove.

Sir Arthur Conan Doyle enjoyed visits to the Brambletye Inn that features in 'The Adventure of Black Peter', in which Holmes and Watson stay at the hotel.

Fowey, Cornwall
Pronounced Foy, as in boy, it is claimed that the young Jesus Christ came here with Joseph of Arimathea who was a tin trader. Other towns in Cornwall make a similar claim, as do locations in Somerset especially around the Glastonbury area, but there are no such claims from Devon tucked between the two counties. In support of this legend what is

now known as the Holy Land did have a tin trade with Cornwall and Somerset some 2,000 years ago but not with Devon.

Daphne du Maurier lived at Menabilly House from 1943 to 1969.The writer Sir Arthur Quiller-Couch, known as Q, is buried in the churchyard of Fowey Parish Church which is dedicated to St Finbarr. Quiller-Couch lived in Fowey from1891 until his death in 1944. He included the town in several of his stories disguised as 'Troy Town'.

Framlingham, Suffolk

Ed Sheeran grew up in Framlingham and it is Framlingham Castle in his hit top-five hit 'Castle on the Hill'. It must be said that the castle is on a bit of a mound rather than a hill and Framlingham is pretty flat like most of Suffolk.

Freckleton, Lancashire

Warton Aerodrome has a 1.5 mile (2.4 km) runway that is partly in Freckleton. During World War Two an aircraft attempting to land at Warton crashed onto the Freckleton Holy Trinity School killing sixty one people. (See Warton)

There is a Quaker graveyard known as Twill Furlong that has only one tombstone.

Freshwater, Isle of Wight

Poet Laureate Alfred, Lord Tennyson, rented Farringdon House in 1853 and purchased it three years later. He moved to West Sussex in 1869 after getting fed up with fans turning up on the Island but he did return to Freshwater during winters.

The poet is remembered in the name of Tennyson

Down where a stone cross stands as his memorial. Hooke Hill takes its name from scientist Robert Hooke who was born in Freshwater.

Fulham, Greater London
Craven Cottage is the home of Fulham FC with Stamford Bridge, the home of Chelsea FC, also in Fulham, not in Chelsea. (See Chelsea)

Aviation pioneer Geoffrey de Havilland built his first plane in Fulham.

Elvis Costello's 'London's Brilliant Parade', Ian Dury's 'What a Waste', Generation X's 'Kiss Me Deadly' and the Pretty Things' 'Take That' all mention Fulham.

To a gambler a Fulham is a loaded die.

G

Gateshead, Tyne and Wear
Much of Gateshead's medieval heritage was destroyed by a massive explosion on the quayside in 1854. A seven-storey bonded warehouse containing thousands of tons of combustible materials was set alight when a neighbouring textile mill caught fire. There was a series of small explosions followed by the major one which killed 53 onlookers and left only one building still standing on the quayside.

Although Thomas Edison is usually given the credit for inventing the electric lightbulb his patent, taken out in 1879, was just an improvement on one designed by Joseph Swan some ten years earlier. Most of Swan's experimental work was carried out at his home, Underhill, at Low Fell, Gateshead, this was the first house in the world to be illuminated by electric lights.

Gateshead's MetroCentre claimed to be the largest shopping centre in the EU until Brexit ruined its record.

The Angel of the North by Antony Gormley cost £800,000 and was mostly funded by the National Lottery

Gerrards Cross, Buckinghamshire
Exteriors for Stanley Kubrick's 'Lolita' were filmed in Gerrard's Cross, 'Inspector Morse', 'The Professionals' and 'The League of Gentlemen' have all included sequences filmed at Hubert's House, just to the southeast of the town.

The first episode of 'Monty Python's Flying Circus' includes the line, 'Sono ingress di Gerrard's Cross', 'I am an Englishman from Gerrard's Cross' and the apostrophe is theirs not mine.

Gillingham, Dorset
Pronounced with a hard G, as in Gift.

An estimated 1,000 of the town's population of 2,000 died as a result of the Black Death at the end of 1348 and start of 1349.

Constable's painting of the town's old bridge with the church beyond hangs in the Tate Gallery

Gillingham, Kent
Pronounced with a J, as in Jill.

Gillingham has witnessed two disasters. In 1929 the local fire brigade put on a public demonstration intended to display their skills but things went tragically wrong, 15 people died. Smoke bombs and other special effects were due to be set off in a tower to give the firefighters the opportunity to show their rescue procedure and then they would put out a real fire. Unfortunately somebody got the timing wrong and the real fire was ignited first resulting in the potential rescuees being burnt to death.

In 1951 a double decker bus ploughed into a company of young Royal Marine cadets aged between 10 and 13, 24 of them were killed.

Glaisdale, North Yorkshire
The Esk Vale Theatre is Glaisdale's own professional theatre company offering an annual August production along with other events through the year.

Beggar's Bridge is a magnet for visitors. The bridge bears the date 1619 and the initials TF for Thomas Ferres who became Sheriff and Mayor of Hull after starting life as the son of a poor Glaisdale farmer. As a youth Ferres had to wade across the river to meet up with his sweetheart, the Squire's daughter, Agnes. The Squire refused to give him her hand in marriage so he went off to make his fortune and eventually returned to claim his bride. When she died Thomas built the bridge as her memorial and to assure that future lovers would not be separated as they had been.

Glastonbury, Somerset

Glastonbury is now best known for the rock festival that isn't held here. Pilton, some seven miles away from the famed town is the home of the festival. (See Pilton. See Wells)

Glastonbury is a place of many mysteries making it a Mecca for the world's remaining hippies and a location where visits by Joseph of Arimathea with Jesus and Arthurian legend take centre stage as historical 'facts'. (See Hayling Island. See Fowey)

Following a catastrophic fire in 1184 much of the ancient abbey was destroyed. It took only four years for a partial reconstruction permitting services to take place again but building work then ground to a halt.

By 1191 pilgrims had virtually stopped visiting the abbey, not only depleting necessary funds to keep the resident monks in the lifestyle to which they had become accustomed, but the inns and lodging houses, some still in business today, outside the abbey grounds, were also suffering.

Fortuitously it was at this very time the tombs of King Arthur and Queen Guinevere were discovered in the Abbey cemetery and pilgrims flocked back. Some say the dig was inspired by information obtained from an ancient Welsh Bard by Henry II. Others say the dig began when a monk died after giving instructions to be buried at this exact spot, his burial resulting in the discovery. Most say it was an outrageous, but very successful, publicity stunt. (See Melrose, Tintagel, South Cadbury, Dolgellau and Carmarthen)

Anyone who knows their myths will instantly write-off the Abbey tombs' authenticity because it is common knowledge that Arthur and his Knights are not dead, they merely sleep soundly beneath Glastonbury Tor waiting to spring to the aid of England in its hour of need.

Glossop, Derbyshire
In a letter Hilaire Belloc wrote, 'Do you know the filthy village of Glossop? It is inhabited entirely by savages. I tried every inn in the place and found each inn worse than the last. It stinks for miles. Rather than sleep in such a den I started to walk back to Manchester with a huge bag.'

Fashion queen Vivienne Westwood and porn publisher Paul Raymond spent part of their childhoods here (not together!) and Glossop was the home of Beatrix Potter's grandfather.

Gloucester, Gloucestershire
Gloucester is the home of Wall's ice cream factory. Wall's started out making sausages but when the sausage trade dropped off during the summer they turned to ice cream. Yes ice cream did contain pork fat which was on the ingredients list, somewhat cryptically, as 'non-vegetable fat'. Almost all ice

creams have replaced pig fat with vegetable oil but contain very little, if any, cream. Ice cream labelled 'Dairy' cannot contain vegetable fats but in 2014 Unilever, the company who own Wall's, Magnum, Ben and Jerry's etc, applied to the Food Standards Agency for permission to produce a diet range of ices using GM technology from the blood of an eel-like creature called an ocean pout. Sounds delicious

Close to Gloucester is Coopers Hill where the famed annual Cheese Rolling takes place.

John Stafford Smith was the British composer of the music that became the US National Anthem, 'The Star Spangled Banner.' Stafford Smith was bon in Gloucester and is buried in Gloucester Cathedral where he played the organ, he allegedly died after getting a grape pip stuck in his windpipe. There were fifteen stars on the Star Spangled Banner when 'The Star Spangled Banner' was written.

Goathland, North Yorkshire

Most of the surrounding land is owned by the Duchy of Lancaster, the Duke of Lancaster, also known as Her Majesty Queen Elizabeth II, has to allow her tenants to graze their black-faced sheep on the village green and on surrounding moorland.

Much of the TV series 'Heartbeat' was filmed here. Set in the 1960s the series was broadcast from 1992 to 2010. The name of the Goathland Hotel was changed to the Aidensfield Arms for TV and, in later years, the pub seen on screen was a set built in a TV studio.

Goathland station doubled for Hogsmeade railway station in 'Harry Potter' films.

Godalming, Surrey
In 1726 a maid, Mary Toft, hoaxed the population and doctors of Godalming into believing she had given birth to rabbits. The story became national news until a porter caught her smuggling a dead rabbit into her room and she confessed to inserting 16 rabbits into herself to fake their births.

In 1881 Godalming became the first town in the world with a public electricity supply.

Golders Green, Greater London
Golders Green boasts almost 50 Kosher restaurants and there are more than 40 synagogues in the area. Japanese and other Asian communities are also increasing in the district with their own places of worship, restaurants and shops.

Golders Green claims to have Britain's first crematorium, opened in 1902, but it wasn't. (See Woking)

In their hit song 'Finchley Central' the New Vaudeville Band give the advice, 'For Golders Green change at Camden Town', (See Finchley).

George Harrison used to visit the band Badfinger here and wrote an unreleased song called 'Going Down to Golders Green'. After the death of Pete Ham, vocalist and songwriter with Badfinger, the band released two albums 'Golders Green' and '7 Park Avenue', which was their address here.

Spike Milligan wrote a poem titled 'Death Wish' in which he pleads, 'But please - don't bury me in Golders Green'.

Gomersal, West Yorkshire
Charlotte Bronte's novel, 'Shirley', is set in the time of the Luddite riots in and around Gomersal. The village's Red House was the home of Charlotte's friend Mary Taylor and features in the novel as Briarmains.

Gomersal has some locations with unusual names; Nutter Lane, Egypt and Monk Ings being just three.

Cleckheaton claims to be the birthplace of 'Mr Men' author and illustrator Charles Roger Hargreaves and there's a blue plaque celebrating this fact on a wall in Halifax Road. Other sources say he spent his childhood at Mill Lane, Gomersal in what is now known as Summerdale. Confused? I am. (See Cleckheaton)

Goole, East Riding of Yorkshire
'Goole' comes from an Anglo-Saxon word meaning 'open sewer' or 'outlet into a river'.

The town's best known landmarks are two water towers, known locally as the Salt and Pepper Pots. Pepper was said to be the biggest in Europe at the time of its construction with a capacity of 750,000 gallons.

Gorleston-on-Sea, Norfolk
Simply known as Gorleston to the locals. The town experienced the highest windspeed (122mph) ever recorded in Britain during the 1987 storm.

Gorleston advertises itself as a 'tourist destination', its two main offerings being an 'Edwardian' beach and a pond on which to sail model boats.

Grantham, Lincolnshire

It was at his home, Woolsthorpe Manor, Grantham, that Isaac Newton formulated his Laws of Gravity after being reportedly hit on the head by a falling apple. Newton himself actually confirmed the 'apple on his head' story but a witness claimed only to have seen the apple fall from a branch without actually striking the scientist. Newton was born at Woolsthorpe Manor, he then moved to Cambridge but returned home when Cambridge University was closed by the Plague.

Grantham gave Britain its first female police officer and first female Prime Minister.

Grasmere, Cumbria

William Wordsworth lived here, at Dove Cottage, once a pub now the Wordsworth Museum, for 14 years and called Grasmere 'the loveliest spot that man hath ever found'.

When it was being built Wordsworth condemned Allan Bank as an eyesore but he came to live in the house with his wife Mary, their three children and Mary's sister Sara. They moved on after two years blaming smokey chimneys and a dispute with the landlord. They moved to Rydal Mount in 1813 (See Ambleside).

The graves of William his wife, his children and his sister Dorothy can be found in the village centre churchyard of St Oswald's where the poet planted eight yew trees. The delightful smell often encountered in the church is gingerbread baking in the shop next door.

Gravesend, Kent

Many come to Gravesend with the sole purpose of visiting the grave of Pocahontas. The Native American saved the life of Englishman, John Smith, by putting her head on top of his as her father raised a club to execute him. The queen of the 1995 Disney movie married tobacco farmer John Rolfe and came with him to England in 1616 where she was presented to high society and royalty as an example of a 'civilised savage,'

The Rolfe's were on their way back to America in 1617 but only got as far as Gravesend when 21-year-old Pocahontas was taken ill and died shortly after. There are claims she was poisoned, or that she died of pneumonia, or possibly smallpox or tuberculosis.

Those tourists looking for her grave will be unlucky as St George's Church was destroyed by fire in 1727 and the grave was lost, although it is said to be below the chancel of the present building. A life-size bronze statue of Pocahontas stands outside the church.

Grays, Essex

On 24th September 1665 Samuel Pepys recorded in his diary that he visited Grays. He 'walked', he 'drank' and he bought a 'great deal of fine fish'.

Grays, also known as Grays Thurrock, stands on the northern bank of the Thames close to Tilbury dockyard. The docks are where John Wayne tackles smugglers in 'Brannigan', the docks stood in for Venice in the 'Indiana Jones and the Last Crusade' boat chase and parts of 'Batman Begins' were filmed here.

Great Dunmow, Essex
The Dunmow Flitch is mentioned by Chaucer in 'The Wife of Bath's Tale' one of his ''Canterbury Tales' and is the oldest recorded competition in the world still taking place. A flitch is a side of bacon which is the prize in this competition. To win the flitch a married couple, from anywhere in the world, must prove to a 'Judge' and his 'jury' of six maidens and six bachelors, that during the preceding twelve months and one day they have 'not wished themselves unmarried again'. The trials take place every four years

Great Torrington, Devon
I have bumped into tourists in Dartington (See Dartington) who had gone there just to visit the home of Dartington Crystal. They're in the right county but 70 miles away from the right town. The beautiful items of modern glass are hand made in Great Torrington.

Like many locations in this area of Devon, Great Torrington cashes in on its position in 'Tarka Country'. Henry Williamson first published his novel 'Tarka the Otter' in 1927. The book achieved new-found fame in 1979 thanks to a film narrated by Peter Ustinov and has since spawned a Tarka industry including the Tarka Trail and Tarka Country.

Lovers of the little otter probably don't know, or conveniently forget, that Henry Williamson was an anti semitic, Nazi promoting, supporter of Fascist leader Oswald Mosley.

Greenstead, Essex
Grinstead boasts the oldest wooden church in the world which is possibly the oldest wooden building

in Europe still standing. Sorry to spoil the illusion of great age that attracts so many visitors but only a very small part of the original construction remains.

Greenwich, Greater London

Shakespeare staged two of his comedies for Elizabeth I at Greenwich Palace and the second wedding in 'Four Weddings and a Funeral' was filmed in the chapel of the Old Naval College. The Old Naval College also stood in for Washington DC in the movie 'Patriot Games'.

What are claimed to be secret tunnels under Greenwich Park are actually old water mains supplying what was the Royal Hospital and is now the National Maritime Museum. The tunnels were closed down in 1917, the same year that saw the closure of Greenwich Park railway station.

The canopy of the 02, originally the Millennium Dome, weighs less than the air inside the dome. The masts, cables and fabric weigh 2,200 tonnes, they enclose air weighing 2,600 tonnes.

Grimsby, Lincolnshire

Residents are known as Grimbarians and it is claimed the town's name comes from a Scandinavian fisherman named Grim who settled here.

The Grimsby Dock Tower was built from one million bricks, its purpose was to create water pressure to power machinery at the docks. There are many fewer than a million Lego bricks in the model of the Grimsby tower at Legoland in Windsor.

Grimsby FC play their home matches away at a ground in Cleethorpes. (See Cleethorpes)

Songwriter Bernie Taupin spent his teenage years here and wrote a song called 'Grimsby' which was recorded by Elton John in 1974.

Guildford, Surrey
In 1995 the remains of the oldest synagogue in Western Europe were uncovered beneath Guildford High Street. It is believed it was built in the 12th century.

Dennis fire engines were built in Guildford until 2007 when production stopped following financial difficulties.

Guildford is a town with a cathedral. Guildford Cathedral is seen in the movie 'The Omen'.

Under his pseudonym Lewis Carroll, Charles Dodgson wrote 'Through the Looking Glass' in Guildford. A statue of Alice can be seen in the castle grounds.

Guiseley, West Yorkshire
In 1928 Harry Ramsden opened a fish and chip shop in a wooden hut in Guiseley. The hut can still be seen in the grounds of the building he moved his business to some three years later. Harry Ramsdens was loved by people from all over Yorkshire. My parents used to take me there for a special treat. The best fish and chips, proper mushy peas that had never seen the inside of a can, china pots of strong Yorkshire tea were served in beautifully carpeted rooms with wood panelled walls and sparkling chandeliers. At one time the pianist tinkling away in the corner was Harry Ramsden's nephew, Harry Corbett of Sooty and Sweep fame. Harry Ramsden's at Guiseley closed in 2012 and has become The Wetherby Whaler.

Harry Ramsden's is now a chain serving food with little or no resemblance to the original product.

H

Hadfield, Derbyshire
Northern club comedian Roy Chubby Brown's real name is Royston Vasey. Royston Vasey is the name of the town in the TV black comedy series 'The League of Gentlemen' and it was Hadfield that became the extremely weird location on screen.

Hadfield is close to the attractively named Bottoms Reservoir.

Hadlow, Kent
Printing pioneer William Caxton is said to have been born here. (See Tenterden)

Hailsham, East Sussex
Hailsham is probably responsible for more deaths in the UK than any other town of its size. This is where hangman's ropes were once made.

Hale, Greater Manchester
Known as the home of footballers and their wives, Hale claims double the percentage of middle class residents compared with the country's average. The Daily Telegraph named Hale as having some of the most expensive property prices in the UK with prices 194% higher than those in surrounding areas.

Halifax, West Yorkshire
Dean Clough Mills was once the world's largest carpet factory, producing Crossley's excellent carpets. The mills no longer operate and their shell is hyped as a 'nationally renowned centre for business, cafes and the arts'. Halifax Piece Hall, which many locals think

is called the Peace Hall, was once a bustling market for local textile producers selling pieces of cloth. The Piece Hall has undergone a £19 million 'regeneration' resulting in it being hyped a 'nationally renowned centre for business, cafes and the arts,' I'm sure I've heard that somewhere before.

Almost all of the town's many mill chimneys have been demolished but one ornate example, Wainhouse Tower, is still an attraction. As in many towns the buildings in Halifax were all entirely black due to the soot from those chimneys but it has now been cleaned up to reveal the original stone colour. The once black Town Hall has a clock that hasn't struck during nighttime hours since 1918 after opera diva Dame Nellie Melba complained it was keeping her awake when she lodged at the nearby White Swan Hotel.

Eureka!, the National Children's Museum, well worth a visit if you have kids, is not far from the former Parish Church, now upgraded to Halifax Minster, and a short walk from the railway station. Halifax railway station, which featured in the movie 'Room at the Top', smells wonderful thanks to the nearby Mackintosh's chocolate and toffee factory. (See New-Biggin-by-the-Sea)

'The Dalesman's Litany' begins with the Yorkshire proverb, 'From Hull, Halifax and Hell, good Lord deliver us'. Hull because of press-gangs, Halifax because heads were removed by the gibbet here for crimes as small as stealing a piece of cloth worth 13 pence and the Hell bit is obvious. (See Hull)

Haltwhistle, Northumberland

Haltwhistle claims to be the exact geographic centre of Britain, as does Dunsop Bridge in Lancashire. The exact centre is found by making a cardboard cut-out of the area and the centre is the point at which this can be balanced on the point of a pin.

An Ordnance Survey study proved that the centre of the island of Great Britain, (excluding other islands) is a field somewhere near Clitheroe in Lancashire. The centre of Great Britain including the smaller islands is at Whitendale Hanging Stones close to Dunsop Bridge. The centre of the UK to include Great Britain and Northern Ireland is somewhere in the middle of Morecambe Bay.

To complicate matters further, if you ignore the above bit about balancing a map on a pin and measure the longest north-south meridian Haltwhistle is indeed in the centre and it is also at the centre of lines through it along the main compass points.

Hammersmith, Greater London
'Guinness Book of World Records' lists the smallest bar in Britain as one at The Dove, Hammersmith, 4 feet by 7ft 10in, but this is one of those records that keeps changing as someone, somewhere, opens a smaller bar just to get mentioned in the record books. I once sank a Scotch at a bar in a phone booth at the Glastonbury Festival. James Thomson wrote the words for 'Rule Britannia' in a room above the bar at The Dove.

The biggest employer in Hammersmith is the BBC.

In 1981 Motorhead released their live album, 'No Sleep 'til Hammersmith', and the Hammersmith Apollo saw David Bowie's first appearance as Ziggy Stardust in 1973.

Hampstead, Greater London
People who live here call it 'The Village'. The Village claims to have more millionaires than anywhere else with a similar area in Britain. If you consider that there are very few places with the same area as anywhere else in Britain just about anywhere can claim to have more millionaires than anywhere with the same area.

John Constable was a regular painter of Hampstead and its Heath, he is buried in the churchyard of St John-at-Hampstead.

Hampstead underground station is the deepest on the entire network at 192 feet below ground level. It has a 300-step emergency spiral staircase and, at 181-feet, the underground's deepest lift.

Dick Turpin is said to have been a customer at the Spaniards Inn and at the Old Bull and Bush which features in a well-known drinking song.

Hampton Court Palace, Greater London
Cardinal Wolsey had Hampton Court Palace built in 1514 as a reward to himself for becoming a Cardinal. Wolsey realised he was going to have problems when he failed to secure Henry VIII a divorce from Catherine of Aragon so he gave the palace to the King before he could take it away from him. Henry married Catherine Parr here in 1543.

Jane Seymour was the only one of Henry VIII's six wives to receive a Queen's funeral. Henry had Jane's heart and lungs buried in a lead box under the altar of the Hampton Court Palace chapel. (See Ludlow) Jane's body is buried beside that of Henry in St George's Chapel, Windsor.

In 1603 William Shakespeare and his company, the King's Men, came to Hampton Court Palace for three weeks to provide Christmas entertainment.

One of the top tourist attractions at Hampton Court is the UK's oldest hedge maze, this was designed in 1700. (See East Molesey)

Hanwell, Greater London

The rector of St Mary's was, at one time, Fred Secombe elder brother of comedian Harry.

The Hanwell Clock Tower was built in 1937 to celebrate the coronation of George VI. In the 1970s a local estate agent claimed the tower was a 'dreadful concrete eyesore' and he announced his intention of raising £5,000 to replace it with something more attractive. The tower was renovated and cleaned but it fell into disrepair and was boarded up. After further restoration it became a monument to the Queen's Golden Jubilee in 2002.

Harleston, Norfolk

(See Redenhall with Harleston)

Harlow, Essex

Harlow became a New Town after World War Two. In the 1960s it was known as Pram Town due to all the young mums pushing their babies around.

'Nearer My God to Thee', allegedly the last song played by the band as the Titanic sank beneath the waves, was written by local resident Sarah Flower Adams.

Harlow had Britain's first pedestrian precinct and in 1951 The Lawn became Britain's first residential tower block, every flat had a south-facing balcony and the block is now a Grade II listed building.

Rupert (Ron Weasley) Grint, comedy actor Rik Mayall and cyclist Laura Trott were born in Harlow.

In their song 'Get 'em out by Friday', Genesis mention both Harlow and Harlow New Town.

Harmondsworth, Greater London
After saying he would lie down in front of bulldozers to stop a third runway at Heathrow, Boris Johnson jetted off abroad to avoid having to stand up and support or vote against his government's 2016 campaign in favour of the issue. At the time of writing the debate goes on.

Half of Harmondsworth was due to be demolished to make way for the airport expansion but lucky residents were assured that the other half of the village, including the 11th century St Mary's Church and a 600-year old barn would be saved. Sounds like an ideal place for those who wish for a quiet retirement! Or maybe not. (See Heathrow. See Hounslow. See West Drayton)

Harpenden, Hertfordshire
Since 1946 Harpenden has hosted an annual Highland Gathering, said to be the largest outside Scotland.

Harpenden was one of the first places in Britain to have a telephone service. Residents expressed their annoyance at the erection of telephone polls in 1893.

Harrogate, North Yorkshire
Charles Dickens visited in 1858 and described Harrogate as 'the queerest place with the strangest people in it leading the oddest lives'.

Harrogate boasts Britain's last, fully operative, 19th century Turkish Bath. In 2011 the council was accused of a cover-up to protect the town's reputation when men-only sessions at the baths were terminated. Councillors claimed the cancellation was due to finances but later confessed this was an attempt to shroud complaints that some bathers had been involved in 'inappropriate behaviour'.

The 1982 Eurovision Song Contest was held in Harrogate. The competition was won by Nicole singing, 'Ein bißchen Frieden' which became 'A Little Peace' in English, this is still the only Eurovision winner to reach number-one in the charts everywhere it was released. Germany didn't win again until 2010.

Betty's Cafe Tea Room of Harrogate has evolved into a chain. Betty's trademarked the Fat Rascal and, in 2017, threatened to take action against a cafe in Whitby with just three tables for using this name for a scone which they subsequently renamed the Whitby Fatty.

Harrow, Greater London
While at Harrow School Lord Byron joined a plot to blow up the headmaster by igniting a trail of gunpowder laid through the corridors. (See Cambridge) The Harrow School uniform includes a black tie, this was originally worn as a symbol of mourning for Queen Victoria and nobody has ever told the boys they can stop wearing them.

In 1899 it is claimed the first fatal motoring accident took place on Grove Hill, Harrow. After lunch at the King's Head (now flats) Edwin Sewell was driving Major James Richer down the hill when the brakes failed and then a wheel collapsed throwing them both into the road. Sewell died on impact and Richer several days later. A plaque marking the spot where the accident took place mentions neither of the victims by name but it does name Alderman Charles Stenhouse, the mayor who performed the unveiling in 1969. (See Purley)

Harrington, Cumbria
Harrington Harbour was closed off to become a reservoir for a secret magnesium works in World War Two. The Magnesite plant extracted magnesium from seawater and this was used in aircraft components and incendiary bombs.

Harrington, Lincolnshire
The garden at Harrington Hall is the one mentioned in Alfred Lord Tennyson's poem 'Maud'. It is also 'The Eden where she dwelt', in his poem 'The Gardener's Daughter'.

Harrington, Northamptonshire
This Harrington was the location of a USAF base in World War Two and later became a Thor missile site. It is now best known for a happier reason as this is the home of the Warner's Edwards Distillery which produces a rather excellent gin.

Hartlepool, County Durham
The people of Hartlepool are still known as Monkey Hangers following an incident during the Napoleonic Wars when a shipwrecked monkey was hanged here because it was thought to be a French spy. Some say the monkey story was fabricated to conceal the fact they had actually hanged a young boy, one of the lads who worked loading cannons on ships who were known as 'powder monkeys'.

In 2002 Stuart Drummond was elected mayor of Hartlepool after campaigning in a monkey costume and promoting the slogan, 'Free bananas for schoolchildren'. He was elected on two further occasions despite never keeping his free bananas pledge.

Harvington, Worcestershire
Harvington Hall boasts Elizabethan wall paintings and claims the largest number (seven) of priests' hiding places (priest holes) in Britain.

Harwich, Essex
Harwich was the likely home port of the Mayflower and claims to have been the birthplace of Mayflower captain Christopher Jones.

From 1979 to 1987 Warner's Holiday Camp was the setting for Maplin's in the TV series 'Hi-di-Hi'.

Haslemere, Surrey
Swan Barn Farm offers a two-mile walk starting at the mediaeval dipping well. Hannah Oakford, Haslemere's last public water carrier, charged a penny-ha'penny to deliver a bucket of water from here to your house.

Between Haslemere and the nearby village of Grayswood can be seen concrete pyramids, each approximately two-feet in height. These were installed during the early years of World War One to keep out German tanks.

Hassocks, West Sussex
David Lloyd George came to nearby Danny House to draw up terms to end World War One.

Two windmills on the Downs above the village are known as Jack and Jill. Jack, a tower mill, is privately owned and Jill, a post mill, is open to the public.

Hastings, East Sussex
Hastings is most famous for the battle that didn't take place here (See Battle).

Hastings now boasts Europe's largest beach-based fishing fleet. The town is home to the True Crime Museum, the Flower Makers Museum and the Shipwreck Museum.

Hatfield, Hertfordshire
Elizabeth Tudor was held at the Old Palace, Hatfield House and it is claimed she discovered she had ascended to the throne while sitting under a tree here in 1558. Her first Council was held in the Great Hall.

Folk musician Martin Carthy and Zombies frontman Colin Blunstone were born in Hatfield, Donovan and temporary Rolling Stone Mick Taylor grew up here.

Hathersage, Derbyshire
A gravestone in the churchyard of St Michael's and All Angels' in Hathersage claims it is the final resting place of Little John, the friend and lieutenant of Robin Hood. Another stone stands over the grave, unreadable due to age, next to the modern one.

Folklore claims that Little John was a huge man and that he asked to be buried beneath a yew tree in the churchyard when he was dying in a nearby cottage (now demolished). There is indeed a yew tree above this grave and, in 1784, Captain James Shuttleworth dug a thigh bone from the grave and it was claimed this had belonged to a man who stood eight-feet tall.

There are those who insist this isn't a grave at all. They say the head and foot stones of what has become known as a grave are in fact the standard measure for a pole, 16-feet and six inches, used by local tradesmen to check materials.

Havant, Hampshire

Havant's old town centre is easy to navigate due it being centred on a crossroads from which run North Street, South Street, East Street and West Street. Part of West Street is pedestrianised.

A row of half-timbered, 16th century, cottages are now the Old House at Home pub. Two of the heavy roof timbers are said to have been recovered from a ship of the Spanish Armada. The Bear Post was allegedly used for tethering the last dancing bear in England.

Haverhill, Suffolk

A nursing home in Haverhill is known as Anne of Cleves House. It is one of the few building to have survived a fire in 1667 and is said to have been part of Henry VIII's marriage settlement with Anne of Cleves. (See Lewes)

Hawkshead, Cumbria

Hawkshead Courthouse is owned by the National Trust and is open to the public but to get in you need to ask to borrow the key from the nearby National Trust Shop.

Following the death of his mother, William Wordsworth was sent to live in Hawkshead and his poem 'The Prelude' is partly based on the time he spent here.

Hawkshead Whigs are oval bread rolls flavoured with caraway seeds, traditionally eaten at Easter. In the early 2000s the Whig Cafe opened serving the rolls stuffed with assorted fillings including sausage, bacon or cheese. The cafe hasn't survived.

Haworth, West Yorkshire
The attractive High Street climbing the hill would make this an attractive tourist town even if it didn't have Bronte connections. The Bronte sisters were born in Thornton but wrote most of their novels at the Parsonage in Haworth. The Parsonage is now a museum where Bronte furniture and tiny handwritten books by the sisters can be viewed. The Brontes were always a star attraction in the USA so the village is frequently busy with American tourists mispronouncing the name of the place. It's 'How earth'. Visitors can still see the pharmacy where Bronte brother Bramwell purchased his regular fixes of opium. Most of the Brontes are buried at the church close to the Parsonage. (See Scarborough). The father of the Bronte sister, Patrick, remains the longest serving (41 years) in Haworth.

Oakworth railway station at the bottom of the hill features in the movie 'The Railway Children', in 'Yanks' which starred Vanessa Redgrave and Richard Gere and in the movie version of Pink Floyd's 'The Wall'.

Haydock, Merseyside
Best known for Haydock Park Racecourse which is equidistant between Liverpool and Manchester.

If you intend placing a bet on a horse at Haydock I am reliably informed by someone who never seems to have any money but claims never to lose any, if the going is soft or heavy and the race is a mile or less put your money on a horse that has come high in the draw. If you intend placing a bet on the weather it does tend to rain a lot in the North West. (See Llanberis)

Hayes, Greater London

The world's top rock bands stand in front of stacks of black speakers emblazoned with the name 'Marshall.' Jim Marshall's first factory employed 15 people in Hayes. Many involved with charities will remember Jim as a very generous, very pleasant man.

Collectors of vinyl records will know that many of these were manufactured at the Hayes Old Vinyl Factory. 'Hayes Middlesex' can be found stamped on the back of such albums including the Beatles' 'Sergeant Pepper's Lonely Hearts Club Band'. The 50th anniversary of 'Sgt Pepper' is celebrated by the 'Gold Disc' installation in the centre of town.

Heinz, Fujitsu and United Biscuits have their UK headquarters here.

Hayle, Cornwall

Hayle stands on a beautiful estuary and was the first town in Cornwall to be awarded 'Walkers are Welcome' status indicating that footpaths are well maintained and signposted.

Only a short walk from the town centre is the Bucket of Blood pub. Legend has it that the pub is so named from the days when this was a haunt for smugglers. The pub landlord went out to draw up a bucket of water from the well and instead pulled up a bucket of blood from a mutilated smuggler's corpse that had been dumped in there. Before you accept the body at the bottom of the well theory it should be pointed out that the run-off from tin mines regularly changed the colour of the water supply to red.

Hayling Island, Hampshire
Hayiling Island has added itself to the list of places allegedly visited by Joseph of Arimathea and the young Jesus. On the back of this it has also made claims to be a part of the Arthurian legend and the possible depository of the Holy Grail. (See Glastonbury and Fowey).

Haywards Heath, West Sussex;
Until a border change in the mid 1970s Haywards Heath was officially in East Sussex. Now actually in West Sussex the town advertises itself as being in Mid Sussex.

Heathfield, East Sussex
The Cuckoo Trail, part of the National Cycle Network, runs along what was once the trackbed of the railway known as the Cuckoo Line. The Cuckoo Line took its name from the Heffle Cuckoo Fair which was held here each April. Tradition had it that a lady would release a cuckoo from a basket at the fair and this was declared to be the first cuckoo of Spring.

Heathrow, Greater London
Everything changed for Heathrow, or Heath Row as it then was, in 1929 when Fairey Aviation purchased land southeast of the hamlet to build an airfield for aircraft testing and then gradually enlarged their property-holding into what became the Great West Aerodrome, which became London Airport in 1944 and then became Heathrow Airport and then, as I keep saying, the rest is history. (See Harmonsworth. See Hounslow. See West Drayton.)

Hebden Bridge, West Yorkshire
The bridge at Hebden Bridge celebrated its 500th anniversary in 2010. Thanks to being a centre for woolen cloth weaving Hebden Bridge was known as Trouser Town.

Hardcastle Crags is a popular local beauty spot.

(See Luddendenfoot)

Helmsley, North Yorkshire
Ryedale leaves the North Yorks Moors here to join the Vale of Pickering.

Understandably popular with walkers Helmsley also attracts bikers who congregate in the Square after negotiating one of their favourite routes along the 19 miles of the B1257 from Stokesley, nicknamed the 'North Yorkshire TT' by 'Rider' magazine.

Helston, Cornwall
Known internationally for its 'Furry Dance' (aka 'The Floral Dance') held on 8th May, or the previous Saturday if the 8th falls on a Sunday or a Monday. In 1977 the Brighouse and Rastrick Brass Band's Christmas recording of the song was kept off the top position in the pop charts by Paul McCartney's 'Mull of Kintyre'. Popular radio and TV presenter Terry Wogan had a hit with a vocal version of 'The Floral Dance' in 1978

Hemel Hempstead, Hertfordshire
Six different traffic routes meet at what has been called the Magic Roundabout. Formerly known as the Plough Roundabout, this Hemel Hempstead landmark was voted the UK's second-worst roundabout in 2005 yet with no changes made it was voted the Best in Britain in 2011.

In the 2013 Crap Towns survey Hemel Hempstead was voted Britain's Ugliest Town.

In the Harry Potter saga Ron Weasley has a tiny pet owl which his sister named Pigwidgeon. Pigwidgeon was born in 1994 in Hemel Hempstead.

Hemingford Grey, Cambridgeshire

During a 1741 hurricane the tower of St James' Church was destroyed, it was never rebuilt and was replaced by eight balls.

The manor house at Hemingford Grey is said to have been built in 1130 making it the oldest continuously occupied house in England. The house looks nothing like as old as this but it has suffered considerable cosmetic work at the hands of the Tudors and Georgians.

Henley on Thames, Oxfordshire

Only known to many for its annual Royal Regatta, rowing is so important here that the town displays statues of oarsmen Sir Steve Redgrave and Sir Matthew Pinsent.

Henley appears as Causton in episodes of 'Midsomer Murders' and the town offers walking tours of places that will be instantly recognisable to fans of the TV series.

Hereford, Herefordshire

Hereford claims to be the home of Miss Piggy, Fozzie Bear and Yoda being the birthplace of Frank Oz who provided their voices.

The Three Choirs Festival is one of Britain's oldest music festivals. It comes to Hereford every third year being also held in Gloucester and Worcester.

The largest medieval map still in existence, the 13th century Mappa Mundi, is on display in Hereford Cathedral.

Hertford, Hertfordshire
Britain's first paper mill was established here in 1488. W E Johns, creator of Biggles, spent much of his childhood in Hertford and his school days in the town are fictionalised in 'Biggles Goes to School'.

Hertford Museum has a collection of 6,000 toothbrushes due to Addis toothbrushes being manufactured in the town from 1919 to 1993.

Heversham, Cumbria
Winston Churchill once commented favourably on the glorious views from here. William Wordsworth wrote his poem 'The World is too Much with Us' while rambling in the area which he visited frequently.

Hexham, Northumberland
The only Roman milestone still located in its original position is at Chesterholm, near Hexham. The remains of a timber palace were excavated nearby, this was dated to around the time of Emperor Hadrian's visit in 122AD so it could have been where the Emperor made a stop.

Heysham, Lancashire
It is claimed that St Patrick's Chapel was founded by St Patrick himself, despite it being dated to 300 years after his death. Graves hacked from the solid rock in the 11th century feature on the sleeve of 'The Best of Black Sabbath' album.

Heywood, Lancashire
Known as Monkey Town, a name thought to have originated in Edwin Waugh's 1855 book 'Sketches of Lancashire Life'. It is said this came from the local pronunciation of Heap Bridge as 'Ape Bridge.'

Singer Lisa Stansfield was born and brought up here and Julie Goodyear, 'Coronation Street's' Bet Lynch, lived in Heywood for many years.

High Wycombe, Buckinghamshire
T S Eliot taught at the Royal Grammar School. Amongst the school's famous pupils have been Blockheads singer Ian Dury, comedian Jimmy Carr and rugby player Matt Dawson. Former pupils at John Hamden Grammar School, known locally as JHGS, include chef Heston Blumenthal and author Terry Pratchett.

Original Windsor Chairs are from High Wycombe, not from Windsor. In honour of the town's furniture making history special occasions are celebrated by the construction of arches from chairs.

Highbridge, Hampshire
The fishing lake in Highbridge is a flooded quarry left behind after the removal of gravel.
Highbridge, Somerset
Frank Foley, the spy known as the British Schindler, who saved thousands of Jews in World War Two, was born in Highbridge and is commemorated by a statue in the town centre.

Highley, Shropshire
Highley is not named after the author of this book. The author of this book comes from Yorkshire and the only, somewhat tenuous, northern link I can find with

the village of Highley is that it has a Colliery Brass Band.

Highley gained notoriety in 1975 when a local resident, 17-year-old Lesley Whittle, was abducted and murdered by Donald Neilson, known as the Black Panther.

Hillingdon, Greater London
In the Church of John the Baptist can be seen a memorial to John, 8th Baron Strange of Knokin, and, even stranger, in 2015 the people of Hillingdon elected Boris Johnson as their MP. Hillingdon was previously the Uxbridge Constituency but in 2010 it became Uxbridge and South Ruislip. (See Uxbridge)

Hinckley, Leicestershire
Shakespeare's 'King Henry IV Part II, Act V, Scene I.' hears a servant say to his master, 'Now sir, a new link to the bucket must need be had; and sir, do you mean to stop any of William's wages, about the sack he lost the other day at Hinckley fair'.

It understandably causes confusion to some visitors that Hinckley is 158 miles away from the Hinckley Point nuclear power stations.

Hilton, Cambridgeshire
Captain Sparrow lived here, but not THAT Captain Sparrow. The Victoria and Albert museum has a wall painting made on plaster for Captain Sparrow at Park Farm, Hilton. This is thought to commemorate his marriage in 1633.

On the village green visitors can negotiate a rare turf maze.

Hilton, Cumbria
Once a centre for lead mining, this village now has an economy mostly based on sheep.

Hilton, Derbyshire
Hilton proudly erected a clock to celebrate the Millennium. Unfortunately the clock was supported on a cast iron column that started to corrode and the whole thing had to be taken down in 2017 due to Health and Safety concerns.

Hitchin, Hertfordshire
The British Schools Museum is in Hitchin. Here you will find the world's only complete Lancasterian Schoolroom, the 19th century Lancasterian Method involved students being taught by members of their peer group. Parts of the 2010 BBC 'Just William' series were filmed at this museum.

The location of the birth of Elizabeth Angela Marguerite Bowes-Lyon, the future Queen Mother, is disputed. Some say she was born in her parents' London mansion or in a horse-drawn ambulance on the way to a hospital from there. Another suggested location for her birth includes her grandmother's home. One thing that is certain is that her birth was registered in Hitchin which is close to the Bowes-Lyon family home, St Paul's Walden Bury, and this, right or wrong, is where the 1901 UK census says she was born. (See Holkham)

Holborn, Greater London
Charles Dickens lived in rented rooms at Furnival's Inn for a while and he commandeered this as the home of John Westlock in 'Pickwick Paper.' It is in Holborn he visited The Old Curiosity Shop. The shop that now attracts so many tourists was originally

a dairy given as a present by Charles II to one of his mistresses. It is now a shoe shop. However, it is unlikely that this shop was the inspiration for Dickens' novel about Little Nell as the name wasn't attached to the building until after the release of the novel. Dickens writes of the building that inspired him: 'The old house had long been pulled down, and a fine broad road was in its place.'

Holkham, Norfolk

Queen Elizabeth, the Queen Mother, had a beach hut at Holkham. (See Hitchin)

Holsworthy, Devon

Several websites place Holsworthy in Cornwall, it isn't too far from the border but it stands firmly in Devon.

Holsworthy celebrates St Peter's Fair eleven days after the feast of St Peter. The right to hold the fair was granted in 1614 by James I. In 1752 we adopted the Gregorian Calendar with the loss of eleven days which explains the date confusion. The fair is announced by the Town Crier from the site of the Great Tree. The Great Tree no longer exists, a plaque can be seen six paces from the site of the tree. This plaque states that the proclamation of the fair has been made from here since 1154. They're obviously not very good with dates in Holsworthy as this is not correct, 1145 is when a Court Leet tribunal was granted by charter.

Honiton, Devon

Honition retains its annual Hot Pennies Ceremony when warmed pennies are thrown to children from balconies in the High Street. The ceremony originated in the days when members of the aristocracy threw hot coins to the poor and gained sadistic amusement when they burnt their fingers.

Since Queen Victoria ordered a Honiton Lace wedding dress, royal brides have almost all included some of the lace as part of their bridal attire and royal babies are traditionally wrapped in a shawl of Honition Lace at their christenings. The making of lace was a Devon cottage industry, small sprigs in the shape of swirls and flowers were sent to Honiton to be stitched together to form lace and this was also the centre from which finished items were marketed to the rest of the country. Hence, Honiton Lace was not necessarily made in Honiton.

Hook Norton, Oxfordshire
Best known for the brewery, which is well worth a visit so long as you are capable of climbing numerous flights of steps to follow the process whereby beer is brewed in a traditional tower system with a different process on each descending floor. (See Steeple Aston) The tour, which ends with a tasting of the brewery's excellent ales, is conducted by knowledgable workers who show a genuine enthusiasm. Local deliveries are often made on a dray pulled by splendid shire horses.

Hope Valley, Derbyshire
Technically this is the Derwent Valley but it is still known as the Hope Valley and a popular destination with local tourists as the Hope Valley Line railway runs between Manchester and Sheffield.

Hope Cement, the UK's biggest cement factory, sits at the middle of the valley in what is a National Park, local people accept this ugly anomaly because the business is a major employer.

Horsley, Derbyshire
Sophia, Rosamund and Blanche are the three fountains donated to the village in 1864 by Reverend Sitwell and named after the Sitwell's daughters.

Horncastle, Lincolnshire
Edward Stanhope MP was born in London but is remembered by the people of Horncastle as a major benefactor to the town when he was MP for Mid Lincolnshire during the late 19th century. When this constituency was abolished in 1885 he became MP for Horncastle. He offered the Market Place, the Wong and the Pig Market their revenue in tolls to the local Board of Health. Wong is a Scandinavian term for common land or pasture, the Horncastle Wong includes the football club's ground.

The Stanhope Memorial stands in the middle of the market place and is the kind of shape that provides an obvious climbing challenge to some who have enjoyed a drink or three.

Horrabridge, Devon
Horrabridge is within the Dartmoor National Park. The Leaping Salmon pub takes its name thanks to its proximity to the River Walkham, famous for its salmon and beautiful packhorse bridge.

Folky Seth Wakeman recorded his 'Kitty Jay' album here but the village has an even bigger claim to fame. In 1898 Francis Frith took a snap of the village which is seen in the opening title sequence of 'Bagpuss'.

Horsham, West Sussex
Horsham's pedestrianised commercial centre is one of three places in Britain with the name Carfax (there are others in Oxford and Winchester). Carfax comes

from the Norwegian 'Quartre Voies' via French 'Carrefour' meaning a place where four roads meet. Interestingly Carrefour, a name adopted by a major French supermarket chain, includes the word' four' but it is the first half of the word that is derived from the Latin for 'four'.

Horsham had a memorial to local poet Percy Bysshe Shelley. The memorial took the form of a water sculpture that occasionally blasted six and a half tons of water into the air. The fountain was turned off in 2006 to save water, it was turned back on to celebrate its tenth birthday in November of the same year but then turned off again that Christmas. After being turned back on for a short period it was turned off in May 2008 when the main pump failed. After being fenced off for repairs it was reopened in full working order in 2009. Further repairs costing £30,000 were undertaken in 2011 but it was permanently removed in 2016 due to the cost of upkeep.

Horsington, Somerset
Horsington means the settlement of horse keepers which is very appropriate considering the village is less than five miles from the Wincanton racecourse.

Hounslow, Greater London
Prior to his march on London in 1647 Oliver Cromwell camped with 20,000 men on Hounslow Common.

As recently as 1802 the bodies of highwaymen executed at Tyburn were brought to Hounslow and hung in gibbets along the road to the west of the town. (See Paddington)

Myrtle Avenue might sound idyllically English but

Myrtle Avenue, Hounslow, has a good claim to be Britain's noisiest street with planes almost touching the rooftops as they land on Heathrow's southern runway which begins at the end of the street. There are more complaints from residents over the difficulty of getting in and out of Myrtle Avenue due to the many plane spotters who gather and park their cars there, than there are about the racket from just above. (See Heathrow.

I was told by a rare resident not complaining about plane spotters that Hounslow is Britain's asbestos fly-tipping capital.

Hove (See Brighton and Hove)

Hoveton, Norfolk
Hoveton is immediately opposite Wroxham on the River Bure. Many people consider the entire settlement to be Wroxham. (See Wroxham)

Huddersfield, West Yorkshire
Rugby League was invented in Huddersfield in 1895 although the game then was very different to what it is now.

The world's biggest nodding dog, which was 11 feet tall, was made in Huddersfield. On the subject of dogs, Huddersfield also claims to be the home of the Yorkshire Terrier with a tiny pooch named Huddersfield Ben being the original of the species.

The Sex Pistols played their last two UK concerts at a nightclub in Huddersfield on Christmas Day 1977. The first of the two gigs, at Ivanhoe's, was a matinee performance for the kids of striking firefighters.

A statue of Harold Wilson, who was born and schooled here, stands outside the railway station.

Hull, East Riding of Yorkshire
I have included this city as Hull because this is what everybody calls the place but it is actually Kingston-upon-Hull. The city stands on the River Hull at its confluence with the Humber Estuary.

Hull Minster is yet another parish church claiming to have the largest floor area of any in the UK. (See Beverley. See Boston)

Coach parties have been known to visit the town just to use the beautiful public toilets which are listed in the 'Lonely Planet' guide.

Lemsip was invented in Kingston-upon-Hull.

'From Hull, Halifax, and Hell, good Lord deliver us' is a Yorkshire Proverb. (See Halifax)

(See Glaisdale)

Hungerford, Berkshire
Very sadly many people of a certain age only remember Hungerford for the massacre that took place here in 1987 when Michael Ryan shot 16 people dead before killing himself. The Hungerford Massacre led to the Firearms (Amendment) Act 1988, which banned the ownership of semi-automatic centre-fire rifles and restricted the use of shotguns with a magazine capacity of more than two rounds.

Hungerford is the only place in Britain to have continuously celebrated Hocktide, or Tutti Day, on the second Tuesday after Easter. This now marks the end of the council's administrative and financial year but was originally an excuse for a general knees up.

Hunstanton, Norfolk
Referred to as 'Sunny Hunny' this is the only East Coast resort that faces west. Locals tell gullible tourists that the land they can see from the cliffs is Holland, it's actually Lincolnshire and the church is St Botolph's, the spire is the one known as Boston Stump. (See Boston)

Huntingdon, Cambridgeshire
Oliver Cromwell was born here in 1599. The coffin of Mary, Queen of Scots, temporarily rested in All Saints Church on its way from Peterborough for reburial in Westminster Abbey. Cromwell would have been 13 at the time so is likely to have witnessed this historic occurrence which was a major attraction in his home town. Opposite the church is the Cromwell Museum in the old grammar school which was attended not only by Cromwell but also by Samuel Pepys.

In the 14th century Godmanchester, just across the Great Ouse, joined Huntingdon in building a bridge to join the two communities. Both sides worked from their own separate set of plans which accounts for the eccentric mixture of styles.

Husbands Bosworth, Leicestershire
Husbands Bosworth is a large village on the crossroads of the routes connecting Northampton to Leicester and the A4304 linking the M1 to Market Harborough.

Solicitor General John Cooke who prosecuted at the trial of Charles I was baptised here in 1608.

From 1943 Wellington Bombers flew from RAF

Station Husbands Bosworth, which is now the home of a gliding club and is used by rapid response helicopters from the East Midlands Air Support Unit.

Hutton-le-Hole, North Yorkshire
Sheep join tourists sauntering along the streets here with their grazing keeping the grass short (the sheeps' grazing not the tourists').

Hyde, Greater Manchester
Moors Murderers Ian Brady and Myra Hindley were arrested at their home in Hyde and the prolific serial killer Harold Shipman had his surgery here. TV presenter and sex offender Stuart Hall was brought up in Hyde.

The dance scene from the 1979 movie 'Yanks', starring Richard Gere, was filmed in Hyde Town Hall.

Hythe, Hampshire
The oldest working pier train in the world takes travellers to the ferry for the ten minute journey from Hythe to Southampton.

Hythe, Kent
Mackeson, a dark-coloured, very sweet stout, known as a milk stout, was brewed in Hythe from 1909 to 1968. The drink was popular in the 1960s and is famous for its early TV commercial voiced by actor Bernard Miles who told us ' It looks good, tastes good, and by golly it does you good'.

St Leonard's Church in Hythe has a very rare ossuary (the only other one in England is at Rothwell in Northamptonshire). An ossuary is a bone store, this one is lined with some 2,000 skulls and an estimated 8,000 thigh bones. (See Rothwell)

I

Ilchester, Somerset
The Ilchester Cheese Company is known to shoppers throughout the nation with most people recognising the brand as a typically English country product. Very few shoppers realise that the Ilchester Cheese Company does not make cheese. Although founded here in 1962 by a local pub landlord the company is not now 100% British, it is part of Norseland, a Norwegian company.

The Ilchester Cheese Company takes ready made cheeses and blends these with other ingredients including beer and fruit. The famed Applewood Cheddar is not smoked as most believe, it is treated with an artificial smoke flavouring and given its smoked appearance by being coated with paprika.

Ilford, Greater London
Britain's finest specimen of a mammoth was discovered in Ilford, said to be the only one with a complete skull. It is on show in the Natural History Museum.

Television inventor John Logie Baird moved to Ilford in the 1920s and did most of the work on his invention in a workshop on the roof of the Plessey building which has now been demolished.

The Ilford photographic company had its headquarters where the Ilford branch of Sainsbury's now stands.

Boxer Nigel Benn was often announced into the ring

as ‘Fighting out of Ilford, England’.

During 2012 Ilford was the fastest growing tourist destination in Europe due to its proximity to the Olympic Park Stadium in Stratford.

Ilfracombe, Devon

Ilfracombe is 35-miles from Swansea, the crossing was first swum in 2009 by Welsh TV presenter Gethin Jones, it took him 22 hours.

Damien Hirst closed his restaurant in Ilfracombe but his controversial 25-ton statue of a bisected pregnant woman, ‘Verity’, still stands on the pier. Hirst loaned ’Verity’ to the town for 20 years in 2012 so it will be interesting to see what happens to her in 2032. (See Combe Martin)

The Landmark Theatre is topped by twin cones known locally as ‘Madonna’s Bra’.

Ilkeston, Derbyshire

Nottingham makes claims that its Goose Fair is the oldest fair in the country. The Nottingham Goose Fair charter was granted in 1284, Ilkeston’s Fair was granted in 1252.

William Roache grew up in Ilkeston. Roache holds the world record for playing the same TV role for the longest period of time having first appeared on ‘Coronation Street’ as Ken Barlow in December 1960. Robert Lindsay, Wolfie in ‘Citizen Smith’, was born here.

After people started sneaking garden gnomes onto a traffic island during the night the island is now officially named Gnome Island.

Weleda skincare products are made in Ilkeston.

Ilkley, West Yorkshire

Legend has it that the song 'On Ilkla Moor Bhat 'at' was written by members of a church choir from Halifax on a picnic outing to Ilkley Moor. 'Bhat 'at' means without a hat and the song tells the story of a headwear-lacking lover pursuing the object of his desire, Mary Jane, who warns him he will catch his death of cold and his body will be eaten by worms which will, in turn, be eaten by ducks. This lyric might sound romantic to someone from Yorkshire but might not start hearts thumping across the county's borders.

The Cow and Calf rocks attract visitors on the moor. This is a rock formation consisting of an outcrop, the Cow, and a boulder, the Calf. Locals insisted there is also a Bull, but none of them could show me where this is situated.

On 12th March 1967 Jimi Hendrix and the Experience played a gig at the Troutbeck Hotel in Ilkley. The hotel is now a care home.

Ingleton, North Yorkshire

This parish includes two of Yorkshire's Three Peaks, Ingleborough and Whernside, the White Scar Caves are another tourist attraction.

Sir Arthur Conan Doyle's mother lived in the nearby hamlet of Thornton-in-Lonsdale which the author visited via Ingleton railway station. When Conan Doyle wrote 'A Study in Scarlet' he intended calling his hero Sherrinford Holmes but later changed this to Sherlock. Reverend Thomas Dod Sherlock was vicar of St Mary the Virgin in Ingleton and the same year

Conan Doyle completed that first novel the church was rebuilt to a design by Walker Gallery architect Cornelius Sherlock so it is likely the name of the world's best known sleuth was inspired by a visit to Ingleton. (See Southsea)

Ipswich, Suffolk

There isn't a museum in Museum Street, Ipswich. The building originally built as a museum became Arlingtons Dance Studio and is now Arlingtons Brasserie.

In St Stephen's Church can be seen a memorial to Robert Leman and his wife who both died on the same day, 3rd September 1637. It is claimed locally that Robert was Lord Mayor of London which is not correct. Robert Leman was the nephew of Sir John Leman who was Lord Mayor of London in 1616.

Ironbridge, Shropshire

The iron bridge, built here in 1779, was the first structure in the world made from cast iron, giving the town its reputation as being the birthplace of the Industrial Revolution.

Ironbridge had the only pink cooling towers in Europe? The towers were constructed from concrete to which a red pigment had been added to make them blend in with the surrounding soil. The power station's main chimney, still standing at the time of writing, is the tallest structure in Shropshire, at 673 feet (205 m) it is taller than Blackpool Tower. Ironbridge B Power Station was turned off in 2015, following some debate, the cooling towers were demolished and 1,000 homes and accompanying shops are planned for the site.

Ironbridge was evacuated during the flooding of winter 2020.

Irthlingborough, Northamptonshire
Until Forest Green Rovers were promoted in 2017, Rushden and Diamonds FC, based in Irthlingborough, made this the smallest town in England with a Football League team. (See Nailsworth)

Whitworths, suppliers of dried fruits, home baking kits and snacks, have been based here since 1886

Isleworth, Greater London
Vincent van Gogh came to Isleworth in 1876 to work as a teacher and assistant preacher at a local school. J M W Turner was also a local resident, he lived at Sion Ferry House and his time spent here inspired several paintings of the Thames.

Ivybridge, Devon
There actually was a bridge covered with ivy here which was immortalised in a painting by J M W Turner.

Ivybridge was elevated from village status to a town in 1977. Between the 1981 and 2001 UK censuses the population more than doubled from 5,106 to 12,056 making this, at the time, the fastest growing town in Europe.

J

Jacobstow, Cornwall
Not to be confused with Jacobstowe some 40 miles away in Devon.

Jacobstowe, Devon
Not to be confused with Jacobstow some 40 miles away in Cornwall. Curworthy Cheese is produced at a farm in Jacobstowe, probably all very good and their Haytor and Devon Oke are excellent.

Jarrow, Tyne and Wear
St Paul's Church, next to the ruins of St Paul's Monastery, has a dedication stone dated 23rd April 685AD, making it the oldest such stone in the country. The church also claims the world's oldest stained-glass window, which I was told dates from about 600AD. Yes I realise this makes the window 85 years older than the building in which it is said to have been installed but these are their claims not mine.

The 'World's Oldest Stained Glass Window' is actually random bits of ancient coloured glass from the monastery, recovered by archaeologist Professor Rosemary Cramp in 1973 and put together to form an abstract, circular mosaic.

The Venerable Bede entered St Peter's, known as St Paul's twin monastery, in around 680 at the age of seven. He wrote more than 60 works including the first known history of the English people. He was buried here after his death in 735. In the 1020s bones, said to have been the Bede's remains, were taken from here to Durham Cathedral.

The Jarrow March to London to protest against unemployment took place in 1936 and inspired Alan Price's 1974 hit record 'Jarrow Song'.

Jesmond, Newcastle upon Tyne
Local legend has it that, shortly after the Norman Conquest, an apparition of the Virgin Mary holding the baby Jesus appeared here. At this point in the story confusion sets in. The suburb had previously been known as Gese Muth, which to me sounds a lot like Jesmond and is said to mean the 'Mouth of the Ouse'. A knowledgable local informed me that the Mary and Child apparition resulted in people renaming this Jesus Mound, which was later abbreviated to Jesmond, but I'll still stick to the Gese Muth theory.

Lennon and McCartney began writing, possibly wrote all of, the Beatles' hit, 'She Loves You' at the Imperial Hotel in Jesmond (now a Holiday Inn) despite somewhat shaky counterclaims that the song was written at the nearby Turk's Head.

Jump, South Yorkshire
Allegedly so called because, in order to get to work, coal miners had to jump over a stream in what is now the Jump Valley.

K

Keighley, West Yorkshire

Americans probably have more difficulty pronouncing Keighley than any other British place name. It's 'Keith Ly'. In support of those Americans with pronunciation problems I cannot find another word where 'gh' becomes 'th' anywhere on the planet but I'm sure someone, somewhere, will find one and contact me to complain.

In 1936 the Zeppelin Hindenburg flew across Yorkshire on its way from the USA to Germany. As the airship passed over Keighley a parcel was dropped from the sky which was picked up in the High Street by two boys. In the parcel was a bunch of carnations along with a small crucifix, postage stamps, a postcard and a letter on Hindenburg notepaper.

The letter was written by John P Schulte who referred to himself as 'the first flying priest'. His note asked for the carnations and crucifix to be placed on the grave of his brother, Lieutenant Franz Schulte, who had died whilst a prisoner of war in Keighley and was buried in Skipton. This last detail was slightly wrong as the soldier had been buried at Morton, two-miles from Keighley.

Kempsey, Worcestershire

Alexander Beckham was Abbot of Cirencester and he was born on the same night as Richard the Lion-Heart, he was brought up by a foster-brother. Beckham was the first Englishman to write about chess, silkworms and the mariner's compass. He died in Kempsey while visiting a friend.

Composer Sir Edward Elgar lived here from April 1923 to October 1927.

Kendal, Cumbria

In a very unscientific survey (guys in the pub) I determined that if you say 'Kendal' to just about anybody, they will reply 'Mint Cake.' Kendal Mint Cake helped Shackleton across the Antarctic and got Hillary to the top of Everest. It was allegedly invented by accident during an experiment to make clear mints by Joseph Wiper. Kendal Mint Cake has to be the best tasting health food on the planet and the variety dipped in dark chocolate is particularly healthy and delicious.

Snuff is the other product for which Kendal is famous.

When the Lake District National Park was mapped out in 1951 it was purposely designed so as not to include Kendal.

Kenilworth, Warwickshire

Sir Walter Scott originally published his novel 'Kenilworth' anonymously.

The field known as Parliament Piece is said to be the site where Henry III held Parliament in 1266 as his army besieged Kenilworth Castle. Elizabeth I visited the Castle on several occasions probably attracted by the lavish banquets and entertainment, known to have cost as much as £1,000 per day, provided by Robert Dudley, 1st Earl of Leicester.

Kensington and South Kensington, Greater London
A fifth of Britain's top 20 most-visited tourist attractions are in Kensington: the Natural History Museum, Science Museum, Royal Albert Hall and Victoria and Albert Museum.

St Mary's Abbots has the tallest church spire (278 feet) in London.

Queen Victoria was born in Kensington Palace, her first name was actually Alexandrina as you will already know if you've read about Banbury.

The first Sumo Wrestling tournament held outside Japan took place at the Royal Albert Hall in 1991. The Royal Albert Hall also hosted the first, one of only two, concerts to include The Beatles and the Rolling Stones on the same bill.

Famous former or current Kensington residents include Madonna, the Beckhams, Kylie Minogue and Nigella Lawson, along with William, Kate, Harry, Megan and their assorted kids.

Keswick, Cumbria
There is no lead in your pencil. The discovery of graphite here some three centuries ago is said to have resulted in Keswick becoming the birthplace of the pencil. The town boasts the world's largest colouring pencil. This 8-metre tall marvel can be viewed at the Derwent Pencil Museum which, at the time of writing, has reopened following closure due to flooding in 2015 and coronavirus in 2020.

Kettering, Northamptonshire
Wicksteed Park in Kettering, which opened in

1921, is the UK mainland's oldest amusement park. Blackgang Chine on the Isle of Wight is the only one older in the UK having been established in the 1840s.

Kettering Tyres' 1976 deal with Kettering Town FC made them the first senior club in England with a sponsor's logo on their shirts.

In his days as a newspaper reporter, Charles Dickens covered the 1835 Kettering by-election which was not without incident. Dickens witnessed a Tory Supporter point a gun at someone in the crowd, he was disarmed and the Tories went on to win.

Kew, Greater London
It is claimed Julius Caesar forded the Thames at Kew during the Gallic wars in 54BC.

Kew Retail Park is on the site of the former factory where Dodge made lorries including a model named Kew. Chrysler cars were also assembled here.

In 1772 George III inherited the Kew Estate and joined it with Richmond so two gardens became one. This is why it is always plural; Kew Gardens, never Kew Garden. The first kangaroo to come to Britain was kept at what was then Kew Menagerie next to Queen Charlotte's Cottage in the Gardens.

Queen Charlotte's Cottage was gifted to Kew in 1898 by Queen Victoria on condition the surrounding land must not be cultivated.

Kidderminster, Worcestershire
I'm not certain this is going to be a big attraction for those hoping to entertain kids on a rainy day but in Kidderminster you can take your family on a visit to

the Museum of Carpet where it is possible to marvel at the Weaving Shed Gallery and a Traditional Office with a selection of typewriters.

The Drakelow Tunnels were originally dug as an underground factory to manufacture engines and guns. After numerous delays in building, the factory went into full production in 1943 manufacturing parts for aircraft including the Sunderland Flying Boat and the Bristol Blenheim. Various uses have been found for the tunnels since then but they last made the news in 2013 when some 30 police officers raided the site to seize 885 cannabis plants.

Kilpeck, Herefordshire

Kilpeck is worth a visit if only to see the superb Norman church of Saint Mary and Saint David dated to around 1140. The church is noted for its wealth of external and internal Norman stone carvings.

King's Cross, Greater London

King's Cross and St Pancras railway stations are just across the road from one another. Families taking selfies with kids can be an inconvenience to passengers at King's Cross due to the Harry Potter gateway to the Hogwarts Express at the fictional platform 9¾. There's a luggage trolley embedded in the wall and, of course, a gift shop. J K Rowling has admitted that when she was writing about the station she was actually thinking about platforms 9 and 10 at Euston. Anyone wanting to take their kids to the actual filming location for the Harry Potter station shots should go to platforms 4 and 5 at King's Cross.

King's Cross is the first station after GO on a UK Monopoly board.

Kings Langley, Hertfordshire
Richard II was buried at the Church of All Saints prior to reburial in Westminster Abbey. The first Duke of York, Edmund of Langley, was buried here and his body remains in the memorial chapel.

Shakespeare's 'Richard II', Act III, Scene IV, is set in the grounds of Kings Langley palace garden.

Swiss chemist George Wander began manufacturing a drink he called Ovomaltine in 1865. His son took over the business and opened a factory in Kings Langley in 1913, he renamed the drink Ovaltine. In 1971 a visitor to the factory was a product endorser who claimed he had drunk Ovaltine since he was a little boy, that visitor? Muhammad Ali.

Kings Lynn, Norfolk
Kings Lynn Town Hall's greatest treasure is the King John's Cup. Made from silver, gold and jewels it is said to be the finest object of its kind in the country. This claim might, or might not, be true but when locals tell you the cup is the oldest of its type in England and was gifted to the town by King John, probably England's worst monarch, this claim should be taken with a very large pinch of salt. John died some 800-years ago but 'his' cup wasn't manufactured until the mid 14th century.

Pocahontas (See Gravesend) is said to have saved the life of John Smith who came from Kings Lynn.

Daniel Defoe's 'Robinson Crusoe' was based on the actual adventures of Alexander Selkirk. Defoe is known to have visited Kings Lynn which he described as 'beautiful, well built and well situated.' In St Nicholas Chapel is a memorial in commemoration of Robinson Cruso (sic) who died in 1794. Although there is no proof that Defoe ever saw this memorial he must have got the name of his most famous character from somewhere.

Kingsbridge, Devon
The royal estates of Alvington and Chillington were once linked by a bridge around which the town developed, hence Kingsbridge.

Kingsbridge is a popular tourist destination in the South Devon Area of Outstanding Natural Beauty with some of the country's finest sailing facilities on the doorstep.

Kingston upon Thames, Greater London
Now known as Royal Kingston.

Many towns and villages have retained at least one old, red phone box. They can be leased for £1 and are used as libraries, tiny clubs, an aquarium and I know one that has been converted to a clock. (See Newton Poppleford). Kingston upon Thames beats them all with its sculpture consisting of twelve phone boxes, each tipped up to lean on the next like a set of falling dominoes. Created by David Mach the appropriate name of the sculpture is 'Out of Order'.

In the grounds of the Guildhall visitors can marvel at the Coronation Stone. This looks like a mounting block, used for climbing onto horses, indeed for a period of time it served just this purpose. Those less cynical claim it was on this stone that many Kings of England were crowned including Athelstan, Edward the Elder, Edmund and Edward the Martyr.

Nipper, the dog on the HMV logo, died in Kingston

upon Thames in 1895 and was buried at a small park in Clarence Street. A branch of Lloyds Bank was built over the grave and nearby is the recently named Nipper Alley.

Kirby Lonsdale, Cumbria
Kirby Lonsdale is a stunning little town on the borders of the Yorkshire Dales and the Lake District. This central location results in it not being quite so crowded with tourists visiting either of the National Parks.

Kirby Stephen, Cumbria
No matter what anyone might tell you, and they probably will, Faraday Road is not named after scientist Michael Faraday but after his uncle Richard who was a local tradesman.

Knaresborough, North Yorkshire
King John distributed the first Maundy Money on 15th April 1210 in Knaresborough.

Mother Shipton's Cave claims to be England's oldest tourist attraction. The prophetess and soothsayer Mother Shipton, aka Ursula Southwell, wife of Toby Shipton, was allegedly born in the cave. Fee paying tourists also get to see the Dropping Well where water, rich in minerals, drips through artefacts suspended there to attract a deposit that it is claimed has turned them into stone.

Knightsbridge, Greater London
In 2018 an apartment at One Hyde Park became Britain's most expensive home when it was sold for £160 million.

Congestion problems at Knightsbridge Underground

station were solved when a separate exit was constructed specifically for Harrods.

Knill, Herefordshire
Knill is a Thankful Village, one that suffered no deaths amongst those who fought in the First World War. Hence the village has no war memorial but a plaque in the parish church gives thanks and records the event.

Knottingley, West Yorkshire
Famous for Bagley's Glassworks with competitors on TV antique shows still snapping up Bagley items and selling them at a profit.

The Ferrybridge Power Station is close by, boasting the largest cooling towers of their type in Europe.

Knowsley, Merseyside
Henry VII is said to have visited Knowsley, Shakespeare apparently performed one of his plays here and Edward Lear was staying at Knowsley Hall when he wrote 'The Owl and the Pussycat'.

The main attraction is Knowsley Safari Park.

Knutsford, Cheshire
The title town in Elizabeth Gaskell's novel 'Cranford' is based on Knutsford where she lived during her childhood, returning here after she married.

Visitors to Tatton Park keep Knutsford busy and you can expect major traffic problems in late July when the park hosts the Royal Horticultural Society flower show.

Krumlin, West Yorkshire
Drivers on the M62 pass signs informing them that, at 1,221 feet - 372 metres, they are on the highest stretch of motorway in Britain. Look to the north from this high point and you can see a line of electricity pylons going down into a valley. The upper pylon is in Krumlin.

Krumlin is the village that hosted the Yorkshire Folk, Jazz and Blues Festival. Now known to most simply as 'Krumlin', the event, held in August 1970, was wiped out by the worst weather ever to hit a music festival. Even though this was mid August rain was horizontal, temperatures dropped to close to freezing, there were thousands of cases of exposure and hypothermia.

The event's organisers were left bankrupt but in the process they gave Elton John his first major gig and he went from Krumlin to the Troubadour in the USA and the rest, as they say, is history.

(See the book 'In Pursuit of Trivia' by Brian Highley, available from Amazon)

L

Lancaster, Lancashire
The Duke of Lancaster is still called a Duke even if female. At the time of writing the Duke of Lancaster is Queen Elizabeth II.

Once known as 'hanging town' because more people were hanged here than anywhere in England outside London.

Lancaster had a reputation for 'lunatics and linoleum'. The linoleum industry has now gone and Moor Mental Hospital, where Alan Bennett's mother was once a patient, has been converted into luxury apartments.

Lancing, West Sussex
In 2019 Lancing applied to have its name changed to Lancing-on-Sea as this sounds more enticing to potential visitors.

Land's End, Cornwall
Sportsmen and charity fund raisers regularly walk or cycle the 874 miles from Land's End to John O'Groats in the belief that these are the most southerly and northerly points in Britain. They are not. Britain's most southerly location is Lizard Point and the most northerly spot is Duncansby Head. (See Lizard) As the crow flies the distance between Land's End and John O'Groats is 603 miles. (See John O'Groats)

The official name for Land's End is Peal Point. It is

known locally as The Peal.

In 2012 Land's End was the UK starting point for the Olympic Torch relay.

Just to the north of Land's End is Cape Cornwall which is England's only cape.

Launceston, Cornwall

Launceston is close to the Devon border and inland so lacks all those tourists who flock to the county for chocolate-boxy fishing harbours and chefs who spend more time on TV and writing cook books than they spend cooking in their restaurants.

The castle here was built by William the Conqueror's half-brother, Robert, and is well worth a visit. Towering over the town the castle is in superb condition considering its age.

Guests at the White Hart Hotel can view a Norman doorway which was allegedly removed from the Friary at St Thomas the Apostle, an Augustine priory in nearby Newport, or possibly from a chapel in the castle depending on the source you choose to believe. At the time of writing the future of the White Hart as a commercial venture was in some doubt following its sale.

Lavenham, Suffolk

'Lavender's Blue, dilly dilly', are the opening words of a folk song said to have originated in the 16th century but lavender isn't blue. Lavender is, well, lavender is lavender. This is entirely my own theory, so might be wrong, but could the song have originally been 'Lavenham Blue'? Originating at about the same time as the song Lavenham Blue was a blue woolen cloth made in this town.

As for 'Dilly Dilly'? I wonder if this could have originally been 'Silly Silly' as Lavenham is in what was known as 'Silly Suffolk', 'silly' originating in the anglo-saxon word 'seely' meaning 'blessed.

I think my interpretation makes far more sense than the folk song.

Leatherhead, Surrey
Leatherhead factories manufacturing Goblin Vacuum Cleaners and Ronson cigarette lighters turned to the production of ammunitions during the Second World War.

Local resident Sir Michael Caine is patron to the Leatherhead Drama Festival and sometimes turns up to hand out prizes. It wasn't until 2016 that Maurice Joseph Micklewhite officially changed his name to Michael Caine.

A mutated alligator in 'Teenage Mutant Ninja Turtles' comics is called Leatherhead.

Leamington Spa, Warwickshire
In 2017 Rightmove declared Royal Leamington Spa the Happiest Place in Britain.

The first lawn tennis club in England was founded here in 1872 and, at the age of eleven, Princess (later Queen) Victoria spent her first night in a public building in the town.

One of Sir John Betjeman's more eccentric works begins; 'She died in the upstairs bedroom By the light of the evening star, That shone through the upstairs window, From over Leamington Spa'.

Lechdale, Gloucestershire
Officially called Lechdale on Thames with the head of the river's navigation being in nearby Inglesham. The river is overlooked by a statue said to be Father Thames and the first stone bridge over the Thames outside London originated here in 1229. It was rebuilt in 1830.

Stone was taken in barges from Lechdale to be used in buildings including St Paul's Cathedral, Windsor Castle and several Oxford colleges.

Ledbury, Herefordshire
John Masefield, Poet Laureate from 1930 to 1967, was born here. Rudyard Kipling was favourite to replace Robert Bridges as the royal poet but George V appointed Masefield after he was recommended by Ramsay MacDonald.

Leeds, West Yorkshire
In 2015 a Leeds DJ was married in a local park. The groom was assisted by a record 103 ushers and his bride was accompanied by a record 230 bridesmaids, there were just 20 people listed simply as 'guests' .

The level of humidity in Temple Mill was once sustained by having grass grow on the roof. A flock of sheep was kept up there to maintain the length of the grass.

Leeds rock band the Kaiser Chiefs take their name from a South African football club. Mel B became Leeds' last minute contribution to Girl Power when the original Scary Spice dropped out because she didn't get on with the other girls.

After supporting them since boyhood, in 2015 actor

Russel Crowe almost bought Leeds United FC but backed out at the last minute because he felt his involvement would result in him spending too much time away from his family. In 2020 Leeds United faced criticism when they were promoted to the Premier League and chose to have players display the trophy from the top of a double deck bus whilst fans had been told to stay at home during the Coronavirus pandemic.

Leek, Stafordshire

Leek's unofficial titles are Gateway to the Peak District and Queen of the Moorlands.

Eric (Crafty Cockney) Bristow lived in Leek. Anna Watkins who won a gold rowing medal at the 2012 Olympics was born here.

Leicester, Leicestershire

When the Anglo Saxons and Vikings began to share trade and ideas in Leicester their languages came together, thus giving the city the claim that the English language was born here.

In 1967 Radio Leicester was launched as Britain's first local radio station.

Leicester was the first city outside London to be blessed with traffic wardens. It is claimed Leicester has more sets of traffic lights than any other city in Britain but cannot produce figures to support this claim.

Leicester hosts the world's biggest annual Diwali celebration outside India.

In 2012 the remains of King Richard III were

uncovered in a Leicester car park and later reburied in Leicester Cathedral. (See Selby. See Carmarthen. See Reading. See Middleham)

Leicester was the first city in the UK to have lockdown reintroduced due to a spike in covid-19 cases in 2020.

Leigh, Greater Manchester
Don't ask me why but Leigh Library had a sign displayed on its door reading, 'No sunflower seeds to be eaten in the library', when I phoned a friend in Leigh to get her to check out the reason for this she said this was the first time she'd realised that Leigh has a library

Arkwright's Spinning Jenny was one of the most important machines in the industrialisation of the textile industry. Richard Arkwright stole the idea for what is looked upon as his most important invention from an employee Thomas Highs. Highs was born in Leigh in 1718.

Leighton Buzzard, Bedfordshire
Leighton Buzzard gave birth to comedy musical group the Barron Knights and 80s glam-poppers Kajagoogoo (ask your grandma).

A local quarry stood in for the city of Hamunaptra in 'The Mummy Returns' and also featured in 'The Da Vinci Code' movie.

Leominster, Herefordshire
Pronounced 'Lemster'. Leominster Priory displays a ducking stool which was the last one used in Britain to torture a poor woman for some petty crime. In 1809 Jenny Pipes was taken in front of a magistrate

to be accused of being a scold after her brother-in-law complained about how she spoke to her husband. She was sentenced to being paraded through the streets of Leominster strapped into the seat of the ducking stool.

Crowds shouted 'Duck the scold' as she was taken to the river. Ducking was supposed to continue until the offender either admitted to her supposed crime, lost consciousness or simply gave up due to exhaustion. Jenny Pipes was still screaming abuse at the magistrate after two duckings and the punishment was stopped.

Letchworth, Hertfordshire

Letchworth was the world's first Garden City and it boasts Britain's first traffic roundabout.

Here you will find the UK's largest colony of black squirrels while muntjac deer have been observed wandering around the town centre.

In 'So Long, and Thanks for All the Fish', the fourth book in the five-part 'Hitchhiker's Guide to the Galaxy' trilogy, Ford Prefect tries to place a phone call from the Pleiades by hacking into the British phone network and telling the operator he is phoning from Letchworth.

Lewes, East Sussex

Lewes (pronounced Loo is) is one of those places that tempts tourists with Anne of Cleves House (See Haverhill)

The world famous Glyndebourne Opera Festival takes place at nearby Glyndebourne House.

Lewes makes a lot of fuss about November 5th when six bonfires are lit around the town. To some it might look like a Ku Klux Klan gathering when seventeen crosses are burnt but these represent the seventeen Martyrs burnt at the stake in Lewes during the period 1555-1557.

Lewisham, Greater London
Lewisham's 'ancient stone circle' was actually erected to celebrate the millennium in 1999. It's hard to explain why Britain celebrated the millennium at midnight on December 31st 1999. You do not celebrate birthdays at the start of each year but at the end, so, like the rest of the world, we should have celebrated the millennium as we went from 2000 into 2001. Shortly after building the stone circle the town opened Europe's largest police station.

The Rivoli Ballroom, has been used to make videos by Tina Turner, Elton John and Oasis. Sid Vicious was born in Lewisham.

Leyland, Lancashire
Undoubtedly most famous for Leyland Trucks, owned by the American Paccar company.

Leyton, Greater London
Spitalfields Market relocated to Leyton in 1991 and is Britain's main horticultural market supplying fruit and vegetables, in 2018 it was judged to be Britain's Best Wholesale Market.

The Parish of Leyton includes Leytonstone. Leytonstone Tube station displays 17 mosaics representing the life and films of Alfred Hitchcock who was born in Leytonstone in 1899.

Lichfield, Staffordshire
Lichfield Cathedral is the only medieval cathedral

in Europe with three spires so that's bound to give Russian visitors something to tell Putin about.

On 11th April 1612 Edward Wightman was taken into Lichfield Market Square and became the last person in Britain to be burned at the stake for heresy.

The Samuel Johnson Birthplace Museum does what it says on the tin. This is where the author of the first authoritative English dictionary was born in 1709. Johnson's father built the house.

Lincoln, Lincolnshire
Thought to be the oldest working canal in the country, the Fosse Dyke Canal was built by the Romans to improve trade links with Lincoln. (See Exeter)

The central tower of Lincoln Cathedral was topped by a spire giving the structure a total estimated height of 525 feet. This was the tallest building in the world until it collapsed during a storm in 1549. (See Salisbury)

The first British prototype tank, Little Willie, was built in Lincoln by William Foster and Co in 1915.

Liskeard, Cornwall
At Stuart House you can visit the room where Charles I slept during two visits to the town in 1644.

You can impress Cornish speaking residents by calling this town Lyskerrys or Lyn Kerwyd and make sure you enjoy the local delicacy, Roadkill Pie.

Littllehampton, West Sussex
It is claimed that Bayford Road in Littlehampton includes the longest uninterrupted stretch of terraced

houses in England, however, the same claim is made for Dorrington Road in Scotforth, Lancaster. Neither can provide me with an actual length so the dispute will continue until I, or one of my readers, can visit both with a tape measure. (See Scotforth)

The Long Bench is 1,000 feet long, can seat more than 300 people and for £150 you can have a message carved on the bench with the money going to a charity.

Liverpool, Merseyside
Everybody, even Russians, know all about Liverpool's musical heritage with more number one hits (56 at the time of writing) coming from Liverpool artists than from any other city, they know all about the ferry across the Mersey and all about the city's maritime history but did you know that Liverpool has the most Grade One listed buildings and more national museums and galleries than any British city other than London.

Liverpool has a group of stones, the Calder Stones, that were once part of a chambered tomb and were erected before Stonehenge. However, the Liverpool stones were originally about four miles from their present site and can now be viewed in a greenhouse at Calderstones Park.

Liverpool has been seen in more movies than any British city outside London. 'The Dark Knight', 'Fantastic Beasts', 'Captain America', and 'Letter to Brezhnev' to name just four.

Lizard, Cornwall
Lizard is a village on the Lizard Peninsula and is mainland Britain's most southerly settlement. Interest

in the unique location has resulted in a village green surrounded by gift shops and cafes. (See Land's End)

Thanks to the village's location, St Winwallow's Parish Church in Lizard is obviously Britain's most southerly church. In 1588 the Spanish Armada was first spotted from the village.

Lofthouse, North Yorkshire
Tourists drop in here on their way to the Nidderdale Caves just to the north of the village.

London
It is very difficult to think of facts about London that most people don't already know but let's give it a go.

The black dot at the 2 on the faces of the two clocks clocks at Horse Guards marks the hour Charles I was executed outside the nearby Banqueting House. Horse Guards is officially the ceremonial entrance to Buckingham and St James's Palaces.

Until 1916 cocaine and heroin were available over the counter in Harrods. The store even produced a gift pack including morphine, cocaine and syringes with which to shoot it up.

Winnie-the-Pooh was a female black bear. During World War One a Canadian regiment was called up to fight in France and they donated Winnie, their mascot, to London Zoo where she lived from 1914 to 1934. A A Milne used to visit the zoo with his son, Christopher Robin Milne. Winnie became one of Christopher's favourites and the rest, as they say ....

Over 300 languages are spoken in London.

You have to look up to see London's smallest permanent sculpture. In Philpot Lane and Eastcheap, EC3, stands a 19th century office block with a Caffe Nero at ground level. It is claimed that when the building was being constructed in the 1860s two of the workmen had a fight after one accused the other of stealing his cheese sandwich. During the brawl one of the men fell to his death at which point his colleague and accuser noticed two mice nibbling the sandwich which the rodents, not his friend, had stolen from his lunch box. To commemorate this tragic occurrence the two mice were sculpted onto the side of the building where they can be seen to this day. Others claim the cheese sandwich incident occurred when two builders died during the building of the nearby Monument? This theory for the tiny mice sculpture does not explain why builders of a 19th century office block would commemorate builders of a 17th century monument to the Great Fire of London.

At the time of writing British pubs are going through a gin craze. It is recorded that during the 1720 to 1751 Gin Craze in London the average consumption was two pints per week for every man, woman and child. Whilst on the subject of booze, in 1814 a vat of beer burst at the Meaux and Co Brewery causing a tidal wave to flood into surrounding streets. Eight people were drowned, five of these were attending a wake.

A subspecies of mosquito has evolved to live specifically in the tunnels of the London Underground. These mosquitos do not need regular water, can live in the dark, do not hibernate and have a ferocious bite. TV talk show host Jerry Springer was born at Highgate Underground station in 1944 while his mother sheltered from a Luftwaffe bombing raid.

Five London tube stations are named after pubs: The Angel, Royal Oak, Elephant and Castle, Manor House and Swiss Cottage.

Long Eaton, Derbyshire
Long Eaton developed along the banks of a stream which now flows through a culvert beneath the High Street.

Dame Laura Knight (nee Johnson) was born in Long Eaton. She was the first female artist to be appointed a Dame of the British Empire as a result of her work.

Longridge, Lancashire
Cromwell halted in Longridge before facing Monarchists in the Battle of Preston.

The Preston and Longridge Railway opened in 1840 to transport stone from the quarries for the building of the Liverpool docks and Lancaster Town Hall.

Looe, Cornwall
In this age of Facebook many will not understand the description of somewhere as being 'picture postcard perfect' but Looe is. East Looe and West Looe are divided by the River Looe and there is also a Looe Island.

Looe is a fishing town with the Shark Angling Club of Great Britain based here.

Lostwithiel, Cornwall
Once the capital of Cornwall and the county's main Stannary Town (a town where tin was refined and assessed), Lotwithiel's tin assets eventually led to its downfall when rubble from the tin mines silted-up the river preventing vessels from reaching the quay to

transport the valuable metal

Loughborough, Leicestershire
The main gates to Loughborough University are called the Bastard Gates. They take their name from a former Chairman of Governors, William Bastard. Sports graduates from Loughborough include Seb Coe, Paula Radcliffe, Tanni Grey-Thompson and Steve Backley.

Loughborough boasts the worlds biggest bell foundry where Great Paul was cast for St Paul's Cathedral. Great Paul was cast in 1881 and weighed 16.5 tons. Until the casting of the Olympic Bell, for the 2012 Olympics, Great Paul was the largest Bell in Britain.

Loughton, Essex
Loughton is in the Epping Forest and has what might best be described as 'tenuous links' to the pop music world. Gladys Mills, known as Mrs Mills, had hits in the 60s and 70s with her piano medleys of singalong songs and Dire Straits frontman Mark Knopfler taught at the local college

Louth, Lincolnshire
Louth had its very own saint, Saint Herefrith. The town once had a shrine to Herefrith but his relics were stolen in around 963AD and taken to Thorney Abbey in Cambridgeshire.

Poet Alfred, Lord Tennyson attended Louth Grammar School.

Lover, Wiltshire
Just take care how you pronounce this. It starts with 'low' as in 'lowver'.

Lowestoft, Suffolk
Lowestoft is the UK's most easterly town, so the first to see the sunrise on days when you can see the sun rise.

In 2009 and 2010 Wessex Foods, Sanyo and Jeld-Wen closed their Lowestoft factories. At the time of writing the Birds Eye frozen foods company employs 700 people in the town.

Composer Benjamin Britten was born here.

Luddendenfoot, West Yorkshire
Probably best known for the confusion the town's name causes when TV and radio newsreaders have to pronounce it. Read it slowly and that is just how it should sound.

Luddendenfoot is the subject of a poem by Simon Armitage in which the frumpy librarian is a witch who is bedding a druid from nearby Hebden Bridge. 'A goat gets killed' and 'Catholics are neutered'.

Ludlow, Shropshire
The heart of Henry VIII's brother, Prince Arthur, is buried in a silver casket beneath the chancel of St Lawrence's Church, Ludlow. Most of these so-called 'heart burials' are actually the interment of all the innards removed during the embalming process.

John Betjeman called Ludlow, 'the loveliest town in England'.

Lulworth Cove, Dorset
One of the gems of the Jurassic Coast (See Exmouth). A major tourist attraction thanks to this being one of the world's most perfectly shaped coves. Stair Hole,

less than half a mile away, is an infant cove showing how Lulworth developed. Durdle Door, a natural arch, is also close by.

Luton, Bedfordshire
It was a TV commercial for Campari and the lady was Lorraine Chase. 'Were you truly wafted here from paradise?' - 'Nah, Luton Airport'.

EasyJet's headquarters are at Luton Airport.

Luton was a centre for the manufacture of hats which is why the football club is known as the Hatters.

Lutterworth, Leicestershire
A model of Britain's first jet aircraft, the Gloster E.28/39 stands on a roundabout to commemorate Frank Whittle who did much of his work on jets here and in nearby Rugby.

Lutterworth's oldest timber-framed building is the Shambles Inn. Dating back to the 16th century this building has been an abattoir, a butcher's, a public house, a private house, then a butcher's again and finally back to a pub in 1982. I have to say it's exciting to mention a pub opening rather than closing.

Lydd, Kent
Lydd Airport, formerly Ferryfield and now London Ashford, even though it is more than 70 miles from the centre of London.

Lydd Parish includes Lydd-on-Sea, a resort built after World War Two consisting mostly of bungalows.

Lyme Regis, Dorset

The harbour wall stretching out into the sea, the Cobb, can be reached down a set of stone steps known locally as Granny's Teeth. In 'Persuasion' Jane Austen has Louisa Musgrave flirting with Captain Wentworth on these steps where she suffers a fall.

Lyme Regis is best known for fossils and 'The French Lieutenant's Woman'.

There is an excellent fossil section in the museum and the town boasts several fossil shops. Mary Anning was born here in 1799 and died here in 1847, she is still revered as one of the greatest pioneering palaeontologists. If you want to guarantee to find fossils with your kids skip Lyme Regis and take them just along the coast to Charmouth.

Posters for 'The French Lieutenant's Woman' still adorn shops with reduced versions available on postcards. The most popular postcard and poster depict Meryl Streep and Jeremy Irons kissing at the end of the Cobb as waves beat around them. I am reliably informed that the person seen walking along the Cobb in the movie is actually a stunt man wearing Meryl's all-concealing cloak. Windows down the steep High Street were replaced with period ones for the film and when the production company returned to replace the originals several shopkeepers preferred the movie version which could still be seen on my most recent visit to the town.

At the time of writing Lyme Regis is, once again, being transformed for a movie. 'Ammonite', a romantic drama about Mary Anning starring Kate Winslet and Saoirse Ronan.

Lymington, Hampshire
In 2008 Lymington came top of a study to find Britain's most desirable seaside resort. The town has two marinas, two yacht clubs and one of the steepest cobbled streets in the country.

The 1980s soap 'Howards Way' was filmed here and locals will tell you Ken Russell lived in Lympington, which he did, and they also say Johnny Depp has a house in the town. The speculation about Johnny Depp's residency could be true but might have evolved from 2013 when the star was photographed in a local pub and a tabloid comic took this visit as an 'obvious sign' he was house hunting.

Lymm, Cheshire
The TV comedy series about the all-female taxi company, 'Candy Cabs', was filmed in Lymm.

The main local tourist attraction is Lymm Dam which was built during the construction of what became the A56 road.

Lyndhurst, Hampshire
The administrative capital of the New Forest boasts Glasshayes House which is the only surviving example of Sir Arthur Conan Doyle's attempts at architecture. He added the third storey and made alterations to the front of the building. More recently this was the Lyndhurst Park Hotel, at the time of writing plans are afoot to demolish the building to create retirement homes.

Another Lyndhurst building is the Queen's House, or the King's House depending on the reigning monarch. This is the main building in the New Forest owned by the Crown and is the local headquarters of the

Forestry Commission.

Lytchett Matravers and Lytchett Minster, Dorset
There were plans to build 2,750 new homes between Lytchett Matravers and Lytchett Minster. At the time of writing villagers along with those from Upton and their local MP had objected to the proposal which was on hold.

Lytham, St Annes, Lancashire
Golfers know this seaside resort for its four courses and links. The Royal Lytham St Annes Golf Club has hosted the Open Championship eleven times.

Few people realise that Lytham and St Annes (also known as St Anne's-on-the-Sea) are two separate places. The landmark windmill is in Lytham. St Annes was the home of ERNIE, the computer that selected winning lottery numbers for 40 years until the operation moved just down the road to Blackpool. Note: St Annes no longer has an apostrophe but St Anne's-on-the-Sea does and, no, I cannot explain the reason for this.

A blue plaque can be seen along the Inner Promenade on the home of George Hoy Booth, better known as George Formby OBE. A bronze statue to local resident Les Dawson was unveiled in 2008 in the gardens next to St Annes Pier.

M

Mabletherpe, Lincolnshire
In 2017 the price of a donkey ride on Mabletherpe beach doubled from £1.50 to £3.00. A cheaper option that can be enjoyed by young and old alike is the Sand Train which travels the length of the beach to the Seal Sanctuary and then back to the start, running in the waves and all for £2.00. (Prices correct at the time of writing, although at the time of writing donkeys and Sand Train were cancelled due to coronavirus.)

Macclesfield, Cheshire
There are 108 steps connecting Water's Green with St Michael and All Angels Church and it is claimed you will have a wish granted if you can get from the bottom to the top without taking a breath.

Macclesfield was once the world's biggest producer of finished silk, in 1832 the town had 71 silk mills.

Maghull, Merseyside
Comedian Ken Dodd topped the bill when the Beatles played at the Albany Cinema in Maghull in 1961. The cinema is now a branch of Lidl.

Frank Hornby, of Dinky Toys and Meccano fame, lived at The Hollies and then at Quarry Brook. In celebration of Hornby The Hollies became the first building outside London to be graced with a blue plaque. Hornby is buried in the grounds of St Andrew's Church

Maidenhead, Berkshire
A 2014 survey revealed Maidenhead to be Britain's capital of infidelity with 1,316 people admitting to being involved in affairs.

For a year prior to their rise to fame, the Spice Girls shared a house in Maidenhead.
Broadcasters Richard Dimbleby and Michael Parkinson both lived in the town.

Maidstone, Ken
Leeds Castle is regularly mislocated to West Yorkshire by TV quiz contestants but it is actually near Maidstone. It is often known as Ladies Castle having been the home of Queen Eleanor of Castile, Margaret of France, Philippa of Hainault, Catherine de Valois, Catherine of Aragon and Elizabeth I.

Maidstone is the county town of Kent. Kentish Men and Kentish Maidens are those born north of the River Medway. Men of Kent and Maids of Kent are born south of the river.

Maldon, Essex
Quite obviously Maldon Sea Salt comes from here.

All Saints church has a memorial window dedicated to George Washington whose great-great grandfather, Lawrence Washington, is buried here.

In 'War of the Worlds' the narrator's brother and two female companions escape across the Channel from Malden.

Malmesbury, Wiltshire
Malmesbury is said to be Britain's oldest borough. It is claimed the town's charter was given by Alfred

the Great in 880AD. However, it must be pointed out there is no concrete validation of this charter and some say a later forgery gave credence to the myth. The first recorded documentation to the 880AD date is in a book published in 1951.

There is no hard evidence to support the claim that Elmer the Monk made one of the first recorded flights when he launched himself from the roof of the old Malmesbury Abbey in around 1000AD with wings strapped to his arms and feet. He is reported to have travelled an estimated 200 yards before crash landing and breaking both legs. (See Stirling)

The churchyard at Malmesbury Abbey is the final resting place of Hannah Twynnoy. The woman who worked at a local inn had teased a tiger exhibited in a travelling wild animal show. On 23rd October 1703 the tiger escaped and mauled her to death.

Maltby, South Yorkshire

Maltby is best known for the colliery which closed in 2013. Cricketer Fred Truman lived in Maltby attending Maltby Hall School.

Other famous residents have included the Chuckle Brothers. In 2017 85-year-old Jimmy Patton, a brother of the Chuckle Brothers, married his 26-year-old girlfriend in Maltby.

Malton, North Yorkshire

In 1138 the Archbishop of York ordered Malton to be burned down to flush out any Scots living there. The town was rebuilt to become New Malton which is its official name today.

Malvern, Worcestershire

One of those 'facts' any trivia geek will tell you is

that Queen Elizabeth II only ever drinks Malvern Water, taking crates of it on overseas tours. In fact the Malvern Spring Water factory was closed down by its owners, Coca-Cola, in 2010 when it was deemed unprofitable. Water from the original source is still bottled by a family-run business under the name Holywell Spring Water which is available from Waitrose.

Franklin D Roosevelt recuperated from a childhood illness at the Alwyn Tower Hotel and Emperor Haile Selassie stayed at the Abbey Hotel for a period during his exile.

Manchester, Greater Manchester
There aren't many things most people don't know about Manchester.

The Romans called Manchester Mamucium, meaning breast-shaped hill.

Manchester University is the only seat of learning in the world to offer a degree in Mummy Studies, the university even maintains a Mummy Tissue Bank (this is as in bodies that have been mummified, not mothers).

Rolls met Royce at the Midland Hotel.

Thanks to its production of cotton during the Industrial Revolution Manchester was known as Cottonopolis, most people know this but few know that, for this same reason, in Australia the textile department of any store is known as the Manchester Department.

Manchester was the first city in the world to celebrate its LGBT history when it commissioned an artist to set rainbow tiles in flagstones across the city. The New Union is one of the oldest LGBT pubs in the country, it was already staging drag shows during World War Two.

Manchester's so-called Curry Mile, in Wilmslow Road, is actually closer to half a mile in length but claims that its 70+ restaurants, takeaways and kebab shops is the largest concentration of Southern Asian food outlets outside the Indian subcontinent.

Until 2019 the only statue of a female in Manchester was one of Queen Victoria. In 2019 the city commemorated the birth of the Suffragette movement here with the erection of a statue of Emmeline Pankhurst in the prestigious St Peter's Square.

Few people can think of a link between Harry Potter and Manchester but it is here, while staying at the Bourneville Hotel, that J K Rowling came up with the concept for the game Quidditch.

Manningtree, Essex
In 2007 the mayor of Manningtree announced that the town's population of 900 living within an area of 20 hectares made this officially the smallest town in England. In 2009 Manningtree merged with Mistily and Lawford to become a single parish, thus losing its identity as a town. (See Fordwich. See Llanwrtwd Wells)

Mansfield, Nottinghamshire
In 'Lady Chatterley's Lover' D H Lawrence refers to Mansfield as 'that once romantic now utterly disheartening colliery town'.

Bernard William Jewry came to Mansfield at a young age and spent most of his childhood here. Bernard changed his name to Shane Fenton and later to Alvin Stardust (another one you might need to ask your grandmother about).

March, Cambridgeshire
March is the only place in the world with a church dedicated to St Wendreda. Wendreda or Wendreth was a 7th century nun who became a saint and who died in March, (this town not the month).

The March March march is marched in March from March to Cambridge.

Margate, Kent
Margate's Dreamland funfair boasts the UK's oldest operating roller coaster. Titled the Scenic Railway the attraction opened in July 1920.

There are secret tunnels underneath Primark at the Westwood Cross shopping centre, but obviously not THAT secret if I can write about them here.

Artist J M W Turner had a long affair with Mrs Sophia Booth of Margate which was the subject of the 2014 movie 'Mr Turner'.
Rockney duo Chas and Dave had a hit record titled 'Margate'.

Market Deeping, Lincolnshire
The Deepings is a group of settlements including Deeping St James, Deeping St Nicholas, West Deeping and Market Deeping

Market Deeping's 15th century church, St Guthlac's, has two sundials. On the south of the tower a sundial is inscribed 'The Day is Thine', and one on the north side is inscribed 'The Night Cometh'.

Market Drayton, Shropshire
Market Drayton's main employer is a sausage factory that was once Palethorpes, then became Pork Farm Bowyers and is currently owned by the Kerry Group from Ireland. Other local industries include the manufacture of Muller yoghurt and a microbrewery.

The town is known as the Home of Gingerbread. Gingerbread production began here in 1793 and at the start of the 20th century four bakers were producing the spicy biscuits which are still popular.

Market Harborough, Leicestershire
After the Battle of Naseby in 1645 Cromwell headed for an inn in Market Harborough to write a letter to the Speaker of the House of Commons boasting about his victory.

Harborough District Council offices are in a building with huge windows. This was once a corset factory and the windows were installed to permit extra light for the sewing machine operators. Owners claimed this was for the sake of the workers' eyesight but it was actually so they could work extended hours. In the same street can be seen a blue plaque commemorating package holiday pioneer Thomas Cook who lived and worked here. (See Melbourne)

Market Rasen, Lincolnshire
Market Rasen is best known for its National Hunt racecourse. National Hunt racing is a winter sport but Market Rasen stages meetings throughout the year. This is Lincolnshire's only racecourse.

The town has strong connections with the music industry, Elton John's lyricist, Bernie Taupin, married here in 1971 with Elton as best man and it has been suggested that Elton's 'Saturday Night's Alright For Fighting' was inspired by a brawl Bernie witnessed at a pub in the town. Rod Templeton who wrote the title track on the world's best selling album, Michael Jackson's 'Thriller' attended school here.

Market Weighton, East Riding of Yorkshire
William Bradley was born in Market Weighton. Bradley, known as the Yorkshire Giant, is the tallest recorded person to have lived in Britain with a height of 7 feet 9 inches. He toured Britain as part of a freak show in which another prized exhibit was the Huge Yorkshire Pig.

Since 1996 Market Weighton has celebrated an annual Giant Community Day dedicated to William Bradley.

Marlborough, Wiltshire
A prehistoric tumulus in the grounds of Marlborough College, said to be the burial place of Merlin, has been dated to 2400BC making it the same age as Silbury Hill. Windmill Hill, Avebury and the West Kennet Avenue and long barrow which are all part of this World Heritage Site, as is nearby Stonehenge. (See Amesbury and Stanton Drew)

Marlborough boasts the second-widest high street in Britain (See Stockton-on-Tees).

Marlow, Buckinghamshire
William the Conqueror gave the Manor of Marlow as a wedding present to his bride Queen Matilda.
Mary Shelley (nee Godwin,) spent time preparing 'Frankenstein' for publication while with her new husband, Percy Bysshe Shelley, here in Marlow.
Jerome K Jerome wrote part of 'Three Men in a Boat' at the Two Brewers pub.

Tom Kerridge's pub, The Hand and Flowers, was the first pub ever to achieve two Michelin Stars. Tom is a TV regular, often referring to himself as a restauranteur, there is no such word as restauranteur, it should be restaurateur without a letter 'n'.

Maryport, Cumbria
John Senhouse began his collection of Roman items in about 1570. The Senhouse Roman Museum is now home to the oldest collection of Roman artefacts in Britain.

In the 18th century the Senhouse family developed the fishing village of Maryport into a coal port.

The Lake District Coast Aquarium can be found on the harbour.

Marston, Cheshire
This Marston is famous for the Anderson Boat Lift. Built in 1875 and, as its name suggests, the purpose of the lift was to raise boats, mostly carrying salt, vertically between the River Weaver and the Trent and Mersey Canal. After closure in 1983 due to corrosion the lift was reopened in 2002 following restoration.

Marston, Lincolnshire
This Marston seems to have little more than a local pub, tourist websites direct visitors to attractions in nearby Grantham.
Marston, Oxfordshire
This Marston is a village situated in the parish of Old Marston close to Oxford.

The Rev John Russell purchased a small female terrier from the milkman in Marston and from this he bred dogs still popular as Jack Russels.

Marston, Wiltshire
There's not much at all in this Marston. The village pub closed in the 1980s and the closest shop is a post office in Potterne.

Matlock, Derbyshire
The county town of Derbyshire, Matlock, consists of several Matlocks and my research reveals that many references to Matlock are actually talking about Matlock Bath, named for its medicinal springs.

A rare mineral discovered here in the 1800s is named Matlockite.

What is now a B&B in Matlock appeared as the home of Gudrun and Ursula Brangwen in Ken Russell's Oscar winning 'Women in Love'.

John Smedley founded a knitwear company at Lea Mills, Matlock, in 1784 and this is now the world's oldest manufacturing company in continuous operation.

Melbourne, Derbyshire
Melbourne Castle was the planned prison for Mary, Queen of Scots, but the place was falling down and was demolished apart from the few remains that can still be seen.

Travel agent Thomas Cook was born here in 1808 (See Market Harborough). Senior citizens are housed in the Thomas Cook Memorial Cottages, built by Cook whose birthplace was demolished in 1968.

Melton Mowbray, Leicestershire
Some buildings in Melton Mowbray still show traces of red paint from the night in 1837 when the Marquis of Waterford led a group of loutish hunters through the town daubing paint on houses and pubs. It is from this event we get the saying 'painting the town red'.

Melton Mowbray is famous for two cheeses, Stilton and Double Gloucester and for the eponymous raised pork pie.

Mexborough, South Yorkshire
Mexborough has had four different teams in the FA Cup, Mexborough Locomotive Works, Mexborough St Johns, Mexborough West End and Mexborough Town. None got close to winning but Mexborough Town did win the Yorkshire Football League in 1973.

Donald Watson who founded the Vegan Society was born in Mexborough as were actors Keith Barron and Brian Blessed.

Middleham, North Yorkshire
Middleham Castle was the home of Richard III prior to his death in 1485 at the Battle of Bosworth. (See Leicester. See Carmarthen)

The Forbidden Corner is a tourist attraction claiming to be the 'Strangest Place in the World'. Modern kids might find this a bit lo-tech but for the full experience you might like to take a torch.

Middlesborough, North Yorkshire
Middlesborough natives are known as Smoggies or Smog Monsters due to the pollution from chemical factories and steelworks.

Explorer Captain James Cook, the discoverer of Australia, was born in Middlesborough.

The Tees Transporter Bridge was the first bridge in Britain where bungee jumping was officially permitted. (See Bristol) It is made from the same north eastern steel as Sydney Harbour Bridge and many others around the world.

A local post-pub delicacy is the Teesside Parmesan or Parmo. A breaded scallop of chicken, the original version was pork, with a layer of béchamel sauce and melted cheese.

Middleton, Greater Manchester
Natives are known as Moonrakers. (See Devizes)

Between 1812 and 1939 the parish church bells chimed for a full ten minutes each evening from 9.50pm, known as the curfew bell, to remind people to go back home.

L S Lowry's painting, 'The Chapel' in Middleton, was stolen in 2000. It famously features a dog with five legs which Lowry swore was not a mistake and was actually there when he created the work.

Middlewich, Cheshire
Salt for icy roads is almost always rock salt and Britain largest salt mine is at Winford, near Middlewich. The constant temperature in the mine has resulted in it being used as storage for National Archives. Around 2.2 million boxes are stored here. (See Winford)

Midhurst, West Sussex
Midhurst Town Council meet in what was once the

library and the library is now in the Leisure Centre.

H G Wells was a pupil and then a pupil-teacher at Midhurst Grammar School. The town features as Wimblehurst in several of his novels.

Midsomer Norton, Somerset
In the 1930s popular children's author Roald Dahl made a living selling kerosene in and around Midsomer Norton.

In 1992 astronomer Duncan Steel discovered an asteroid that is now called 9767 Midsomer Norton (1992 EB1).

Milton Abbas, Dorset
In 1780 Joseph Damer, the first Earl of Dorchester, owner of Milton Abbey, complained that the small town of Middleton was ruining his view of rural life. He commissioned landscape gardener Capability Brown and architect Sir William Chambers to design a village at Luccombe Bottom. Most of Middleton was demolished and the villagers moved to the new, prettier village, Milton Abbas.

Minehead, Somerset
The name Minehead comes from the Welsh, mynydd, meaning mountain.

The UK's longest countryside walking trail (630 miles), the South West Coast Path, runs from here to Poole in Dorset.

In Monty Python's 'Mr Hitler' sketch the National Bocialist Party aims to unite Taunton and Minehead.

Mirfield, West Yorkshire
The Miller and Carter Steak House in Mirfield,

formerly The Three Nuns, hides an interesting secret. Not far from the pub stands Kirklees Abbey, legend has it that Robin Hood fired an arrow from his deathbed on the upper floor of the Abbey with instructions to his followers that he should be buried where the arrow landed.

Robin's cousin, the Prioress of Kirklees, had arranged blood letting to cure a sickness from which Robin was suffering and it isn't clear whether she accidentally or purposely allowed him to bleed to death.

Near the pub is what appears to be a grave with an epitaph dedicated to 'Robert Earl of Huntington' who apparently died in 'Dekembris 1247,' This all ties in with the Robin Hood legend. However, the inscription was made when the 'grave' was restored in 1850. A TV documentary crew found no indication of ground disturbance, as would be expected if this was indeed a grave. Ground penetrating radar has found no trace of human remains. (See Nottingham)

Mitcham, Greater London

Elizabeth I made several visits to Mitcham, Sir Walter Raleigh had a home here.

Mitcham gained its reputation thanks to its lavender fields. Lavender is pictured on the town's coat-of-arms. Distilled oils from the fragrant plant were included in cosmetics from as early as the mid 18th century.

Modbury, Devon

With its population of approximately 1,500 Modbury could be officially called a town under the Local Government Act of 1972 but has not elected to adopt this status so there is no town council and no mayor.

In 2007 Modbury became one of the first places, arguably the very first place, in the UK to ban plastic bags.

Morecambe, Lancashire
TV antique valuers always get excited when they see furniture stamped with the name Gillow. Leighton Hall, just to the north of Morecambe was, indeed still is, the home of the Gillow family.

From 1956 to 1989 Morecambe was the venue for the Miss Great Britain beauty competition.

As a child Alan Bennett was taken on regular summer holidays to Morecambe and later speculated he was conceived in a local boarding house.

Moretonhampstead, Devon
W H Smith lived here but there isn't a branch of W H Smith's in Moretonhampstead. This was also the home of engineer George Stephenson's assistant, George Bidder who was so clever when it came to mental arithmetic that he was known as the Calculating Boy.
The tombstones of two Frenchmen stand in the entrance to the church. A nearby copper beech tree grows where an earlier tree was the centre for village celebrations through the ages and became known as the Dancing Tree when French prisoners, on parole from Dartmoor Prison, played music here to entertain themselves and the local populace.

Moreton-in-Marsh, Gloucestershire
Probably the oldest building in Moreton-in-Marsh is the 16th century Curfew Tower (See Middleton). A local man, Sir Robert Fry, was once lost in the fog and the sound of the curfew bell guided him

home. In gratitude he donated money for the tower's maintenance.

Charles I sought shelter at the White Hart Royal Hotel during the English Civil War. A plaque in the hotel entrance commemorates his visit along with a copy of his unpaid bill.

Morley, West Yorkshire
Morley, like Rome, is built on seven hills, the Seven Hills of Morley. (See Chiddingly)

Morley Town Hall contains a disused magistrates' court that occasionally pops up in episodes of TV series such as 'Heartbeat' and 'Emmerdale'.

Everyone knows that Eric Morecambe came from Morecambe but Morley boasts a statue to his partner, Ernie Wise, who was born here and won a local talent competition in 1936.

Morpeth, Northumberland
Admiral Nelson's second-in-command at Trafalgar was Lord Collingwood from Morpeth.

In 2008 more than 1,000 homes in Morpeth were flooded when a month's rain fell in 12 hours. It is not known if any rain got into the 'top secret' nuclear bunker that everyone will tell you is underneath the former council building.

Desperate tourists looking for kicks on a rainy day might consider a visit to England's only bagpipe museum.

Much Wenlock, Shropshire
Local surgeon William Brookes, who is credited with

introducing physical education to Britain's schools, promoted a forerunner of the Modern Olympics in Much Wenlock. The first games were held in 1850 and it is claimed Baron de Coubertin was inspired to create the actual Modern Olympics, first staged in 1896, after a visit to Much Wenlock. Coubertin's games failed to include one of Much Wenlock's best-loved events, The Old Women's Race which was contested for a pound of tea. (See Chipping Campden)

N

Nailsea, Somerset

Nailsea is best known for its glassworks, they mostly manufactured bottles but decorative items made by workers at the end of their shifts became very collectable. The famous glassworks stood in the area now occupied by Tesco's car park.

It was once possible to walk from Nailsea to Nowhere. Nowhere being the name of a hamlet demolished in 1967 for development.

Nailsworth, Gloucestershire

At the time of writing Nailsworth is the smallest English town with a Football League Club. Forest Green Rovers finished 21st in League Two at the end of the 2017-18 season. Their ground, The New Lawn, has a capacity of 5,141 which is almost all of the 5,794 people living in the town at the most recent census. In 2017 Forest Green Rovers was officially recognised as the world's first vegan football club.

Nantmawr, Shropshire

Various gazeteers and websites place Nantmawr in Wales and its name does sound extremely Welsh but it is actually just over the border in Shropshire.

Jones Rough Nature Reserve is a breeding place for the rare pearl-bordered fritillary butterfly.

Nantwich, Cheshire

The International Cheese Awards take place at the Nantwich Show each year. It is often claimed that

Cheshire Cheese is the oldest named cheese in Britain having first been mentioned by Thomas Muffet in his 'Health's Improvement' from around 1580. This ignores the fact that in this same tome Muffet also mentions Shropshire Cheese.

Nantwich's other annual events include a jazz and blues festival, a food festival and the Worm Charming Championships.

Needham Market, Suffolk
It took Needham Market 200 years to recover when two-thirds of its population died between 1663 and 1665 after chains were placed across exit roads to prevent residents from leaving to spread the plague.

Nelson, Lancashire
The West Indian cricketer Sir Learie Constantine played for Nelson Cricket Club during the inter-war period. When he became the first person of African descent to be awarded a life peerage in 1969 he chose the title Baron Constantine of Maraval in Trinidad and Tobago and of Nelson in the County Palatine of Lancaster.

Bernie Calvert and Tony Hicks from the Hollies were both born here.

Nether Stowey, Somerset
There are claims that Samuel Taylor Coleridge wrote 'Kubla Khan' in Nether Stowey, however there is evidence that he was at a farm between Porlock and Linton when he dreamed the drug induced words to the poem and was only part way through writing this down when he was interrupted by the infamous 'person from Porlock' and forgot what came next. (See Porlock)

Coleridge did live in Nether Stowey and often walked through the Quantocks with brother and sister William and Dorothy Wordsworth. Their route is now known as the Coleridge Way. 'The Rime of the Ancient Mariner' was almost certainly written in Nether Stowey. (See Watchet)

Newark-on-Trent, Nottinghamshire
In the spire of St Mary Magdalene Church in Newark-on-Trent can be seen a perfectly round hole created by a six-pound Parliamentary cannon ball in one of the last sieges of the Civil War. The cannon ball that created the hole is one of many exhibits in the nearby National Civil War Centre.

Newbiggin-by-the-Sea, Northumberland
The first telegraph cable from Scandinavia was laid in 1868 from Jutland to Newbiggin-by-the-Sea.

The brass statue by Sean Henry in the middle of the bay is titled 'Couple'.

John Braine wrote his best-known novel, 'Room at the Top', while working at Newbiggin library. (See Halifax)

Newbury, Berkshire
Highclere Castle, near Newbury, provided the setting for 'Downton Abbey.' Highclere was the home of Lord Carnarvon who funded the legendary 1922 excavation of the tomb of Tutankhamun. Carnarvon died in Cairo in April 1923, some say of a curse he picked up in the tomb of the Boy King, but he actually died due to pneumonia resulting from blood poisoning following a mosquito bite aggravated by a razor cut.

When rock band The Who were due to play at Newbury Corn Exchange in 1966 drummer Keith Moon and bassist John Entwistle arrived two hours late to discover guitarist Pete Townshend, and singer, Roger Daltry, had already taken to the stage and were performing with members of the support group. A brawl ensued amongst the four members of the headline act during which Keith Moon suffered a broken ankle and a black eye.

Paddington Bear author, Michael Bond, was born in Newbury.

Newcastle-under-Lyme, Staffordshire
Newcastle-under-Lyme is hyphenated.

In 2008 Newcastle-under-Lyme was given a £2.8 million government grant intended for Newcastle upon Tyne some 185 miles to the north and not hyphenated. (See below)

The New Vic was Europe's first purpose-built theatre-in-the-round.

Arnold Bennett attended the Middle School here and in his 'Clayhanger' trilogy Newcastle-under-Lyme appears as Oldcastle.

Newcastle upon Tyne, Tyne and Wear
Newcastle upon Tyne is not hyphenated. (See above)

Town Moor in Newcastle Upon Tyne is larger than Hyde Park and Hampstead Heath combined.

Newcastle upon Tyne is on the same line of latitude as Copenhagen.

The first covered railway station in the world was opened here in 1850 by Queen Victoria. In 1879 Mosley Street became the first street in the world to be illuminated by electric lamps. Taunton was the first town with its entire centre lit by electricity. (See Taunton)

Lucozade was invented in Newcastle upon Tyne. Newcastle Brown Ale was brewed here from the 1920s to 2005 when brewing moved to Dunston, it is now produced at the Heineken Brewery in the Netherlands. In the late 1990s Newcy Brown was the most widely distributed alcoholic product in the UK but by the 2000s the majority of the sweet, dark beer was imbibed in the USA.

Newent, Gloucestershire

Puff's Alley is not far from Newent Community School and is said to get its name from being where pupils gathered for an illicit smoke.

The International Centre for Birds of Prey is just down the road in Boulsdon.

Since 1996 Newent has hosted an annual Onion Fayre which includes an onion eating competition.

Newent was the birthplace of legendary record producer Joe Meek who was celebrated by a festival held in the town each year from 2007 to 2014.

Newhaven, East Sussex

Yacht owners will be delighted to know that Newhaven has two marinas but the snobbish ones amongst them should be warned that the one on the West Quay is considered to be more upmarket than the one on a branch of the Ouse.

New Haven's West Beach is owned by NPP (Newhaven Port and Properties), a French company who fenced off the beach in 2008 rather than pay for insurance to cover visitors being injured on the crumbling breakwater which the company hadn't bothered repairing.

New Holland, Lincolnshire
This port on the Humber estuary is the only place I can find in Great Britain to be named after a brand of gin. The village was a smuggling centre with spirits being brought in by the barrel-load, one of the favourites being New Holland gin.

Newmarket, Suffolk
In 1671 Charles II became the only reigning monarch to ride a winner at Newmarket.

Newmarket is the home of Tattersalls, the world's oldest bloodstock auctioneers and also the only place in the world with two turf racecourses, The Rowley Course and the July Course. The Rowley Mile is actually 1.25 miles and is the longest turf straight in the world of horse racing. In 1965 Newmarket became the first place in Britain to introduce starting stalls.

New Mills, Derbyshire
New Mills is the home of Swizzles Matlow, manufacturers of Love Hearts, Parma Violets and Drumsticks lollies.

New Milton, Hampshire
Milton is listed in the Domesday Book, 1086, New Milton originated as a New Town, the name first

being used with the arrival of the railway station in 1888. The first recorded written use of the name came in 1895 when the owner of the post office erected a sign reading 'New Milton Sub Post Office'.

The main local tourist attraction is the Sammy Miller Motorcycle Museum which was established in 1964 when former championship trial rider, Sammy Miller, opened a parts business in the town. The museum houses some 300 motorcycles and three-wheeled vehicles.

Newport, Shropshire
Newport was the first town in Britain to win six gold Britain in Bloom awards in consecutive years.

In January 1982 the nearby village of Edgmond suffered the lowest temperature ever recorded in England, -26 C.

Newport Pagnell, Buckinghamshire
Although many only know Newport Pagnell as a motorway service station this is a town in its own right.

Pickford Bridge was built in 1810 and is Britain's only iron bridge that continues to carry main road traffic. It is the oldest iron bridge in the world still in constant use for vehicles.

Aston Martin cars were built in Newport Pagnell from 1954 to 2003.

Newquay, Cornwall
Fistral Beach is a major big-wave location for surfers. This is the home of the British Surfing Association, Newquay Surf Life Saving Club and the Newquay

Boardriders Club. A reef at the northern end of the beach known as the Cribber causes waves to break when the swell is high. As well as Fistral, Newquay has eight other easily accessible sandy beaches.

The last bank in Bank Street Closed in 2020 and, at the time of writing, Newquay is scheduled to become a Spaceport.

New Romney, Kent
A metal mooring ring in front of the church is a reminder of when New Romney, now more than a mile from the sea, was once one of the Cinque Parts. The Norman church once stood on the harbourside.

Newton Abbot, Devon
Ye Olde Cider Bar in Newton Abbot is one of very few British pubs serving no beer. I remember when women and holiday makers were limited to a half pint of cider but this rule has now gone along with the sawdust that was once spread across the floor. Country wines and perry are available for those who don't enjoy cider. (At the time of writing the Cider Bar is up for sale.)

Newton Aycliffe, County Durham
Newton Aycliffe was founded under the New Towns Act in 1947. Along with Aycliffe Village and part of School Aycliffe it forms Great Aycliffe.

Newton Aycliffe has a Central Avenue, several Roads, Places, Crescents and a Parade but it does not have any Streets.

Mark Gatiss's father worked at Aycliffe Mental Hospital and this gave Gatiss some ideas for his 'League of Gentlemen' scripts.

Newton-le-Willows, Merseyside
Haydock Park Racecourse replaced the one at Newton-le-Willows in 1898. The Old Newton Cup is the oldest continually competed for trophy in horse racing.

Newton Poppleford, Devon
The A3052 is squeezed to its narrowest at both ends of this linear village. To the east by a narrow bridge over the River Otter and to the west it is even narrower due to the road passing between Devon's oldest toll house and a thatched, listed cottage.

King Alfred Way, one of the main streets off the High Street, is not named after the ancient King of Wessex but after the King Alfred Daffodil which was developed here, although, it has to be said the daffodil was probably named after the king.

For 27 years all UK and several international editions of the board game Trivial Pursuit were written in Newton Poppleford.

No Place, County Durham
Included here purely because of its name. (See Pity Me. See Sandy Balls)

Normanton, West Yorkshire
In an episode of the TV series 'A Touch of Frost' the police find a body in a brick kiln. The sequence was filmed at Normanton Brickyard which has since been. demolished. The demolition was in no way linked with the finding of the 'Touch of Frost' body.

Northallerton, North Yorkshire
The industrial estate at nearby Leeming Bar is the home of R&R Ice Cream. By volume this is Europe's biggest manufacturer of ice cream products and second-largest in the world after Unilever. Fab and Rowntree's Fruit Pastilles ice lollies are made here.

Northam, Devon
The only famous person I can track down as having come from Northam is serial killer Rosemary West.

Northampton, Northamptonshire
Pub landlords like to impress customers with the many 'foreign' beers they have on their shelves. Brooklyn American Ale, Poretti Luppoli, Celia Czech Lager, Skol, Holstein Pils, and, of course, to remind you of that holiday in Spain, San Miguel. If it's available in your local pub it has probably either been brewed or bottled in Northampton by Carlsberg.

Comedian Alan Carr grew up in Northampton. His dad, Graham, played half-back for Northampton Town FC (aka the Cobblers) and then managed the club from 1985 to 1990. Singing comedian Des O'Connor also played for the Cobblers.

Northampton Tower can be seen from just about everywhere in the town. It's the testbed for elevators made by the Express Lift Company and was opened in 1982 by Queen Elizabeth II.

Northwood, Greater London
Northwood stood in for location shots of Surbiton in 'The Good Life'.

Norwich, Norfol
Norwich claims to be the only British city to contain

part of a National Park, the Norfolk Broads. It is also the most complete medieval city in the nation. (See Sheffield)

It was once claimed that Norwich had a Church for every Sunday in the year and a pub for every day. In 1870 there were actually 780 pubs in the city. In 1966 the Chief Constable informed the Licensing Court that the number of pubs had dropped to 355 so the claim of a pub for each day of the year was lost. By 2019 there were only about 100 pubs still trading.

If you are wondering why I haven't mentioned mustard see Durham and Tewkesbury.

Nottingham, Nottinghamshire

The tourist industry of Nottingham relies heavily on a somewhat debatable connection with Robin Hood. Although Robert Fitzooth, Earl of Huntingdon (aka Robin Hood) was allegedly born in Nottinghamshire history suggests that he and his Merry Men were based in Yorkshire. (See Mirfield)

Claims are made that Ye Olde Trip to Jerusalem was established in 1189 making it the oldest pub in Britain. Other Nottingham pubs claiming to be the oldest in the land are Ye Olde Salutation and The Bell Inn.

There are those who maintain that caves in the rocks behind Ye Olde Trip to Jerusalem were used as a brewhouse in the twelfth century but the oldest parts of the building can only be dated back to the seventeenth century.

The Nottingham rock band Baby Godzilla had to change their name following a lawsuit by Japanese film company Toho, the band became Heck. (See Heck)

(See Ilkeston)

Nuneaton, Warwickshire
Mary Ann Evans, better known as George Eliot, was born just outside Nuneaton in 1819, her novel, 'Scenes of Clerical Life' was based here.

In 1992 Nuneaton made history when the world's first free-standing outdoor condom machine was installed at a taxi rank next to the town's bus station. Anti-porn campaigner Mary Whitehouse, who was born here, is not known to have ever used the condom machine. Mary Whitehouse is also not known to have referred to the landmark, Mount Judd, a conical spoil heap, by its local name, the Nuneaton Nipple.

O

Oakham, Rutland
Members of the royal family and peers of the realm visiting or passing through this, the county town of Rutland, are required to make a token payment in the form of a horseshoe.

More that 200 horseshoes are displayed on the walls of the castle, some are dated and some were specially made to a giant size. It is traditional to display horseshoes with the points upwards so the hollow can collect good luck but here they all point downwards, reputedly to prevent the devil from sitting in them.

Okehampton, Devon
For many years Okehampton was infamous as a traffic bottleneck during holiday weekends. The chaos was alleviated in 1988 when the A30 was rerouted around the town centre.

Following major disruption due to damage to the railway line at Dawlish in 2014, there have been suggestions that the Exeter to Plymouth rail route via Okehampton might be reopened. (See Dawlish)

Oldbury, West Midlands
In 1864 Lloyds opened their first bank here, the original building is now a branch of the Subway sandwich chain.

Jack Judge, composer of 'It's a Long Way to Tipperary' was born in Oldbury as was photographer Martin Elliot who is best known for the iconic 1970s

'Tennis Girl' poster. His 18-year-old girlfriend Fiona Butler posed for the photograph, they split up three years later and she is now the mother of three children.

Oldham, Greater Manchester
Park Cake Bakeries in Oldham sell 90% of their cakes to Marks and Spencer. Yates Wine Lodge was founded here and it is claimed the town had Britain's first chip shop with John Lees serving deep-fried chipped potatoes from around 1858. In 1900 Oldham claimed the country's highest concentration of chip shops with one for every 400 members of the population.

Louise Brown, known as the world's first test tube baby, was born on 25th July 1978 at Oldham General Hospital. Louise wasn't technically a test tube baby as her conception took place in a Petri dish. Louise's sister Natalie became the world's 40th test tube, or should that be Petri dish, baby in 1982.

People who tuned in to early ITV programmes will undoubtedly remember the slogan 'I told 'em - Oldham', advertising a brand of car battery. (See Denton)

Ollerton, Nottinghamshire
Ollerton is in the Dukeries, so called because there were four ducal seats here, Worksop Manor, Welbeck Abbey, Thereby Hall and the now demolished Clumber
House.

In 1984 hundreds of pickets stayed overnight in Ollerton following the death here of miner David

Gareth Jones. He had been hit by a brick thrown by a local youth but the postmortem put the cause of his death down to being crushed against the colliery gates earlier in the day.

Olney, Buckinghamshire

John Newton and William Cowper collaborated on what are known as the 'Olney Hymns'. Newton, best known as author of the lyrics for 'Amazing Grace' is buried in Olney.

Olney is undoubtedly best known for its Pancake Race, held annually on Shrove Tuesday. Competitors toss their pancakes as they run 400 yards from the market place to the Church of St Peter and St Paul where the winner's prize is a kiss from the verger.

Ormskirk, Lancashire

Ormskirk's twice-weekly market (Thursday and Saturday) has been held here since 1286.

Ormskirk hosts an annual classic car rally each August and the Christmas lights switch-on always attracts crowds with former 'celebrity' switcher-onners including 'Coronation Street's' Les Battersby and a rapping vicar.

Orpington, Greater London

Romani people first came to Orpington to find temporary work picking hops and fruit.

Eric Lubbock made headlines in 1962 when he won Orpington, considered to be a safe Tory seat, for the Liberal Party at a by-election. His win saw a revival in the Liberal Party. In 1967 Lubbock promoted a Private Member's Bill in Parliament to provide permanent Gypsy Sites for travellers and in 1971 the Orpington Congress took place marking the foundation of the International Romani Union.

Osset, West Yorkshire
When ten high-explosive bombs were accidentally dropped on Osset in 1940 the only fatalities were several chickens.

Author Stan Barstow lived here and attended the local grammar school. He referred to Osset and nearby Horbury as the 'border country' at which point the north-western tip of the coalfield met the south-east corner of the woolen towns.

Electronic band The KLF mention Osset in their 1991 top-ten hit, 'It's Grim Up North'.

Oswestry, Shropshire
Due to its border location, Oswestry has some Welsh street names.

Rev William Archibald Spooner, originator of Spoonerisms, was educated at Oswestry School, which doesn't say a lot for Oswestry School. Spooner himself only admitted to one Spoonerism when he referred to 'Kinkering Kongs'. However, I have also found reference to 'The Lord is a shoving leopard', 'It is kisstomary to cuss the bride', and referring to Queen Victoria, 'Three cheers for our queer old dean.'

In 2018 Oswestry had Britain's highest per capita crime rate with 76 crimes per 1,000 people.

Otley, West Yorkshire
Thomas Chippendale was born in Otley and quite a lot of people know that. It is a lesser-known fact that J M W Turner's painting 'Hannibal Crossing the

Alps' was not inspired by glimpses of the European mountain range but by the view of the Otley Chevin Ridge close to Farnley Hall where Turner was a frequent visitor.

Otley is Hotton in the TV farming soap 'Emmerdale'

Ottery St Mary, Devon

St Mary's in Ottery St Mary is a scaled-down version of Exeter Cathedral. The church's weathercock is allegedly the oldest in Britain but the tail had to be replaced after Cromwell's troops used it for target practice. This was once a whistling cock with two tubes that whistled increasingly louder according to the strength of the wind. The whistles are now blocked to preserve the sanity of nearby residents.

On November 5th blazing Tar Barrels are carried through the town centre attracting thousands of spectators from around the world. Locals know not to try to visit the doctor on November 6th as the waiting room is likely to be crowded with burn victims.

Oundle, Northamptonshire

The Talbot Inn in Oundle, formerly the Tabard and now the Talbot Hotel, was rebuilt in 1626 with stones and fixtures from nearby Fotheringham Castle where Mary, Queen of Scotts, was executed. The imprint of a crown on the staircase balustrade is said to have been made by the ring on Mary's finger as she gripped for support on her way to the execution block.

Outlane, West Yorkshire

Outlane sits on the M62. Objections in the early 1960s that the motorway would run through the local golf club received little sympathy.

Oxford, Oxfordshire

Due to being a major attraction for tourists and an easy day-trip from London there's not a lot people don't know about Oxford.

Oxford is the second-oldest functioning university in the world after Bologna. Oxford's first colleges opened in the 13th century but female students weren't admitted until 1878.

Several colleges have their own pet tortoise and every year, in May, a circle of lettuce is arranged in an 8 metre circle with the tortoises placed back-to-back in the centre, the winner of the race being the first tortoise to reach the lettuce. The earliest evidence I can find of this 'tradition' dates only back to the 1970s. There are several accounts of tortoise kidnappings and tortoises simply going missing but I guess they must have had help to get away as they're not exactly speedy. The current record for the race is held by Balliol College whose tortoise completed its thrilling run in a time of 4 hours in 2004. To celebrate the victory students took their tortoise out for a night in the city and lost it.

A copy of the Cambridge Mathematical Bridge crosses the Iffy Lock. (See Cambridge)
Hitler ordered that Oxford must not be bombed during World War Two as he wanted it to be his capital when he conquered England. (See Brighton)
Oxford was temporarily the capital of England during the Civil War, 1642 - 1646.

The Ashmolean is the world's oldest purpose-built museum, opened in 1683, and the Queen's Lane Coffee House is the oldest continually functioning coffee house in Europe. (See Settle)

Oxford's motto, 'Dominus Illuminatio Mea', means 'The Lord is my light' which is the opening line of Psalm 27.

Great Tom, a bell in the tower over Tom Gate, is rung 101 times each night. 100 times for the first 100 students at the college plus an additional one, added in 1663. Oxford is one degree west of the Greenwich Prime Meridian which puts it five minutes behind UK time, thus explaining why Great Tom's marathon nightly bong takes place at five past nine. (See Sandford on Thames)

P

Paddington, Greater London
Many will tell you the Tyburn Gallows was situated where Marble Arch now stands. I even heard an official tour guide giving his admiring audience this information. The execution spot was actually on the small pedestrian island at the southern end of Edgware Road in Paddington. It is marked by a plaque set in the cobbles. In the 18th century a Paddington Fair Day was a day when public executions took place. To Dance the Paddington Frisk was when a hanged person twitched at the end of the rope. (See Hounslow)

The last hanging at Tyburn was that of highwayman John Austin in 1783.

Padstow, Cornwall
Padstow's May Day is not to be missed with the Obby Osses frantically pirouetting around the harbour and the constant beating of drums.

Thanks to Rick Stein's fishy presence in pubs and restaurants the town has been dubbed Padstein. Paul Ainsworth at Number 6 is a great restaurant with a Michelin Star and for something traditionally local you could do far worse than a pasty from Chough's Bakery.

Paignton, Devon
Ask anyone of a certain age who had a hit with 'Born Free' and they will tell you it was Matt Monro.

Believe it or not Matt Monro's 1966 version of the song never made it into the UK charts and it wasn't until 1991 that 'Born Free' became a huge hit for comedian Vic Reeves accompanied by the Roman Numerals.

Ask anyone of a certain age what happened to Elsa, the lioness star of the movie 'Born Free', and they will relate romantic dreams of the much-loved animal dying of old age surrounded by tearful cubs in a jungle clearing somewhere in Africa. In fact Elsa died in 1987 in the pen at Paignton Zoo where she had spent most of her life.

Quaywest Splashdown at Goodrington Sands Beach, Paignton, advertises itself as the largest outdoor waterpark in the UK.

Pant, Shropshire
Pant is close to the Welsh border. (See Pant, Merthyr Tydfil). In Welsh Pant means hollow and there are many Welsh connections here.

The village is home to the Llanymynech Golf Club and the Bryn Offa Church.

Pateley Bridge, North Yorkshire
Locally just called Pateley but known nationally to boys and girls who haven't grown up as the town with The Oldest Sweet Shop In The World, established in 1827.

Penistone, South Yorkshire
Penistone is the highest market town in Yorkshire but the size of the market has been much reduced since Tesco took over part of its traditional footprint in 2011. It is amazing how many historic places in this

book have had Tesco stores dumped on them. (See Fforestfach)

The Penistone Railway Viaduct has 29 arches.

Local people get quite cross when visitors mispronounce the name of their town (It's Penis to rhyme with Dennis). For a time mentions of the town were automatically blocked by some social media sites. (See Scunthorpe)

Penrith, Cumbria
The Roman road linking Manchester to Carlisle came through the area and the Roman fort of Voreda is five miles to the north of the town.

The town has many links with Richard III who lived at Penrith Castle for a time and is also said to have resided at the Gloucester Arms when it was a private house. (See Middleham See Reading)

Skirsgill Auction Mart in the Agricultural Hall was once famed for its 18ft statue of King Kong, now removed.

Penrith has its own dialect known as Penrithian.

Penryn, Cornwall
Penryn was once a very busy harbour town in its own right but it is now ignored by most visitors who head straight for nearby Falmouth.

Penzance, Cornwal
In 1973 a national newspaper conducted a survey revealing that 32% of the readers who took part thought that Penzance was in Scotland. An unscientific survey carried out in my local pub at the

time of writing revealed that 40% of the locals who had heard of him believed Humphry Davy, inventor of the miner's safety lamp, was from Yorkshire, he was from Penzance.

Sir John Hawkins introduced tobacco to England in 1564 and it is claimed Sir Walter Raleigh smoked his first pipe at the Dolphin Inn, Penzance.

Perranporth, Cornwall
Perranporth is possibly unique in being able to boast three miles of beautiful surfing beach right at the end of its main street, St Piran's Road.

Manchester-born author Winston Graham came to live in Perranporth at the age of 17 and it became the setting for his 'Poldark' series of novels.

Pershore, Worcestershire
Pershore Purple, Pershore Yellow Egg and Pershore Emblem are all types of plum celebrated at the annual Pershore Plum Festival with local lasses vying for the coveted title, Plum Princess.

Peterborough, Cambridgeshire
A showcase in Peterborough Museum contains the skeletons of a man, woman and child buried between 5,000 and 6,000 years ago. The man has an arrowhead lodged between his ribs making him the earliest known murder victim in Britain.

Catherine of Aragon, is buried in Peterborough Cathedral.

Now for something quite controversial. On the subject of Henry's wives he had three, not six! Three of his marriages (Catherine of Aragon, Anne Boleyn just prior to her execution and Anne of Cleves) were annulled, an annulment means the marriage never existed.

Petworth, West Sussex
Petworth House is set in Petworth Park which boasts England's largest herd of fallow deer.

Pickering, North Yorkshire
Legend has it that in around 270BC King Peredus lost his precious ring here and accused a young girl of stealing it. Later that same day the King was served a pike, caught in the local river, for dinner and inside the pike was the missing ring. The King was so happy he married the girl and - have you already guessed the next bit? - he renamed the village Pike Ring which gradually morphed into Pickering. There are those who think it more likely that the town took its name from the followers of an Anglian leader called Picer, they were the Picer-ingas.

Piercebridge-on-Tees, Durham
The York to Newstead Roman road crosses the River Tees at the point where this village stands. The excavated Roman fort is open to the public and nearby can be seen the remains of the bridge.

Pilton, Somerset
For five days at the end of June this sleepy Somerset village with a population of less than 1,000 is transformed into by far the largest town in Somerset as some 200,000 people descend on the Glastonbury Festival. The festival usually takes place in four out of five years, the fifth and fallow year being to allow the ground at the dairy farm to recover. The 50th anniversary festival in 2020 had to be cancelled due to the Coronavirus pandemic. (See Wells. See Glastonbury)

Pimlico, Greater London
Being so close to the Houses of Parliament Pimlico is a centre for politicians. The Labour Party and Trades Union Congress shared offices here until 1928 and it was in Pimlico the 1926 General Strike was organised.

It can be hard to find buildings in Pimlico that do not sport blue plaques in honour of people born here or who were former residents. Winston Churchill lived here as did Isadora Duncan, Laura Ashley and Old Man Steptoe, actor William Bramble.

Pity Me, County Durham
Included here purely because of its name. (See No Place. See Sandy Balls)

Plymouth, Devon
Many will tell you that America's Founding Fathers, the Pilgrim Fathers, came from Plymouth and that is as much, or as little, as they know about this city without a cathedral.

The Pilgrim Fathers were religious fanatics mostly from Nottinghamshire (that's about 250 miles north of Plymouth) but with some from East Anglia (about 350 miles to the east). Following various debacles in Holland a group set sail in a boat named Speedwell (formerly the Swiftsure), which they intended keeping in the USA when they got there to use it as a fishing vessel. They had arranged to meet up with the Mayflower, its passengers and crew, in Southampton Water.

It wasn't too long before the Speedwell started to take in water so a repair stop was made at Dartmouth. Approximately 40 miles along the Devon coast their feet once again started to get wet so they pulled in to Plymouth.

On the first attempt to cross the Atlantic with the Mayflower the Speedwell sprang yet another leak so both ships returned to Plymouth. Mayflower then made the historic crossing with 102 passengers plus a crew of approximately 30.

Speedwell was sold and reportedly made many future voyages. Some claim the captain of the ship purposely caused the leaks to abort the voyage and thus avoid the starvation he expected would occur in America.

However …

When American tourists are not taking selfies with the replica of a statue of Francis Drake (See Tavistock) they are standing in line on Plymouth's Barbican to take more selfies on what they believe to be the 'historic' Mayflower Steps.

The admiring 'gees' and 'wows' that emanate when they see the steps they have travelled some 4,000 miles to visit deters most locals from spoiling their obvious excitement by telling them the truth. The Doric portico above the steps was erected in 1934, the small stone pier was built approximately 100 years ago.

Books and knowledgable local residents suggest that the seaward side of the Barbican has been rebuilt over the centuries, gradually moving further out into the water. If American visitors want to take photos of the actual spot from which the Pilgrim Fathers set sail my research puts this in one of the toilets, or possibly the beer cellar, at the Admiral McBride pub. (See Retford)

Polesworth, Warwickshire
It is claimed that William Shakespeare worked for a time as a pageboy alongside poet Michael Drayton at Polesworth Hall.

Polperro, Cornwall
Regularly featured on jigsaw puzzles and chocolate boxes, thousands of tourists flock to Polperro during the summer. Visitors are not permitted to drive their cars into the village and must leave these in a car park at the nearby hamlet of Crumplehorn. For those who don't wish to walk there are milk floats disguised as trams and a few horse-pulled carts.

One of the houses in the village is entirely covered with shells and this is known as (bet you can't guess!) The Shell House.

The use of fingerprints in criminology was developed after a study of fingerprints in Polperro. The village was selected for the experiment because of the heavy incidence of intermarriage between residents due to the isolated location which might have been expected to result in some having identical prints but none had. (See Blackburn)

Polzeath, Cornwall
Sir John Betjeman based several of his works here and Laurence Binyon wrote 'For the Fallen' whilst in Polzeath. Binyon's seven-verse poem is best known for verse four:

'They shall not grow old, as we that are left grow old,
Age shall not weary them, nor the years condemn.

At the going down of the sun and in the morning
We will remember them.'

Poole, Dorset

Brownsea Island in Poole Harbour was the location for a camp in 1907 that led to Robert Baden-Powell forming the Boy Scouts the following year. (See Studland) In 2020 a statue of Baden-Powell on Poole Quay was boarded up amid rumours it would be removed to a museum. During Black Lives Matter protests campaigners had criticised the statue due to Baden-Powel's racism, homophobia and support for Adolf Hitler. Some supporters claim his only admiration for Hitler was because they shared ideas about the education of boys. Say what you like Baden-Powell did describe Hitler's 'Mein Kampf' as a 'wonderful book.' When he was an army officer in South Africa at least three Zulus were killed when he lost control of his men and when an injured African chief was promised safe return if he surrendered, Baden-Powell claimed he wouldn't be able to survive the journey so he was immediately tried, found guilty and shot dead.

Poole Harbour cockles are the largest, sweetest and least gritty I have ever tasted.

Porlock, Somerset

In 2010 Porlock registered the most elderly population in Britain with more than 40% being pensioners.

At low tide the remains of an ancient forest emerges from the waves on Porlock Beach.

(See Nether Stowey)

Porthleven, Cornwall
Porthleven is known as Britain's Most Storm-Battered Town. I cannot find evidence to support that claim but photographs of fifty-foot waves battering the harbour-side granite tower adorn the national press whenever there is a named storm.

Of course wind and waves attract surfers to the nearby beach and gourmets can enjoy several fish restaurants, the closure of one owned by Rick Stein was announced in 2020.

Portland, Dorset
Mention Portland and the majority of the world's population think of a city in Oregon although the USA has at least 24 other Portlands, Australia and Canada have several and all of them took their name from the Isle of Portland, a tied island that forms the southernmost point of Dorset. (See Weymouth)

Portland stone, used for many famous buildings, including St Paul's Cathedral, is still quarried here.

When American pedestrian crossings display their DON'T WALK warning the colour of the flashing light is Portland Orange.

Portsmouth, Hampshire
After Central London, Portsmouth is Britain's second most densely-populated city, it is also the 13th most densely-populated place in Europe.

H G Wells described the two years he spent in Portsmouth as 'the most unhappy, hopeless period of my life.'

The first model to display full-frontal nudity in an

international magazine was Marilyn Cole who was the 1973 'Playboy' Playmate of the Year. Marilyn was born in Portsmouth.

Sir Henry Ayers, five times premier of South Australia, was the, son of a Portsmouth dockyard worker. He gave his name to Ayers Rock, now known as Uluru.

Jonas Hanway of Portsmouth is acknowledged to have been the first person in England to use an umbrella.

(See Southsea)

Postbridge, Devon
Famous for the ancient clapper bridge and the Hairy Hands. (See Two Bridges)

Potters Bar, Hertfordshire
Potters Bar railway station is the highest between York and King's Cross.

Acker Bilk, who became the first British artist to top the US Billboard singles chart with his hit 'Stranger on the Shore, lived in Potters Bar for many years before retiring to Pensford in Somerset. Although it is always referred to in Britain as a 'Number One', 'Stranger on the Shore' peaked at number two in the UK charts.

Prescott, Gloucestershire
The Bugatti Owners Club purchased land here in 1937 and this is now the home of the Prescott Speed Hill Climb. Most events use the 1,128 yards (1,031 m) Long Course. There is also an 880 yards (804.7 m) Short Course used mainly by the Vintage Sports-Car Club.

Preston, Lancashire
Britain's first motorway, now part of the M6, was built to by-pass Preston in 1958.

Preston became England's 50th city when it received its charter to celebrate the 50th year of Elizabeth II's reign.

Nick Park, creator of Wallace and Gromit, was born in Preston. In 2007 it was announced that funds were being raised to erect a bronze statue of the two animated characters in Preston but, at the time of writing, this was still a dream. The robot dog in 'A Close Shave' who becomes Lady Wendolene's butler in 'The Curse of the Ramsbottoms' comic book is named Preston.

Purley, Greater London
No matter what it tells you on a plaque in Grove Hill, Harrow, (See Harrow) Henry Lindfield of Brighton became the first person to die in Britain from injuries received in what is recorded as the nation's first fatal car crash. He ran into a tree in Russell Hill Road, Purley in February 1898. Russell Hill now has speed humps.

Pyrford, Surrey
Poet John Donne lived here, as did Australian driver Jack Brabham, the only person to win a Formula One world championship driving one of his own cars.

H G Wells mentions Pyrford as the landing site for the third of ten Martian cylinders in 'The War of the Worlds'. (See Woking)

Q

Quarry Bank, Cheshire
Quarry Bank is an industrial heritage site centred around a mill. At the time of writing entry for an adult is £20.25 with most reviewers saying this is good value with plenty to do and view.

Quarry Wood, Kent
Mainly known for a large industrial estate and a nature reserve.

Quebec, County Durham
The Roman Road, Dere Street, passes through the village on its way from Hadrian's Wall to Yorkshire.

Locals in the Hamsteels Inn tried to tell me that Quebec in Canada is named after the village but it's actually the other way around. The name was adopted when fields in the area were enclosed in 1798 at about the same time as Quebec in Canada was captured from the French. Just down the road you will find Toronto which did not give its name to the most populous city in Canada. The name of Toronto most likely comes from an Iroquoian word, 'tkaronto', meaning a place where trees stand in the water.

Queensbury, West Yorkshire
Queensbury stands high on a hill on the road from Bradford to Halifax.

This is the Home of Black Dyke Mills and the Black Dyke Brass Band. The Black Dyke Band had problems when posters for a concert at New York's Carnegie Hall were considered to be racist and sexist.

Queen's Nympton, Devon

Although Queen's Nympton, aka Queensnympton, is listed in various gazetteers, I'm not saying it doesn't exist but a tour of the area resulted in me being unable to find anywhere actually called by either of the above names. There are other Nympton's in North Devon. (See Bishop's Nympton)

Quernmore, Lancashire

Quernmore is in the River Conder Valley, Roman pottery kilns have been found in the area and at one stage this was a Royal Forest.

This was the first village to be connected to the Broadband 4 Rural North network.

Quidhampton, Wiltshire

Quidhampton apparently means 'home farm with good manure'.

The village has a pub but no church.,

Quorn, Leicestershire

Vegetarians devour a pretend-to-be-meat product called Quorn. Quorn is named after this village which is most famous for its not-very-vegan-friendly fox hunt.

R

Radcliffe, Greater Manchester
Oscar-winning film director Danny Boyle was born in Radcliffe, as was snooker world champion John Spencer.

Radstock, Somerset
The Writhlington Site of Special Scientific Interest was once a colliery spoil heap. Coal was first discovered here in 1763 leading to several pits being sunk around the town where pit-head lifting-gear wheels and other mining memorabilia still decorate the streets. The last two mines closed in 1973.

Ramsey, Cambridgeshire
The ancient history of Ramsey is a mystery. A single Palaeolithic axe head was discovered in the town centre and evidence suggests this was brought here by glacial movement in the Ice Age. Odd bits of Roman pottery have been discovered but not sufficient to suggest a settlement and nothing has been found connecting the town with the early or Mid Saxon periods.

Ramsey, Isle of Man
The second-biggest town on the island is the northern terminus for the Manx Electric Railway and also the start of the TT race's Snaefell Mountain Course.

Ramsgate, Kent
I'm not sure if this is a reason for visiting Ramsgate, or possibly an even better excuse for staying away but, at the time of writing, the town boasts Britain's

biggest Wetherspoons pub.

If the massive pub and the fact that Nigel Farage once stood for election as MP here aren't sufficient to attract visitors there will undoubtedly be those who cannot wait to get to St Augustine's Church which boasts a shrine holding a fragment of bone that might, just possibly, have belonged to St Augustine who it is claimed landed close to here in 597AD bringing the Gospel to Britain. Ramsgate has a Pugin and St Augustine Visitor Centre celebrating the saint and the architect Augustus Welby Northmore Pugin who designed several local buildings including St Augustine's Church where Pugin is buried.

Rawtenstall, Lancashire

Rawtenstall boasts Britain's only remaining Temperance Bar. Mr Fitzpatrick's was established in 1890 and still serves non-alcoholic drinks including Root Beer, Sarsaparilla and Blackcurrant with Liquorice.

Reading, Berkshire

Reading is Britain's largest town without city status (See Bolton). in 1958, the nation's first Little Chef opened here.

The Royal Berkshire Hospital in Reading was originally built to attend to the many people injured during the construction of the Great Western Railway.

At the time of writing archaeologists were planning to dig in a Reading car park where it was thought they would discover the remains of King Henry I. Henry was said to have been buried in the area and graves had been discovered by ground-penetrating radar. (See Leicester. See Selby)

Redbrook, Gloucestershire
This village is on the border with Monmouthshire which probably accounts for it being located in Wales according to some websites and gazetteers.

The Offa's Dyke Footpath and the Wye Valley Walk run through the village which is connected to Wales by a footbridge. (See Clun)

Redcar, North Yorkshire
Redcar Museum houses Zetland, the world's oldest surviving lifeboat.

In 2018 the town was the location for the four-part BBC documentary 'The Mighty Redcar' which followed students looking for work after completing their studies.

Redditch, Worcestershire
Ninety per cent of the world's needles were once manufactured in Redditch, the town is now better known for springs. The Flying Flea, a motorbike that could be dropped by parachute during World War Two was made here.

Duran Duran guitarist John Taylor went to school in Redditch and Led Zeppelin drummer John Bonham was born here. Bonham's report from Redditch Secondary Modern School forecast he would either be a dustman or a millionaire.

Redenhall with Harleston, Norfolk
This civil parish consists of the town of Harleston and the village of Redenhall.

The two most notable people from here were Samuel and Edward Fuller, passengers on the Mayflower.

Sam became a much respected physician and deacon for the Plymouth Colony whilst Edward and his wife both died shortly after arriving in the New World. (See Plymouth)

Redhill, Surrey

During the 16th century this was known as Reigate Foreign with the first reference to Red Hill being recorded during the English Civil War (1642 to 1651). A nearby hill was described as being rich in red clay. Red Hill became Redhill with the opening of Redhill Post Office in 1856.

Repton, Derbyshire

The Viking Army arrived in Repton in 873-74 making this one of the very few places in the UK where a Viking winter camp has been found. The Vikings used the Christian graveyard to bury some of their dead but there was also a mass grave containing the remains of 264 individuals. Coins found with the remains date this tomb to the previously mentioned winter of 873-74. There were four males to every female, mostly aged between 25 and 40, and the lack of injuries to the bones suggests there had been some type of disease. It is known from excavated sewage samples that there were serious intestinal infections due to poor sanitation.

Retford, Nottinghamshire

Retford stands on the Idle River, an important habitat for eels. The river is prone to flooding with many inundations being recorded throughout the history of the town.

Locals will tell you that the Broad Stone in the market square in front of the Town Hall was once filled with vinegar to disinfect coins during plague times but it is more likely to be the upturned base of a boundary marker.

The Pilgrim Fathers (See Doncaster, See Plymouth, See Redenhall with Harleston) had strong connections with local villages Babworth and Scerooby and in 2018 the Bassetlaw Museum was given £450,000 of National Lottery Funding towards a gallery dedicated to the Pilgrim Fathers.

Architectural historian Nikolaus Pevsner described Retford as 'a singularly unattractive town'.

Ringwood, Hampshire
There are websites and even maps that place Ringwood in Dorset, it is in Hampshire. Ringwood sits on the A31 at a point where many motorists turn south for Bournemouth Airport.

Richmond, North Yorkshire
I found 56 Richmonds around the world, the Yorkshire Richmond was the UK's Town of the Year in 2009.

In the 18th century the entrance to a tunnel was discovered beneath Richmond Castle. An adult would not fit into the tunnel so a young drummer boy was sent in and told to keep beating his drum as he walked so the rest of the troops could follow him above ground. After walking for three miles the soldiers noted that the drumming had abruptly stopped. The disappearance of the boy has never been explained.

Ask just about anyone 'Who performed the song 'Walking in the Air' in the TV movie 'The Snowman'' and it's worth putting a bet on that they will name Aled Jones. Aled Jones did have a hit record with the song but in the movie it is performed by 13-year-old Peter Auty from Richmond.

Richmond-upon-Thames, London

Richmond-upon-Thames is the only London borough situated on both sides of the River. The coat-of-arms includes a light blue and a dark blue oar, these are there to indicate that the annual University Boat Race ends at Mortlake which is within the borough.

Rickmansworth, Hertfordshire

Rickmansworth is the first location mentioned in Douglas Adams' 'Hitchiker's Guide to the Galaxy'.

Ripon, North Yorkshire

Ripon was the first chartered city in Britain with a charter dating back to 886.

Ripon Racecourse, known as Yorkshire's Garden, staged the first ever race for female riders in 1723.

Robin Hood's Bay, North Yorkshire

There is absolutely no evidence connecting Robin Hood with this location but Bram Stoker's 'Dracula' does include scenes set in Robin Hood's Bay.

'Phantom Thread', the 2017 Daniel Day-Lewis period drama about the haute couture world in the 1950s, is set in London but includes many location shots filmed at Robin Hood's Bay.

Rochdale, Greater Manchester

Two top singers from very different eras are linked with Rochdale. Lisa Stansfield moved here in 1977, two years before the death of Dame Gracie Fields who was born above a fish and chip shop in the town but the big coincidence is that Dame Gracie's surname was actually Stansfield.

Rochdale was the original location for the BBC TV drama series 'Waterloo Road.' (See Greenock)

Rock, Cornwall
In 1303 this village was known as Penmayn, by 1337 it had become Black Tor and in the 18th century it was Black Rock to soon be shortened to Rock. The ferry to here from Padstow is the Black Tor.

Rock is a favourite destination for the rich with the likes of Mohamed Al-Fayed dropping in by helicopter.

Doom Bar ale is named after the sandbank close to Sharp's Brewery at Rock. Some connoisseurs claim to have noticed a blandness in the beer, David Cameron's favourite, since the brewery was taken over by Molson Coors in 2011. Bottled Doom Bar is now brewed in Burton upon Trent.

Romsey, Hampshire
Romsey stood in for the town of Kingsmarkham in the 'Ruth Rendell Mysteries' TV series and in 'Absolutely Fabulous' there is a reference to the 'underground car park in Romsey'. I have been unable to locate an underground car park anywhere in Romsey.

Ross-on-Wye, Herefordshire
In 1745 John Egerton began taking friends for boat trips along the Wye from his rectory in Ross. News of the beauty of this stretch of waterway soon spread and by 1808 there were eight boats taking visitors to enjoy the trip. This is why Ross-on-Wye is hyped as

the birthplace of British tourism.

Rotherham, South Yorkshire
The Romans came here for iron but it was the Industrial Revolution and the Rotherham area's abundance of coal that boosted the revenue and population.

Rotherham hit the headlines in 2007 due to summer flooding and again in 2012 following a child sexual abuse scandal. Jayne Senior, who had been a youth worker in the town, spent more than a decade trying to expose child abuse here but was ignored. She was awarded an MBE in the 2016 Birthday Honours.

The Arctic Monkeys' song 'Fake Tales of San Francisco' includes the line, 'You're not from New York City, you're from Rotherham'.

In his TV series 'Jamie's Ministry of Food' the TV chef Jamie Oliver set out to turn Rotherham into 'the culinary capital of the United Kingdom'. He failed miserably.

Rotherhithe, Greater London
Degenerating towards slumdom in the 1960s-80s, with the arrival of the Jubilee Line in 1999 and the London Overground in 2010 this is now emerging as an upmarket residential area in what was once The Docks but has now morphed into Docklands.

Actor Michael Caine and entertainer Max Bygraves were born in Rotherhithe. The famous Thames Tunnel was built by Marc Isambard Brunel with help from his son Isambard Kingdom.

Rothweil, Northamptonshire

Holy Trinity Church in Rothwell attracts tourists to a macabre display in its 13th century crypt or Charnel House. The bones of around 2,500 people can be seen here, they were piled in a broken mass on the floor when discovered but have now been organised with skulls on shelves and thigh and other bones stacked in piles at the centre of the room. (See Hythe)

Rothweil, West Yorkshire
Rothweil is on one corner of the Rhubarb Triangle. (See Wakefield)

Royston, Hertfordshire
Situated on the Hertfordshire Chalk Downs, Royston was the crossroads for the ancient Icknield Trackway (now the A505) and the Roman Ermine Street (now partly the A10).

A character in the 'Thunderbirds' sci-fi puppet series was Deborah the Duchess of Royston.

Rugby, Warwickshire
Charles Dickens' story 'Mugby Junction' is set at a little-disguised Rugby Junction which was once a very important railway link.

Legend has it that the game of rugby was invented in 1823 during a game of soccer when a Rugby School pupil, William Webb Eliis, 'picked up the ball and ran with it'. This is fiction as the boys at the school were already playing a version of rugby but official rules for the game weren't written down until 1845 by three of the school's pupils.

Ruislip, Greater London
Despite being so far inland, Ruislip has a beach. This is an artificial beach at Ruislip Lido. A 19th century

reservoir now boasts the beach and a narrow-gauge railway. It became a leisure resort in 1933.

What is now one of Whitbread's Beefeater chain was once a top class restaurant popular with pilots celebrating World War Two battle successes, the landlord would pour them a bottle of champagne for every German plane they shot down.

Runcorn, Cheshire
Norton Water Tower is a Grade II listed building, it holds 672,000 imperial gallons which is supplied to Liverpool.

In 1972 the Queen opened Runcorn Shopping Centre which, at the time, was Europe's largest covered shopping plaza.

Ryde, Isle of Wight
Ryde Pier is the oldest and fourth longest in the United Kingdom, it is a listed structure.

The Ryde Minghella Film Festival celebrates the life of Anthony Minghella who was born here. Minghella won the Best Director Oscar in 1996 for 'The English Patient'

Rye, East Sussex
Spike Milligan was Vice President of Rye Rugby Club. Paul McCartney lives in the nearby village of Peasmarsh and his children attended local schools.

Names like Wish Street and Mermaid Street might give you some idea of how dreamy this town actually is.

St Mary's claims the oldest, still-functioning church

turret clock in England. At the time of writing there was a £4 charge for climbing the tower to view the clock mechanism with this £4 giving admission for twelve months.

S

St Just, Cornwall
St Just is mainland Britain's most westerly town. A delve into the knowledge of local residents found nobody who could tell me who St Just actually was.

In 1478 William of Worcester said he believed the church here contained the bones of St Justus of Trieste but this boast might be contested by various locations in Italy also claiming the saint's relics.

St Albans, Hertfordshire
The earliest recipe for a hot cross bun came from St Albans in the 14th century. A monk at St Albans Abbey distributed the buns to the poor on Good Friday. In 2009 St Albans Cathedral campaigned for the bun to return to its original name, the Alban Bun, on which the cross is not piped but cut into the top.

During World War One, following an attack on St Albans, the German Zeppelin SL11 was the first airship brought down over England.

Nicolas Breakspear, who became the only English pope, Adrian IV, was educated at St Albans Abbey School.

Scientist Stephen Hawking received at least a part of his education at St Albans School but it is a lesser known fact that he also spent some time at St Albans School for Girls when a few younger boys were accepted there.

In the opening shots of the TV sitcom 'Porridge' the main gate of Slade Prison is actually the Gate House in St Albans.

(See Whitchurch Canonicorum)

St Austell, Cornwall

St Austell is a misspelling of the name of Saint Austol who came to Cornwall from Brittany to spread his Christian message.

The St Austell Bay Hotel, now the Carlyon Bay Hotel, was the first large hotel built on the Cornish Riviera. Most tourists visiting St Austell include the nearby Eden Project in their itinerary.

Edward Prince of Wales used to come here for sneaky weekends with Mrs Simpson.

Wallpaper from the White Hart Hotel depicting the Bay of Naples is now in London's Victoria and Albert Museum.

St Austell is the home of Cornwall's largest brewery producing several ales including the truly superb Proper Job.

St Issey, Cornwall

In 1942 a British tug, HMS St Issey, was sunk by a torpedo fired from a German submarine off the coast of Libya.

St Ives, Cornwall

The St Ives Society of Artists was founded in 1927. Sculptor Barbara Hepworth and potter Bernard Leach lived and worked here. St Ives now boasts one of Britain's four Tate Galleries.

St John's Wood, Greater London
Lord's Cricket Ground is in St John's Wood as is the Abbey Road recording studio.

St John's Wood is mentioned in the Rolling Stones song, 'Play With Fire'.

St John's, Isle of Man
Although only a small village St John's is extremely important in the history of the island. Tynwald Hill, home of the Isle of Man's original parliament, was in the village. Tynwald Day attracts thousands of visitors here each year and takes place on July 5th, St John's Day. (See Douglas)

St Leonards-on-Sea, East Sussex
Although residents of St Leonards maintain it has its own, somewhat superior, identity, it is actually part of Hastings.

St Mawes, Cornwall
St Mawes is less than a mile from Falmouth by ferry but is 30 miles away by road.

St Pancras, Greater London
Best known for the railway station, St Pancras is named after a Roman citizen, aged just fourteen, who was beheaded for converting to Christianity in around 304AD.

Salcombe, Devon
In the 1970s Salcombe was high on the Soviet Union's hit list for nuclear attack as they'd got it into their heads this would become a seat of government after they'd wiped out London.

Tourists and yachtsmen flock to Salcombe Estuary

with few, if any, of them realising there is no such thing as an estuary at Salcombe. No river feeds what is a ria, or drowned valley, which is tidal at Salcombe and has an almost entirely marine system.

Salford, Greater Manchester

When Greater Manchester was formed in 1974 what is now Salford almost became Irwell until someone pointed out that the river flows through two other boroughs.

The Lowry Centre is in Salford and almost anyone will tell you the artist was born here (See Stretford).

The Gunpowder Plot was allegedly planned in Salford's Ordsall Hall.

More than 200-years ago the unfortunately-named Rev William Cowherd from the even more unfortunately-named Beefsteak Chapel in Salford became the first person to preach the virtues of a meat-free diet. His followers were originally known as the Cowehrdites but became the Vegetarian Society.

Salford is Ewan MacColl's 'Dirty Old Town' and the BBC relocated here in 2006.

Salisbury, Wiltshire

For the sake of Russian and other visitors I should maybe point out that you do not pronounce the 'i' in Salisbury.

Everyone in Russia apparently knows that the spire of Salisbury Cathedral is the tallest spire in Britain at a height of 123m, or 404ft, and also Britain's tallest stone structure. (See Introduction. See Lincoln) The clock was installed in 1386 and is the oldest in Britain and said to be the oldest mechanical device of any complexity anywhere in the world.

William Golding taught at Bishop Wordsworth School in Salisbury and it's here he wrote 'Lord of the Flies'. (See Camberley)

Despite all the history and beauty Salisbury has to offer, a 2017 survey revealed that more than 70% of the visitors who come here arrive as what they consider to be a superfluous side-trip from nearby Stonehenge. (See Amesbury)

Sampford Courtenay, Devon
On Whit Sunday 1549 the Act of Uniformity came into effect making it illegal for churches to use the Latin liturgical rites. The parishioners of Sampford Courtenay rebelled and forced their priest to revert to the traditional service, arguing that the new liturgy was 'like a Christmas game'.

This was the start of the Prayer Book Rebellion. Troops were sent from London, battles were fought across Devon and Cornwall. At least 2,000 civilians were killed along with more than 300 soldiers. (See Clyst St Mary)

Sandbach, Cheshire
Fodden and ERF trucks were originally built here but both companies have now gone. Fodden's brass band won the National Championship 12 times.

The 9th century Anglo-Saxon crosses, erected in the market place, are two of the largest and most elaborate examples of their type and are designated Grade 1 listed structures and a scheduled monument.

Sandford on Thames, Oxfordshire
In 1943 the second wartime University Boat Race between Oxford and Cambridge was staged at Sandford. (See Ely)

Sandhurst, Berkshire
Known worldwide for the Royal Military Academy Sandhurst which most people refer to simply as Sandhurst. (See Camberley)

Sandown, Isle of Wight
This is a Victorian seaside resort which, until the 19th century, was considered a problem because it was feared that invading forces would enter Britain via the beaches around the bay.

I actually know two people who came all the way here hoping to watch the racing at Sandown Park. (See Esher)

Sandwich, Kent
'Sandwich' is found in languages across the world thanks to the bread-based snack allegedly invented by John Montagu, 4th Earl of Sandwich, so that he could eat without taking a break from card playing.

Approximately 2.5 miles down the road is a village named Ham giving visitors the opportunity to take a selfie next to a road sign pointing towards HAM-SANDWICH.

Sandy, Bedfordshire
The headquarters of the Royal Society for the Protection of Birds relocated to here in 1961.

Sandy Balls, Hampshire
A popular holiday area in the New Forest. (See No Place. See Pity Me)

Sawtry, Cambridgeshire
Sawtry makes several halfway claims. Halfway between Huntingdon and Peterborough. Halfway between Stansted and Luton Airports.

Between the 1911 and 2011 censuses the population of Sawtry soared from 994 to 6,536 thanks to the nearby A1(M) converting this to classic commuter country.

Sawbridgeworth, Hertfordshire
There is no proof that Anne Boleyn ever came here but Henry VIII bought Pishiobury Manor in 1534 as a gift for her.

It is claimed, that at the time of the Norman Conquest Sawbridgeworth was the richest village community in the country. At the time of writing Sawbridgeworth is the 645th largest town in the UK and you can't get much more trivial than that.

Scarborough, North Yorkshire
Thousands of visitors flock to Haworth every year for its Bronte connections but very few of them realise that Anne Bronte, author of 'Agnes Grey' and 'The Tenant of Wildfell Hall', is buried at St Mary's Church in Scarborough at the northern end of the churchyard overlooking the sea. Anne was given a new gravestone in 2013, not only was the old one deteriorating, it also included her age at the time of death as 28 when she was, in fact, 29. The new stone is placed over the grave in front of the old headstone. (See Haworth)

Scarborough Conservative Club runs bingo sessions where winners are required to shout 'Government' instead of 'House'.

Kids, and most adults, will love the miniature naval battles fought out during the summer on the boating lake at Peasholm Park.

Scotforth, Lancashire
It is claimed that Dorrington Road in Scotforth is the longest uninterrupted row of terraced houses in Europe. (See Littlehampton)

Scotch Corner, North Yorkshire
This is the junction of the A1(M) and A66. In the title track of their 'Too Old to Rock 'n' Roll: Too Young to Die!' album, Jethro Tull sing about an old rocker reaching 120 on his bike before taking his leave by Scotch Corner.

Scunthorpe, Lincolnshire
For some time Scunthorpe could not be accessed on several search engines. (See Penistone)

A Sainsbury's store now stands where Scunthorpe United used to play.

In a 2013 Hotels.com poll Scunthorpe was named the Least Romantic Town in the UK, Bradford and Blackpool came in second and third places.

Seahouses, Northumberland
The annual Seahouses Festival began as a showcase for sea shanties but has developed to cover other types of music since receiving an EU grant in 2005.

It is claimed that in 1843 John Woodger, a local fisherman, left a stove smoking overnight in a room full of herrings and accidentally invented the kipper. (See Great Yarmouth)

Seascale, Cumbria
Seascale is a lovely name for a lovely village until you realise it stands right next to the not-so-attractive Sellafield nuclear fuel reprocessing and nuclear decommissioning plant.

Seaview, Isle of Wight
The Isle of Wight Tourist Association advertises Seaview as a 'unique village.' I doubt there are two identical villages anywhere on the planet so Seaview is not unique in being unique.

Sedbergh, Cumbria
Although Sedbergh is in Cumbria it still manages to squeeze into the Yorkshire Dales National Park.

In 1652 George Fox, founder of the Religious Society of Friends (Quakers) spoke in the church here and also on nearby Firbank Fell giving Sedbergh the claim to be the birthplace of Quakerism.

Sedbury, Gloucestershire
Listed in some gazetteers and on several websites as being in Wales, Sedbury is in the Forest of Dean on the English side of Offa's Dyke. (See Clun) The village does have a Welsh postcode. NP for Newport.

Selby, North Yorkshire
Most people know that Richard III's remains were uncovered in a Leicester car park in 2012 (See Leicester) but it's not quite so well known that Selby claims King Henry I was born here in 1086, in the car park at the back of the library. Obviously it wan't a car park at the time of his birth and the family were only here on a temporary basis as Henry's father, William the Conqueror, was busy doing a bit of conquering up north. If current research is correct,

Henry I is the only British monarch to have been born in and then laid to rest in what became car parks. (See Reading)

Settle, North Yorkshire
There are claims that Ye Olde Naked Man is the oldest cafe in England however it has been a private house and has also served as an undertakers. (See Oxford)

Victoria Cave is so named because its inner chamber was discovered on the day of Queen Victoria's accession to the throne.

Sevenoaks, Kent
The seven oak trees in the town's name have been replanted many times over the centuries. Seven new oaks were planted to the north of The Vine cricket ground in 1902 but six of these were blown down in the Great Storm of 1987. The replacements were vandalised leaving just one mature tree in situ. Someone made a miscalculation when it came to replanting and there are now eight oaks at Sevenoaks.

Shaftesbury, Dorset
Shaftesbury is the only settlement of any importance in Dorset to be built on a hilltop. The 1973 TV commercial for Hovis, directed by Ridley Scott, was filmed at Gold Hill. In 2018 the commercial was voted 'most iconic UK advert of all time'. The boy on the bike was Carl Barlow who was paid £60 for his appearance in the advert. (See front cover)

Shanklin, Isle of Wight
There are many versions of 'The Three Little Pigs' with almost all being based on Joseph Jacobs' 1890 version in which the Pigs and the Wolf live near Shanklin.

Shap, Cumbria
Shap is a village with a population of just over one thousand but officially it is classed as a market town having a charter that dates back to the 17th century. Shap Fell is famous for a type of pink rock known as Shap Granite.

Shardlow, Derbyshire
Shardlow is the most complete remaining example of a British canal village. In the 18th century it was a river port for goods being transported from the River Trent to the Trent and Mersey Canal. It was known as 'Rural Rotterdam' or 'Little Liverpool'.

Sheerness, Kent
Dr Beeching, famous for destroying the British rail network, was born in Sheerness as was Rod Hull, famous for his Emu.

Sheffield, South Yorkshire
Sheffield FC, founded in 1857, is the world's oldest Association Football club. Sheffield Hallam is the second oldest football club in the world being just three years younger than Sheffield FC. Hallam play home games at Crosspool, the oldest football ground in the world. Matches between the two clubs are known as a Rules Derby as the games are played according to the Sheffield Rules.

Sheffield claims to be the only city in the UK with part of a National Park within its boundaries. The Peak District became the country's first National Park in 1951. (See Norwich)

Sheffield's graffiti artist equivalent to Bristol's Banksy is called Phlegm.

Park Hill Flats is the largest, and possibly ugliest,

listed building in Europe.

Shepherds Bush, Greater London
The official distance for the marathon was set at the White City Olympics in Shepherds Bush in 1908. Prior to this race the marathon distance had been precisely 26 miles but the additional 385 yards was added so the finishing line was in front of the royal box from where Queen Alexandra was viewing.

Steptoe and Son's junkyard was at the fictional 24 Oil Drum Lane, Shepherds Bush.

Shepperton, Surrey
Best known for the film studios, 'Captain America,' 'Anna Karenina,' 'The Da Vinci Code,' 'Batman Begins,' 'Bridget Jones's Diary,' etc, etc.

Shepperton is destroyed in H G Wells' 'War of the Worlds.'

Shepton Mallet, Somerset
Shepton Mallet is famed for its cider but, until closure in 2013, it was also the home of Britain's oldest working prison which was once the home of the Krays. Shepton Mallet Prison is now known as Britain's Most Haunted Prison with the ghosts of former inmates; including rapists, gangsters, murderers and those executed within its walls, wandering the dank corridors in the night.

Sherborne, Dorset
Sherborne has two castles. The Old Castle, which Elizabeth I once leased to Sir Walter Raleigh, is a 12th century ruin set in grounds next to New Sherborne Castle. The New Castle is a 16th century Tudor mansion that has developed from what was originally a compact lodge built by Raleigh for use as

accommodation during his visits.

Sheringham, Norfolk
This parish was originally two villages, Upper Sheringham and Lower Sheringham. The current town is what was originally Lower Sheringham.

The town's museum is called The Mo, taking its name from a young girl who lived in the village more than 130 years ago. The museum tells the story of Mo and other residents across the centuries.

Shifnal, Shropshire
One of the English Romantic movement's most influential works, 'The Relique of Ancient English Poetry', published in 1765, is based on a manuscript found in Shifnal.
Bishop Thomas Percy discovered the folio at the home of his friend Humphrey Pitt. The pages were spread across the floor, many were missing as Pitt's maid had been using the paper to light fires.

Shipley, West Yorkshire
The village of Saltaire is located in Shipley. Saltaire is a UNESCO World Heritage Site. Built by Sir Titus Salt in 1851, the model village created to house workers in Salt's textile mills, takes its name from its founder and the River Aire.

Shipton-under-Wychwood, Oxfordshire
One of three villages named after the ancient forest of Wychwood. Milton-under-Wychwood and Ascott-under-Wychwood being the other two. (See Charlbury)

Shoreditch, Greater London
James Burbage built England's first playhouse, known

as The Theatre, here in 1576 and one year later built the Curtain Theatre 200 yards away. 'Romeo and Juliet,' 'Henry V' and an early version of 'Hamlet' were first performed in Shoreditch.

Shrewsbury, Shropshire
Is it pronounced 'Shrews-bry' or is it 'Shrows-bury'? A debate I couldn't settle by talking to local people who seem to be equally divided.

Shrewsbury is the county town of Shropshire, a very rare county that does not have a city within its borders.

Local people will tell you that summer officially ends when the final firework falls at the annual Shrewsbury Flower Show in August.

Sidmouth, Devon
Sidmouth boasts one of the world's most beautiful cricket clubs. The Fortfield Cricket Ground overlooks the sea and has an exceptionally attractive thatched pavilion. A blue plaque on the pavilion commemorates the fact that Somerset County Cricket Club was founded here, in Devon, following a match in 1875.

Sidmouth has hosted a folk festival during the first week of August almost every year since 1955. The only cancellation I could find was 2020 due to the Coronavirus pandemic. In addition to advertised concerts in marquees the festival offers hundreds of impromptu performances in the streets and pubs.

Sittingbourne, Kent
Sittingbourne was famous for paper and bricks.

The town is now better known for large housing developments thanks to its one-hour train journey time to London.

Skegness, Lincolnshire
Skegness (known to all as Skeggie) is named after a beard, due to its position on a beard-shaped headland. 'Skeg' being a Norse word for 'beard'. Barbados also takes its name from a European word connected with beards but there is no similarity between Skegness and Barbados.

The first Butlin's holiday camp opened here in 1936.

Skegness was advertised on posters, published by a railway company, showing a fat fisherman dancing along with the strapline 'So Bracing.' Not likely to attract 21st century holidaymakers more interested in Caribbean sunshine.

Skelmersdale, Lancashire
Skem, as it it called by locals, has a population of 40,000 but no hospital, no railway station and no recognisable town centre other than a shopping mall, The Concourse, known locally as The Connie..

Skipton, North Yorkshire
Skipton is Anglo Saxon for Sheep Town which explains why there is still a Sheep Street and The Wooly Sheep Pub.

There are plenty of signs in this attractive town to remind you that Skipton is the self-appointed Gateway to the Dales.

Sleaford, Lincolnshire
Sleaford is the home of eight malthouses, the largest

group in England. The malthouses were built between 1901 and 1907 for the Bass brewery in Burton-upon-Trent. Malting ceased here in 1959 and the buildings have not been occupied since then, other than for a large chicken farming business. Three of the malthouses were severely damaged by fire in 1976 and all have been derelict since the 1990s. There were plans to convert the buildings into retail, office and accommodation space but a major backer pulled out in 2015 and there are ongoing delays over planning permission.

Slough, Berkshire
Although most people realise that Mars is an American company, in 1932 founder Frank Mars gave his son, Forrest, the money to set up a chocolate business in the UK. Forrest came to Slough and it is here the Mars Bar was invented. The Slough factory is also responsible for Topic, Twix, Malteser's and Opal Fruits (now called Starburst).

Wheelie bins were invented here and Slough was also the test ground for zebra crossings.

Soho, Greater London
Great Marlborough Street in Soho was the British home of the Phillip Morris tobacco company. With typical American ignorance of spelling the name of this street was used for the name of Marlboro Cigarettes, originally advertised as a 'lady's cigarette.'

The upper floor of what is now the Quo Vadis restaurant and members' dining club in Dean Street was once the home of Karl Marx.

Solihull, West Midlands
The name of this town derives from 'Soily Hill', it is

said that the parish church of St Alphege was built on the said, soily hill.

The largest collection of British motorcycles in the world is housed at the National Motorcycle Museum in Solihull.

Birmingham Airport is at Solihull, as is the Genting Arena, formerly the National Exhibition Centre Arena, which has staged hundreds of exhibitions and concerts by some of the world's top pop and rock acts.

South Benfleet, Essex
In 894 King Alfred's Saxon army, commanded by his son, Edward the Elder, beat Vikings here in the Battle of Benfleet.

Benfleet, or Benflet, became South Benfleet in Saxon times when Little Benfleet developed, the area where Little Benfleet once stood is now the rural community of North Benfleet.

South Brent, Devon
Brent Hill gives its name to the village, not the other way round. Brent came from Brant, an Old English word for 'steep'.

Restorations to St Petroc's Church have resulted in what was once a central tower now standing at the western end of the building. The outline of a door can be seen in the church wall. This was blocked up in 1436 after Rev John Hay was dragged out through the door and murdered.

South Cadbury, Somerset
Cadbury Castle is a Bronze Age/Iron Age hillfort

formerly known as Camelet. Evidence of a Great Hall has been uncovered and this is the prime contender for the location of King Arthur's Camelot. (See Glastonbury. See Melrose. See Dolgellau. See Carmarthen.)

South Littleton, Worcestershire
There are three Littletons, North and Middle Littleton are both smaller than South Littleton.

The maximum security men's prison Long Lartin is situated here.

South Molton, Devon
In 2018 the Tour de France went through South Molton Pannier Market, the first time any part of the race had been held indoors.

South Ruislip, Greater London
The Polish War Memorial stands on the A40 next to RAF Northolt airfield commemorating all the Polish airmen who died during World War Two when Polish fighter pilots were based here.

South Shields, Tyne and Wear
A very unscientific survey conducted amongst visitors to a local agricultural show gave me evidence that most people think Barbour waxed jackets, as worn along with Hunter wellies by upper-class countryfolk, come from Scotland. The founder was indeed from Scotland but the jackets have always been made in South Shields. Also interesting to note that the waxed clothing, even worn by members of the royal family when viewing their estates during damp weather, was originally made for motorcyclists.

South Shields is the only constituency in existence

since the Great Reform Act of 1832 to have never elected a Tory MP.

Southall, Greater London

In 1979 the police violently attacked people demonstrating against a National Front march in Southall. Dozens were injured and anti racist school teacher Blair Peach was killed. A police investigation narrowed down the list of suspects for the killing to six officers but nobody has ever been held responsible.

Jazz singer Cleo Laine was born here. Punk pioneers the Ruts and reggae band Misty in Roots formed in Southall. Trevor Baylis, inventor of the clockwork radio grew up here.

Southam, Warwickshire

In 'Henry VI, Part 3': Act 5, Scene 1, William Shakespeare has Somerset saying to Warwick, the Mayor of Coventry: 'At Southam I did leave him with his forces.'

Saint Fremund was allegedly beheaded while celebrating victory in a battle. He picked up his head and carried it away, his sword touched the ground and at that point a well sprang up. He washed the blood from his body and severed head, turned to the east, and dropped dead. It is a historical fact that Saint Fremund did die in this area and was buried at Offa's Church, in 936 his body was moved to Prescote, near Cropredy, Fremund is patron saint of Prescote, and in 1203 his remains were moved again, this time to Dunstable Priory. The spring where legend says he died is Southam's Holy Well.

Southampton, Hampshire

The legendary Spitfire aircraft first took to the air in

1936 from Southampton Airport.

Southampton boasts the UK's only commercially viable geothermal power station which heats a number of buildings in the city centre and makes this a city with very low C02 emissions.

After her father's death Jane Austen moved to Bugle Street, Southampton.
Many people know that RMS Titanic set sail from Southampton just before noon on 10th April 1912 but not so many can tell you that the ship made stops at Cherbourg, France and Queenstown, Ireland before its fatal encounter with the iceberg on 14th April.

A circular shelter in Southampton is thought to be 600 years old. The interior is divided by walls into four sections, hence it is called the Crosshouse.

Southampton Civic Centre was the first building in the country to be called a Civic Centre.

Clarence Birdseye did most of the market research for his Herring Savouries and Battered Cod Pieces on shoppers in Southampton making this the first place to taste what is now universally known as a Fish Finger. (See Great Yarmouth)

Southend-on-Sea, Essex
Prittlewell was a small fishing village with a southern area that grew to become Southend, hence the name, it is now the largest town in Essex.

At 1.34 miles (2.16 km) Southend Pier is the longest pleasure pier in the world. In World War Two the pier was commandeered by the Navy to act as a departure point.

Records list Southend as the driest and warmest place in the UK. Despite the likelihood of high temperatures, Adventure Island theme park will not admit men with bare chests.

Southport, Merseyside
In 1838 Prince Louis Napoleon spent some time in Southport and fell in love with the town's long, straight streets and ornate buildings. He returned to France as Emperor and replicated his memories of Southport to become Paris's most beautiful boulevards. The Avenue des Champs-Elysees is said to be modelled on Lord Street.
Southport is the home of the British Lawnmower Museum with a collection including the thrilling ride-on mower used by Prince Charles and Princess Diana.

Britain's second-longest pier is at Southampton (See Southend-on-Sea).

Southsea, Hampshire
'A Study in Scarlet', the very first Sherlock Holmes story, was written by Sir Arthur Conan-Doyle when he was working as a doctor in Elm Grove, Southsea. Dr Watson was based on a friend of Conan-Doyle's who was President of the nearby Portsmouth Literary and Scientific Society. (See Ingleton)

Sowerby Bridge, West Yorkshire
It's pronounced 'sore' not 'sower'. 'Sore bi Bridge'

17th century Archbishop of Canterbury John Tillotson came from here.

The BBC TV series 'Happy Valley' is set in Sowerby Bridge. The town now has several businesses that have cashed in by embracing the name of the popular programme.

Stafford, Staffordshire
The Elizabethan Ancient High House in Stafford town centre is listed as the largest timber-framed town house in England.

St Chad's Church, dating back to the 12th century is the oldest building in the town.

The triple-looped Stafford Knot is the traditional symbol of the town and the county of Staffordshire, it appears on the badges of many local organisations and is also the name of a pub.

Stamford, Lincolnshire
Stamford was the first designated conservation area in England and Wales.
The Rutland and Stamford Mercury claims to be Britain's oldest continuously published newspaper. The weekly publication has been available since 1710/1712 (exact date disputed) when it was titled the Stamford Post but its masthead claims it was established in 1695. (See Worcester)

Composer Michael Tippet and conductor Malcolm Sargent went to school here.

Stansted, Kent
This Stansted should not be confused with Stansted Mountfitchet or Stansted Airport which are both in Essex. However, British Airways did manage to confuse Stansted in Kent with the airport on their inflight electronic maps apparently showing passengers where they weren't.
Stanton Drew, Somerset
Stanton Drew's stone circles are an ancient attraction

worth visiting. The Great Circle is the second largest stone circle in Britain. The landowner asks for a £1 donation and entry is at his discretion although during my visit, on a sunny afternoon, I put my donation in a box and didn't see another person. (See Avebury)

Steeple Ashton, Wiltshire
Bannerdown Gliding Club is situated at what was Keevil Airfield where the RAF and United States Army Air Forces operated during World War Two. This was a launch site for gliders taking part in the Normandy Invasion and Montgomery's failed Operation Market Garden.

Steeple Aston, Oxfordshire
If you're looking for a pub the White Lion is now closed but the Red Lion survives and is operated by the Hook Norton Brewery. (See Hook Norton)

Steeple Bumpstead, Essex
If you're searching for the steeple on Steeple Bumpstead Parish Church of St Mary the Virgin there isn't one and the Congregational Church only has a small Victorian steeple.

Bumpstead comes from the Anglo Saxon word Bumsted, meaning a place of reeds and it is believed there once was a steeple along the A1307 close to what is now a pumping station.

Edith Cavell was governess to the four children of the Steeple Bumpstead vicar before she became a nurse. She is commemorated by a plaque in the church and a road here is named after her.

Some locals will regale you with the 'fact' that corrugated iron was invented in Steeple Bumpstead by Colonel J.C. Humphrey who was son of the village wheelwright. This is a myth, corrugated iron was patented in 1829 by civil engineer Henry Robinson Palmer of London.

Stevenage, Hertfordshire
Stevenage's history can be dated back to Roman times, a hoard of 2,000 silver Roman coins was discovered here in 1986, in 1946 Stevenage became the first New Town under the New Towns Act.

Stewkley, Buckinghamshire
Stewkley High Street is the longest in Britain, with its continuously populated length of 1.7 miles (2.7 km) (See Combe Martin)

Al Murray, aka The Pub Landlord, was born in Grove Cottage on High Street South.

Stilton, Cambridgeshire
In 1722 Daniel Defoe said that Stilton was famous for its cheese yet for many years Stilton Cheese was never produced here. Stilton Cheese was served at the village's inns, including the famous Bell Inn, along the Great North Road, and this is said to be the origin of the cheese's name.

Stilton Cheese could not now be made here as its production is limited to Derbyshire, Leicestershire and Nottinghamshire. However an 18th century recipe for a creamy cheese made in Stilton has been discovered so it is possible a blue version of this also existed. At the time of writing Stilton has applied for an amendment to the Stilton Protected Geographical Status to include the village. The PGS is an EU scheme so will probably be dropped after Brexit.
Stockbridge, Hampshire

Obviously a bridge over the River Test led to the second part of the name. Locals might tell you that 'Stock' came from this being where coaches stocked up with goods during their journey from London to Devon and Cornwall but the full name actually comes from the fact that the bridge was made from stocks (tree trunks).

Edward VII's mistress, Lily Langtry, lived in what is N J Stokes Garage, now a restaurant.

Stockport, Greater Manchester
The viaduct, prominently featured in numerous L S Lowry paintings, is the Stockport Viaduct over the River Mersey.

10cc built their Strawberry Studios in Stockport. Paul McCartney, Joy Division and the Stone Roses have all recorded here.

Stockton-on-Tees, County Durham
Stockton boasts the world's oldest railway station and England's widest High Street.

Chemist John Walker invented the safety match at his shop in the High Street in 1826 and did not consider his invention important enough to warrant a patent.

Stoke-on-Trent, Staffordshire
Stoke-on-Trent's culinary speciality is an oatcake, similar to a thick pancake, served with cheese and canned tomatoes slathered with brown sauce it actually tastes much better than it sounds.

Local pop stars include Robbie Williams and Lemmy. Slash of Guns 'n' Roses fame lived here during his childhood and fictional Murdoc Niccals from the animated band Gorillaz is from the city.

Stone, Staffordshire
The etymology of many place names is confusing but in this case Stone means stone.

Stonehouse, Gloucestershire
Yes you guessed. There was a Stone House here.

Stourport-on-Severn, Worcestershire
The Stourport Ring is a 74-mile connected series of canals with 105 locks around Worcestershire.

Stow-On-The-Wold, Gloucestershire
In 1646 the final battle in the first phase of the English Civil War took place just up the road from Stow-on-the-Wold with final action taking place in the Market Square where the Parliamentary forces routed the Royalists.

It can be a bit breezy here which has led to the couplet, 'Stow-on-the-Wold where the winds blow cold.'

Stowmarket, Suffolk
The Museum of East Anglian Life opened here in 1967.

The River Rat joins the River Gipping just to the south of Stowmarket.

Stratfield Mortimer, Berkshire
The main settlement is Mortimer Common which, at the time of writing, has three pubs and a Chinese chip shop.
Stratford-upon-Avon, Warwickshire

Everyone knows about the Shakespeare connections and you don't need to be in Stratford for long before someone will tell you that the young William went to their school, the boy's grammar school, and likely sat at their desk in their classroom and he proposed to Anne Hathaway in what is now the girls' grammar school's music room. But do any of those who come here realise that Kylie Minogue once pulled a pint in the Dirty Duck pub?

Visitors come from all over the world to see 'Shakespeare's House' where he allegedly wrote many of his best known works and personally planted a mulberry tree in the garden. Rev Francis Gastrell purchased Shakespeare's House, New Place, in 1753 and became so fed up with people peering through his windows that he cut down the tree, which was turned into souvenirs, and demolished the house leaving just the foundations. What the thousands of visitors now see is a reconstruction based on an 18th century sketch.

Stratford, Greater London

The 2012 Olympic Park was renamed Queen Elizabeth Olympic Park to celebrate the Diamond Jubilee. The site has the postcode E20 which had previously only been used in the TV soap 'EastEnders'.

Despite Honest Boris Johnson claiming credit for the 2012 London Olympics it was, in fact, Tony Blair and Ken Livingstone who brought the Games to the UK.

Stretford, Greater Manchester

In Gorse Hill Park you will find the Great Stone which gave its name to Great Stone Road. The Great Stone is a very big stone with hollows in its top that some claim once held vinegar and holy water in which coins were cleansed during the plague years.

Ian Curtis of Joy Division, Jay Kay leader of Jamiroquai and artist L S Lowry were all born in Stretford. (See Salford)

Stroud, Gloucestershire

The lawnmower was invented here in 1830 by Edwin Beard Budding. The mower was based on a machine used to put a finish on woollen cloth. The woollen cloth that covers Wimbledon tennis balls is still made in Stroud. E B Budding is also recorded as the inventor of the adjustable spanner.

Laurie Lee was born in Stroud and set much of 'Cider With Rosie' in and around the town.

Studland, Dorset

Studland is at the most easterly end of the Jurassic Coast, World Heritage Site. (See Exmouth. See Weymouth). Studland Parish includes Brownsea Island. (See Poole)

The opening sequence of the first 'Monty Python's Flying Circus' saw Michael Palin staggering from the sea onto Studland beach and saying, 'It's ...'.

The sea area around Studland claims the highest density of seahorses anywhere in the world.

Sunderland, Tyne and Wear

Residents of Sunderland, especially supporters of the local football club, are known as Makems. Makem is thought to have come from the city's shipbuilding industry and is a corruption of 'make them'.

'Carry On' star Sid James died of a heart attack in April 1976 while on stage at the Sunderland Empire Theatre.

Surbiton, Greater London
Surbiton is probably best known as the setting for 'The Good Life', but it wasn't? (See Northwood)

Surbiton Station makes an appearance in Agatha Christies 'The Adventure of Clapham Cook,' a TV adaptation of a Poirot short story. The station also appears in 'Harry Potter and the Half-Blood Prince'.

Sutton Coldfield, West Midlands
Since Henry VIII granted a charter in 1528 this has officially been Royal Sutton Coldfield.

Everyone knows about the wild ponies on Dartmoor and Exmoor but few realise that wild ponies also rome in Sutton Park.

Sutton-in-Ashfield, Nottinghamshire
Described as 'formerly Europe's largest sundial', the Sutton-in-Ashfield sundial originally had 42 Roman numeral characters around the Portland Square pavement to indicate the time. At the time of writing five of these characters have gone missing, reportedly having been removed by vandals.

Swadlincote, Derbyshire
Swadlincote is within the South Derbyshire constituency. Edwina Currie was MP here from 1983 to 1997. During this period she became a Junior Health Minister and issued a warning against British eggs. She announced that 'Good Christians don't get AIDS' and she rubber stamped Jimmy Savile's

appointment to head a task force to run Broadmoor psychiatric hospital giving him a set of keys allowing access to 800 severely disturbed patients including many young girls.

Swaffham, Norfolk
Stephen Fry's TV series 'Kingdom' features Swaffham as the fictional location Market Shipborough. The Greyhound Inn is renamed the Startled Duck for the series.
Egyptologist Howard Carter spent much of his childhood here as Swaffham was the birthplace of his parents. A collection of antiquities in Didlington Hall sparked Carter's interest in Egypt.

Swanage, Dorset
Queen Victoria reportedly spent one night in Swanage but nobody can tell you where she laid her royal head.

To prevent the German's using Swanage Pier as an aid to an invasion it was blown up to be rebuilt after World War Two and then used as a docking point for steam ships. The last steamer left the pier in 1966 and the structure fell into disuse. A trust took over ownership of the pier which reopened to the public in 1998.

In 'Fawlty Towers' Basil names Swanage as his hometown.

Swindon, Wiltshire
Swindon is the home of the Magic Roundabout. Having negotiated this on several occasions I believe the British Government should introduce a negative version of the knighthood, maybe a knothood, for idiots who devise things like this. Basically it's a large ring junction surrounding five mini roundabouts

with another roundabout in the centre. Sounds simple but try driving to your destination via this. Also do not even attempt this roundabout if relying on satnav which is just not quick enough to spot your mistakes before you make them.

Britpop band Oasis took their name from the Oasis Leisure Centre in Swindon after Liam Gallagher saw the name of the venue on a poster for an Inspiral Carpets gig when he worked with the band as a roadie.

T

Tamworth, Staffordshire
Reliant cars and vans originated in Tamworth. When founder Tom Williams built the prototype car in his shed the vehicle was too big to fit down the alley at the side of his house and had to be taken apart and then rebuilt on the pavement. Numerous quiz books claim that Del Boy Trotter drove a Reliant Robin, his yellow van is in fact a Reliant Regal.

For several centuries Tamworth was split in two and had two town halls. From 1563 until 1885 the town also had two MPs.

In 1949 Tamworth's librarian had chairs removed from the library to prevent old men from using the facility to snooze while drying their recently laundered underwear on the radiators.

Taplow, Buckinghamshire
Dusty Springfield and Terry Wogan lived in Taplow but not together.

Tarporley, Cheshire
Since 1980 Prince Charles has been patron of Tarporley Hunt Club, the oldest surviving hunt club in Britain.

Taunton, Somerset
In 1881 Taunton became the first town in England to be permanently lit by electric street lights. (See Newcastle Upon Tyne)

Somerset County Cricket Club's home is at the

County Ground (See Sidmouth). The County Ground is the home of England's women's cricket team..

The New Look clothing retail chain opened its first store in 1969 in Taunton.
Taunton is mentioned in John le Carré's 'Tinker, Tailor, Soldier, Spy' and in the 'So Long, and Thanks for All the Fish' book of Douglas Adams' 'The Hitchhiker's Guide to the Galaxy' series.

Tavistock, Devon
The first recorded (997AD) cream tea was served during the restoration of Tavistock Abbey when there was a butter shortage. Obviously if the cream was replacing butter it went on first no matter what anyone in Cornwall tries to tell you. (See Bude)

Sir Francis Drake was born at Crowndale Farm near Tavistock. The Statue of Drake on Plymouth Hoe, alongside which thousands of tourists take selfies each week, is a replica of the original in Tavistock. (See Plymouth)

Telford, Shropshire
Telford is the largest town in Shropshire and was named after the engineer Thomas Telford who engineered many of the roads and railways in the area.

The Ironbridge Gorge is on the town's southern boundary. (See Ironbridge)

Temple Sowerby, Cumbria
Local people successfully campaigned for a bypass which was opened in 2007 but Temple Sowerby is a very pretty village surrounding a traditional village green so worth the detour.

Tenterden, Kent
Printing pioneer William Caxton is said to have been born in Tenterden. (See Hadlow)

Tetbury, Gloucestershire
On the last Bank Holiday Monday in May, Tetbury hosts the annual Woolsack Race with competitors carrying a 60-pound (27KG) sack of wool up and then down the steep Gumstool Hill.
At the time of writing Brian (Jet Black) Duffy from the punk band The Stranglers lives here and Prince Charles resides just down the road at Highgrove. There is no evidence of the two enjoying dainty afternoon teas together.

Tettenhall Wood, West Midlands
The working men's club is more than a hundred years old and is known locally as The Institute.

Tewkesbury, Gloucestershire
Tewkesbury Abbey lays claim to the largest Norman tower still in existence but this is disputed by Norwich Cathedral.

Shakespeare refers to Tewkesbury Mustard on several occasions and the Battle of Tewkesbury features in 'Richard III'. Tewkesbury Mustard is a mixture of English mustard and horseradish. (See Durham. See Norwich)

Thame, Oxfordshire
Named after the River Thame, a tributary of the Thames. Budget hotel company Travelodge has its UK headquarters at Sleepy Hollow, Thame.

Bee Gee Robin Gibb lived here until his death in 2012.

Thetford, Norfolk
Much of 'Dad's Army' was filmed in and around Thetford which explains why the town boasts the 'Dad's Army' Museum. The Bell Hotel is where most of the cast lodged during filming. The British Comedy Society announced the unveiling of a 'Dad's Army' blue plaque and luncheon at the hotel in 2018 but this was cancelled due to lack of interest.

Thirsk, North Yorkshire
James Alfred White, better known by his pen name James Herriot, was the vet here from 1941 until his death in 1995. In his books and on the 'All Creatures Great and Small' TV series, Thirsk becomes Darrowby.

Streets in Thirsk include Cod Beck and Finkle Street.

What is now Thirsk Museum was the birthplace, in 1755, of Thomas Lord who is best known for having given his name Lord's Cricket Ground. (See St John's Wood)

Threlkeld, Cumbria
A very unscientific survey revealed that Threlkeld is the least-known location in this book and that the river on which it stands, the River Glendermackin, is the least-known river.

The 2ft-gauge Threkfeld Quarry Railway is an attraction to anyone who has heard of it and the village has two pubs directly opposite one another.

Timperley, Greater Manchester
The name Timperley comes from Anglo-Saxon, Timber Leah, meaning clearing in a forest.

Ian Brown and John Squire lived just around the corner from one another in Timperley and went to school together at Altrincham High. In the early 1980s they formed a band called Patrol which developed into The Stone Roses.

Tintagel, Cornwall

Tintagel thrives on its Arthurian-based tourist industry. Excited history buffs snap selfies outside King Arthur's Hall without realising it was built in the 1930s by a custard powder magnate.

Excavations at Tintagel Castle, a 12th century ruin on the headland, have uncovered finds dating back to Roman times and foundations of what could have been a 5th or 6th century Celtic monastery, or maybe a princely fortress, depending on which group of diggers you choose to believe.

The earliest I can date the Arthurian link with Tintagel is from around 1136. Geoffrey of Monmouth's 'Historia Regum Britanniae' sees Gorlois, Duke of Cornwall, install his wife Ingrain in Tintagol (sic) when he goes to war. Wizard Merlin disguised Uther Pendragon as Gorlois and Uther impregnated Ingrain who gave birth to Arthur.

If you believe any of that proves a link with a King called Arthur you'll believe anything. (See Glastonbury. See Melrose. See Dolgellau, See South Cadbury and See Carmarthen)

Tiverton, Devon

Tiverton suffered two great fires. In 1596 much of the

town was destroyed following a frying pan fire. In 1612 the 'Dog Fight Fire' caused further destruction when men who were supposed to be keeping an eye on a furnace were distracted by a dog fight.

In 1944 'Catcher in the Rye' author J D Salinger spent three months in Tiverton during the build-up to D-Day.

Tonbridge, Kent
Until 1870 this town was called Tunbridge but the GPO changed this to Tonbridge to avoid confusion with nearby Tunbridge Wells.

Britain's largest cash theft took place here in 2006 when over £53 million was stolen from the Securitas depot. Around half the money was recovered and five people were convicted of the robbery.

Torquay, Devon
Agatha Christie's Torquay connection is well known but it's not so generally recognised that Irish Nationalist Sean O'Casey, the first playwright of note to write about the Dublin working classes, whose works include 'Shadow of a Gunman' and 'Juno and the Paycock' died in Torquay in 1964. (See Totnes)

Torquay and its neighbouring resorts are famous for their 'palm trees', known as Torbay Palms or Torquay Palms. These are, in fact, Cordyline Australis, a tree that originated in the lowlands of New Zealand and not a member of the palm family. (See Scourie. See Plockton. See Ullapool)

Totnes, Devon
Sean O'Casey lived in Totnes from 1938-1954. (See Torquay)

Totnes claims to have more listed buildings per-head of population than any other town in Britain.

Tottenham Court Road, Greater London
'The March of the Guards to Finchley' by William Hogarth is set outside the Adam and Eve pub at the end of Tottenham Court Road.

Pink Floyd were the house band at the UFO Club. The Road is mentioned by the Pogues in 'Transmetropolitan.

In the Lerner-Loewe musical 'My Fair Lady' Eliza Doolittle sells flowers at the corner of Tottenham Court Road. (See Covent Garden)

Tregony, Cornwall
Tregony was once called Tregoney but the 'e' was dropped. Tregoney was a port which closed when clay mining along the River Fal at St Austell caused the river to silt up.

Trevone, Cornwall
Trevone boasts a fine beach without the restaurants, pubs and crowds associated with nearby Padstow.

The Sink Hole is a blowhole formed when the roof of a sea cave collapsed into the sea.

Tring, Hertfordshire
Only 30 miles from London and in a gap in the Chiltern Hiils, an Area of Outstanding Natural Beauty, property in Tring is not cheap. The town boasts various industries including egg packing.

The Natural History Museum at Tring was originally

the private museum of Lionel Walter, the 2nd Baron Rothschild. It is now controlled by the London Natural History Museum.

Trowbridge, Wiltshire
Trowbridge is the county town of Wiltshire. Although there is no longer a castle it is thought Fore Street runs along what was once the castle ditch which probably explains why the town has a Castle Place Shopping Centre and a Castle Street.

In the 1820s the scale of woolen cloth production in Trowbridge was to such a scale it was known as the Manchester of the West.

Isaac Pitman who developed the Pitman Shorthand System was born here. (See Wotton-under-Edge)

In 2006 Trowbridge became the first English town to twin with an Arab Muslim city, Oujda in Morocco.

Truro, Cornwall
There are towns called Truro in Canada, USA and South Australia but none of them seem to know the origin of the Cornish City's name. Some claim that 'tru' derives from a Cornish word meaning 'three' but it is more likely the name comes from 'tre-uro' meaning a settlement on the river Uro.

Tunbridge Wells, Kent
This has been Royal Tunbridge Wells since 1909 when Edward VII recognised how popular the town was with his relatives including Queen Victoria.

The bridleway across the Common was once a racecourse but racing was banned due to 'drunkeness and riotous behaviour.'

In Charles Dickens' 'Bleak House' the children find a mug decorated with the slogan 'A Present From Tunbridge Wells'.

Two Bridges, Devon
Once known for its potato market Two Bridges is now a popular picnic spot in the summer.

The road between here and Postbridge is famous for the Hairy Hands. Motorists claiming to have been stone-cold-sober have become involved in accidents when they claimed their steering wheel was grabbed by a pair of hairy hands which steered them off the road. (See Postbridge)

U

Uckfield, East Sussex
The hoax 'missing link' collection of bones, named Piltdown Man, was discovered in the nearby village of Piltdown and the last sighting of nanny murderer Lord Lucan was at Grants Hill House, Uckfield.

Ullsawater, Cumbria
(See Ambleside)

Up Holland, Lancashire
Although the country known as Holland is very flat, this village was once known as Holland which means land on the spur of a hill. It became Upholland in the 13th century

Richard Ashcroft of the Verve comes from Up Holland.

Upminster, Greater London
In 1709 the Reverend William Derham, Rector of Upminster, improved on Newton's estimates to become the first person to accurately calculate the speed of sound. From the top of the Church of St Laurence, he observed the flash from a shotgun being fired and then measured the time it took for the sound to reach him. He made his measurements from several locations, the distance was known thanks to triangulation and from this he calculated the speed of sound. Derham calculated the speed of sound in air to be 344 metres or 1,127 feet per second, the current accepted speed of sound is 343 metres or 1,125 feet per second.

Uppingham, Rutland
For one day each November Uppingham stages the only fatstock show held in temporary pens in a traditional market town.

Upton-upon-Severn, Worcestershire
Guests at the White Lion Hotel can lodge in rooms referred to in Henry Fielding's 'Tom Jones'. Fielding describes the hotel as, 'a house of exceeding good repute'.

Uttoxeter, Staffordshire
Listed as Wotocheshede in the Domesday Book the town has had over 70 different spellings since then.

'Coronation Street' sent its residents on a day out at Uttoxeter races and the town was regularly mentioned in 'A Bit of Fry and Laurie.'

Uxbridge, Greater London
Uxbridge is hugely Conservative and even went so far as to voting for Boris Johnson as its MP. At the 2019 election his majority was halved. (See Hillingdon)

V

Vauxhall, Greater London

Vokzal, pronounced 'Vauxhall', is the Russian word for any large railway station. This resulted from a delegation of Russian politicians visiting Britain to see the newly invented railway train when they were taken from the House of Commons to the closest station which was Vauxhall. When the Russians asked what this was called, meaning what was the English word for a station, they were told 'Vauxhall' and their spelling of this, 'Vokzal', is still used to mean a railway station in Russia.

Some argue that the French word for a pleasure garden, 'Vauxhall', came from the Vauxhall Gardens in London and the Russians adopted their word from the French for a park but it still originates here.

Ventnor, Isle of Wight

In the late 19th century Ventnor was known as Mayfair by the Sea and the English Mediterranean due to its popularity as a holiday resort.

Ventnor is now very much a retirement region with the average age in 2011 being 47.3 years compared with 39 across England.

W

Wadebridge, Cornwall

I know it sounds obvious, but I'm still going to tell you that, until the bridge over the River Camel was built this town was known as Wade.

The Royal Cornwall Show takes place here and also a five day folk festival around the August Bank Holiday.

At the time of writing Andrew Ridgley, the other half of Wham!, lives in Wadebridge with Karen Woodward from Bananarama.

Wakefield, West Yorkshire

The Museum of Mental Health can be found on the Fieldhead site, Wakefield. Entry is free with a suggested donation of £2 to the museum's charity.

There is a Theatre Royal in Drury Lane, Wakefield.

Nursery rhymes with Wakefield connections are 'Here We Go Round the Mulberry Bush' said to have originated with female inmates walking around the exercise yard at Wakefield prison and 'The Grand Old Duke of York' is thought to be about the Battle of Wakefield in 1460. (My proof reader looked at the first four words here and informed me 'But 'Nursery' does not rhyme with 'Wakefield'.')

Wakefield is the capital of the Rhubarb Triangle. This 9-square-mile triangle, which produces most of the country's early forced rhubarb, includes the area between Wakefield, Morley and Rothwell but originally encompassed the the much larger area between Wakefield, Leeds and Bradford.

Wallasey, Merseyside
During the 16th century horse races took place on the nearby sands to entertain the Earls of Derby and this is said to be the forerunner of the modern, annual Derby. (See Wirral)

Wallingford, Oxfordshire
Anglo-Saxon Archbishop of Canterbury, Stigand, surrendered to William the Conqueror here in 1066 which took William to the throne and to the creation of Wallingford Castle.

Wallingford is now better known for its annual Festival of Cycling and the Vintage Car Rally.

Wallingford stands in for the fictional town, Causton, in 'Midsomer Murders' and features in Ronnie Corbett's 'Sorry'.

Walsall, West Midlands
Princess Anne, the Princess Royal, opened the Walsall Leather Museum in 1988. The museum's collection includes a display of saddles and harnesses which could explain HRH's interest.

Slade singer Noddy Holder became a freeman of Walsall in 2014.

Walsall gained fleeting fame in 2000 when a statue of Princess Diana, carved in black wood, appeared in the town and was reportedly condemned by the Queen. The statue went through a green period due to the growth of moss in times of neglect and was last heard of standing outside the headquarters of a funeral memorial company in nearby Bloxwich. (See Bloxwich)

Waltham Forest, Greater London
The northern part of the Queen Elizabeth Olympic Park, including the three swimming pools, is in Waltham Forest.

The first British motor car was built by Frederick Bremer in his garden shed at Waltham Forest in 1892. The first all-British aeroplane was successfully tested here in 1909 by A V Roe.

Wandsworth, Greater London
Wandsworth Category B Men's Prison is the largest in London and one of the largest in Europe. When the building was originally constructed in 1851 there were toilet facilities for every prisoner. The toilets were removed to make space for more prisoners and were not reinstalled until 1996.

Between 1878 and 1961 Wandsworth was the site for 135 executions. The gallows was tested every six months until 1993 with the execution suite now being used as the prison officers' tea room. Execution boxes for the whole of Britain were kept at Wandsworth. These contained everything required by the executioner: 2 ropes, a block and tackle, 2 straps, a sandbag to test the trapdoor, a measuring rod, chalk, thread to hold up the rope and designed to snap when the prisoner fell, copper wire and a cap.

Wantage, Oxfordshire
Alfred the Great and Lester Piggot were born here and Alice Fitzwarin, wife of Dick Whittington, grew

up in the town.

John Betjeman lived at the Old Rectory for many years and made Wantage the subject of several poems. The Betjeman Millennium Park was opened in his honour in 2002.

Ware, Hertfordshire
From 2012 the Great Bed of Ware was on loan to the local museum but it is usually to be seen in the Victoria and Albert Museum. As its name suggests, his is a very large bed, it is mentioned in Shakespeare's 'Twelfth Night'.

Wareham, Dorset
Clouds Hill was the home of T E Lawrence who kept a sleeping bag here for visitors. The sleeping bag was stolen shortly after Lawrence returned to hero status following the release of the 'Lawrence of Arabia' movie in 1962. It was returned in 2001.

Warkworth, Northumberland
Warkworth boasts St Lawrence's Church, an almost completely Norman structure making it unique in Northumberland.

Warrington, Cheshire
Warrington was the first place to have a Social Democratic Party election candidate. Roy Jenkins, former Home Secretary, stood for the party in 1981 and lost to Labour's Doug Hoyle. (See Abersychan)

Ian Brown of Stone Roses fame was born here as was radio and TV presenter Chris Evans.

Warton, Lancashire
Warton sprang to national attention when someone

named Jay Gardner lost his left shoe down a toilet and then got involved in all kinds of publicity stunts before running as mayor (at the time of writing) with policies including cheaper beer.

(See Freckleton)

Warwick, Warwickshire
Warwick is an ancient town but most of the medieval buildings were destroyed by the Great Fire of Warwick in 1694.

Warwick Castle is a 12th century stone reconstruction of a wooden motte-and-bailey castle built by William the Conqueror in 1068.

Wasdale, Cumbria
The civil parish and valley of Wasdale are in the west of the Lake District and much of the valley is taken up by Wastwater, England's deepest lake at 258 feet.

Washington, Tyne and Wear
William de Wessyngton, a forbear of the USA's first president, George Washington, lived here and Washington Old Hall still celebrates Independence Day each 4th July.

Washington, West Sussex
Composer John Ireland spent his final years in a windmill at Washington.

Watchet, Somerset
Watchet is a harbour town on the Bristol Channel.

Samuel Taylor Coleridge wrote 'The Rime of the Ancient Mariner' in the area and he is commemorated by a harbourside statue of the Mariner. (See Nether

Stowey)

Waterloo, Merseyside
Crosby Beach begins in Waterloo and is the location of Antony Gormley's 'Another Place' which consists of 100 naked figures, based on Gormley's own body, looking out to sea.

Watford, Hertfordshire
In 2009 Watford was proposed as a transport hub for the Eurostar service between London and Paris. The scheme was dumped and is currently on hold.

Watford Grammar School for Boys and Grammar School for Girls featured in scenes for the movie 'The History Boys'.

In the TV series 'Benidorm' Donald and Jacqueline Stewart belong to the Watford Swingers' Association.

Simon Le Bon, of Duran Duran fame, was born in Watford.

In his 'Step Into Christmas' video Elton John holds up his Watford AFC supporter's club card.

Wellingborough, Northamptonshire
Sir Frances Drake's ship, The Pelican, was renamed The Golden Hind after the heraldic symbol of the Hatton family from Wellingborough when Sir Christopher Hatton sponsored his expeditions.

Sir David Frost attended Wellingborough Grammar School.

At the time of writing Thom Yorke of Radiohead lives here.

Wellington, Somerset
A memorial to the Duke of Wellington's victory at the Battle of Waterloo stands in the Blackdown Hills to the south of Wellington. At a height of 175 feet (53m) it is the tallest three-sided obelisk in the world.

Wells, Norfolk
Officially known as Wells-next-the-Sea, the sea is now approximately a mile away from the town centre due to the harbour having silted up.

Still just close enough to the North Sea to be classed as a seaside resort, Wells employs a World War Two siren to give a ten minute warning of when the notoriously unpredictable tide is likely to take over the beach.

The town boasts the world's smallest public railway.

Wells, Somerset
Water bubbles up from the ground here. Hence the name Wells.

Wells is the closest city to Britain's biggest and best music festival. (See Glastonbury. See Pilton)

Although Wells has boasted a cathedral since the 12th century it wasn't until 1974 that Elizabeth II confirmed its city-status. By area Wells is the smallest free-standing city in the UK, (2.1 sq miles) that is a city that is not part of a larger urban area such as the City of London (1.12 sq miles). (See St Davids. See St Asaph)

The west front of the cathedral is decorated with what is almost certainly the finest collection of statuary in Europe with around 300 medieval effigies. The cathedral also has the most incredible fan-vaulted ceiling and a well-worn stone staircase that is sculptural in its beauty. At the Bishop's Palace a pair of mute swans ring a bell when they require feeding.

Despite all of the above, tourists can often be found wandering around St Cuthbert's Parish Church in the belief that this is the cathedral.

Welwyn, Hertfordshire
Residents debate over whether this should be known as Old Welwyn or Welwyn Village, both names intended to distinguish it from Welwyn Garden City.

Welwyn boasts a 3rd century Roman bath-house, once part of a villa. The bath-house is preserved in a vault beneath the A1 and is occasionally open to the public.

Welwyn Garden City, Hertfordshire
Welwyn Garden City was England's second garden city (founded in 1920) and an early new town (designated in 1948). It is unique in being both a garden city and a new town. (See Letchworth)

Wembley, Greater London
The original Wembley Stadium was officially opened for the 1923 FA Cup Final and remained in use for 77 years. The current stadium, opened in 2007, seats 90,000 making it the largest football stadium in the UK and second largest in Europe after Barcelona's Camp Nou which has a capacity of approximately 99,400. Wembley boasts 2,618 toilets, including urinals. Camp Nou claimed not to know how many toilets they provide but recent reviews on a well known website revealed complaints about the smell. Due to the Coronavirus pandemic there were some

tiny crowds for major sporting events in 2020 with the Rugby League Challenge Cup Final being watched by just 50 lucky fans.

Weobley, Herefordshire
The first thing you need to know is that you do not pronounce the 'o' in Weobley.

The building known as the Throne is where Charles I spent the night after the Battle of Naseby during the English Civil War.

As a commemoration of Weobley becoming the Village of the Year in 1999, a magpie, the village's emblem, was sculpted by Walenty Pytel.

West Bromwich, West Midlands
Best known for West Bromich Albion FC. The club has won the FA Cup on five occasions but has only been League Champions once, 1919-1920. Their ground, the Hawthorns, is the highest in the Football League at 551 feet above sea level.

Westbury-on-Severn, Gloucestershire
Shortly after the steeple of the Church of St Peter and St Paul was built the old wooden church was destroyed by fire resulting in this being a rare example of a church with a stone tower topped by a wooden spire not attached to the main building.

West Drayton, Greater London
West Drayton is allegedly insulated from Heathrow Airport noise thanks to the East/West runway configuration but as someone not used to being THAT close to a major airport (approx three miles) I can assure you the racket from jets on the ground is constant and there are flightpaths for very low flying

aircraft immediately overhead. (See Heathrow. See Hounslow)

Rolling Stone Ronnie Wood was born here.

West Ealing, Greater London
West Ealing hamlet was first recorded in 1234 but it then became Ealing Dean so the current West Ealing is actually approximately one hundred years old in its present form.

Westcliff-on-Sea, Essex
Westcliff touts itself as a holiday resort but beware. The Thames estuary has been transformed into a series of beaches with imported sand between a series of groynes and at low tide the water goes out to a distance of 600m leaving unattractive, somewhat smelly, mud flats exposed. (See Weston-Super-Mare)

Westminster, Greater London
Simon de Montfort's Parliament, the first English Parliament, originally met here on 20th January 1265.

This became the City of Westminster in 1965, until the 16th century fields separated the City of London from Westminster.

The UK's oldest surviving blue plaque commemorates Napoleon III and was erected in 1867 in King Street.

Westminster Abbey is actually the Collegiate Church of St Peter.

Weston-Super-Mare, Somerset
I have visited Weston on many occasions whilst living in Bristol and never managed to find the energy to

walk all the way to the sea. I am assured the Bristol Channel does bring the waves close to the town's beaches but I failed to witness this phenomenon. (See Westcliff-on-Sea) Weston has the second highest tidal range in the world at 15 metres, beaten only by the Bay of Fundi in Canada.

The pier burnt down in 2008 and it took 2 years to rebuild at a cost of £39 million.

Wetherby, West Yorkshire
Goldenfry Gravy, available from most supermarkets, is made here at what was once a fish and chip shop.

The Horsefair Centre might sound like an ancient equine auctioneering market but is actually a large, modern shopping complex.

Weymouth, Dorset
Thomas Hardy lived in Weymouth on and off between 1869 and 1872 working on 'Under the Greenwood Tree' whilst here.

Weymouth is situated approximately half way along the Jurassic Coast UNESCO World Heritage Site. (See Exmouth. See Studland)

Weymouth and Portland Harbour were the venues for the 2012 Olympic sailing events.

Whitby, North Yorkshire
Known by most for jet, the hard, black stone popular in Victorian jewellery, and for 'Dracula' but not so many realise that Captain Cook gained his love for the sea while sailing coal ships out of Whitby.

The whale jaw bone arch, on West Cliff,

commemorating the town's whaling history was donated by Alaska in 2003 to replace an arch originally erected in 1853.

Whitchurch, Shropshire
Whitchurch is the oldest continuously inhabited town in Shropshire.

Whitchurch Canonicorum, Dorset
St Wite, also known as St Candida, is the patron saint of Dorset. The Church of St Candida at Whitchurch claims to be the only church in England to house the bones of the saint to whom it is dedicated. This is not quite correct as at least a part of the skeleton of St Alban was returned to St Albans Cathedral in 2002, however St Candida's was the only church to retain the relics of its saint in the original shrine following the Reformation, other than those of Edward the Confessor in Westminster Abbey.

Whitehaven, Cumbria
In the 1720s Daniel Defoe came to Whitehaven and wrote about its coal trade.

People from Workington refer to the people of nearby Whitehaven as Jam Eaters, thought to be an insult suggesting that, due to poverty, they could not afford to put beef in their sandwiches.

Whitley Bay, Tyne and Wear
The town was known as Whitley until 1901 when Bay was added.

Whitley Bay is mentioned in Dire Straits' song 'Tunnel of Love'.

Whitstable, Kent

You will often be told to never eat oysters during a month without an R in it. Whitstable produces probably Britain's best-known oysters and the Whitstable Oyster Festival takes place in July.

The extremely narrow Squeeze Gut Alley was once known as Granny Bell's Alley, locals will tell you this is the narrowest street in Britain but it isn't. (See Exeter)

What was once known as Tankerton Towers is now called Whitstable Castle but it isn't actually a castle.

Widnes, Cheshire
It is claimed that Paul Simon wrote the Simon and Garfunkel classic, 'Homeward Bound,' at Widnes station. Simon said he wrote the song whilst feeling homesick on his way home from a gig in Liverpool, waiting for the late night milk train to London 'at a station close to Widnes'. A blue plaque and then its replacement, commemorating the origin of the song, were stolen from the Liverpool-bound platform at Widnes. A new brass plaque made by students is supposedly theft-proof. However, and here's the rub, at the time Paul Simon wrote the song direct trains to London departed not from here, but from the other station in the town.

Screenwriter Alan Bleasdale and Spice Girl Melanie Chisholm went to school in Widnes.

Wigan, Greater Manchester
Wigan Pier, famous thanks to George Orwell's 'The Road to Wigan Pier,' was a wharf on the Leeds/Liverpool Canal. It once included a museum dedicated to Victorian life in the town but this closed in 2007 due to lack of interest. The Wigan

Pier nightclub shut up shop in 2011 and the building was demolished in 2015. At the time of writing The Orwell pub was also closed. A ten-year redevelopment plan was launched in 2015. (See Coatbridge)

Wilmslow, Cheshire
Lindow Man, the centrepiece of the British Museum's Iron Age exhibit, was discovered in Lindow Moss, a peat bog close to Wilmslow. Preserved for more than 2000 years by the peat, the body was excavated in 1984,

During the previous year fragments of the body of Lindow Woman had been found here. Prior to dating it was assumed that the skull and other body parts were those of a missing woman called Malika de Fernandez. As a result of the bog discovery the husband of the lost wife thought her body had been found. He confessed to her murder and was duly convicted.

Wilmslow is one of the most desirable and expensive areas for property in the north of England.

Wilton, Wiltshire
Trivial Pursuit was once sued by Axminster Carpets due to a question on the lines of: 'Where was your carpet made if it was manufactured after 1835 on the original Axminster looms?' The answer given was 'Wilton.' Rather than spend a fortune defending a court case the manufacturers of the board game settled out of court.

FACT: In 1835 Samuel Rampson Whitty, grandson of the founder of Axminster Carpets, was declared bankrupt. The Axminster remaining stock and looms were sold to Blackmores of Wilton whose carpets were then manufactured under the brand name, Axminster. (See Axminster)

Wimbledon, Greater London

It's hard to mention Wimbledon without making reference to tennis and the price of strawberries.

Wimbledon's history goes back to the Iron Age. The remains of the second-largest Iron Age hillfort in London can be seen on Wimbledon Common. Although the Common is, of course, much more famous as the home of the Wombles.

The All-England Croquet Club opened at Worple Road in the 1870s. Interest in croquet was waning and the club adopted the upcoming sport of tennis to become the All England Lawn Tennis and Croquet Club in 1922.

Wimborne Minster, Dorset

Wimborne Minster boasts a memorial to 16th/17th century politician Sir Edmund Uvedale. Observant visitors will note that, if the reclining statue is correct, Sir Edmund had two left feet.

Winchcombe, Gloucestershire

Winchcombe means 'valley with a bend' and it still has streets that bend along the valley. Winchcombe was once a centre for tobacco growing but this was made illegal in 1619 to protect the interests of America and other colonies.

Christopher Merrett, who was born here in 1614 (some sources say 1615), wrote the first list of British birds and butterflies but, far more importantly, no matter what claims the French make for Dom

Perignon in 1697, it was Merrett who documented his invention of sparkling wine, made by precisely what the French named the method champenoise, in 1662. The English had also invented much stronger glass bottles so the English were producing and bottling sparkling wines 35 years before the French.

5 North Street, Winchcombe is a restaurant that has held a Michelin Star for ten years at the time of writing.

Winchester, Hampshire

Winchester Cathedral boasts the longest nave and overall length of any Gothic cathedral in Europe. When people talk about the bride and groom walking down the aisle they are obviously unaware that the aisles in a church are at the sides. It is the central nave the bride and groom traditionally walk down after plighting their troth.

Winchester College is the UK's oldest public school still operating from its original premises.

In a 2016 survey carried out by the Lloyds Banking Group, Winchester was voted the Best Place to Live in the UK. (See Fleet)

Winchester has 24 traffic bollards painted with topical scenes or in the style of famous artists.

Background material published about the 1960s TV series 'Captain Scarlet and the Mysterions' identifies Winchester as the birthplace of Captain Scarlet.

Windermere, Cumbria

Windermere sits on the shores of England's largest natural lake. Now merged with Bowness-on-

Windermere there are two distinct town centres. (See Bowness-on-Windermere)

Windsor, Berkshire
Windsor Castle is the largest inhabited castle in the World and the longest-occupied castle in Europe. Typhoid fever, blamed on the plumbing at Windsor Castle, is usually given as the cause for the death of Prince Albert but from his reported symptoms modern scholars believe he is more likely to have been killed by stomach cancer.

Until 1917 the Royal House of Windsor was the House of Saxe-Coburg-Gotha and when German Emperor Wilhelm II heard of the name change he joked he was looking forward to going to see Shakespeare's 'Merry Wives of Saxe-Coburg-Gotha.'

'The Merry Wives of Windsor' is the only Shakespeare play to mention cabbage.

Windsor Chairs come from High Wycombe, not Windsor. (See High Wycombe)

(See Hampton Court Palace)

Winnersh, Berkshire
From 1975 to the early 1990s the UK headquarters of Hewlett-Packard was in Winnersh.

Winscombe, Somerset
Max Bog Site of Special Scientific Interest is next to the village. The Bog is important for rare plants including orchids.

Having been built on land that originally belonged to Quakers, Winscombe only has one pub but there are a couple of clubs and a wine shop.

At one time Kildare House was the British headquarters of Moose International, a fraternal organisation founded in Mooseheart, Illinois.

Winsford, Cheshire
Winford boasts the UK's largest rock salt mine. If you are driving along a salted road in the winter the salt probably came from here. (See Middlewich)

Winterbourne Stoke, Wiltshire
Winterbourne Stoke is surrounded by ancient burial mounds. The Bell Inn is an excellent village pub, a useful refreshment stop for visitors to Stonehenge and I can recommend their Full English.

Winterslow, Wiltshire
There are West Winterslow, Middle Winterslow and East Winterslow. Modern road signs put Middle and West together as West Winterslow.

Wirral, Cheshire/Merseyside
The northern section of the Wirral Peninsula, including Birkenhead and Wallasey, is in Merseyside and the southern third in Cheshire.

Parts of 'Chariots of Fire' were filmed here, as were scenes in the TV series 'Peaky Blinders'. (See Birkenhead. See Wallasey)

Wisbech, Cambridgeshire
Samuel Pepys and Daniel Defoe both wrote about visiting here.

Rev W Awdry of 'Thomas the Tank Engine' fame,

was vicar of nearby Emneth from 1953 to 1965. One of his characters, Toby the Tram Engine, is based on a small steam train that transferred farm produce along the Strawberry Line between Wisbech and Upwell.

Witney, Oxfordshire
Witney is such a safe Tory seat that it has been gifted to former Foreign Secretary Douglas Hurd and former Prime Minister David Cameron.

Woking, Greater London
Woking takes its name from Saxon chieftain Wocca who also gave his name to other towns with names beginning Wok.

In 1876 Woking became the site for Britain's first purpose-built crematorium. (See Golders Green)

In 'The War of the Worlds' the narrator lives in Woking and this is one of the towns close to where the first of the ten cylinders falls. (See Pyford)

Wokingham, Berkshire
For a period during Victoria's reign the town became known as Oakingham which accounts for the acorns and oak leaves on the town's coat-of-arms. (See Woking)

Tom, the child chimney sweep in Charles Kingsley's 'The Water Babies', is based on the story of James Seaward, a boy from Wokingham who swept Kingsley's chimneys when he resided at the Rectory in Eversely.

Wolverhampton, West Midlands
Natives of Wolverhampton are called Wulfrunians. Wolverhampton was granted city status along with

Brighton and Hove to celebrate the Millennium.

In 1927 Wolverhampton became the first town in Britain to install automated traffic lights.

Wolverhampton footballer Billy Wright was the first player in the world to win 100 caps playing for his country.

Woodbridge, Suffolk
6th and 7th century burial sites close to Woodbridge include the mound in which the Sutton Hoo burial ship and its associated treasures were found.

Brian Peter George St John le Baptiste de la Salle Eno, better known to early Roxy Music fans as Brian Eno, was born at Phyllis Memorial Hospital one mile to the north of Woodbridge.

Woodbury, Devon
In the heart the East Devon Area of Outstanding Natural Beauty the village of Woodbury is situated below Woodbury Common with its impressive Iron Age hillfort.
Much of The Common is a nature sanctuary with a diverse variety of animals and birds.

Woodbury Park Golf Club, originally founded by Nigel Mansel, boats a hotel and health centre.

The village has a chapel and the ancient St Swithun's Church. Two pubs, The Maltsters Arms and The White Hart attract locals and visitors.

Woodcroft, Gloucestershire
Woodcroft is one of several communities listed in gazetteers and online as being in Wales when it is, in

fact, in England. Okay so it is only two miles from Chepstow but it is still in England, in the Forest of Dean to be precise.

When the Wye Valley Railway was being built Sophia Morgan, from Tidenham House, organised evangelic services in Woodcroft in an attempt to cut down drunkenness amongst Irish labourers working on the project. A strict no alcohol policy still applies at what is now the Woodcroft Christian Centre.

Woodford Bridge, Greater London
Reston Park housing estate and gymnasium stand on the site of Clayburn Hospital. This was a psychiatric hospital, opened in 1893 and listed by Historic England as the most important asylum in Britain,

Woodford Green, Greater London
Labour Prime Minister Clement Attlee lived in Woodford Green at the time Winston Churchill was the MP here.

Woodstock, Oxfordshire
Winston Churchill was born at nearby Blenheim Palace which is now a UNESCO World Heritage Site, he is buried just down the road at Bladon.

Historically far more important was Woodstock Manor, or Palace, which was destroyed during the Civil War with most of the remaining structure being used to build Blenheim.

Woodstock Palace saw the marriage of William the Lion, King of Scots, to Ermengarde de Beaumont in 1186. The Treaty of Woodstock between Henry III and Llewelyn the Last was signed here in 1247. Edward I's youngest son, Edmund, was born at the

Palace, Edward, the Black Prince, was born here and Mary Plantagenet, daughter of Edward III married John, Duke of Brittany, here in 1361. The future Queen of England, Elizabeth 1st was imprisoned in the lodge at Woodstock Palace after being transferred from the Tower of London in 1554.

Wool, Dorest

The name of Wool has nothing to do with a sheep's overcoat. This was once Wyllon, then became Wille and Welle, all names derived from the wells, or springs, to be found here.

Obviously unaware of the above story, in 2018 the animal rights group, PETA, unsuccessfully campaigned to have the village renamed Vegan Wool.

Woolbridge House was the location of Tess's honeymoon in Hardy's 'Tess of the D'Urbervilles.'

The parish includes Bovington Camp army base

Woolacombe, Devon

'Coast' magazine named Woolacombe beach the best in Britain in 2012. In 2015 TripAdvisor voted it the 4th best beach in Europe and the 13th best in the world.

The winter population here is around 1,000 but the high quality of the sea water and surfing conditions makes Woolacombe a popular resort for summer holidaymakers.

Wooler, Northumberland

Wooler sits on the edge of the Northumberland National Park. It is hyped as the Gateway to the Cheviots and attracts visitors to guest houses, a youth hostel and campsites.

In 1107 the town was described as being 'situated in an ill-cultivated country under the influence of vast mountains, from whence it is subject to impetuous rain.'

Wootton Bassett, Wiltshire
In 2011 this became Royal Wootton Bassett in recognition of the populace turning out en masse to salute military repatriation funeral processions which passed through the town when British personnel, killed in Iraq and Afghanistan, were landed at nearby RAF Lyneham.

Worcester, Worcestershire
Worcestershire Sauce was created here by John Wheeley Lea and William Henry Perrins.

Edward Elgar was born in the nearby village of Lower Broadheath.

Worcester's Berrow's Journal claims to be the oldest newspaper in the world. Published weekly since 1709 with some claims it has been around since 1690. (See Stamford)

Workington, Cumbria
When Mary, Queen of Scots, fled over the Solway Firth with sixteen companions she arrived with very few possessions and requiring shelter. A Scottish laird remained loyal to his Queen and sent a message to his friend, Sir Henry Curwen of Workington, asking him to help Mary. Sir Henry gave her shelter until she could be taken to Carlisle Castle. All she could give the family by way of thanks was a small agate cup, thought to be Mary's travelling communion cup, and

this became known as the Luck of Workington. Mary was executed less than eight months after giving the cup away.

For seventy years the cup remained with the Curwen family when they moved away from here and it is said many misfortunes fell upon Workington while the cup was elsewhere. It was returned in 2012 to be displayed at the Helena Thompson Museum where it is reportedly insured for £50,000

Worksop, Nottinghamshire
Worksop is still known as the Gateway to the Dukeries even though the Dukeries no longer exist. The Dukeries were Clumber House, Thoresby Hall, Welbeck Abbey and Worksop Manor.

Worth, Kent
C S Forester's hero Horatio Hornblower was born in Worth. Hornblower's biographer, Cyril Northcote Parkinson claimed the village name was Word or Worde before becoming Worth. Parkinson also said there was a smuggling business based at a farm called Blue Pigeons which could be based on fact as the village has a Blue Pigeons Hotel.

Worth, West Sussex
Although almost swallowed by Crawley, Worth does have an interesting history of its own.

Robert Whitehead built Worth Abbey. The house now combines a public school with a Catholic monastery. Whitehead was an industrialist best known as the inventor of the torpedo. Ironically Whitehead's granddaughter and heiress married a German Naval Commander which resulted in the Royal Navy being torpedoed by a British invention.

Worthing, West Sussex
Worthing Lumps are a series of three-metre high chalk cliffs about five miles off the coast.

Jane Austin and Harold Pinter have lived in Worthing and it is here that Oscar Wilde wrote 'The Importance of Being Earnest.'

Wotton-under-Edge, Gloucestershire
Sir Isaac Pitman, inventor of the famous shorthand system and vice president of the Vegan Society, married a widow and moved to Wotton-under-Edge in 1836. Pitman Place is named after him. (See Trowbridge)

Wrotham, Kent
Wrotham boasts three pubs within one hundred yards of one another, a fourth ceased trading in 2009.

Wroxall, Isle of Wight
Appuldurcombe House was once the grandest house on the Isle of Wight but it is now a shell with the falconry centre, still advertised on several websites, closed down at the time of writing.

Wroxall, Warwickshire
In 2006 it was announced that a huge motorsport facility, The Fulcrum, would be built at the former RAF Honiley airfield. At the time of writing a change in the rules of Formula One has resulted in the project being put on hold.

Wroxham, Norfolk
Wroxham calls itself the Capital of the Broads, although Hoveton challenges this claim. A bridge here is so difficult to navigate that a pilot is available,

currently at a fee of £12 each way, to assist boats through. (See Hoveton)

Yarmouth, Norfolk
Also known as Great Yarmouth, with a floor area of 2,752 square metres Great Yarmouth Minster, St Nicholas, is England's third-largest Parish Church after Beverley - 3,489 square metres and Christchurch Priory - 2,815 square metres but fans of Great Yarmouth ignore the competition and claim theirs to be the largest.

In 1599 Thomas Nashe wrote about a fisherman in Lothingland, near Yarmouth, who accidentally invented the kipper. (See Seahouses)

American explorer and scientist Clarence Birdseye invented the fish finger and this was first produced in Yarmouth in 1955. The product was not a success when launched as Herring Savouries, they then became known as Battered Cod Pieces until female workers at the factory explained the problem with this title and came up with Fish Fingers. (See Southampton)

Charles Dickens stayed at the Royal Hotel and described Yarmouth as 'the strangest place in the wide world' and complained he could smell the fish. Daniel Defoe claimed the South Quay was 'the finest in all of Europe'.

In 1845, as a publicity stunt for a visiting circus, Nelson the Clown attracted a massive crowd as he set off to travel in a barrel pulled by four geese along the River Bure in Great Yarmouth. An estimated 400 spectators watched from the suspension bridge. As Nelson passed underneath, the crowd rushed to the other side to follow him, their collective weight causing the chains to snap dumping them in the water. 79 people died in the tragedy.

Yelverton, Devon
A terrace of houses in Yelverton had their upper storey's removed during World War Two to ease the approach of planes to the nearby RAF Harrowbeer. The tower of St Paul's Church wasn't removed and was hit by an aircraft resulting in the fitting of a warning light. President Roosevelt landed here when his intended destination was fogbound.

Yeovil, Somerset
In Tomas Hardy's Wessex Yeovil becomes Ivell. The town also features in Stephen Potter's series of novels, 'School of Lifemanship,' 'Gamesmanship' etc, etc.

Yetminster, Dorset
The first recorded vaccination was carried out here in 1774. Local farmer Benjamin Jesty realised that inducing cowpox would bring immunity from the far more dangerous smallpox as sufferers of the former disease had been noticed not to get the latter. He scratched the arms of his two sons and his wife with an old darning needle covered with pus from a neighbour's cowpox-infected beast.

York, North Yorkshire
It is legal to shoot a Scotsman within York City's walls so long as you use a bow and arrow and never on a Sunday.
The Kit Kat chocolate bar was invented in York. 47 are consumed every second. (See Girvan)

Lancelot Blackburne was a pirate who became Bishop

of York from 1724 to 1743. He was once ejected from a church for demanding a pipe of tobacco and a jug of beer. Blackburne's wife objected when he requested that his mistress should move in with them.

(See: Clifton-Without)

Z

Zeal Monachorum, Devon
The village's name is Latin for 'Cell of the Monks.' The manor was given to Buckfast Abbey by King Cnut (aka Canute).

The turreted house to the south-west of the village is Reeve Castle which was built in 1900, fell into ruin and was rebuilt in the late 20th century.

The school closed in 1954 and the car park was once the site of the Church Hall.

Zeals, Wiltshire
Zeals is on the edge of Salisbury Plain and archaeologists have discovered signs of life here dating back to neolithic times.

The Zeals almshouses look to be Tudor but were built in 1865.

RAF Zeals, known as HMS Hummingbird, was used during World War Two as an airfield for fighters including Hurricanes and Spitfires. It then became a base for glider training.

Zelah, Cornwall
Zelah is named after the burial place of King Saul in Judea.

Until the opening of the by-pass in 1992, the A30, Land's End to London road, ran through the village

Zennor, Cornwall
Alphabetically Zennor is the last parish in Britain.

Megalithic burial chambers Zennor Quoit and Sperris Quoit stand close together.

D H Lawrence and his wife, Frieda, lived near the village from 1915 to 1917 and it is here he completed 'Women in Love'. The Lawrences were forced to leave Cornwall following accusations that they were spying and sending signals to German submarines.

Zennor's name comes from the Cornish saint St Senaera. Legend tells that a mermaid visited St Senara's Church and enticed a singer away. Dye`an Thomas's friend Vernon Watkins wrote a poem titled 'The Ballad of the Mermaid of Zennor'. The whole mermaid story probably originates thanks to a 15th century carving of a mermaid on a pew end in the church.

Zouch, Nottinghamshire
The name of the hamlet derives from an Old English term for poor ground and it comes last on any list of settlements in England that I can find.

The few dwellings grew around the canal, the Zouch Cut, but there was a mill here before the canal became navigable.

SCOTLAND

As England is divided into Counties and Regions, Scotland is divided into Council Areas and Lieutenancy Areas. Where possible I have listed locations with their Lieutenancy Area but some locations fall within two separate areas so please don't complain on those rare occasions where I fail to name the Lieutenancy Area.

A

Aberdeen, Aberdeen
Much of Aberdeen is built from silver-grey local granite, hence it is known as the Granite City.

The Aberdeen area has the highest number of whisky distilleries of any area in Scotland with 17.

Donald Trump loves the local coastline so much that he spoilt it by building a
golf resort here.

The nearby Cairngorms National Park is twice the size of England's Lake District.

Brig o'Balgowne is Scotland's oldest bridge with its construction starting in the late 13th century and completion in 1320.

Aberfeldy, Perth and Kinross
Robert Burns wrote a song lyric titled 'The Birks of

Aberfeldy', the chorus goes: 'Bonnie lassie, will ye go, Will ye go, will ye go, Bonnie lassie will ye go to the Birks of Aberfeldy,' which possibly explains why he has never been that significant outside Scotland.

Aberlour, Moray
Although rarely used, the full name of the village is Charlestown of Aberlour.

Aberlour distillery is famed for its Speyside single malts, the town's other distillery, Glenallachie, is best known for whisky used in blends such as Chivas Regal and Clan Campbell.

Abernethy, Perth and Kinross
Said to have been the capital of the Picts, Abernethy boasts one of Scotland's only two round towers. (See Brechin)

Achnasheen, Ross-shire
The Achnasheen Hotel burnt down in the early 1990s and hasn't been rebuilt.

Alloa, Clackmannanshire
Alloa is the county town of Clackmannanshire. (See Clackmannan)

The Alloa Brewery proudly produced Graham's Golden Lager until the 1950s when it was renamed Skol.

John Jameson, founder of the Irish Whiskey company, was born in Alloa. Jameson was the great grandfather of Guglielmo Marconi, joint recipient of the 1909 Nobel Prize in Physics for his pioneering work in radio,

Alva, Clackmannashire
The Alva Games have been held here for more than 150 years.

The Harviestoun Brewery produces a variety of ales at the Alva Industrial Estate.

Anstruther, Fife
There are two halves to this town, Anstruther Easter and Anstruther Wester.

Anstruther is the home of the Scottish Fisheries Museum. The Anstruther Fish Bar won the Fish and Chip Shop of the Year award in 2001-2002.

Appin, Argyll and Bute
The West Highland branch of the Clan Stewart is the Clan Stewart of Appin. Their chiefs descend from James Stewart of Perston who was a grandson of Alexander Stewart, his cousin, Walter, married Marjorie Bruce, daughter of Robert the Bruce and their son, also called Robert, became the first Stewart Monarch.

Ardgay, Sutherland
Pronounced Ard-guy, the National Cycle Track passes through the village.

Arisaig, Inverness
Several places in England have streets named after Arisaig. A small passenger ferry sails from here to Eigg, Muck and Rùm.

The 'Ian and Sovra' series of children's books by Elinor Lyon are set on a fictional Ardnish peninsula and in the village of Arisaig.

Armadale, West Lothian
Armadale Stadium promotes speedway and previously attracted crowds for stock car and greyhound racing. The stock cars didn't race against the greyhounds, this was two separate events. The town has a football club and a flute band.

Arrochar, Argyll and Bute
The mountains overlooking the village are known as the Arrochar Alps and the main summit is the Cobbler.

Auchencairn, Dumfries
Princess Anne officially opened the community shop and post office in 2008. Ten years later a cafe was added in an attempt to rescue the failing business and, with no royalty available, this was officially opened by the oldest man in the village.

Parts of 'The Wicker Man' movie was filmed in the area and, until 2016, the Wickerman Pop Festival took place in the village on land owned by Jamie Gilroy who died in a firearms incident in 2014.

Auchencairn is also the name of a hamlet further north in Dumfries and of a village on the Isle of Arran.

Aultbea, Ross and Cromarty
The Isle of Ewe is just across the water with the Isle of Lewis visible in the distance. The area is scattered with World War Two military buildings and a NATO base sees large ships coming in to refuel.

The Ewe Distillery at the Drumchork Lodge Hotel was opened in 2006 and was up for sale at the time of writing with buyers showing interest from as far away as Japan. The bar at the Aultbea Hotel offered great views of bird life. In April 2019 complaints were being received from potential customer who failed to receive refunds when the Aultbea Hotel closed without notice.

Aviemore, Inverness-shire
Britain's only freely grazing reindeer herd can be found here at Glen More.

Parts of the 25th James Bond movie, 'No Time to Die' were filmed at Aviemore in 2019.

Ayr, Ayrshire and Arran
A road at Sauchie House near Ayr was the first in the world to be tarmacked. The house belonged to John McAdam who was deported from America for showing loyalist sympathies during the War of Independence.

Ayr is the home of the Scottish Grand National and boasts some of the finest beaches in the country.

B

Balivanich, Western Isles
Balivanich is the largest settlement and administrative centre of Benbecula, an island in the Outer Hebrides.

Ballater, Aberdeenshire
Ballater is famed for its spring water which was once claimed to be a cure for scrofula.

Thanks to its proximity to Balmoral many local shops were bestowed with Royal Warrants. Although members of the royal family still shop here most Warrants expired five years after the death of the Queen Mother and some shopkeepers are still sulking over the requirement to remove HM the QM's arms from above their doors.

Ballantrae, South Ayrshire
It doesn't take a lot of guesswork to conclude that R L Stevenson's 'The Master of Ballantrae' is set here.

On a clear day Ireland can be seen from Ballantrae.

Ballantrae hosts an annual festival of food and drink on the second weekend of June.

Balmaha, Stirling and Falkirk
Popular with day trippers from Glasgow. The B837 is the only road that runs through the village.

Conic Hill sits on the east bank of Loch Lomond next to the village of Balmaha.

Baltasound, Shetland
Baltasound is notable for Bobby's Bus Shelter. The shelter, close to the village, is named after six-year old Bobby Macaulay. Bobby saved the small glass shelter from closure after writing to the council to let them know he kept his bike there when he caught the bus to school. The shelter is maintained by Shetland Islands Council and is equipped with a sofa, computer and TV. (See Unst)

Banchory, Aberdeenshire
Known as the Gateway to Royal Deeside, Banchory is close to two castles, Crathes and Drum.

Archaeologists discovered what are said to be the world's oldest bottle openers in Banchory.

Bathgate, West Lothian
Bathgate is mentioned in 'Letter from America' by the Proclaimers. 'Bathgate no more, Linwood no more' (See Linwood)

Beauly, Inverness
In 1994 the 15th Lord Lovat, Simon Fraser, sold Beaufort Castle to Ann Gloag, director of the Stagecoach transport group.

Bettyhill, Caithness
The cafe at Bettyhill is creatively called The Cafe at Bettyhill.

Biggar, Lanarkshire
The Biggar Little Festival takes place in October each year. Biggar is the home of a Gasworks Museum and the nearby village of Broughton has a museum commemorating John Buchan. The 'Thirty Nine Steps' author spent much of his childhood here.

Birkhill, Angus
(See Muirhead)

Birnham, Perth and Kinross
Birnham is opposite Dunkeld on the south bank of the Tay. It is claimed that the Birnham Oak is the only remaining tree from Birnham Forest, mentioned in Shakespeare's 'Macbeth'.

The Birnham Games feature the World Haggis Eating Championships.

Blackwaterfoot, Ayrshire and Arran
Blackwater is on the Isle of Arran and boasts one of Europe's only two, twelve-hole golf courses.

Robert the Bruce reputedly hid in the village at King's Cave.

Blairgowrie and Rattray, Perth and Kinross
Raspberries and strawberries grow well here resulting in a Smedleys cannery and a jam factory. Prior to Brexit the summer population was boosted by many East Europeans employed to pick the fruit.

Songwriter, folk music enthusiast and poet Hamish Scott Henderson was born here.

Bonnybridge, Stirling and Falkirk
Bonnybridge is close to the Bonny Water. A very well preserved section of the Antonine Wall stands close to the village along with what remains of Rough Castle which is the most complete of the remaining Roman forts on the wall.

Brae, Shetland
Brae stands on an island confusingly called Mainland.

The Delting Dolphins swimming club is believed to be the most northerly swimming club in the UK.

Braemar, Aberdeenshire
The Braemar Gathering, known locally as The Games, takes place on the first Saturday in September and usually attracts assorted members of the royal family but they are much more likely to be seen sitting looking bored rather than tossing cabers.

Brechin, Angus
Brechin has a famous cathedral but this is not a city (See Elgin and Perth). To be perfectly precise, as a Presbyterian congregation of the Church of Scotland this is not, strictly speaking, a cathedral.

The church has a rare Scottish example of a round tower. There are many of these in Ireland but the only other in Scotland is at Abernethy. (See Abernethy)

Broadford, Ross and Cromarty
This is the second-largest settlement on Skye, part of the village is called Waterloo, a reminder of Napoleonic War veterans who settled here.

It is claimed that James Ross, proprietor of the Broadford Inn (now the Broadford Hotel) made improvements to the Drambuie recipe given by Bonnie Prince Charlie to Clan McKinnon. Initially Ross served the drink just to friends but its popularity spread and it was trademarked in 1893.

Broadford has been celebrated in song by Jethro Tull in 'Broadford Bazaar' and by the Waterboys in 'The Trip to Broadford'.

Brodick, Ayrshire and Arran
Brodick is the main village on the Isle of Arran and

is the most important hub thanks to the ferryport connecting Arran to the mainland.

The Isle Be Wild adventure park can be found in the grounds of Brodick Castle.

Broomhouse, Edinburgh
Scotland's first guided busway was opened in 2004 and ran parallel to Broomhouse Drive. Guided buses can be steered externally with the guidance system being the kerb or guide band. (See Wester Broom)

Brora, Sutherlan
The woolen industry brought electricity here making Brora the first places in northern Scotland with this form of power, resulting in the nickname 'Electric City'.

Stone from the Brora quarry was used in the construction of Liverpool Cathedral and London Bridge.

Brother's Point, Ross and Cromarty
In 2020 a line of depressions was discovered at this location on the Isle of Skye and a palaeontologist identified these as the footprints of a stegosaurus. This is the first time evidence has been found to suggest that these cow-sized dinosaurs existed in Scotland.

Burravoe, Shetland
The Old Haa Museum is located in Burravoe on the Isle of Yell. The museum displays a collection of historic items and visitors can also enjoy the garden and tearoom. (See The Haa. See Yell)

Burghead, Moray
The nearby hillfort has been attributed to the Romans

but actually dates back much further, to the Picts.

January 11th sees the annual Burning of the Clavie. The Clavie is a barrel filled with tar which is set alight then carried around the town. (See Ottery St Mary) The barrel is then taken to the ramparts of the fort where more fuel is added. It usually takes around 90 minutes for the Clavie to burn out and fall down the hill where locals eagerly collect the smouldering embers for reasons only they can explain.

Burntisland, Fife

A volcanic plug known as The Binn is a local landmark and the town has an award-winning beach.

C

Cairndow, Argyll
The school closed in 1988 when only three pupils were attending. In the same year the Loch Fyne Oyster Bar opened across the Head at Clachan.

Caithness, Caithness
Caithness is a historic county, registration county and lieutenancy area. There is also the Earldom of Caithness and the Caithness Parliamentary constituency. These areas have assorted boundaries so visitors might be in one interpretation of Caithness whilst not in another.

Callander, Inverness-shire
Your Granny will remember Callander as the setting for the fictional town of Tannochbrae in the TV series 'Dr Finlay's Casebook.' Have you noticed at this point that your Granny gets almost as many mentions in this book as Tesco's car parks.

Campbeltown, Argyll and Bute
Once self-styled as the 'Whisky Capital of the World' with over 30 distilleries, Campbeltown now concentrates on quality rather than quantity and only three distilleries remain active.

The annual Mull of Kintyre Music Festival takes place here.

Canonbie, Dumfries
In 2001 Foot and Mouth was first spotted at a local market resulting in all the surrounding farms losing their herds.

Carbost, Ross and Cromarty
This village on the Isle of Skye attracts tourists thanks to it being the home of the Talisker distillery.

Talisker House became the home of the eponymous single malt whisky in 1831.

Talisker was the favourite whisky of Robert Louis Stevenson and is the favourite whisky of the author of this book. Talisker is not like a medicine but it does have a back taste of iodine which I am told comes from sheep that eat seaweed and their urine then flavours the peat over which the malted barley is smoked. I do realise I'm not helping to sell this but it is delicious.

Carinish, Western Isles
Carinish is on the island of North Uist, Outer Hebrides. The Battle of Carinish was fought in 1601 between Clan MacLeod of Dunvegan and the Clan MacDonald of Sleat. A MacDonald victory led to an enforced peace. This is the last battle in the UK recorded as having been fought with bows and arrows.

Carluke, Lanarkshire
Known to locals as Kirkstyle, Carluke is Clydesdale's largest town.

One of the town's main employers is the jam factory but most working residents are commuters to nearby Glasgow.

Carnoustie, Angus
Sea bathing first attracted visitors to here in the 19th century and the arrival of the railway in the early 20th century boosted the tourist influx.

Locals have been playing golf on the Barry links since the 16th century and a more formal 10-hole course was laid out in 1850. Carnoustie has four courses and has hosted the Open Championship on several occasions.

Carrbridge, Inverness
'Carr' means boggy area and locals tell me the name should be hyphenated, Carr-Bridge. The 'bridge' part of the name comes from the packhorse bridge which is the oldest stone bridge in the Highlands.

The village hosts an annual chainsaw carving competition and the Golden Spurtle World Porridge Making Championship. A spurtle is a peculiarly Scottish porridge stirring implement.

Castle Douglas, Kirkcudbrightshire
Castle Douglas is designated a Scottish Food Town, it boasts some 50 businesses producing or selling food and drink.

Clackmannan, Clackmannanshire
There are those who will assure you that this is the county town of Clackmannanshire, however this title was handed over to Alloa as long ago as 1822. (See Alloa)

Clydebank, Dunbartonshire
The strength of the Socialist movement here in the early 20th century led to the town being called Red Clydesdale.

Wet Wet Wet formed at Clydebank in 1982, originally going by the name Vortex Motion, they are best known for their cover of The Trogg's hit 'Love Is All

Around'. The Wet's version of the song was featured on the soundtrack of 'Four Weddings and a Funeral' and had spent 15 weeks at the top of the UK singles chart when it was withdrawn from sale, reportedly so it wouldn't attract negative criticism if it didn't equal or even better the record 16 weeks spent at number-one by Bryan Adams' 'Everything I Do' three years earlier.

Coatbridge, Lanarkshire
In 1845 Robert Baird said of Coatbridge, 'There is no worse place out of hell than that neighbourhood.'

George Orwell''s 'The Road to Wigan Pier' was illustrated with a photograph of houses in the Rosehill area of Coatbridge. (See Barnsley - See Wigan)

Cockburnspath, Berwickshire
The lands of Cocksburnspath were once held by the Crown and were part of James IV's dowry to Mary Tudor in 1503.

John Broadwood, founder of piano manufacturers Broadwood and Sons, was born in Cockburnspath in 1732.

Cockenzie and Port Seton, East Lothian
This is a unified town on the coast of the Firth of Forth. Originally two small fishing villages with Port Seton still laying claim to be Scotland's largest fishing port. The fishing industry here is in decline with the catch now consisting mainly of prawns.

Coldstream, Berwickshire
Edward I of England invaded Scotland at Coldstream in 1296. General George Monck founded the Coldstream Guards in 1650.

The England/Scotland border runs down the middle of the River Tweed except for a small field between the Coldstream village of Cornhill and the English village of Wark. Local tradition saw men from the two villages play an annual local version of football known as ba, with each team consisting of as many men as the villages could muster. The winning side claimed the field, called Ba Green, for their village for a year and therefore for their country. Coldstream gained a much larger population than Wark and it reached a stage where, due to numbers, they couldn't possibly be defeated at the game so Ba Green permanently became a part of Scotland.

Colintraive, Argyll and Bute
Colintraive's name stems from the Gaelic for 'swimming strait' as cattle were driven into the water to swim from here to pastures on the Isle of Bute.

Corrour Railway Station, Inverness-shire
One of the UK's most remote stations, Corrour Railway Station, is not accessible by any public roads. The station in unstaffed and there are no facilities to purchase tickets.

Corrour Railway Station features in a scene in the movie 'Trainspotting' and also shows up in an episode of 'Paul Merton's Secret Stations' TV series.

Cowdenbeath, Fife
Burke and Hare are said to have taken bodies from Beath Cemetery, resulting in coffins being placed in iron safes or with graves having heavy, flat stones on top to deter body snatchers. (See Edinburgh)

Craignure, Argyll and Bute
The main ferry port on the Isla of Mull, Craignure, has a population of approximately 200 and it boasts two castles, Duart and Torosay.

Crainlarich, Stirling and Falkirk
Crainlarich hypes itself as The Gateway to the Highlands. The village is in the Glen of Strath Fillan at the north west of the Trossachs.

Crieff, Perth and Kinross
Crieff is the home of the Caithness Glass Visitor Centre and the Glenturret Distillery. Both well worth visits, these are the main attractions for many visitors to the area.

Rob Roy MacGregor came regularly to Crieff to sell cattle. His outlaw son was pursued through the streets by soldiers who killed him.

Self-styled 'poet and tragedian' William McGonagall wrote a poem titled 'Crieff' which includes the immortal lines: 'Ye lovers of the picturesque, if ye wish to drown your grief. Take my advise and visit the ancient town of Crieff.'

Actor Ewan McGregor was born here
Cromarty, Ross and Cromarty
From 1987 to 2009 the port was linked to Nigg by Britain's smallest, public vehicle ferry. The Cromarty Rose held fifty foot passengers and two cars.

The name of Cromarty is better known than the names of many much larger locations thanks to Cromarty being a sea area frequently mentioned on radio in the Shipping Forecast.

In 2012 the death of Bobby Hogg made national news. Bobby was the last remaining speaker of the local North Northern Scots dialect.

Cullen, Banffshire
Smoked haddock, milk, potatoes and onions become the delicious soup known as Cullen Skink. Proper smoked haddock is light brown. The fluorescent orange stuff originated in fish that had gone off being dyed this colour to warn people not to buy it.

Cumnock, Ayrshire and Arran
According to the poem 'The Wallace' by Blind Harry, William Wallace spent three months here in 1296.

Robert Burns is also said to have spent time in Cumnock.

Cupar, Fife
Cupar Golf Club is described as 'probably the oldest nine-hole club in the world'.

D

Dalbeattie, Kirkcudbrightshire
This was the home town of William McMaster Murdoch, First Officer on the RMS Titanic.

Granite quarrying played an important part in Dalbeattie's economy and Craignair Quarry is a local landmark. Granite from here was used to build the Eddystone Lighthouse. (See Eddystone Lighthouse)

Deeside, Aberdeenshire
Known locally as Royal Deeside, a title encouraged by the tourist industry.

Doune, Stirling
Fourteenth century Doune Castle dominates the landscape and legend has it that Bonnie Prince Charlie visited the town in 1745.

Dingwall, Ross and Cromarty
Dingwall once had a harbour but now lies inland.

Ross County FC are based in Dingwall. In 2012 they won promotion to the Scottish Premiere League and are the most northerly full-time football squad in the British Isles. In 2016 they won the Scottish League Cup.

Drumnadochit, Inverness
Drumnadochit relies heavily on tourism with nearby Urquhart Castle being one of the most visited sites. The castle's main attraction is its connection with

alleged sightings of the Loch Ness Monster. It is managed by Historic Scotland and Nessieland. As might be expected the castle features a Nessie-based exhibition. (See Inverness)

Drymen, Stirling and Falkirk

Close to Drymen stands Buchanan Castle, used as a hospital during World War Two, it housed senior Nazi officer Rudolf Hess.

Dufftown, Banffshire

The town's four main roads meet at the Clock Tower, once a prison it is now a tourist information centre.

Dufftown stands on the River Fiddich and is the location for several whisky distilleries, the most famous being Glenfiddich.

Hogwarts, the main setting for the Harry Potter series, is mentioned by Hermione Granger in one of her Daily Prophet articles as being close to Dufftown.

Dumfries, Dumfries

The locals are known as Doonhamers and their town was nicknamed Queen of the South by poet David Dunbar, a name adopted by the local football club.

Robert Burns lived here from 1791 until his death in 1796.

Dunbeath, Caithnes

In 1942 Prince George, Duke of Kent, died when his Short Sunderland flying boat crashed on a hillside in Dunbeath.

Dunblane, Stirling and Falkrik

Stringent national laws banning the ownership of several types of weapon were passed following the massacre of 16 children and their teacher at Dunblane Primary School in 1996.

The Murray tennis family come from Dunblane.

Dunfermline, Fife
The first Carnegie Library was opened in Dunfermline in 1883. Andrew Carnegie had emigrated from the town to the USA as a child. His foundation went on to fund 2,509 libraries around the world.

Dunkeld, Perth and Kinross
Dunkeld, on the north bank of the Tay, suffered almost total destruction during the Battle of Dunkeld in 1689.

Dunoon, Argyll and Bute
In 1961 the Cold War saw the US Navy basing Polaris ballistic missiles in Holy Loch with accompanying CND protests making international news. For thirty years Dunoon became a garrison town.

Percy James Patrick Kent-Smith was born in Dunoon. Percy changed his name to Sylvester McCoy and became the seventh incarnation of The Doctor in 'Doctor Who'.

Dunvegan, Ross and Cromarty
Dunvegan is on the Isle of Skye and is best known for Dunvegan Castle, seat of the chief of Clan MacLeod. The name of the village has nothing whatsoever to do with failed vegetable eaters.

E

Earlston, Berwickshire
An apparently 13th century keep known as Rhymer's Tower is traditionally said to have been the home of Thomas Learmonth aka Thomas of Ercildoune or Thomas the Rhymer. Thomas was a friend of the elves as well as being a poet and a prophet. Thomas almost certainly predates the tower so is more likely to have been born in a cottage on, or close to, the site.

East Linton, East Lothian
This was originally called Linton, with the East being a later addition to avoid confusion with West Linton in Peebleshire.

Ecclefechan, Dumfries
This village is where Thomas Carlyle was born, his birthplace, The Arched House, is a tourist attraction. The Fechan blended whisky has an image of The Arched House on its label. The author of this book was threatened with forced removal from an English pub when, purely in the cause of research, he asked for a Fechan Whisky.

Robbie Burns composed a song titled 'The Lass O' Ecclefechan'.

At Christmas 2007 the Sainsbury supermarket chain promoted Ecclefechan Tart as an alternative to mince pies. Ecclefechan Tart is a mix of spices, butter, sugar, nuts and dried fruits in a pastry case.

Edinburgh, Edinburgh

Thousands of American tourists visit Edinburgh each year even though most of them cannot pronounce the city's name. Many come here for the Edinburgh Festival which is the largest arts festival in the world. Edinburgh is known as Auld Reekie (Old Smoky) due to the many coal and wood fires that once burned in the city.

Edinburgh Castle stands on a section of a volcanic plug. Arthur's seat is the summit of another section of this plug in the Holyrood district of Edinburgh. The area was once used for archery practice and the gaelic name for the ground was 'Ard-na-said', meaning 'the height of arrows'. 'Are-Na-Said' sounds suspiciously like 'Arthur's Seat' if slurred in a Scottish accent after numerous pints of Tennent's so any suggestion of a link with King Arthur can be forgotten.

Burke and Hare began their shady career as body snatchers and went on to murder at least 16 people in the city, selling the bodies for dissection at the medical college. Burke was hanged, Hare escaped prosecution by turning King's Evidence, he was last seen walking over the border to England. The Surgeons' Hall Museum displays Burke's death mask and a wallet made from his skin. (See Cowdenbeath)

Charles Dickens is said to have found the name Ebenezer Scrooge on a tombstone in Canongate Kirkyard, Edinburgh. If he did he made two major errors. The memorial is actually for Ebenezer Scroggie, not Scrooge. Scroggie was a corn trader, so is described on his memorial as a Mealman. Dickens thought this was 'Meanman' and every mean man since has been called a Scrooge.

The Guinness Book of World Records lists Elaine

Davidson of Edinburgh as the world's most pierced woman. At the last count she had more than 9,000 piercings.

An old Edinburgh cure for baldness was to burn the droppings of a dove and then rub the ash into the bald spot. Don't try this at home.

At the time of writing there are more statues of animals in Edinburgh than of women. The only statue of a woman is one of Queen Victoria.

Elderslie, Renfrewshire

It is claimed that William Wallace was born and brought up here but no proof exists. A commemorative ceremony takes place each August at the Wallace Monument, the Wallace Yew tree stands close by.

Elgin, Moray

Daniel Defoe referred to Elgin as, 'A very agreeable place to live in.'

In the 1960s Elgin's Two Red Shoes dancehall hosted gigs by The Beatles, The Who, Cream and Dusty Springfield.

Until the late 1990s Elgin was a city. (See Brechin and Perth) (See Lossiemouth)

Ellon, Aberdeenshire

The North Sea oil boom turned Ellon into a dormitory town for nearby Aberdeen and in 2006 Ellon was ranked as having the fourth most rapidly-increasing average house prices in Scotland.

Iain Sutherland of the Sutherland Brothers folk duo was born here. Brother Gavin Sutherland is undoubtedly best known for his song 'Sailing' which became an international best seller for Rod Stewart. (See Peterhead) No matter how hard he tries to cultivate a Scottish image, Sir Roderick David Stewart was born at 507 Archway Road, Highgate, London.

Erskine, Renfrewshire
Erskine Bridge is the most westerly crossing point on the River Clyde.

Eyemouth, Berwickshire
Eyemouth hosts an annual Herring Queen Festival which originated in the Fisherman's Picnic held to celebrate the end of the First World War.

Fair Isle, Shetland
This is the most remote inhabited island in the United Kingdom.

Fair Isle knitting, known as the Fair Isle Technique, is a colourful, patterned woolen fabric popularised by Edward, Prince of Wales who later became Edward VIII.

Falkirk, Stirling and Falkirk
In 1228 William Wallace fought his final battle against the English during the War of Independence at Falkirk. (See Wallacestone)

Residents of Falkirk are known as Bairns thanks to an 18th century motto 'better meddle with the diel than the bairns of Falkirk', 'bairns' being children and 'diel' being Scottish for devil.

The Falkirk Wheel is the only boat lift connecting two canals.

Falkirk has won the Most Beautiful Town in Scotland award on two occasions.

Falkland, Fife
American country singer Johnny Cash traced his ancestry back to the Falkland area of Scotland.

Falkland is the home of the first racket sport, Real Tennis, formerly known as Royal Tennis, it is is said to have been played here by 15th century Stuart Kings.

The Falkland Islands took their name from Anthony Cary the 5th Viscount Falkland.

Findhorn Ecovillage, Moray
Findhorn is a commune with its own currency.

Fochabers, Moray
Fochabers is in the delightfully named Parish of Bellie and is home to the Bellie Kirk.

The Baxters food company is based here.

Forfar, Angus
The Forfar Bridie is similar to a Cornish Pasty minus the potato and swede.

Glamis Castle, ancestral home of Queen Elizabeth the Queen Mother and birthplace of Princess Margaret is just down the road.

Prince Edward is the Earl of Forfar and although the band AC/DC are generally acknowledged to be Australian, their lead singer until his death in 1980 was Bon Scott who was born in Forfar. (See Camden)

Forres, Moray
Sueno's Stone is said to be of Pictish origin and was erected to commemorate victory in a battle against Norse invaders. The 20-foot-tall stone is encased in a glass box to protect it from graffiti-daubing vandals.

In Shakespeare's 'Macbeth' Duncan's castle is in Forres and the Three Witches cast their spell on a heath close to the town.

Roy Williamson, member of the Corries and writer of 'Flower of Scotland' lived in Forres and died here at the age of 54 in 1990.

Forsinard, Sutherland
The RSPB operates a 38,000 acre nature reserve here with the old station building serving as their visitor centre.
Fortingall, Perth and Kinross
Fortingall claims to be the birthplace of Pontius Pilate. Pilate was actually born long before Romans came to Scotland so this claim is extremely doubtful. Fortingall also claims to be the home of the oldest living thing in Europe in the form of a 5,000-year-old yew tree in the churchyard.

Fort Augustus, Inverness-shire
Although the village has a population of less than 700 it is a popular tourist destination thanks to spectacular views of Loch Ness and stunning walks along the Great Glen Way.

Fort William, Inverness-shire
Fort William is on the Road to the Isles and is a major centre for tourism due to the town's proximity to Glen Coe, Ben Nevis, Aonach Mor and Glenfinnan.

Films made in or around Fort William include 'Braveheart,' 'Highlander,' 'Rob Roy' and 'Harry Potter'. I'm coming to the conclusion there isn't a place in Britain that doesn't have at least some tenuous connection with the boy wizard.

Fortrose, Ross and Cromarty
Fortrose was the home of the Brahan Seer (Coinneach Odhar). Although many will tell you that he predicted the future there are no contemporary records of his prophecies, in fact he is first mentioned in the works of Alexander MacKenzie (1838 to 1898) who wrote long after the events he said the Seer predicted had actually happened.

Fraserburgh, Aberdeenshire
Fraserburgh boasts one of the largest shellfish ports in Europe and by far the largest in Scotland.

The town has an award winning beach and a golf club founded in 1777.

G

Gairloch, Ross and Cromarty
The Gulf Stream brings warm waters attracting sea bathers here but swimmers beware, with the warm waters come jellyfish, mostly harmless.

Gairloch is the home of Two Lochs Radio which claims to be the UK's smallest local radio station.

Galashiels, Roxburgh, Ettrick and Lauderdale
Locals regularly shorten the name of their town to Gala.

The two foxes eating plums on the town's coat-of-arms commemorate an occasion in 1337 when a group of English soldiers were caught and killed while picking plums here.

Robbie Burns' songs 'Sae Fair Her Hair' and 'Braw Lads' are set in Galashiels.

Girvan, Ayrshire and Arran
Grant's whisky has been distilled just to the north of Girvan since 1964.

Everyone believes that Nestlé's chocolate is made in York but a factory at Girvan manufactures chocolate which is then taken to York for use in the production of Kit Kats and Yorkie bars. In 2010 this became the UK's first zero-waste factory. (See York)

Glasgow, Glasgow
Eleven fossilised trees in Glasgow's Victoria Park are twice as old as the oldest known dinosaur.

Despite its boozy reputation, or perhaps as a result of it, Glasgow has some weird and wonderful drinking laws. For example kids aren't permitted in premises after 8.00pm if alcohol is being served. This results in some restaurants kicking kids out at 8 and others completely stopping alcohol service at this time.

It is claimed that the Glasgow Tower is the only structure on Earth with the ability to rotate 360 degrees to face into the prevailing wind. The Tower is listed in Guinness World Records as the tallest, fully rotating, freestanding structure.

Glasgow hosted the first international football game between two different countries, Scotland and England in 1872. (See Bishop Aukland)

The Whyte and MacKay whisky company, now owned by a Philippines-based organisation, has its headquarters in Glasgow. The phrase 'The Real McCoy' is a corruption of 'The Real MacKay', coming from the Glaswegian phrase 'a drop of the real MacKay'. (See Grangemouth)

The nursery scenes in the children's TV series 'Balamory' are actually filmed in Glasgow with children from four of the city's nurseries taking time off each week to visit the Balamory Nursery. (See Tobermory)

Gourock, Renfrewshire
The name of this town comes from a Gaelic word meaning 'pimple'. The Pimple is a hill close to the town.

A flight of steps leads from the main shopping street to St John's Church at the top of the hill. On the way climbers pass Granny Kempock Stone. This is a megalithic stone which sailors used to walk around for luck prior to a long voyage and couples about to be married walked around seven times hoping for a similar helping of good fortune.

Grangemouth, Stirling and Falkirk
Grangemouth grew around a port which is why natives are known as Portonians.
The renowned Soap Works was demolished in 2005 to be replaced by the much more desirable Whyte and Mackay blending and bottling plant. (See Glasgow)

The Grangemouth Refinery is the only crude oil refinery in Scotland and one of only six in Europe.

Grantown-on-Spey, Moray
None of the churches in the town has a burial ground. There are two cemeteries away from the churches. Inverllan is the original burial ground which is now only available to those who own an existing plot. Local people refer to Grantown as the New Cemetery even though it has been used since early in the 20th century.

Greenock, Renfrewshire
The most obvious landmark in Greenock is the Italianate tower of the Municipal Buildings which could have been lifted straight out of Venice. The tower was completed in 1886 after a competition won by architects H & D Barclay. Although it has never been officially admitted as the reason for their design being the winner, it is interesting to note that the tower is one metre taller than that of the Glasgow City Chambers. The town was left in debt after paying £197,061 to construct the Municipal Buildings, a debt that wasn't cleared until 1952.

Greenock's most famous son is undoubtedly engineer James Watt who was born here in 1736.

The BBC drama series 'Waterloo Road' was relocated to Greenock from Rochdale. (See Rochdale)

Gretna Green, Dumfries

In 1754 Lord Hardwicke's Marriage Act came into force in England and Wales making it possible for a parent to object to the marriage of an offspring under the age of 21. In Scotland it was still possible for boys to marry at 14 and girls at 12 so long as two witnesses were present. The construction of a toll road made Gretna Green the most easily reached village across the Scottish border. In 1856 Scottish law was changed requiring 21 days' residence prior to marriage, this residential requirement was dropped in 1977. The age for marriage was increased to 16 for both parties in 1929.

Weddings were conducted at the Famous Blacksmith's Shop and Gretna Hall Historic Marriage House. Gretna is still looked upon as a romantic venue for marriages.

Haddington, East Lothian

The Royal Burgh of Haddington retains almost all of its historic street plan.

The town has a much-photographed statue of two fighting goats. Since the 13th century the goat has been Haddington's seal or coat-of-arms. There is no accepted reason for the town's connection with goats so I cannot explain why athletes take part in an annual Goats Gallop or why there is a Goatfield housing estate.

Halkirk, Caithness

Locals claim that Halkirk was Scotland's first planned village.

Canadians all know of Alexander Keith's beers. Alexander Keith was born in Halkirk in 1795 and in 1817 emigrated to Halifax, Nova Scotia, where he established a brewery in 1820.

Hamilton, Lanarkshire

Originally known as Cadyou or Cadzow, Hamilton gained its current name following the Hamilton family's change of allegiance from England to their support of Robert the Bruce during the Wars of Scottish Independence.

In 1659 building began on Hamilton Palace which became the largest non-royal residence in the Western World. Ground subsidence resulted in the palace being demolished in 1921.

Hamilton Old Parish Church is the only church built by William Adam. Adam was beloved by Scotts who referred to him as their 'Universal Architect'. Someone else described his work as being 'varied to an extreme in degree.'

Hatton, Aberdeenshire
Sometimes known as Hatton of Cruden, this village was once the home of Simmers who supplied their biscuits to the likes of Marks and Spencer.

Hawick, Roxburgh, Ettrick and Lauderdale
Hawick (pronounced Hoyk) claims to be the furthest town from the sea in Scotland. The furthest point from the sea can be disputed according to whether or not lochs and estuaries are taken into consideration. (See Pitlochry. See Coton in the Elms)

At the end of Hawick High Street stands an equestrian statue which locals know as Ken. Ken the Horse has his own Facebook page.

Heck, Dumfries and Galloway
Heck is a small village not known for very much at all, but what the heck?

The rock band named Heck are not from Heck. (See Nottingham)

Helensburgh, Dunbartonshire
In 2015 Colquhoun Square was redesigned as an outdoor museum. Around 120 plinths were originally intended to direct the traffic but it is planned for the plinths to be filled with objects, or replicas of objects, associated with the town's past. Plinths currently in use include two displaying items associated with

previous residents of Helensburgh. The bell from Henry Bell's paddle steamer Comet and the puppet seen in John Logie Baird's first TV broadcast.

Helmsdale, Sutherland
The Earl of Sutherland and his Countess, Marie Seton, were poisoned by Isobel Sinclair in 1567 at the historic Helmsdale Castle. What was left of Helmsdale Castle was demolished in the 1970s as it stood in the way of the A9 road bridge.
David Mackay joined Virgin Galactic in 2009. His suborbital flights as a test pilot on an SS2 (Space Ship 2) made him the 569th person into space and the first Scots-born astronaut.

Hilton, Inverness
During post-war years a large number of council houses were built in this village which has now been swallowed-up by the city of Inverness.

Holywood, Dumfries and Galloway
The 'wood' part of the name of the village refers to an oak copse and it is thought the 'Holy' part refers to a disciple of Saint Mungo called Convallus.

Anyone with the ability to count will note that the nearby Twelve Apostles stone circle consists of eleven stones.

Houston, Renfrewshire
The symbol of this village is a Celtic cross dating back to the 8th century. This was moved from its original position near the Mill of Barochan to a site close to the village centre but has now been relocated to Paisley Abbey to protect it from further weathering.

Humbie, East Lothian
In 1939 a Luftwaffe bomber crashed near Humble

after becoming the first German aircraft to be shot down by the RAF over British soil. It is referred to locally as the Humbie Heinkel.

Huntly, Aberdeenshire
Huntly stands on the River Bogie and was once known as Milton of Strathbogie.

Huntly is the historic home of the Gordon Highlanders regiment. Dean's delicious shortbread, available in most British supermarkets, is baked here.

Prime Minister David Cameron's father, Ian, was born at Blairmore House.

I

Invergarry, Inverness-shire
The River Garry flows into Loch Oich at Invergarry in the Great Glen.

Invergordon, Ross and Cromarty
During the 1970s and 80s nearby Nigg became known for the construction of oil rigs which could be seen lined up in the Cromarty Firth awaiting repair.

The deep water port allows cruise liners to dock here with many of their passengers taking coach tours of the Highlands.

Tourists come to Invergordon to see the many murals, seventeen at the most recent count, depicting the history of the town.

Invergordon's distillery produces the grain whisky found in many internationally known blends.

Invermoriston, Craic
In 1813 Thomas Telford built a bridge here crossing the River Moriston Falls. Traffic now uses the newer bridge, constructed in the 1930s but tourists still visit Telford's bridge for the views and glimpses of salmon leaping.

Spectacular views of the Great Glen can be enjoyed from the hill above the village, Sròn Na Muic in Gaelic, which translates into English as Nose of the Pig.

Inverness, Inverness-shire
Inverness, the Capital of the Highlands, didn't become a city until 2001, unlike other cities it has no officially defined boundaries. It is the most northerly city in the UK.

In 1921 the first Cabinet Meeting outside London took place at Inverness Town House. Prime Minister, David Lloyd George, was taking a holiday at Gairloch when Ireland rejected the King and Empire. As his deputy was at nearby Beaufort and King George V was on a shooting holiday at Moy, the Prime Minister called the meeting in Inverness.

In Shakespeare's 'Scottish Play' King Duncan is murdered by Macbeth as he descends into madness at Inverness Castle.

Inveraray, Argyll and Bute
Inveraray's coat of arms depicts a net in which five herrings are entangled. The Latin motto, 'Semper Tibi Pendeat Halec' allegedly translates into English as 'May a herring always hang to your pants.' A classics scholar translated this for me as 'Always have your herring', Latin for herring being either Halec or Alec, so if your name is Alec you now know what it means!

Inveraray Jail is advertised as 'One of the finest tourist attractions in Scotland.'

(See Inverurie)

Inverurie, Aberdeenshire
Inverurie used to be spelled Inverury but with increased use of the postal service many letters for this town were ending up on the opposite coast at the similarly spelled Inveraray (See Inveraray). To avoid

confusion the town council changed the spelling to Inverurie which was officially accepted in 1866.I can find no records to show if the postal service improved after this change of spelling.

Aberdeenshire is divided into six Committee Areas. One such area is Garioch and Inverurie is known as the Heart of the Garioch.

Isle of Arran, Ayrshire and Arran

Being divided into Highland and Lowland, the Isle of Arran is known as Scotland in Miniature.

Lochranza Castle, Arran, was the model for the castle in Tintin's adventure 'The Black Island.'

No matter what some local knitwear sellers might try to tell you, Aran sweaters (only one 'r') have nothing whatsoever to do with the Isle of Arran, they originated in the Irish group of Aran Islands.

Natives of Arran are known as Arranachs. (Note: that is not anoraks)

Isle of Harris, Western Isles

In 1968 Harris stood in for Jupiter in the movie '2001: A Space Odyssey.'

In 1998 Tony Blair became the first serving Prime Minister to visit the Outer Hebrides when he opened the Scalpay Bridge to replace the ferry service from Harris to Scalpay. (See Isle of Lewis)

Isle of Islay, Argyll and Bute

Islay is the southernmost of the Inner Hebrides and is known as the Queen of the Hebrides.

There are nine distilleries on Islay the more famous being Laphroaig, Ardbeg and Bowmore.

Isle of Lewis, Western Isles

Harris and Lewis are actually one island, known as the Long Island, despite the two locations claiming to be two totally separate land masses. Lewis and Harris is Scotland's largest island and is the third largest of the British Isles after Great Britain and the island of Ireland.

The Butt of Lewis, the most northerly spot on the island, is recorded as being the windiest location in the UK.

Isle of Mull, Argyll and Bute

Tourism in Mull has seen a considerable boost thanks to its fame as the location for the children's TV series, 'Balamory.' (See Tobermory)

Isle of Mull cheese is actually a type of Cheddar.

Isle of Skye, Ross and Cromarty

Skye has approximately ten sheep (100,000) for every human resident (10,000). Portree, Skye's largest town and capital, has a population of just 2,000.

Locals will inform you that you will be granted eternal beauty if you put your face into the water under the old Sligachan Bridge for seven seconds then let it dry naturally. It might be unkind to suggest that it's immediately obvious that many of the 10,000 natives have either not followed this procedure, or it just doesn't work.

J

Jamestown, Dunbartonshire
Estate agents have started treating Jamestown as part of Balloch.

Jamestown, Fife
The northern approach to the Forth Bridge is the Jamestown Viaduct.

Jedburgh, Roxburgh, Ettrick and Lauderdale
The Scots name for Jedburgh became part of the expression 'Jeddart Justice' whereby a man was hanged prior to his trial.

There is some dispute as to whether or not Mary, Queen of Scots, actually stayed in the building now a museum known as Queen Mary's House.

Jemimaville, Ross and Cromarty
Tourists come here to watch dolphins jumping around in the bay. They are said to go through this performance every day but please do not take my word for it and beware, the village is seven miles from the closest shop.

John O'Groats, Caithness
John O'Groats takes its name from a 16th century Dutch immigrant called Jan de Groot. Jan had seven offspring who constantly argued over their precedence. Jan solved the problem by building an octagonal house with eight doors so he and each of his family could leave or enter at the same time. He sorted out who sat at the head of the table by creating an octagonal table. This unusual building stood on the

mound close to what is now the John O'Groats House Hotel.

Natives of John O'Groats are known as Groaters. (See Land's End)

Johnsonshaven, Aberdeenshire

A coastal village where flax, sailmaking and fishing were of historic importance.

Johnstone, Renfrewshire

In 2008 Johnstone History Museum opened, it was the world's first museum inside a supermarket.

Chef Gordon Ramsay was born in Johnstone as was serial killer Peter Tobin.

Johnstonbridge, Dumphries and Galloway

Scottish drivers best know Johnstonbridge as the location of the Annandale Motorway Services on the A74(M).

Joppa, Edinburgh

Seawater was once evaporated to produce salt at Joppa Pans.

The first enemy casualties of the Second World War to be buried on British soil were interred at St Philips Church in 1939 after two German pilots were shot down during a daytime raid to bomb British warships at Rosyth.

Jordanhill, Glasgow

There are a basketball player and a singer called Jordan Hill but neither has any connection with this town of mostly terraced houses.

Juniper Green, Edinburgh
Juniper Green was officially absorbed into the City of Edinburgh in 1920. Its main industries were the manufacture of snuff and paper.

Jura, Argyll and Bute
Pap is a slang word for breast and the hills called the Paps of Jura do indeed look like a pair of breasts. They are the subject of William McTaggart's 1902 painting, 'The Paps of Jura', which can be seen in the Kelvingrove Gallery.

Jura is Scotland's 8th largest island but with a population of only 196 in the latest census it comes 31st on the population list.

George Orwell completed 'Nineteen Eighty-Four' here. It is on Jura that the band KLF famously burned £1 million of banknotes.

K

Keith, Banffshire
Sounds painful but Keith is split into three distinct parts. Keith Old Town is where the original settlement was established in the 12th century, Fife Keith was once a separate town and Keith is the modern main commercial area.

Anyone called Keith might not be so delighted to learn that their name, and the name of this town, is said to come from a Celtic word meaning 'wood.'

With three distilleries, Keith is the starting point of the Scottish Malt Whisky Trail.

Kelso, Roxburgh, Ettrick and Lauderdale
From 1881 to 1982 Kelso held the record for the UK's lowest January temperature at -26.7 C. From 1879 to 1995 it also held the December record.

Locals boast of having roses in their gardens which sprang from cuttings taken from a bush planted in the town by Charles Edward Stuart, the Young Pretender, in 1745. In Roxburgh Street the outline of a horseshoe can be seen on the pavement which is said to be where Charles' horse cast a shoe as he rode through the town on his way to Carlisle.

Sir Walter Scott attended Kelso Grammar School for six months in 1783 whilst staying with his Aunt Jenny. It is at the school he met James and John Ballantyne who joined him as business partners and went on to print his books.

Kenmore, Perth and Kinross
Kenmore Hotel originated as a tavern, built in around 1500, and has a strong claim to be the oldest inn in Scotland. (See Tweedsmuir)

Kilmarnock, Ayrshire and Arran
Kilmarnock is known to many people outside Scotland only because its football club, the oldest professional club in Scotland, is mentioned during the football results.

Kilmarnock has a museum and library called the Dick Institute.

Charlie and Craig Reid, The Proclaimers, have a song titled 'The Joyful Kilmarnock Blues.' 'Ballroom Blitz' by The Sweet was inspired by a performance the band gave at Kilmarnock Grand Hall when the crowd drove them off stage by pelting them with bottles. In 2006 Kilmarnock was voted the UK's Friendliest Shopping Town.

Kilmore, Ross and Cromarty
Kilmore is on the Isle of Skye's Sleat Peninsula and most locations in the village take the name Sleat. There is a Sleat Medical Centre, Sleat Parish Church and it is the home of the clan MacDonald of Sleat.

Kincraig, Perth and Kinross
Kincraig was once called Boat of Insh as the ferry across the Spey, close to Loch Insh, operated here. The name was changed when the ferry became redundant due to the building of a bridge in 1871.

Kingussie, Inverness-shire
Kingussie Camanachd Shinty team was listed in

the Guinness Book of Records as the world's most successful sports team of all time having won 20 consecutive league titles and for remaining unbeaten for four years in the 1990s. Despite all of this success and a 2014 win in the Camanachd Cup the team was narrowly saved from relegation in 2015 by a play-off victory against Kilmallie.

Kingussie is mentioned in Compton Mackenzie's comic novel 'The Monarch of the Glen' with the 'Monarch of the Glen' TV series being filmed here. The village also features in 'Slumdog Millionaire.' (See Laggan)

Kinloch Rannoch, Perth and Kinross
Kinloch (Ceann Loch) means the end of the loch and usually indicates a location at the end where the water flows out. It is, therefore, self explanatory that this Kinloch is at the end of Loch Rannoch.

Locals will tell you that the bridge over the River Tummel is the work of Thomas Telford. However, a plaque on the bridge gives its date as 1764 when Telford was only seven years old.

Kinlochbervie, Sutherland
For the meaning of the name see Kinloch Rannoch and you will then be quite correct if you assume that this village stands at the end of Loch Bervie.

Kinlochbervie was shortlisted by the Oxford Dictionary as a definition for the word 'remote.'

This is the most northerly port on the west coast of Scotland. Morrison is the most common surname here and the locals are known as Greeks for reasons lost in time.

Kinross, Perth and Kinross
T in the Park rock festivals were held at the former Balado airfield, Kinross, from 1997 to 2014. Although there are those who believe the T stood for a hot drink from India and China, the T actually stood for Tennent's, the sponsoring brewery. (See Motherwell)

Kippen, Stirling
The Kippen Vinery closed in 1964. Until then it was famous as the location of the Kippen Vine which grew to become the largest in the world. This tourist attraction covered an area of 5,000 square feet and was housed in four large greenhouses.

Kirkcaldy, Fife
Kirkcaldy is known as the Lang Toun (Long Town). In the 16th century the town had a 0.9 mile main street which eventually grew to a length of over 4 miles.

Kirkcaldy became the world's top producer of linoleum. The town had long been a manufacturer of linen cloth which was later covered with materials such as pine resin to form the floor covering.

Raith Rovers Football Club is based here.

Former Prime Minister Gordon Brown was brought up in the town. Coldplay bass guitarist Guy Berryman was born and brought up here as was World Champion darts player John Thomas Wilson, known to all as Jocky.

Kircudbright, Kirkudbrightshire
Billy Marshall's gravestone in St Cuthbert's churchyard says he died in 1792 at the age of 120. If

this is correct it would make him Britain's oldest man.

John Paul Jones, known as the father of the American Navy, was detained in the town's Tollbooth jail after landing at Kircudbright where he stole the Earl of Selkirk's silver. The Tollbooth is now an arts centre.

The Stewartry Museum displays what it claims is Britain's oldest sports trophy. The Siller (Silver) Gun was presented to the winner of a shooting competition in 1587 by King James VI. (See Musselburgh)

Although the movie 'The Wickerman' sets its action on a small island, much of it was actually filmed in Kirkudbright.

Kirkwall, Orkney
Kirkwall is the largest island town in Scotland.

The kirk at Kirkwall is an 11th century church dedicated to Norwegian Saint Olaf.

Kirkwall is one of several places in Scotland to host an annual Ba Game. A rough and tumble game of football played in the streets usually on Christmas Day and New Year's Day.

Kyle of Lochalsh, Ross and Cromarty
Kyle of Lochalsh is almost precisely 500 miles due north of Land's End.

The village is situated opposite Kyleakin on the Isle of Skye. The two villages were connected by ferry prior to the opening of the Skye Bridge, about a mile away, in 1995.

Kyleakin, Ross and Cromarty

Situated on the Isle of Skye, Kyleakin is the site of Castle Moil. Local legend claims this castle was built to replace an earlier castle erected for a Norwegian princess known as Saucy Mary. Mary allegedly charged a toll for boats using the channel between Skye and the mainland. She had a chain placed across the strait to prevent anyone from crossing without payment. The Saucy nickname came about because she thanked the crews of boats who paid the toll by flashing her breasts at them.

L

Laggan, Invernes
Parts of the TV series, 'Monarch of the Glen' were filmed in Laggan. (See Kingussie)

The Laggan Communities website calls this 'The Centre of Scotland.' (See Loch Garry. See Schiehallion. See Newtonmore)

Largs, Ayrshire and Arran
I visited Nardini's having been told this was Scotland's most famous cafe. It is hard to define 'most famous' but I must acknowledge their ice cream is pretty special.

Brisbane in Australia is named after Sir Thomas Brisbane who lived and died in Largs.

Largs stages an annual festival to mark the town's historic links with the Vikings.

Lasswade, Midlothian
Lasswade claims to be the most ancient parish in Scotland with evidence that the burial ground was in use as early as the 9th century.

Lauder, Berwickshire
The Lauder Common Riding is held annually on the first Saturday in August. Highlights of the event include Election of the Cornet who leads the ride. The Cornet gets to select his own Lass and he serves for one year then becomes the Right Hand Man for a year and serves a further year as Left Hand Man. (See Selkirk)

If you got confused by all that, further bafflement arises for the uninitiated due to the Common Riding's requirement for a Lady Busser and a Wreath Giver.

Laurencekirk, Kincardineshire
Laurencekirk was always a sleepy town but it became even sleepier when by-passed in 1985.

Snuff takers will know of the Laurencekirk hinge, an airtight construction on a snuff box, invented here by James Sandy.

Lerwick, Shetland
Lerwick is the capital and main port of the Shetland Islands. It is the most northerly and most easterly town in Scotland. (See Peterhead)

Leuchars, Fife
RAF Leuchars was used for ballooning prior to the establishment of Montrose Air Station coming into operation so can claim to be Britain's oldest military aviation facility. (See Montrose)

Leven, Fife
Leven's beaches are a tourist attraction which accounts for the town's caravan parks, guest houses and hotels. The promenade is part of the Fife Coastal Path.

Coal mining collapsed here in 1969 and to compound Leven's problems the railway link was closed in the same year. At the time of writing the Kingdom of Fife Railway Preservation Society is showing interest in re-establishing the railway as a heritage line.

Linlithgow, West Lothian
Linlithgow was once West Lothian's county town.

Linlithgow Palace, now in ruins, was the birthplace of James V (1512) and Mary, Queen of Scots (1542).

Livingston, West Lothian
Livingston was built as part of the 1946 New Towns Act to relocate people from the overcrowding in Glasgow.

The Almondvale Shopping Centre is named after the River Almond which flows through the town.

(See West Calder)

Linwood, Renfrewshire
The Hillman Avenger and Sunbeam cars were built here. The Proclaimers' song 'Letter From America' refers to the closure of the car factory, 'Linwood no more'. (See Bathgate)

Loch Awe, Argyll and Bute
Loch Awe is obviously the name of a loch, the longest freshwater loch in Scotland, but also of a village on the loch's banks. The village is alternatively known as Lochawe.

Tourist are attracted here for the trout fishing.

Loch Garry, Inverness-shire
If you drive along the A87 keep your eyes open and your camera ready for the lookout point from which the view shows Loch Garry to have the same outline as Scotland has on a map.

In 2002, using the centre of gravity method, whereby

a cardboard cut-out of Scotland is balanced on a pin, the exact centre of Scotland was calculated to be close to Loch Garry. (See Laggan, Schiehallion and Newtonmore)

Loch Lomond, Stirling/Argyll and Bute/West Dunbartonshire

Carved out by glaciers Loch Lomond sits on the Highland Boundary Fault and is considered to be the boundary between the Lowlands of Central Scotland and the Highlands.

The Loch includes 30+ islands, Inchmurrin being the largest island set in freshwater in Britain.

Loch Lomond attracts thousands of tourists each year, many admit to having first been attracted here by the old song 'On The Bonnie Banks o' Loch Lomond.'

Loch Ness, Inverness-shire

Loch Ness is the most voluminous lake in the UK containing more water than all the lakes in England and Wales combined but Loch Lomond is bigger by area and Loch Morar is deeper. The water remains at a temperature of 6C year round.

Visitors are unlikely to catch a glimpse of the legendary monster but the Corrimony chambered burial cairn is worth a visit.

Some guides will tell you that the only island in the loch is Cherry Island. This is not an island, it is a man-made crannog, and it isn't called Cherry, it's actual name is Eileen Mhuireach or Murdoch's Island.

During futile searches for the monster divers have found thousands of golf balls.

Lochcarron, Ross and Cromarty
Lochcarron is a group of small villages along the sea loch, Loch Carron.

The company Lochcarron of Scotland claims to be the country's leading manufacturer of tartan.

Loch Ryan, Wigtown
(See Stranraer)

Lochearnhead, Stirling and Falkirk
As its name suggests, the village is on the banks at the head of Loch Earn. Villagers claim a water horse, each-uisge, lives in the loch from where it entices people to climb on its back. The creature's neck is said to be so sticky that the victim cannot release his/her hands and is dragged beneath the water to drown. The loch does have very strong and unpredictable tides which could have brought about this legend.

One of Britain's largest sheep shearing competitions takes place at Lochearnhead each June.

Lochgilphead, Argyll and Bute
Although hardly heard of outside Scotland, since 1975 Lochgilphead has been the administrative centre of Argyll and Bute.

Lochgilphead features in the James Bond movie, 'From Russia with Love.' During filming the rushes were viewed in the local cinema.

Lochinver, Sutherland
Lochinver is Scotland's second largest fishing port. (See Port Seton)

Lochinver features in Oscar Marzaroli's 1973 documentary film, 'The Highlands and Islands,' about a visit by Prince Charles to Scotland.

Lochmaddy, Western Isles
Lochmaddy is the main ferry port and administrative centre of North Uist in the Outer Hebrides.

Lockerbie, Dumfriesshire
It will be impossible for Lockerbie ever to shake off its tragic notoriety as the village devastated by the wreckage of Pan Am Flight 103 when it was blasted out of the sky on 21st December 1988.

In 1593 Clan Johnstone fought Clan Maxwell at the Battle of Dryfe Sands, two miles to the west of Lockerbie. The Johnstones practically exterminated the Maxwells leading to the expression 'Lockerbie Lick', meaning a downward sword cut delivered from horseback to the head of enemy foot soldiers. It is recorded that one fighting warrior at this bloody battle was Robert Johnstone, aged eleven.

Lossiemouth, Moray
This was originally the port for Elgin.

James Ramsay MacDonald, the first Labour Prime Minister, was born in Lossiemouth, the illegitimate son of a farm labourer, John MacDonald and a housemaid, Anne Ramsay.

Just outside Lossiemouth is Gordonstoun School. Gordonstoun is famous for former pupils Prince Philip the Duke of Edinburgh and his son Prince Charles. Charles made news by escaping to a local pub and being caught drinking cherry brandy while underage. Gordonstoun School has the only UK fire service that can employ under 18-year-olds and also a very rare circular square.

M

Macduff, Banffshire

Originally a settlement by the name of Doune (meaning hillfort) the place was purchased in 1733 by William Duff, the first Earl of Fife. The second Earl built the harbour in 1783 and renamed what had now become a burgh after Macduff, the character from Shakespeare's 'Macbeth' who was almost certainly fictional but who James Duff maintained was his ancestor.

Macduff was the last place in the UK still building deep-water wooden fishing boats.

Mallaig, Inverness-shire

In the 1840s Lord Lovat divided up one of his farms into seventeen areas and encouraged tenants to move to the western area of the peninsula, Mallaig, to take up fishing.

Mallaig is at the end of the West Island railway line and the Hogwarts Express is seen at the Mallaig station in the Harry Potter films. The West Island Line was voted the world's top railway journey by readers of the Wanderlust travel magazine in 2009.

Maybole, Ayrshire and Arran

Culzean Castle, near Maybole, became Scotland's first Countryside Park in 1969. The castle contains a six-bedroomed flat, known as the National Guest Flat, given to General Eisenhower to use whenever he wanted for the rest of his life as a gesture of thanks for the USA's part in World War Two.

Melrose, Roxburgh, Ettrick and Lauderdale
Melrose is known worldwide as the birthplace of Rugby Sevens. Greenyards hosts the Melrose Sevens each year on the second Saturday in April.
The Eildon Hills which overlook the town are said to be the final resting place of King Arthur. (See Glastonbury. See Dolgellau. See South Cadbury. See Tintagel. See Carmarthen)

Milton, Everywhere
Scotland has seven Miltons, in Moray, Dumfries and Galloway, Perth and Kinross, Stirlingshire, Glasgow, Highland and Dunbartonshire. Plus a further 14 Miltons with additions such as Milton of Balgonie and Milton of Cultoquhey. Milton quite obviously means Mill Town.

Milton of Balgonie, Fife
The village is well worth a visit for the nearby Balgonie Castle and the ruins of Balfour House an occasional residence of Mary, Queen of Scots. (See Windygates)

Moffat, Dumfries
A hollow in the hills to the North of the town was used by members of Clan Moffat and later by Clan Johnstone to hoard cattle they had stolen. The hollow is known as The Devil's Beef Tub.

Since the 17th century Moffat has been a spa town thanks to its sulphur-smelling water. Robbie Burns came here, allegedly for the water but was known to frequent the inns with the Black Bull being a favourite.

Moffat Toffee, available from the Moffat Toffee Shop, is not a chewy confection but a hard, boiled sweet.

Moniaive, Dumfries and Galloway
Almost all of the towns and villages in this book are twinned with one or more locations, usually of a similar size to themselves and usually at some distant spot on another continent. In 2020 the powers that be in Moniaive cancelled plans to twin with a town in Europe due to uncertainty following Brexit. The Moniaive Twinning Association took the decision to twin with Penpont. Penpont is 6.2 miles down the road from Moniaive.

The Community Council described this as ' a perfect solution' with visits between the twinned villages involving no more than a short bus trip. At the time of writing the formal twinning ceremony was on hold due to Coronavirus but there were plans to bury a time capsule.

Montrose, Angus
The Montrose Air Station, which is now a Heritage Centre, claims to be the oldest operational military airfield in Britain. The Royal Flying Corps founded the airfield in 1913. (See Leuchars)

Montrose has the widest High Street in Scotland. (See Stockton-on-Tees. See Marlborough)

Motherwell, Lanarkshire
T in the Park music festival was held in nearby Strathclyde Park until 1996. (See Kinross) Next to the park is the popular M & D's Amusement Park with its four roller coasters.

The North Lanarkshire Heritage Centre, formerly the Motherwell Heritage Centre, is next to the railway station and displays items covering the history of the town from Roman times.

Muirhead, Angu
Muirhead is invariably listed as one half of a village-duo along with Birkhill.

Templeton Woods is home to one of the UK's largest populations of red squirrels.

Locals call the small hill close to the villages The Round and the pub/restaurant is known as the Birkie Inn.

There are other villages called Muirhead in Fife, North Lanarkshire and South Ayrshire.

Mull of Kintyre, Argyl and Bute
The British Board of Film Classification denies that it ever applied the legendary Mull of Kintyre Test to movies it reviewed. Allegedly the test was the guideline as to whether or not an image of a penis could be shown in a film. It is claimed that, under requirements of the test, an erect penis could not be depicted if the angle it rose from the vertical was more elevated than that of the Kintyre peninsula as seen on a map.

It is said the test was first applied to the movie 'Caligula' released in 1979, two years after Paul McCartney and Wings scored the Christmas number one with a song named after the location of McCartney's Scottish home. 'Mull of Kintyre' was the first single to sell over two million copies in the UK. The song is still the UK's biggest-selling, completely non-charity single, of all time.

Murrayfield, Edinburgh
The Murrayfield area of Edinburgh is best known

for its stadium, home of the Scottish national rugby squad. Close to the stadium is the Murrayfield Ice Rink and a Lawn Tennis Club.

Musselburgh, East Lothian
This is the only town in the book named after a shellfish.

The Royal Company of Archers compete annually for the Musselburgh Silver Arrow which is claimed to be the oldest sporting trophy in the UK. The arrow dates back to 1603. (See Kirkudbright)

N

Nairn, Nairn
Actress Tilda Swinton lives here, she generated worldwide publicity for the town when she inaugurated 'The Ballerina Ballroom Cinema of Dreams,' a film festival held in the Nairn Public Hall.

Charlie Chaplin took annual holidays at the Newton Hotel, Nairn, and a street is named after former Deputy Prime Minister Willie Whitelaw who was born in the town.

Ness, Western Isles
Ness consists of a group of villages in the north of the Isle of Lewis. 75% of the population can speak Scottish Gaelic.

Gannet is considered to be a delicacy here and each year ten men sail from Ness to the island of Sula Sgier where they live for two weeks harvesting as many as 2,000 young gannets which are known locally as Guga.

Netherton, Lanarkshire
Scotland's national soft drink, Irn Bru, was once bottled here.

There are also Nethertons in Glasgow, Stirling and Perth and Kinross.

Nevis, Inverness-shire
There's a river Nevis a Nevis Gorge and a Glen Nevis but most come here to view or climb Britain's highest

mountain, (1,344.527 m / 4,411.18 ft), Ben Nevis, known to locals as The Ben.

The summit of Ben Nevis is the collapsed dome of an ancient volcano but very few of the 100,000 or so who ascend to this point each year are aware of that fact. The ruined building at the summit was an observatory in use from 1883 to 1904.

At the foot of the mountain can be found the Ben Nevis Distillery.

Newport-on-Tay, Fife
From the 1700s until completion of the Tay Road Bridge in 1966 a ferry service connected Newport-on-Tay to Dundee and for a time the town was known as New Dundee.

At the bottom of Boat Hill can be seen the former ferry terminal buildings and slipways, now used as a boat repair yard.

Newton Stewart, Wigtownshire
Known as the Gateway to the Galloway Hills, the New Town of Stewart was founded in the 17th century by William Stewart.

In 1329, whilst on a pilgrimage to the shrine of St Ninian at Whithorn, Robert the Bruce forded the river at the point where the bridge now stands. The bridge was built in 1813 to a design by John Rennie the Elder. An older bridge, opened in 1745, was destroyed by flooding in 1806.

'The Wicker Man' was mostly filmed on location around Newton Stewart.

Newtonmore, Inverness-shire
A stone set in a wall close to the village claims this to be the exact centre of Scotland. A similar claim is made by nearby Loch Garry, Schiehallion and by Laggan. (See Laggan. See Loch Garry. See Schiehallion))

North Berwick, East Lothian
The North Berwick Witch Trials took place from 1590 to 92. At least 70 people were tried. Many were tortured until they confessed then burnt at the stake. Shakespeare adapted aspects of the trials in 'Macbeth', the trials inspired Burns' 'Tam o' Shanter.' Mollie Hunter's novel for young adults, 'The Thirteenth Member', is based on the trials

Two sandy bays made North Berwick a popular destination for visitors from nearby Edinburgh in the 19th century.

O

Oakbank, Perth and Kinross
In 1890 the Sheriff of Edinburgh was petitioned regarding the unsatisfactory sanitary conditions in the village of Oakbank, owned by the Oakbank Oil Company.

Fracking supporters know Oakbank for its Museum of the Scottish Shale Oil Industry.

Oban, Argyll and Bute
Oban is known as the Seafood Capital of Scotland, the town boasts some celebrated fish restaurants.

Oban's official population is just in excess of 8,500 but in the holiday season this is boosted to 25,000+.

In the 18th century Oban was a small group of fishermen's cottages, the town was built around a distillery which is currently listed in the world's top twenty of single malt sales.

Oich Old Bridge of Tilt, Inverness-shire
Bridge of Tilt is a village named after a bridge over the River Oich. English engineer James Dredge designed the bridge using his patented 'taper principle'. The principle is far too complicated to go into here but apparently the bridge looks exactly like a normal suspension bridge but isn't.

Onich, Inverness-shire
St Bride's Church, Onich, is one of only two designed by J Garden Brown who died at the age of 27. Built in

1874 St Bride's Church is noted for its Arts and Crafts interior.

Oronsay, Argyll and Bute
Known as Oransay by the locals this is a small island to the south of Colonsay in the Inner Hebrides.

The 2001 census listed Oronsay as having a population of five but by 2011 this had rocketed up to eight.

The Oronsay air strip is described as 'fighting a losing battle with rabbits'.

Orkney, Orkney
(See Brae)

Ormiscaig, Ross-shire
Ormiscaig is a remote village on the shores of Loch Ewe, the village Mellon Charles is just down the road. Ormiscaig is famed for being close to Mellon Charles and Mellon Charles is famed for being close to Ormiscaig.

Out Skerries, Shetland
Known to the locals as Da Skerries or simply Skerries. The 'Out' part of the name comes from Norse for 'east'. This is an archipelago of islets, the easternmost group of the Shetlands.

Overtown, Lanarkshire
A busy mining village in the 19th century, the population of Overtown declined after the mines closed along with the railways in the 1950s.

P

Paisley, Renfrewshire
Paisley is Scotland's largest town (population 77,210). Although it does not have city status at the time of writing Paisley has put in an application to become the 2021 UK City of Culture. (Stop press: See Coventry)

Since 1987 Paisley has hosted Scotland's biggest annual beer festival.

Paisley Abbey boasts a gargoyle in the shape of the monster from the 1979 movie 'Alien'. It is believed this was carved by a sci-fi fan in the 1990s. The Abbey stood in for Westminster Abbey in the 2008 movie 'Stone of Destiny'.

In 1966 James Goodfellow OBE created the very first PIN number system in Paisley.

Peebles,Tweeddale
Gutterbluid is the name traditionally given to those born in Peebles, a Stoorlift is a resident of Peebles who wasn't born here. There are few genuine modern Gutterbluids as the Peebles Hospital and its maternity unit are closed down.

Lynn Church, some four miles from Peebles, is a Tardis in reverse. The walls are more than a metre thick making it much smaller inside than it appears to be from outside and qualifying it as Scotland's smallest church. (See Dover)

Penpont, Dumfries and Galloway
See Moniaive.

Perth, Perth and Kinross
The early importance of Perth was enhanced by nearby Scone Palace where kings were crowned. (See Scone)

For many years road signs welcomed visitors to the City of Perth but when a new definition of a city was introduced in the 1990s Perth was not included on the list. (See Brechin and Elgin) To celebrate the Queen's Diamond Jubilee then First Minister Alex Salmond led a bid to renew city status and Perth became Scotland's seventh city.

Perth in Australia and Perth in Canada were named after this city.

Peterhead, Aberdeenshire
Peterhead is the most easterly town in mainland Scotland. (See Lerwick)

The statue of a fisherwoman in the town centre is known as Jessie.

Peterhead fishermen traditionally wore blue stockings, locally called moggins, which is why residents of Peterhead are known as Bloo Tooners (Blue Towners) or Bloomogganners.

Bram Stoker began writing 'Dracula' while staying at the Kilmarnock Arms Hotel in Peterhead.

Gavin Sutherland of the Sutherland Brothers folk duo was born here. He is undoubtedly best known for his song 'Sailing' which became an international best seller for Rod Stewart. (See Ellon)

Pitlochry, Perth and Kinross
Pitlochry lays claim to being the furthest place from the sea in Scotland. This depends on what you consider to be the sea, the furthest point differs according to which, if any estuaries and/or lochs, are included in your definition of the sea. (See Hawick. See Coton in the Elms)

Pitlochry's Edradour Distillery is the smallest in mainland Scotland with a production of just 12 casks a week.

Plockton, Ross and Cromarty
The self-styled 'Jewel of the Highlands' probably lives up to its name. Set at the side of Loch Carron most people will recognise this beautiful place as the setting for the TV series 'Hamish Macbeth'.

At the time of my visit there were three hotels with public bars and I found the natives to be extremely friendly. They like pointing out 'the most northerly palm trees' but they're not. (See Torquay. See Scourie)

Port Ellen, Argyll and Bute
Port Ellen is the largest town on Islay.

Most of the distilleries on Islay take their malt from the Port Ellen Maltings. The Port Ellen Distillery started production in the 1820s and closed in 1983.

Port of Menteith, Stirling and Falkirk
Port of Menteith (also known as Loch Inchmahome) is the only settlement of any significance on Lake Menteith, it was originally known simply as Port.

Locals will tell you this is the only Scottish loch

known as a lake but this is not correct, there are several lakes in Scotland. If ice on the lake reaches a thickness of seven inches an outdoor curling tournament, known as a Bonspiel, should take place. The last was held in 1979, one planned for 2010 was abandoned due to health and safety issues.

In 1991 Nick Nairn, at the age of 32, became the youngest Scottish chef to hold a Michelin Star. He operates a cooking school near to his birthplace at Port of Menteith.

Port Seton, East Lothian
(See Cockenzie)
Portree, Ross and Cromarty
Portree is the largest town on Skye and the island's capital. The Portree pier was built by Thomas Telford.

In 1746 Flora MacDonald had her final meeting with Bonnie Prince Charlie at Macnab's Inn, a bar in what is now the Royal Hotel.

In 'Harry Potter' one of the Quiditch teams is the Pride of Portree.

Prestonpans, East Lothian
A Mercat Cross is Scotland's equivalent of the English Market Cross with Prestonpans boasting the only one in Scotland remaining in its original form and location.

Prestonpans styles itself as 'Scotland's Mural Town' with its local history depicted with murals on buildings throughout the location.

In 2010 the Prestonpans Tapestry was unveiled. It is 100ft (30m) longer than the Bayeux Tapestry which, like the Prestonpans piece, is an embroidery not a tapestry. At the time of writing this was the longest such work in the world, it depicts Bonnie Prince Charlie's journey from France, through the Highlands, to victory in the Battle of Prestonpans. The first significant battle in the Jacobite Rising which is also known as the Battle of Gladsmuir.

Tam Paton who managed the Bay City Rollers was born here.

Q

Quaich, Perth and Kinross
There is a Glen Quaich situated on the River Quaich and there is a two-handled drinking bowl called a quaich.

Quarrymill, Perthshire
There have been quarries and mills here since the 14th century. Robert, King of Scots, wrote to the monks of Scone Abbey in 1328 requesting permission to use stone from the quarries for the Kirk of Perth and several bridges.

Stone from Quarrymill was almost certainly used to build nearby Scone Abbey.

It is interesting to note that the Stone of Destiny, now housed in Edinburgh Castle and allegedly the stone on which Jacob laid his head in the book of Genesis, is exactly the same type of stone found in this quarry. (See Perth. See Scone)

Queensferry (South), Edinburgh
South Queensferry also known simply as The Ferry stands opposite North Queensferry across the Firth of Forth.

South Queensferry stages an annual Burry Man procession in which a man covered from head to foot in burrs from the burdock plant walks through the town assisted by two men in normal clothes and fortified by tots (or should that be lots?) of whisky.

Queensferry (North), Fife
North Queensferry is the southernmost settlement in Fife and, like South Queensferry, stands close to the Forth Bridge and Forth Road Bridge.

North Queensferry boasts one of Britain's most spectacular public aquariums, Deepseaworld.

Former Prime Minister, Gordon Brown, lives in North Queensferry.

Quoich, Inverness-shire
Quoich is the name of a loch and a river but best known to tourists for the Linn of Quoich. The Linn is a waterfall at a point where the River Quoich flows through a narrow ravine crossed by a bridge at its narrowest point.

R

Rabbit Islands
Not officially in a Lieutenancy Area as the three islands are uninhabited. The islands take their name thanks to the sandy soil which is favoured by rabbits.

Ramsburn, Moray
Research for Ramsburn turned up a wedding planner, septic tank repairer, tooth implanter, skip hire and an accountant.

Ramscraig, Caithness
Ramscraig is a scattered group of crofts 2 miles to the southwest of Dunbeath.

Ratagan, Ross and Cromarty
Ratagan is a hamlet situated on the shore of Loch Duich, a sea loch in Lochalsh.

Ratagan boasts a Youth Hostel with superb views towards Skye.

Ravenscraig, Lanarkshire
Ravenscraig is currently in the process of major redevelopment and is due to become a New Town. This was the site of the largest hot strip steel mill in western Europe, the mill closed in 1992.

At the time of writing, prior to redevelopment, Ravenscraig includes a derelict site the area of 700 football pitches.

Redford, Edinburgh
A suburb of Edinburgh, Redford is best known for the Redford Barracks

Renfrew, Renfrewshire
Celebrated as the Cradle of the Royal Stewarts thanks to its link with the former royal house. The Stewarts were based at the former Renfrew Castle which was the site of the Battle of Renfrew in 1164.

The Castle was demolished in the 18th century with the stone being used to build a soap factory. The castle is said to have stood on a mound in what is now Castlehill Gardens but a 1997 archaeological dig found no evidence of this.

Renfrew attracts shoppers to the Braehead shopping centre and its connected leisure facilities. When first opened in 1999 Braehead was the subject of a boundary dispute between Glasgow and Renfrewshire as the council boundary went straight through the middle of the complex. A Local Government Boundary Commission ruled that the boundary should be redrawn to place the entire shopping centre in Renfrew.

Roberton, Roxburgh, Ettrick and Lauderdale
Roberton is situated by Ale Water which isn't as interesting as it sounds, (See Beer) it is a tributary of the River Teviot which flows through the Alemoor Loch.

Half a mile from the village stands the Borthwick Mains Symbol Stone. This is a 1.5 metre-high stone bearing a carving of a fish, said to be a salmon. Locals will tell you that the stone is very ancient, probably 6th or 7th century, but evidence suggests it is a much more recent creation.

Rosebank, Lanarkshire
One of the least-populated settlements in southern Lanarkshire, Rosebank is renowned as the home of the largest independent garden centre in the Clyde Valley.

Rosewell, Midlothian
The village was established around a colliery in the mid to late 19th century by mining engineer Archibald Hood.

Whitehill House, half a mile to the south-east of the village was a hospital for children with learning difficulties. The nuns and their pupils were visited by Pope John Paul II in 1982. The house is now privately owned and boasts a 20-hole golf course.

Roslin, Midlothian
Formerly known as Roskelyn, Rosslyn or Roslyn, the village was painted by J M W Turner, Wordsworth penned a poem whilst sheltering from a storm in the chapel, his sister Dorothy wrote, ' I never passed through a more delicious dell than the glen of Rosslyn' but William Morris said the landscape was 'much spoiled by the misery of Scotch building and a manufactory or two.'

Roybridge, Inverness-shire
Okay so you've probably already guessed that Roybridge is where the River Roy was crossed by a bridge. To be specific it is at the point where the Roy meets the River Spean.

Mary MacKillop's parents lived here before emigrating to Australia. She was beatified in 1995 and canonised in 2010 to become the first Australian recognised as a saint by the Catholic Church, St Mary of the Cross. St Margaret's Church in Roybridge has a shrine dedicated to her.

S

St Andrews, Fife

St Andrew was a fisherman and the brother of Simon Peter, they were Jesus's first disciples. Originally called Kilrymont, the name of this town became St Andrews in AD357. Legend has it that a Greek Monk, St Rule, was told by an angel to take the remains of St Andrew to the 'ends of the earth' and this instruction led him to this point in Scotland.

St Andrews University is the oldest in Scotland and the third oldest in the English-speaking world.

St Andrews Old Course had eleven holes which were played out and back again, making a total of 22 holes. In 1764 it became nine holes out and the same nine holes in. It was turned into a proper 18 hole course in 1832 with nine holes out and a different nine back. The holes out and then back convention originated at St Andrews due to the layout of the Old Course.

In 2000 Tiger Woods won his first Open Championship at St Andrews in 269 strokes. When playing at the course now he will only stay in room 269 at the hotel.

Salen, Inverness-shire

Salen stands on the coast of the Ardanmurchan peninsula which is the most westerly point of mainland Britain.

Salen, Argyll and Bute

Sàilean Dubh Chaluim Chille is the full name of this village on the Isle of Mull. It was once a stopping-off point for the ferry from Craignure to Tobermory.

Scalloway, Shetland
Scalloway on Mainland was once the capital of Shetland. (See Lerwick)

Schiehallion, Perth and Kinross
Although this book does not make a habit of listing hills and mountains Schiehallion does warrant its own inclusion. This Munro (Any Scottish mountain over the height of 3,000 feet is classed as a Munro) was used for an 18th-century experiment to 'weigh the world'. Scientist Charles Mason set out to estimate the mass of the Earth in 1774. The mass of a mountain deflects a pendulum, the distance of the deflection can be used to measure the mean density of the Earth and from this the total mass of the Earth can be calculated. Schiehallion was selected for the experiment due to its isolation and almost perfectly conical shape when viewed from the west.

Schiehallion is yet another of those places laying claim to be at the exact centre of Scotland. (See Laggan. See Loch Garry See Newtonmore)

Scone, Perth and Kinross
Scone is pronounced Scoon.

Many Scottish, and later English and UK monarchs, were crowned on the Stone of Destiny from Scone Palace. For a time it lived on a shelf beneath the Coronation Chair in Westminster Abbey where it was located during the coronation of Elizabeth II. The stone now displayed at the Palace is a replica, it is claimed the real stone can be seen in Edinburgh Castle but there are those who say it is actually built into the foundations of Scone Palace. The Stone of Scone is said to be the stone used as a pillow by Jacob when he had his Biblical vision. (See Quarrymill)

Scourie, Sutherland
The 'palm trees' in the grounds of Scourie House are claimed to be the most northerly 'palms' anywhere in the world growing naturally out of doors, but they're not. (See Torquay. See Plockton)

Selkirk, Roxburgh, Ettrick and Lauderdale
Natives of Selkirk are known as Souters, which means cobblers (as in shoemakers not as in a load of old ....)

Selkirk is known for its bannocks. A bannock is a somewhat dry flat bread which is sometimes improved by the addition of dried fruits.

Selkirk's Common Riding takes place on the second Friday after the first Monday in June. (See Lauder)

Shetland, Shetland
The Largest of the Shetland Islands is called Mainland.

Until Princess Margaret of Denmark married James III of Scotland in 1496, Shetland belonged to Denmark.

(See Brae. See Fair Isle. See Lerwick. See Scalloway. See Out Skerries.)

Sleat, Ross and Cromarty
Sleat Peninsula is known as the Garden of Skye. (See Kilmore)

Sligachan, Ross and Cromarty
Sligachan on the Isle of Skye is a small settlement

centred around a hotel built in 1830. The hotel has a microbrewery and nearby are a bunkhouse and a campsite.

South Uist, Western Isles

South Uist is the second-largest of the Outer Hebrides. This is the only place in the British Isles where prehistoric mummies have been discovered. It is believed that in the Bronze Age the mummified body of a man was put on display on the island with fragments replaced as the body deteriorated over the centuries. Several hundred years later the man was joined by a mummified woman. They were eventually buried with a row of roundhouses being built over their graves. The remains of the mummies were excavated in 2001 along with the skeletons of another woman and a baby. The mummified woman was, in fact, parts of three different people arranged to appear to be one. The remains were at least 500 years older than the houses beneath which they had been buried.

Stanley, Perth and Kinross

Richard Arkwright, inventor of the water frame for spinning cloth, was persuaded by local MP George Dempster to set up a cotton mill in Stanley powered by the waters of the River Tay. The village was built to house mill workers.

Stirling, Stirling and Falkirk

In 1507 the first recorded attempt at flight took place here. John Damian donned a pair of false wings and flung himself from the top of Stirling Castle. A dung heap broke his fall and his only injury was a broken thigh. (See Chard. See Malmesbury)

Dated to around 1540, what is allegedly the world's oldest football was found behind an oak panel in

Stirling Castle.

Mel Gibson fought for Stirling Castle in 'Braveheart'. Mary, Queen of Scots, spent much of her life here and was crowned in the castle's Royal Chapel.

Stonehaven, Kincardineshire
The ruins of Duntottar Castle stand on a nearby outcrop. In 1650 the castle was attacked by Oliver Cromwell in an attempt to find the Scottish Crown Jewels after he had destroyed the English Crown Jewels. The jewels had been smuggled out by a group of women who took them to a small church along the coast where they remained hidden for eleven years (the jewels not the women).

Stonehaven hosts an annual fireball ceremony during Hogmanay when crowds gather to see balls of fire swung around on chains until they are finally tossed into the harbour.

Stornoway, Western Isles
Stornoway, the capital of Lewis and Harris, is the second-largest island town in Scotland. (See Kirkwall)

The MacKenzie River in Canada is named after Alexander MacKenzie who was born here. Donald Trump's mother came from Tong, a village four miles from Stornoway.

In Tom Clancy's novel 'Red Storm Rising' RAF Stornoway features as the base for Allied air operations over the North Atlantic and against Soviet-held Iceland.

Strachur, Argyll and Bute
Strachur is a small village situated on the coast of

Loch Fyne. The heart of the village is half a mile inland

Visitors here took thousands of photographs of two roan trees with branches intertwined to form a circle. These trees were moved to a lochside location to make room for road improvements but the move killed them. Two other saplings have been trained into a similar shape to replace them.

Stranraer, Wigtown
Locals call this The Toon, at the time of writing it was unknown how much difference Brexit would make to EU's financial help towards the Stranraer and Loch Ryan Waterfront project.

Stranraer's football club is referenced in the Proclaimers' song 'Cap in Hand': 'I can understand why Stranraer lie so lowly, they could save a lot of points by signing Hib's goalie'.

The Duchess of Stranraer makes an appearance in the Alan Partridge 'Knowing Me, Knowing You' radio series. There is no such person as this Duchess.

Strathpeffer, Ross and Cromarty
Strathpeffer is on the upper reaches of the Strath Peffer valley.
This village looks very un-Scottish thanks to Anne, Duchess of Sutherland and the Countess of Cromartie, who wanted Strathpeffer to look more like the spa towns in Europe. It has been described as a cross between Harrogate and a Bavarian mountain resort.

Until recently the waters could be sampled in a room, now a cafe, on the car park and later in the pump room a little further up the hill.

Stromness, Orkney
The outsides of many homes in Stromness are decorated with whale bones and the town's museum displays many whaling relics.

Sir Peter Maxwell Davies's 'The Yellow Cake Review' was written as a protest at plans to open a uranium mine in this area and includes a piano piece titled 'Farewell to Stromness'.

Strontian, Inverness-shire
Spell Check insists upon changing Strontian to Strontium and there is a connection. Doctor Adair Crawford recognised in 1790 that there was a considerable difference between ores from Strontian and those normally seen elsewhere. He concluded that he had discovered a 'new species of earth' and this was named strontites. The main use for strontites was in the production of sugar from beet, a process used in Germany into the 20th century. The name was changed to strontium to keep in line with other alkaline earths. Strontium is the only element named after a place in the United Kingdom.

T

Tannach, Caithness

Men of Clan Keith and Clan Mackay fought against men of Clan Gunn and probably their allies Clan Oliphant and Clan Sutherland at the Battle of Tannach in what some say was 1438 and others have dated to 1464. There were heavy casualties on both sides but the Keith-led group claimed victory.

Tannochside, Lanarkshire

Tannochside is an area of Uddingston. (See Uddingston)

Taransay, Western Isles

This was once three separate villages, Paible, Raa and Uidh. Since 1974 the island has been uninhabited except on a temporary basis by the cast of 'Castaway 2000' and now a few tourists come to use the facilities the TV show left behind.

The Haa, Shetland

A Haa was a ground-hugging crofthouse.

The Old Haa Museum is in a house built in 1672 for merchant Robert Tyrie. There is a room devoted to the collection of naturalist Bobby Tullock in the museum. (See Burravoe. See Yell)

Thornton, Fife

Thornton's main street has the River Ore at one end and a stream, Lochty Burn, at the other.

Thurso, Caithness

Thurso boasts the UK's most northerly passenger

railway station. Princess Street Station has three car parking spaces and racks for three cycles.

Martin Carr, lead guitarist and song writer with the Boo Radleys rock band, was born in Thurso.

Tobermory, Argyll and Bute
The brightly coloured buildings along Main Street make Tobermory, on the Isle of Mull, popular as a film location. It is probably most familiar from the children's show 'Balamory'. (See Glasgow. See Isle of Mull) Prior to 'Balamory' the town was probably best known for an appearance in the 1963 007 movie 'From Russia With Love'.

People from the Isle of Mull are known as Mullochs.

Troon, Ayrshire and Arran
Famous for Royal Troon, the town has six golf courses. Royal Troon has the longest and the shortest holes in Open Championship golf. The par-5 6th hole, Turnberry, has a length of 601 yards (550 m) while the par-3 8th hole, Postage Stamp, is 123 yards (112 m) with a minuscule 293 sq yard (245 square metres) green.

Tweedsmuir, Tweedale
The Crook Inn claims to be the oldest inn in Scotland. Robbie Burns wrote 'Willie Wastle's Wife' here. (See Kenmore)

Tyrie, Aberdeenshire
The Pictish Raven Stone was discovered in the foundations of the old parish church at Tyrie and was displayed in the porch of the new church. In the 1890s it was built into the interior wall close to the vestry. It takes its name, the Raven Stone, from a bird carved into it but this is more likely meant to be an eagle.

U

Uachdar, Western Isles
Uachdar is a village on the island of Benbecula in the Outer Hebrides. Uachdar is the home of MacLean's, Benebecula's only bakery, where there is also a small shop.

Uddingston, Lanarkshire
From 1947 to its closure in 2003, Glasgow Zoo was located in Uddingston.

Uddingston is famed as the home of Tunnock's, manufacturers of caramel wafers and marshmallow tea cakes. The Tunnock's factory has a candy shop and tea room.

Uig, Ross and Cromarty
Uig is situated on the Trotternish Peninsula, the most northerly point on the Isle of Skye.

The River Rha and River Conon enter the bay at Uig. The lower courses of these two small rivers have attractive waterfalls.

Uigg, Prince Edward Island, Canada, was named by settlers from Uig who apparently had problems with spelling.

Ullapool, Ross and Cromarty
Ullapool's 'palm trees' aren't actually palm trees. (See Torquay. See Scourie. See Plockton.)

Ullapool was founded in 1788 as a herring port, fish is still brought into the harbour at the edge of the town.

In the video game 'Team Fortress 2' Ullapool is the hometown of the Demoman and in the 'X-Men' series of Marvel Comics, Rahne Sinclair, the mutant werewolf, comes from here.

Ullinish, Ross and Cromarty
The only promontory fort on the Isle of Skye is at Ullinish.

The largest building in the area is the Ullinish Country Lodge hotel with just six bedrooms (adults only) which was originally a farmhouse. During their literary tour of the Hebrides Doctor Johnson and James Boswell stayed at this farm.

Ulsta, Shetland
The car ferry from the island of Yell to Toft on Mainland departs from here.

Unst, Shetland
Uist is the northernmost of the inhabited British Isles with its tiny hamlet of Skaw being the most northerly settlement in the UK. The main village is Baltasound, formerly a major herring port, it is the location of the island's airport. (See Baltasound)

Tourists often make a beeline for the Muckle Flugga Lighthouse where they can brag about being the Most Northerly Person in Britain.

Upperton, Lanarkshire
The charmingly-named Hulks Road and Fannyside Road run close to Upperton.

The Upperton tuberculosis sanatorium was converted to a remand centre which has now been demolished.

A three-bedroom flat here was offered with a starting price of £1 in a 2016 online auction, it eventually sold for £20,000.

Urquhart, Inverness
(See Drumnadochit)

V

Vacasay Island, Western Islands
This island in the Outer Hebrides is listed in gazetteers as having a population of 0 persons, which represents 0.00% of the population of Scotland and 0.00% of the population of the UK.

Verran Island, Western Islands
Vera Island has the same population profile as Vacasay.

Vorogay, Western Isles
It would seem that all Scottish islands beginning with V have the same population profile.

Voy, Orkney
Voy is a settlement three miles to the north of Stromness. (See Stromness)

Walkerburn, Tweeddale

Walkerburn was founded in 1854 for workers in the Tweed factories. There is evidence of Bronze Age activity and the Romans came here but the lack of their structures shows they didn't hang around for long.

Wallacestone, Stirling and Falkirk

It is known that William Wallace fought his final battle of the War of Independence somewhere in the area of Falkirk. (See Falkirk) Although the actual battle site hasn't been located, a stone pillar replacing a much older one stands in Wallacestone and is said to mark the place where Wallace stood to view the approaching English Army and to command the battle.

Walston, Lanarkshire

Walston Primary School has so few pupils (approx 40 across the ages 5 to 11 at the current count) that teachers have to double up as caretaker and lunch cook.

Wanlockhead, Dumfries

Wanlockhead is the highest village in Scotland so everything here claims to be the highest. Highest inn, highest shop, highest library, etc, etc.

Robbie Burns stopped here with a friend during the winter of 1789-90 when the weather became so bad they needed to have their horses' shoes sharpened for a better grip. While they waited for the blacksmith to complete his task the two men sheltered at Ramage's Inn and it was here Burns wrote his poem, 'Pegasus at Wanlockhead'. Pegasus being the name of Burns' horse.

Burns returned here in 1792 to explore the lead mines. He travelled with poet Maria Riddell. Riddell mentions what happened in a letter but Burns makes no record of the visit, probably being embarrassed due to having to turn back when he became distressed due to the poor air in the mine.

Waterloo, Lanarkshire
Waterloo was once a village in its own right but is now accepted to be a suburb of Wishaw.

Waterloo, Perth and Kinross
There is also an East Calder and a Mid Calder (See Livingston)

Some claim that this Waterloo took its name from the battle, others say it was named by soldiers from the battle who settled here, and then there are those who believe this to be a hamlet created for widows of those who were killed in the battle.

Close to Waterloo are the Staredam standing stones. Viewed from the road, the right-hand of the two stones bears a carving of a cross that is assumed to be one of the earliest examples of the Christian symbol in Britain.

West Calder, West Lothian
West Calder is the northernmost centre of the Dogs Trust, formerly known as the National Canine Defence League.

Mountaineer Dougal Haston was a pupil at West Calder High.

West Kilbride, Ayrshire and Arran
Although, strictly speaking, a village, West Kilbride is usually considered to be a town along with neighbouring Portencross and Seamill.

The Ministry of Defence lists West Kilbride as one of the UK's leading spots for UFO spotting.

West Linton, Tweeddale
West Linton hosts a traditional festival known as the Whipman Play during which nobody gets whipped.

Linton was considered to hold the largest markets in Scotland which accounts for the Scottish description of any sizeable gathering as being 'Big as Linton Market.'

The railway that first came through here in 1864 was designed by Thomas Bouch who is more famous as the architect of the Tay Bridge which witnessed the deaths of at least 59 people (some records say 75) in the calamitous rail disaster.

Wester Broom, Edinburgh
Wester Broom borders Broomhouse and is sometimes considered to be part of Corstophine or South Gyle, all are districts of Edinburgh. (See Broomhouse)

Whiting Bay, Ayrshire and Arran
Situated on the Isle of Arran, Whiting Bay is a short walk from Eas a' Chrannaig, better known to tourists as Glenashdale Falls.

Scotland's longest pier was once to be found at Whiting Bay.

Whitecraig, East Lothian
Whitecraig's best known eatery is the Mercat Grill. The restaurant owner refers to himself as Head of Happiness and the locals know his father as Pork Chop. Pork Chop enjoys red wine, the chef likes beer and the Head of Happiness's mother drinks rosé wine with her curry.

Wick, Caithness
Robert Louis Stevenson stayed in Wick when his Uncle Alan came to oversee the building of the Noss Head lighthouse. In a letter about the town the author describes it as having 'no beauty'.

Wick Harbour is an isosceles triangle with the mouth of the river at its apex.

Caithness Glass originated here in 1961, production has been moved to Perth.

The first town reached by walkers from John O'Groats to Land's End is Wick. (See John O'Groats. See Land's End)

In 2006 Guinness World records confirmed Ebenezer Place in Wick as the world's shortest street at a length of 2.06 metres with one door leading into it, a door is required to qualify as a street. In previous years it had failed to qualify for the record as it did not have an official postal address.

Wigtown, Wigtownshire
The name Wigtown may come from Wigca's Farm but is more likely to have Norse roots. Vic meaning bay, so it is the town on the bay. The name has absolutely nothing to do with hair pieces.

This is Scotland's National Book Town thanks to the many second-hand book shops and an annual book festival.

After closure in the 1990s Bladnoch distillery is now up-and-running again producing its own single malt.

Windydoors, Roxburgh, Ettrick and Lauderdale
Windydoors Tower was built in the 16th century but only its lowest storey remains and is now part of a farmstead with modern buildings at either end.

Windygates, Fife
Windygates is the sister village of Milton of Balgonie. (See Milton of Balgonie)

Until the late 19th century there were toll gates at the village crossroads close to the Windygates Hotel. The tolls were removed when the village was extended to encompass the Cameron Bridge Distillery.

Withorn, Wigtownshire
Robert the Bruce came here to visit St Ninian's shrine. (See Newton Stewart)

Wishaw, Lanarkshire
Wishaw was the site of the first Christian church in Scotland, Candida Casa, meaning the White House after the stone from which it was made or possibly because it was coated with whitewash, was built in about 397AD by Saint Ninian.

A 12th century enamelled bishop's crozier was found here and is loaned back to the Whithorn Visitor Centre each summer from its home in the National Museum of Scotland.

Yell, Shetland
Yell is the second-largest island in Shetland after Mainland.
(See Burravoe, The Haa and Ulsta)

Windhouse is claimed to be the most haunted building in Shetland. During renovations in 1880 skeletons were discovered beneath the floor and this is probably the main reason why it remained empty for 80 years. An English couple purchased the house in 2003 but, at the time of writing, they have put it back on the market.

WALES

Wales is divided into 22 Principal Areas which are used in this book rather than counties.

A

Aberaeron, Ceredigion
Abaraeron south beach was awarded a Blue Flag in 2005 but the beaches here are mostly steep banks of pebbles with a small area of sand only visible at low tide.

Bass-baritone opera singer Sir Geraint Evans lived in Aberaeron for more than 30 years.

A new-found interest in regional cooking has seen some Welsh restaurants resurrecting Aberaeron Broth. Traditionally served with freshly baked, crusty bread as a main course, the broth is thickened with oatmeal and includes bacon, beef, cabbage, carrots, leeks and swede.

Abercarn, Caerphilly
(See Newbridge)

Aberavon, Neath Port Talbot
Aberavon is a district of Port Talbot. Aberavon Beach, aka Aberavon Sands, holds a Blue Flag and is popular with surfers

Aberbargoed, Caerphilly
Between Aberbargoed and Bargoed was the largest-ever colliery waste tip in Europe. This has been levelled and is now a country park. At the time the colliery closed in 1977 the tip had a height of 400 feet (122 m).

Aberbargoed is in Monmouthshire, neighbouring Bargoed is over the border in Glamorgan. (See Bargoed)

Abercarn, Caerphilly
In September 1878 268 miners died in an explosion at the Abercarn Prince of Wales Colliery. (See Gresford)

Aberdovey, Gwynedd
Also known locally as Aberdyfi. The river here is the Dyfi but to add to the confusion the yacht club on the Dyfi is the Dovey Yacht Club.

In 1597 a ship from the Spanish Armada, the Bear of Amsterdam, missed Milford Haven and ended up in the estuary at Aberdovey/dyfi. Due to high winds the ship was stuck here for ten days but the locals couldn't get to her due to their lack of boats. They attempted to set fire to the ship but the winds blew out the flames. The ship eventually escaped only to be captured by the English off Cornwall.

A 19th century song titled 'The Bells of Aberdovey' refers to the bells of the lost kingdom of Cantre'r Aberdyfi said to ring out beneath the waters of Cardigan Bay.

Aberfan, Merthyr Tydfil
In 1963 local authorities raised their concerns about the millions of tons of mining debris that had been

deposited on the hillside above Aberfan.

After several days of heavy rain a massive section of the debris broke away on the morning of 21st October 1966. A farm and twenty terraced houses were destroyed and the landslide struck the Pantglas Junior School and part of the senior school. 116 children and 28 adults were tragically killed.
The immediate aftermath of the disaster is remembered by few but at the time people were shocked when the Queen refused to visit the village, instead Prince Philip was dispatched to express royal sorrow. The Queen eventually made it to Aberfan eight days after the disaster and in 2002 said her greatest regret in life was not going there immediately.

Abergavenny, Monmouthshire
Abergavenny was the capital of Wales until 1905. It is claimed that it lost its position after failing to pay the five shillings (25p) government City Status tax when a letter requesting the payment got mixed up with junk mail and was binned.

Shakespeare refers to Lord Abergavenny in 'Henry VIII'.

In 1968 a song titled 'Abergavenny' by English pop singer Marty Wilde (Real name Reginald Leonard Smith) reached the top ten in the UK. The song was also a hit in America where Reg's name was inexplicably changed to Shannon.

Abergele, Conwy
'Prince Valiant', starring Edward Fox, was filmed at Gwyrych Castle, Abergele and the castle was used as a training gym in the 1940s by heavyweight boxing

champion Bruce Woodcock and in the 1950s by middleweight champ Randolph Turpin.

A gravestone in St Michael's parish church has an undated inscription reading: 'Here lieth in St Michael's churchyard a man who had his dwelling three miles to the north'. The sea is approximately one mile to the north of the church so the mystery man either had a submarine home or the sea has since advanced in by some considerable distance.

The 33 victims of what was then the worst rail disaster in Britain were buried in the churchyard in 1868.

Abersoch, Gwynedd
Abersoch was once a sleepy fishing village but is now a popular and fashionable seaside resort with excellent beaches. Visitors can take boat trips around St Tudwall's Islands. One of these islands is owned by TV survival presenter Edward Michael (Bear) Grylls.

The Afon Soch River reaches the sea here and the village is also at the end of the A499.

In the 2011 UK Census 51.1% of the village's population registered they were born in England.

Abersychan, Torfaen
Roy (known as Woy) Jenkins was born here. Later in life Jenkins became leader of the SDP but his more important contributions to the nation were when, as Labour Home Secretary, he tried to build what he called a 'civilised society' with the abolition of capital punishment, theatre censorship and the partial

decriminalisation of homosexuality. (See Warrington)

Abertillery, Blaenau Gwent
Abertillery was a major coal mining centre but when the mines closed the area was transformed to a much greener environment thanks mostly to EU funding. 62% of the grateful population of Blaenau Gwent who bothered to vote in the 2016 referendum wanted out of the EU.

Aberystwyth, Ceredgion
Although St David's College awarded degrees before Aberystwyth it was still a college so Aberystwyth University is the oldest University in Wales.

A seafront shelter near Constitution Hill, popular with fish and chip eaters, stands at the former location of the town gallows.

Capel Bangor, three miles east of Aberystwyth, is listed in the Guinness Book of World Records as having the world's smallest commercial brewery. The brewery is in a former toilet and supplies its beers to just one customer, the pub next door.

Afonwen, Flintshire
Afonwen is overlooked by the Moel-y-Park transmitting station which, at a height of 771 feet (235 metres), is the tallest structure in North Wales.

Amlwch, Anglesey
Amlwch is the most northerly town in Wales. It once had a global trade in copper thanks to the world's biggest copper mine at Parys Mountain but it now relies on tourism.

In the late 1950s the Ysgol Syr Thomas Jones

bilingual secondary school at Amlwch was attended by Ian Fraser Kilmioster aka Lemmy of Hawkwind and Motörhead fame.

Ammanford, Carmarthenshire
One of many Welsh towns that built its fortune around a now lost coal mining industry.

Right-wing former MP Neil (Cash for Questions) Hamilton grew up here. (See Saron)

B

Bala, Gwynedd

Bala has hosted the National Eisteddfod on several occasions. The 2009 Eisteddfod made news due to the decision that none of the entrants reached a standard worthy of being awarded the traditional victor's chair.

Actor Christopher Timothy was born here.

Bangor, Gwynedd

Bangor is the oldest city in Wales, there are also two towns in Wales called Bangor. This Bangor claimed city status thanks to its cathedral but wasn't officially confirmed as a city until 1974.

Recreation in Bangor takes place on King George V Field and to confuse things for visitors there are two of these.

During the Blitz sections of the BBC relocated to Bangor.

In 2016 Bangor became the first city in the UK to impose a night-time city centre curfew on under-16s. Civil rights groups opposed the six-month trial introduced by Gwynedd Council.

Pop star Duffy was born here. (See Nefyn)

Bargoed, Caerphilly

Caerphilly County Borough Council defines Greater Bargoed as being the towns of Bargoed and Aberbargoed along with the village of Gilfach. (See Aberbargoed)

When the Bargoed coal mine closed, a factory producing parts for Austin cars and later on specialising in children's pedal cars, became the first in the world where every employee was registered disabled.

The town's Emporium Snooker Club is used for practice by snooker champion Mark Williams. (See Cwm)

Barmouth, Gwynedd
The first area of land donated to the National Trust was Dinas Oleu (Citadel of Light) on the hillside close to Barmouth.

Brummie accents are not rare here as Barmouth is one of the closest seaside resorts to the English West Midlands.

Barry, Vale of Glamorgan
In 1913 Barry was the largest coal port in the world.

Barry Island Pleasure Park began as a few temporary carousels in the late nineteenth century. Since then it has gone through ups and down in popularity but since 2007 has seen a boost thanks to the TV series 'Gavin and Stacey'. 'Gavin and Stacey' families are named after serial killers, the Wests, the Shipmans, with a 2008 Christmas special introducing a character called Peter Sutcliffe. Fred West's ashes were scattered on Barry Island beach. Barry Island offers a 'Gavin and Stacey' bus tour.

The Small Space with just 20 seats is the smallest theatre in the UK. It also converts to become the smallest commercial cinema in the UK. (See Gorseinon. See Parkmill)

Bethlehem, Carmarthenshire
The village celebrates an annual Christmas market which attracts many visitors who come here just so they can post their Christmas cards with a 'Bethlehem' postmark. (See Nasareth)

Beaufort, Blaenau Gwent
Thomas John Woodward was calling himself Tommy Scott when he performed with the Senators beat group in the Beaufort village ballroom. He is now better known as Sir Tom Jones.
Beaumaris, Anglesey
In 1403 Owain Glyndŵr led Welsh forces to take Beaumaris Castle. Glyndŵr was the last native Welshman to hold the Prince of Wales title. Beaumaris Castle is now a World Heritage Site. J M W Turner painted the castle in 1835.

Red Hill is so named due to the blood spilled there in 1648 during the Civil War.

Beddgelert, Gwynedd
Close to this attractive village is Gelert's Grave. Beddgelert means Grave of Gelert. Local legend has it that 13th century Prince Llewelyn had a palace in this village and returned home one day to discover blood all over his infant son's cot and bedroom. Suspecting the worst Llewelyn plunged his sword into his dog, Gelert. The boy then turned up at home unharmed and the body of a wolf that Gelert had killed protecting the boy was discovered. I cannot find another location named after a pet animal's burial place.

Bethesda, Gwynedd
Europe's longest zipline, just short of a mile in length, is in Penrhyn Quarry, Bethesda.

Just down the road from Bethesda can be found the Popty Bakery which supplies traditional Welsh cakes such as Bara Brith to supermarkets across the UK.

Betws-y-Coed, Conwy

Betws-y-Coed is known as Snowdonia's principle village or the Gateway to Snowdonia. Many villages around the UK calling themselves the Gateway to somewhere have little to offer other than their proximity to a location you actually want to visit. Betws-y-Coed, on the other hand, is a beautiful destination in its own right and well worth spending a few nights here in one of the many B&Bs or small hotels.

Swallow Falls, about two miles from the village, is understandably one of the UK's most-photographed waterfalls. A lovely walk through the woods but if you're not feeling active the Falls does have its own small car park plus a pay-and-stay car park across the road. (See Rhydlanfair)

Blackwood, Caerphilly

Blackwood was originally intended to be a model village but shocking working conditions during the Industrial Revolution resulted in this becoming a centre for the Chartist movement in the 1830s. Leading Chartist Zephaniah Williams was from Blackwood and he held regular meetings with other senior figures from the organisation at the Coach and Horses public house.

Before the Titanic disaster became public knowledge the distress signals were picked up in Blackwood by amateur radio enthusiast Artie Moore. Moore later became a senior scientists for Marconi.

The Ancient Druid Inn, Hollybush, Blackwood, was owned by wool merchant Evan James. James and his son James James are credited with writing the words for 'Land of My Fathers' ('Hen Wlad fy Nhadau'), the Welsh national anthem.

Blackwood's modern claim to fame is that it's the home of top Welsh rock band Manic Street Preachers.

Blaenau Ffestiniog, Gwynedd
The Ffestiniog Narrow Gauge Railway and the Slate Mines are top tourist attractions. The railway is owned by the oldest surviving railway company in the world.

During World War Two the National Gallery stored many of its treasures in the local mines. Steel gates installed to protect the artworks can still be seen.

Blaenavon, Torfaen
Parts of the town and surrounding industrial landscape became a World Heritage Site in 2000. Attractions in the town include the Big Pit National Coal Mine Museum.

In 2003 there was a failed attempt to make Blaenavon the second Welsh 'book town'. (See Hay-on-Wye) The main reason for failure of the project was said to have been the town's distance from other principal areas of population.

Blaenffos, Pembrokeshire
This small village developed around a drovers' track that has evolved into the A478.

Bronze Age burial mounds can be seen on nearby hill,

Frenni Fawr, and it is said that a chest of treasure lies in one of these, although excavations have resulted in nothing so exciting.

Local legend claims that fairy folk live on Frenni Fawr and they once took a local shepherd boy to their own country. It was a beautiful and magical land where he was told he could stay for ever so long as he did not drink from a particular well. Of course curiosity got the better of him and, after just one sip, he was transported back to his sheep on Frenni Fawr and nobody had even noticed his absence.

Prince Charles' former official personal harpist (don't snigger), Claire Jones, grew up in the village and was married here in 2012.

Blaina, Blaenau Gwent
Blaina is a small town between Abertillery and Brynmawr. (See Abertillery. See Brynmawr)

Until 1962 Blaina had a railway station on the GWR line.

Bontnewydd, Denbighshire
In 1978 archaeologists working in a cave at the Bontnewydd palaeolithic site discovered teeth and part of a jawbone from a Neanderthal boy who died at approximately the age of eleven some 230,000 years ago. This is the only site in Britain that has produced the remains of a classic Neanderthal.

Borth, Ceredigion
More than 50% of the residents at this attractive seaside resort were born in England. At low tide the stumps of an ancient forest emerge from the waves.

In 1983 the village war memorial had to be

reconstructed after it was struck by lightning.
(See Ynyslas)

Brecon, Powys
Brecon Cathedral began life in 1093 as a Benedictine priory. Brecon is one of several towns in the UK with cathedrals but no city status.

Sarah Siddons is revered as the greatest tragic actress of the late 18th-early19th century. Sarah was born at the Shoulder of Mutton Inn in Brecon High Street when her father's travelling theatre company were performing in the town. The pub is now renamed The Sarah Siddons Inn.

Bridgend, Bridgend
In 1944 a camp was set up at Bridgend to house 1,600 captured German officers. The camp had no sentry towers or perimeter lighting which encouraged inmates to attempt regular escapes. In March 1945 a tunnel was dug from Hut 9 allowing 83 prisoners to make a successful break-out. None of the 83 made it back to Germany, the most fortunate escapees being a group who stole a car and got as far as Birmingham.

Bridgend sand dunes stood in for some of the desert scenes in David Lean's movie 'Lawrence of Arabia', starring Peter O'Toole.

Bridgend's most popular tourist attraction is the McArthur Glen designer outlet shopping mall.

Broad Haven, Pembrokeshire
Broad Haven is a seaside resort with a popular west-facing Blue Flag beach.

In 1977 the town became a Mecca for UFO fanatics

after several claimed sightings and a report in a downmarket tabloid claiming an alien had been spotted in what the paper labelled 'The Terror Triangle'.

Broad Haven South, Pembrokeshire
Not to be confused with the former-mentioned Broad Haven. Broad Haven South is one of the most popular beaches in Wales, it is south-facing, has great views and is backed by woodland belonging to the National Trust.

Brynamman, Carmarthenshire
Split into Lower and Upper Brynamman by the River Amman this village was once known as Y Gwter Fawr or The Big Gutter.

Ynys Dawela Nature Park is to the west of Brynamman with its northern section in the Brecon Beacons National Park.

Welsh anthracite miners had their first union branch at the Tregib Arms in Brynamman.

Brynmawr, Blaenau Gwent
Brynmawr means Big Hill. Most Welsh towns are situated in valleys but Brynmawr is 1345 feet (410 metres) above sea level making it the highest town in Britain. (See Buxton)

Brynmawr furniture is popular with collectors. In 1929 a group of Quakers set about attacking local mass unemployment by opening a furniture factory. A group of skilled men made bespoke furniture designed by a Polish immigrant, Paul Matt, whose designs were inspired by Charles Rennie Mackintosh. Their first order was for 400 chairs for a Quaker school in York. They charged £1 per chair.

Buckley, Flintshire
One of the very few places on the planet that boasts a nearby cement kiln as its most prominent landmark.

In 1420 Henry V gave the manor of Ewole and its pastorage of Buckley to his wife, Catherine of Valois, as a wedding present.

A small lake, The Trap, is stocked with fish for local anglers. During World War Two a German Messerschmitt bomber was shot down as it returned from bombing Liverpool, one of its engines ended up in The Trap.

A ceremonial march, The Jubilee, takes place on the second Tuesday in July. The March is led by the Royal Buckley Brass Band, one of only two in the UK permitted to use 'Royal' in their name.

Buckley's nightclub, The Tivoli, known locally as The Tiv, has hosted bands including Led Zeppelin, Oasis and Super Fury Animals. The Tiv features on the DVD reissue of the Oasis album 'Definitely, Maybe'.

Builth Wells, Powys
Builth Wells has the only working post office in the UK with a contemporary inscription to Edward VIII. (See Bradford-on-Avon)

Bulith Wells claims to be famous as the home of the Royal Welsh Show but, strictly speaking, it isn't. (See Llanelwedd

Burry Port, Carmarthenshire

In 1928 Amelia Earhart became the first woman to fly across the Atlantic. The seaplane, Friendship, landed at Pwll near Burry Port and there is a plaque here commemorating the event. The plaque fails to point out that Earhart was a passenger in the plane piloted by Wilmer Stultz who had help from his mechanic and copilot Louis Gordon. Earhart, acclaimed as the first woman to fly across the Atlantic, later confessed: 'Stultz did all the flying' and she was 'just baggage like a sack of potatoes.'

C

Caernarfon, Gwynedd

In 1955 Caernarfon was in the running to become the Capital of Wales on grounds of its history but Welsh authorities voted 11 for Caernarfon against 136 for Cardiff. (See Cardiff)

Caernarfon became a Royal Borough in 1963 and the Queen upped this status to Royal Town in 1974.

Caernarfon Castle and the town walls are part of the Walls of King Edward in Gwynedd World Heritage Site. The castle hosted the 1969 investiture of Prince Charles as Prince of Wales.

Caerphilly, Caerphilly

Caerphilly is obviously most famous for the eponymous cheese but how many realise that Caerphilly Castle has a tower that leans at an angle of 10 degrees to the vertical, the Leaning Tower of Pisa only leans 3.99 degrees having been slightly straightened from 5.5 degrees due to fears it would topple. The castle is second in size in the UK only to Windsor.

Caersws, Powys

In modern Welsh, Caersws means Fort (caer) Kiss (sws), but it is doubtful that this is what it was originally known as. Some claim the 'sws' part of the name has links with the Roman God Zeus or, more likely, with the British queen Swswen.

Caerwent, Gwent

The Ministry of Defence site at Caerwent was the site used for the World War Two battle in the 'Captain America' movie. 'Dr Who' and 'Torchwood' have also been filmed here, as has the 2006 comedy 'Big Nothing' which starred Simon Pegg and David Schwimmer.

Cardiff, Cardiff

Cardiff has a reputation for rain but there are multiple claims that the city enjoys more hours of sunshine in the average year than Milan. Then there are those who quote actual figures which show Cardiff's average 1553 hours of sunshine compared with Milan's 1900.

Captain Henry Morgan, who gave his name to a popular brand of rum, was born in Llanrumney, Cardiff, other famous people born in the Welsh capital include Shirley Bassey, Charlotte Church and Roald Dahl. (See Llandaff)

The world's first £1 million deal was secured at Cardiff Coal Exchange in 1907.
The world's oldest record store, Spillers, opened in 1894 selling phonograph cylinders and it is still trading.

The 74,500-seat Principality Stadium is the second-largest in the world with a fully retractable roof. The AT&T Stadium in Arlington, Texas, is the largest with its capacity of 80,000. A planned renovation of the Principality Stadium will raise the capacity to a record equalling 80,000.

Much of 'Doctor Who' has been filmed in and around Cardiff. (See Llandaff)

On St David's Day 2004 Cardiff was named the world's first Fair-trade Capital City.

Cardigan, Ceredigion

The wooly cardigan was named after the Earl of Cardigan who was English and had nothing to do with the Welsh town. The Cardigans are a Swedish pop band who, like the Earl, have no links with this town..

Cardigan Bay is the largest bay in the British Isles.

The first eisteddfod took place at Cardigan Castle over the 1176 Christmas period.

The Saturday following the last Friday in April is Barley Saturday when farmers came to town to recruit workers and to hire horses for stud.

Carmarthen, Carmarthenshire

Some supporters of the Arthurian legend claim that Merlin was born in a cave near Carmarthen. The Welsh version of the town's name, Caerfyddin, is said to mean Merlin's Fort. (See Glastonbury. See Melrose. See South Cadbury. See Dolgellau. See Tintagel)

Most people know that Richard III's body was found in a Leicester car park in 2012 (See Leicester) but not many know who put him there. Sir Rhys ap Thomas was the Mayor of Carmarthen. He was a supporter of Richard III but changed sides when Henry Tudor made him a better offer. During the Battle of Bosworth Field in 1485 Rhys killed Richard III with a blow to his head by a long-poled axe.

EU labelling regulations mean that only ham from Parma can be labelled 'Parma Ham'. When the

Romans came to Carmarthen they tasted and enjoyed the local salt-cured ham. They took the recipe back to Italy so Parma Ham was actually invented by the Welsh.

Cemaes, Anglesey
Cemaes is situated on Cemaes Bay which is an Area of Outstanding Natural Beauty partly owned by the National Trust. From your own home you can watch the tide roll in at Camaes via a live webcam.

Chepstow, Monmouthshire
Chepstow is at the Welsh end of the old Severn Bridge. Striguil (or Strigoil) is a Norman castle, the name was also attached to the port. (See Newchurch)

J K Rowling was head girl at Wyedean School and College in Chepstow. Several locations in Harry Potter books are said to be based on the town. Rowling's sixth-form friend owned a turquoise Ford Anglia, there's a flying version of such a car in the Potter books. Rowling's long-haired chemistry teacher, John Nettleship, is claimed to be the inspiration for Severus Snape.

The Welsh Grand National is held at Chepstow racecourse. During World War Two the racecourse became RAF Chepstow.

City, Powys
City is a hamlet and has never been a city.

City, Vale of Glamorgan
Another City that has never been a city.

Clynderwen, Pembrokeshir
The bluestones for Stonehenge were quarried in the

Presell Hills, close to Clynderwen. (See Amesbury)

The railway station goes by the Welsh name for the village, Clunderwen.

Colwyn Bay, Conwy
Colwyn Bay pier was closed in 2009 after the County Borough Council made the owner bankrupt over unpaid business rates. In 2012 the Council purchased the pier from the Receivers and applied for a Lottery Grant to save the pier but their request was turned down. The Council then applied for permission to have the pier's listed status removed so they could demolish it. They were refused permission. Sections of the pier collapsed in 2017 and since then the rest has been demolished for safety reasons. Plans are now afoot to rebuild.

North Wales Police train at Llety'r Dryw, a Grade II listed house, originally built for the uncle of Prime Minister Anthony Eden.
'Monty Python' star Terry Jones was born at Colwyn Bay in 1942.

Conwy, Conwy
Visitors flock to Conwy to see the castle and Thomas Telford's road bridge, the bridge having been designed to match the architecture of the castle, it was one of the world's first suspension bridges. Conwy Suspension Bridge can now only be crossed by pedestrians. The railway bridge was by Robert Stephenson.

The smallest house in Britain is easy to spot as it is painted bright red. The house is 72 inches across, 122 inches tall and has a depth of 120 inches. It was declared unfit for habitation in 1900. It has a bedroom

and living area with basic cooking facilities.
(See Llanrwst)

Corntown, Vale of Glamorgan
(See Ewenny)

Cowbridge, Vale of Glamorgan
To the east of Cowbridge is the claimed site for Owain Glyn Dwr's victory over Henry IV in 1405.

TV presenter Anneka Rice was born in Cowbridge, Sir Anthony Hopkins attended the local school.

Criccieth, Gwynedd
Criccieth is the self-styled 'Pearl of Wales on the Shores of Snowdonia.'

David Lloyd George, a Criccieth solicitor, became a Liberal Member of Parliament in 1890 and served as Prime Minister from 1916 to 1922.

A chain of family-run cafes, Calwalader's, originated as a general store in Criccieth and went on to find fame thanks to their home made ice cream.

Crickhowell, Powys
Crickhowell has a somewhat eccentric 18th century bridge over the River Usk. Said to be the longest stone bridge in Wales it has twelve arches upstream and thirteen downstream.

In 2015 Crickhowell was revealed as the first British settlement to use tax avoidance tactics previously adopted by multinational businesses. This was the town's protest at these large corporations exploiting legal loopholes to avoid UK corporation tax, their philosophy being, if you can't beat them, join them.

Surveyor George Everest, after whom the mountain is named even though he had nothing to do with its discovery, was probably born in Crickhowell. There is some doubt as to where Everest was born but it is a fact that his surname was pronounced Eve-rest.

Royal nanny/companion Tiggy Legge-Bourke spent her childhood at Glanusk Park stately home and now runs the Tŷ'r Chanter B&B.

Cwm, Blaenau Gwent
Cwm is a Welsh word for valley, locals often refer to their home village as The Cwm.

Until its closure in 1989 Marine Colliery in Cwm was the last deep mine work in the Ebbw valleys.

Snooker World Champion Mark Williams was born in Cwm in 1975. (See Bargoed)

Cwmbran, Torfaen
Cwmbran is a new town which was designated in 1949. Older maps show Cwmbran as a single farm in the area now known as Upper Cwmbran. (See Upper Cwmbran)
Burton's biscuits turn out Jammie Dodgers and Wagon Wheels from their factory here.

Cwmtwrch, Swansea
Cwmtwrch means 'Valley of the Wild Boar' and is yet another Welsh location with an Arthurian link. Legend claims that Arthur had a task to clear a pack of wild boar from the Brecon Beacons. Arthur threw a large stone, which can still be seen on the hillside. The stone killed the boar and its body rolled into the river.

Cyfartha, Merthyr Tydfil

The Cyfartha Ironworks are celebrated as one of the greatest industrial enterprises of the late 18th/ early 19th centuries. Although there are claims that Cyfartha was the first major ironworks in the World it was actually the third of five in the Merthyr Tydfil area. (See Vaynor)

D

Dafen, Carmarthenshire

Dafen Welfare Ground is known locally as Dafen Park. The Park was opened in 1926. Workers in the area each subscribed a penny a week towards the project, as a contribution towards maintenance and as a fee for using the facilities. The Park was handed over to Llanelli Borough Council in 1976 but at the time of writing the council was looking at making savings by offloading their interest in the Park.

Dale, Pembrokeshire

Before becoming Henry VII, Henry Tudor landed at Mill Bay, near Dale, prior to the Battle of Bosworth.

RAF Dale was decommissioned after the Second World War and became the Fleet Air Arm's RNAS Dale.

The village is at the entrance to Milford Haven and it is here that, in 1996, the oil tanker Sea Empress grounded spilling more than 70,000 tonnes of crude oil. (See Milford Haven)

Defynnog, Powys

Defynnog is situated in the Brecon Beacons National Park.

The church is dedicated to Saint Cynog and attracts history enthusiasts to see an ancient stone carved with Ogham inscriptions.

Y Gaer, a small hillfort, stands on a ridge close to the village.

Deganwy, Conwy
The hill on which the ruined Deganwy Castle stands has been fortified many times over the ages with the original stronghold dating back to the 6th century. The castle seen today is what is left of Henry III's rebuilding between 1245 and 1250.
In the spirit of Henry's reconstruction of the castle the town has recently rebuilt its Victorian seafront shelter which was damaged in winter storms during 2013/14.

Deiniolen, Gwynedd
It is claimed the Wicklow Mountains in Ireland can be seen from here but a local resident informed me the only mountain he'd ever been able to spot was Holyhead Mountain on Holy Island, Anglesey. Admittedly the said local was on his way out of the Wellington Inn.

Huw Robert Jones was born here and successfully campaigned for the name of the village to be changed from Ebenezer to Deiniolen. In 1924 Jones founded the Welsh Home Rule Army and, as one of the leaders, he attended the founding meeting of Plaid Cymru.

Denbigh, Denbighshire
Denbigh once stood at the top of the hill but, following its destruction in the Wars of the Roses, the town moved to the area which is now the market.

Sir Henry Morton Stanley, who claimed he did actually say 'Dr Livingstone I presume', despite this being disputed by many sources, was born in Denbigh and he is likely to be remembered long after everyone has forgotten another of the town's natives, Amber Davies, who won 'Love Island' in 2015. (See Barnet. See St Asaph)

Denbigh's cinema in Love Lane had an up and down history. In 1928 it opened as the Scala before being renamed the Wedgwood in the 1970s. The Wedgwood Cinema closed in 1980 and was reopened in 1982 as the Futura. This closed in the 1990s to become a video shop. In 1995 it reopened as a cinema but didn't last long due to Peter Moore, the new owner, being convicted of the murder of four men.

Dolgellau, Gwynedd
There are over 200 listed buildings in Dolgellau, the highest concentration anywhere in Wales.

Close to Dolgellau there are three hillforts. Roman coins have been found in the area but it is doubtful there was ever a Roman fort here as, at the time Romans were in Britain, this was an area of bogland.

A field to the south of the village is known as Camlan, which sounds a bit like Camelot, and it is claimed this field was the site of King Arthur's final battle. (See Carmarthen. See Glastonbury. See South Cadbury. See Melrose. See Tintagel.)

Dolwyddelan, Conwy
Prior to World War I this was Dolyddelen and until 1980 the local station was Dolwyddelen. So this has been Gwyddelan's Meadow, Gwyddelan being a saint born some 200 years after the town allegedly got that name so this seems unlikely. It has also been Elen's Meadow, Elen Luyddog founded churches in Wales in the 14th century. To confuse things further the town has Dolwyddelan Castle and Elen's Castle Hotel.

Drefach Felindre, Carmarthenshire
The National Wool museum can be found here. Thanks to the wool trade that once boomed in Drefach Felindre the village is known as the Huddersfield of Wales.

Dulas, Anglesey
Known locally as City Dulas this is a small village that has never been a city. (See City, Powys. See City, Vale of Glamorgan)

Earlswood, Monmouthshire
Earlswood boasts the oldest Methodist chapel in Wales. It was inspired by an occasion when John Wesley preached at nearby Devauden Green. There is a kitchen at the side of the chapel in what was originally a small stable for the preacher's horse.

Ebbw Vale, Blaenau Gwent
Ebbw Vale Steelworks, known locally as The Works, provided steel for the Sydney Harbour Bridge. In the 1930s and 40s this was the largest steelworks in Europe. In the 1960s 14,500 workers were employed here but by the time of its closure in 2002 there were only 450 employees.

In 2010 Ebbw Vale was officially abolished to become Ebbw Vale North and Ebbw Vale South.

Fashion designer Jeff Banks was born in Ebbw Vale.

Edwardsville, Merthy Tydfil
Edwardsville is the area around Quakers Yard Station. The railway came before Edwardsville and Treharris so, although not close to Quakers Yard, this was the only local place with a name at the time. (See Treharris and Quakers Yard)

Elan Valley, Powys
Not a town or even a village but the Elan Valley attracts many tourists and is known as the Welsh Lake District.

Ely, Cardiff
In 1863 a home for orphaned, pauper children, mostly from Cardiff, was opened in Ely. Although now part of Cardiff in the 1880s Ely was an isolated village.

In the 1920s Ely expanded considerably to provide homes for 'heroes' after World War One.
Ely Racecourse closed in 1939 after a fire had destroyed the main stand two years earlier. The last race here was won by Grasshopper, ridden by Lester Piggott's father, Keith Piggott.

In September 1991 a dispute began between a white shopkeeper and an Asian who had started selling bread, allegedly in an attempt to put his competitor out of business. It is claimed this was the spark that fired what became known as the Ely Petrol Riots (or Bread Riots) which made national headlines for several days and resulted in the destruction of a number of homes and shops.

Ewenny, Vale of Glamorgan
Corntown and Ewenny were once distinctly separate villages, now they are one.

The Ewenny Pottery was opened in 1610 and is the oldest working pottery in Wales. Since the early 1800s the pottery has been owned and run by the Jenkins family. Horace W Elliot, a leading figure in the Arts and Crafts movement, made many visits here and designed pots for the Jenkins family. These are highly collectable, especially if they carry Elliot's fleur-de-lys stamp mark. Caitlin Jenkins is the 8th generation of the family, she achieved a ceramics degree from the University of Wales, Caitlin works here with her parents Alun and Jayne (7th generation).

Ewloe, Flintshire
Ewloe is almost in Cheshire.

Liverpool and Real Madrid striker Michael Owen, who now breeds racehorses, grew up in the area and purchased a house here in 2004.

(See Buckley. See Hawarden)

F

Fairwood, Swansea
Fairwood electoral ward is between Gower and Pennard. (See Upper Killay)

Felinfach, Powys
Felinfach is in Felin-fach. The FelinFach company that produces Welsh Blankets and other gifts is not in Felinfach.

Fennifach, Powys
Fennifach is sometimes spelled Fenni-fach or Venni-Vach. In Welsh F is pronounced V.

Fennifach has a celebrated menhir (standing stone) which recent reports claim might easily be missed as the side closest to the road is concealed by ivy.

Ferndale, Rhondda Cynon Taf
At 300 metres above sea level this is the highest town in Rhondda Cynon Taf. Walk a little further up the hill for views of Exmoor in Devon.

A blue plaque in the town centre commemorates the birthplace of actor Sir Stanley Baker.

Fishguard, Pembrokeshire
The last invasion of Britain took place in Fishguard in 1797 when French invaders were allegedly repelled after being frightened by a bunch of scary women wearing Welsh national costume. Armed only with a pitchfork, Jemima Nicholas (Aka Jemima Niclas or Jemima Fawr) rounded up twelve drunken Frenchmen.

The majority of visitors to Fishguard are passing through on their way to the ferry that departs from here for Rosslare in Ireland.

The Richard Burton, Elizabeth Taylor, Peter O'Toole film of Dylan Thomas's 'Under Milk Wood' features Lower Fishguard as Llareggub (which makes much more sense when read backwards). (See Solva) Parts of Gregory Peck's 'Moby Dick' were also filmed here.
Fishguard is immediately to the east of Goodwick. (See Goodwick)

Flint, Flintshire
As the crow flies Flint is less than twelve miles from Liverpool with the Wirral easily seen across the River Dee. It is almost 22 miles between Flint and Liverpool by road.
The name of the town is taken from the platform on which the first castle was built. The original name was le Chaylou which is French for gravel.

Although many people in Flint identify themselves as being Welsh one of my unscientific surveys appeared to show shops displaying more signs in Polish and English than in Welsh.

Fforestfach, Swansea
Fforestfach boasts the largest Tesco Extra store in Wales. Tesco's receive numerous mentions in this book, mostly due to historic sites being buried beneath their carparks.

This is probably as good a point as any to tell readers a few things about Tesco's, if they don't know already.

Tesco heiress Dame Shirley Porter was leader of Westminster City Council. Every time you shop at Tesco you are contributing towards her legacy. Porter oversaw what became known as the 'Homes for Votes' scandal in which rented council houses in marginal wards were sold off to buyers more likely to vote Tory. Shirley called it her 'Building Stable Communities' policy. Some of the people she made homeless were dumped in condemned properties but there is no evidence any of them were moved into stables despite what Porter's name for the project might suggest. Porter was eventually ordered to pay £42 million including interest and costs. At the time, Porter had been found guilty of wilful misconduct, and I can find no evidence of her ever denying reports that she had £70 million in offshore accounts and investments. Porter transferred most of her wealth to other members of her family and then claimed she had assets of only £300,000. The Conservative Party and Audit Commission took pity and agreed to accept a total of £12.3 million in full settlement. Porter then returned to the UK from Israel and purchased a £1.5 million flat in Westminster.

During the Tesco heiress's time as leader of Westminster City Council the Council sold off three cemeteries, three lodges, a flat, a crematorium and more than 12 acres of prime London development land for a total of 85p. (Yes that said 85p)

Shirley Porter grew up in a former council house purchased by her father, Tesco founder Jack Cohen, with the help of a £1,000 loan from the council.

Ffosyffinn, Ceredigion
Maps tell me this is Ffosyffinn but locals pop in two hyphens to make it Ffos-y-ffin. The name means

Boundary Ditch and the said ditch can be viewed from the bridge close to the Red Lion pub.

Birdwatchers gather in Ffosyffinn to view red kites which gather at several feeding stations in this part of Wales.

Four Mile Bridge, Anglesey

Four Mile Bridge is a village spread across both sides of the Cymyran Strait which connects Holy Island with Anglesey. The actual Four Mile Bridge is not four miles long, it gets its name because it is approximately four miles from Holyhead.

G

Ganllwyd, Gwynedd
With just 179 residents at the 2011 Census Ganllwyd has the smallest population of any Welsh council. (See Ysbyty Ifan)

Gelligaer, Caerphilly
St Catwg (aka St Cadoc) is said to have been born here in 500AD and the local church is dedicated to him. (See Glynneath) St Catwg's Church is ancient, probably having been dedicated in 1266, but what you see today has undergone major restoration. Catwg apparently lived with his mother, Gwladys, at Capel Gwladys, the remains of which can still be visited.

Gelligaer's other ancient buildings include the ruins of a Roman fort dated to somewhere around 103-111AD.

Glynneath, Neath Port Talbot
Another one of those Welsh places with a disputed spelling. some have it as Glyn Neath and the Welsh version is Glyn-nedd.

The Brecon Beacons classic waterfall walk starts here with the rivers Melite, Hepste, Nedd and Pryddin all plunging over a series of picturesque waterfalls. The most falls you will find in such a small area anywhere in Wales.

Rhys ap Siancyn, patron of poets, once owned Aberpergwm House which is now in ruins. In the grounds of the house stands St Cadoc's Church. (See Gelligaer)

Goodwick, Pembrokeshire
Goodwick is on the Pembrokeshire coast to the west of its twin town, Fishguard. (See Fishguard) At the time of writing, Fishguard and Goodwick Marina is in the planning stages.

Stop-and-Call, aka Stopancall, was once a separate settlement but it is now contiguous with Goodwick.

The first flight from Britain to Ireland departed from Goodwick's Harbour Village on 22nd April 1912, one week after the sinking of the Titanic.

Gorseinon, Swansea
If not in a pub the locals like to spend their evenings in the Llwchr Workingmen's Club, known to the regulars as The Bug.

Welsh rugby winger/fullback Leigh Halfpenny was born and brought up here. I found it difficult to find anyone in the town who didn't claim to know him.

Gorseinon was the home of the world's smallest cinema (See Barry and Parkmill). For more than 50 years films were shown in a converted railway carriage known as La Charrette. The last film shown at La Charrette was the premiere of Danny Boyle's 'Love Triangle', an event attended by Kenneth Branagh.

Gowerton, Swansea
Gowerton is the self-appointed Gateway to the Gower Peninsula.

This was once the upperclass area of Swansea with white collar workers from the steel industry living here. The white collars have resulted in local residents being known as Starch.

Gresford, Wrexham
Gresford is close to the border with Cheshire and over the years the town has been both English and Welsh.

All Saints' Church in Gresford has more surviving medieval stained glass than any other church in Wales and the church's bells are listed as one of the Seven Wonders of Wales. This is described as the finest parish church in the country.

In 1934 266 men died in an explosion and fire at Gresford Colliery.(See Abercam) Robert Saint composed the hymn titled 'Gresford' to commemorate the disaster. The hymn has no words and is popular with brass bands.

Halfway, Carmarthenshire
An obelisk stands here commemorating the occasion when a mail coach crashed 130 feet down a slope. The coach was a write-off but the driver and passengers survived.

Harlech, Gwynedd
The 13th century Harlech Castle was constructed at the orders of Edward I. There is now a golf course where the sea once came right up to the hill on which the castle stands. 1,000 workers were employed to build the castle at a cost of £10,000 which was 10% of Edward's entire military budget. The castle is so strong it once withstood a seven-year siege. The song 'Men of Harlech' is about this siege.

For many years Baldwin Street in Dunedin, New Zealand, was listed as the steepest street in the world with a gradient of 35%. In 2019 measurements were carried out on Fford Pen Llech in Harlech and this took the title away from its antipodean competitor with a gradient of 37.45%. In 2020 both streets were remeasured along their centres and the title returned to New Zealand when the Welsh contender was downgraded to a slope of 28.6%.

Haverfordwest, Pembrokeshire
Until the Cleddau Bridge opened in 1975 Haverfordwest was the western end of the River Cleddau's lowest crossing point making it strategically important since Roman times and

explaining why the defensive castle was built here in 1100.

Several play centres for children can be found in Haverfordwest along with an adventure farm and Wales' first trampoline park. (See Merlin's Bridge. See Tangiers)

Hawarden, Flintshire
Hawarden is contiguous with Buckley and Ewloe. (See Buckley. See Ewloe)

America is littered with former Presidents' libraries but Britain's only Prime Ministerial Library is Gladstone's Library in Hawarden. This residential library, founded by William Gladstone in 1894, known as St Denial's Library until 2010, has a collection of more than 250,000 printed items. Gladstone's home is known as Hawarden Castle, not to be confused with the medieval Old Castle.

English actress Lady Emma Hamilton, Nelson's mistress and George Romney's muse, was brought up in Hawarden and worked here as a maid from the age of twelve.

Hay-on-Wye, Powys
Thanks to its many book shops (Between 24 and 30 according to who you listen to) and its annual literary festival, Hay-on-Wye is known as the Town of Books. (See Blaenavon). There is a children's section of the Hay-on-Wye Literary Festival known as Hay Fever.

Richard Booth takes the credit for blessing Hay-on-Wye with its literary image when he opened a second-hand book shop here in 1962. Booth proclaimed Hay an independent kingdom, was crowned its king and named his horse Prime Minister. All of this on April 1st 1977.

Hay is twinned with Timbuktu. (Coincidentally Timbuktu has a 'buk' at its heart.)

The late, lamented rock star Ian Dury reworded 'Hit Me With Your Rhythm Stick' when he made one of his final concert performances here: 'From Bombay to Santa Fe' became 'From Bombay', to lovely Hay.'

Tony Benn said the Hay-on-Wye Festival had replaced Christmas in his mind. American Playwright Arthur Miller asked: 'Hay-on-Wye, is that some kind of sandwich?'

Hendy, Carmarthenshire
At Hendy you will find one of the world's leading suppliers of medical leeches. Biopharm UK supplies around 50,000 leeches each year to hospitals mostly in the USA and Japan.

Holt, Wrexham
Holt is linked to Farndon in England by a Grade 1 listed sandstone bridge. The bridge was constructed in 1339 by monks from Chester and was originally topped by a fortified gate house.

Several Bronze Age burial urns have been discovered in the village. Holt Castle was begun by Edward I in 1277 soon after the English invaded Wales. The Church of St Chad has parts dating to the 15th century and there is a medieval market cross in the village centre.

Hollybush, Newport
Hollybush is an area of Newport and is situated just

off the very busy Malpas Road.

Holyhead, Anglesey
St Cybi's Church stands inside a rare three-walled Roman fort. The fourth side was once protected by the sea which came right up to the fort.

The port of Holyhead is a major employer now that Anglesey Aluminium has closed down.

Comedy actress Dawn French was born here and politician Glenys Kinnock attended Holyhead High School.

Holyhead County School became Britain's first comprehensive in 1949 when Holyhead Grammar and neighbouring St Cybil Central School amalgamated.

Holywell, Flintshire
The town takes its name from St Winefride's Well which claims to be the oldest continually visited site of pilgrimage in Britain and has been dubbed 'The Lourdes of Wales'. Until 1930 St Winefride's Brewery stood next to the well.

Some locals claim that Thai Boxing originated in Holywell and, reportedly, impromptu demonstrations of this marshall art break out at pub closing time on occasional weekends.

Actor Jonathan Pryce and TV presenter Gareth (Gaz Top) Jones come from here. If you don't know who Gat Top is ask your granddad.

Hook, Pembrokeshire
Sixty years ago Hook was an important mining village, supplying anthracite across the world. It now has a population of less than 700.

I

Idole, Carmarthenshire
Idole boasts a small housing estate, a primary school and a chapel. I could find no shops, pubs or restaurants in the village and only included it because Wales is very short of locations beginning with I.

Iet-y-bwich, Carmarthenshire
Not much happening here either and they didn't even bother giving it an English name but it does begin with I.

Ilston, Swansea
Ilston is in the heart of the Gower Peninsula and boasts a limestone quarry now owned by the National Trust.

The 'Ilston Book' was taken to America in 1663 by religious leader John Myles (or Miles) and it now resides in the library of Brown University, Providence, Rhode Island. The book is the earliest record of a Baptist church in Wales.

Isallt Bach, Anglesey
225.8 miles (363.4 km) from London and it begins with I.

Islawrdref, Gwynedd
Also known as Islawr Dref, a 2.5 hour walk beginning here is listed as one of the best hikes in the UK.

Isycoed, Wrexham
Isycoed Parish Church, St Paul's, was built in 1827

but there have been two previous churches on this same site. The Grade 2 listed building is unusual in being constructed from brown bricks.

Isycoed is not to be confused with Bangor Isycoed, a few miles to the south, or with Iscoyd parish in Flintshire.

J

Wales has just about as many places beginning with J as it does with I. I can't wait to get to Ll.

Jamestown, Pembrokeshire
Jamestown is alternatively spelled Jameston. In the 17th century Jamestown was recorded as having seven farms, ten houses and one cottage, apart from a small 20th century housing development, things haven't changed much.

Jeffreyston, Pembrokeshire
Jeffreyston is also known as Jefferson. The parish church, dedicated to St Jeffrey and St Oswald, is built on what is said to be an Iron Age enclosure. Saint Oswald was a seventh century king of Northumbria but the Catholic Church claims no knowledge of a Saint Jeffrey.

Jersey Marine, Neath Port Talbot
Jersey Marine includes Pant y Sais Matinal Nature Reserve, an area of reed and sedge beds that is home to many species of birds and insects including Britain's biggest spider, the fen raft spider. Visitors can cross a boardwalk to the centre of the fen.

The Jersey Marine Tower was built in the Victorian era as a viewing platform with a camera obscura. A camera obscura projects an image through a lens onto a wall or screen.

Jersey Marine Beach can be very dangerous due to the tide going out a long way and then cutting off visitors when it sneaks back in concealed behind a number of sandbanks.

Johnston, Pembrokeshire
Johnston is in South Pembrokeshire which is known as Little England Beyond Wales. St Peter's Church has a very English look about it.
If you travel here by rail be aware that trains only stop by request.

Johnstown, Carmarthen
The internet is peppered with houses for sale in Johnstown but some say there aren't enough shops. In 2018 permission was refused for the building of a Co-op and two smaller shops on the site of a closed care home.

Johnstown, Wrexham
Johnstown is on Offa's Dyke. (See Clun)

Yr Hafod in Johnstown is a country park on what was once the former coal tip.

K

Kemeys Commander, Monmouthshire
This was once a commandery. A commandery was a small administrative division, hence the 'Commander' part of the name. Kemeys comes from the Welsh, cemais, meaning a bend in the river and the village does stand at a bend in the River Usk.

Kemeys Inferior, Monmouthshire
Kemeys Inferior is just over ten miles to the south of Kemeys Commander. The old manor house is now a farm.

Kenfig, Bridgend
Kenfig Pool is a National Nature Reserve. Local legend tells us the lake is bottomless but it is actually only about twelve feet deep at its deepest point. This is a part of the largest active sand dune complex in Europe.

Legends from the area of Kenfig village and Sker House were the inspiration for R D Blackmore's three-volume novel 'The Maid of Sker'.

Kerry, Powys
In 1228 Llewelyn Fawr, King of Gwynedd, and Hubert de Burgh, first Earl of Kent, led their troops into the Battle of Kerry. Llewelyn fended off the English army and Hubert was forced to demolish a castle he'd started to build in the town.

The Kerry Hill sheep breed takes its name from this village.

Kilgetty, Pembrokeshire
Kilgetty was the site of Pembrokeshire's last coal mine which closed in 1950.

Pembrokeshire has two versions of the Miners' Walk. The long version of this, six miles, starts and ends at the Kilgetty Community Centre car park. For those who are daunted at the very thought of a six-mile walk, shortly after you begin there's a hotel with a bar and restaurant.

Killay, Swansea
Killay is considered to be an affluent area of Swansea. The village is well above sea level and the southern area is on the common which is used for grazing. The common is part of the Gower Area of Outstanding Natural Beauty.

Wetland habitats are the star attraction at Killay Marsh Nature Reserve. This was once a much larger area of wetland which was reclaimed to be used for housing. What is left of the wetland has been managed by the Wildlife Trust of South and West Wales since 1995.

Kingcoed, Cardiff
Kingcoed (aka Cyncoed) is a suburb of Cardiff and it boasts some of the highest house prices in Wales.

In addition to several churches, Kingcoed has an active synagogue thanks to the large Jewish community here and in neighbouring areas.

Kinmel Bay, Conwy
Kinmel Bay is a coastal resort with views of Rhyl on the opposite banks of the River Clwyd. (See Rhyl). Also known as Sandy Cove, Kinmel Bay has

a popular sandy beach with grey seals sometimes providing entertainment nearby.

The small promenade close to the beach leads to the Kinmel Dunes Nature Reserve. (See Towyn)

Kinnerton, Powys
Kinnerton has two standing stones, one with a rounded top that looks as though it was shaped to mimic a distant hill but this could just be a coincidence.

St Mary's Church looks ancient and the churchyard is partly surrounded by an earthwork but the church is, in fact, a late 19th century building with a 20th century extension.

Knighton, Powys
Although Knighton is in Wales, its railway station is in Shropshire, England, and the town actually stands on the eastern, English, side of a well preserved section of Offa's Dyke. (See Clun)

Knighton has the remains of two castle mottes (mounds) one at Bryn-y-Castell the other in a private garden at the back of the fire station.

Knighton was the venue for a 1970 rock festival. (See Krumlin)

The observatory just outside Knighton is part of the Spaceguard UK project searching for asteroids, it includes a planetarium and Europe's largest camera obscura.

Knighton is mentioned in A E Housman's 'A Shropshire Lad'.

Knucklas, Powys
Knucklas is just three miles away from Knighton and is best known for its 13-arch railway viaduct.

The National Museum of Wales houses three Bronze Age torcs (neck ornaments) found here in 1991.

In 1989 someone set fire to a tyre dump in nearby Heyope and this broke a British record by continuing to burn until 2001.

L

Lampeter, Ceredigion
With a population of less than 3,000 Lampeter is the UK's smallest university town, students add approximately 1,000 to the population. In 1850 the university formed the first rugby team in Wales.

Lampeter might not have the throbbing nightlife of most university towns but students can always look forward to an exhilarating tour of the Welsh Quilt Centre.

Little Haven Pembrokeshire
Little Haven was the first resort in Britain to trial 'No Smoking' signs on its beaches.

Llanaelhaearn, Gwynedd
Llanaelhaearn is the smaller half of a community that includes Trefor. (See Trefor)

Tradition has it that the village takes its name from its Patron Saint, Aelhaiarn, who was a follower of Saint Beuno. In 1865 workers in the churchyard discovered a gravestone with a Latin inscription dedicated to Aliortus of Elmet which suggests a religious settlement here even before Bueno's followers arrived.

Llanbadrig, Anglesey
The name of this village means Church of St Patrick and local legend has it that the church at nearby Cemaes was founded by the saint himself. It is claimed that in 440AD the Patron Saint of Ireland was shipwrecked on Ynys Badrig, the most northerly point in Wales, which can be seen from the churchyard.

Demi Moore's 2006 movie, 'Half Light' is set in Scotland but scenes were filmed in Llanbadrig. (See Onllwyn and Porthdinllaen)

Llanberis, Gwynedd

Welsh landscape painter Richard Wilson and the great J M W Turner painted the ruined Dolbardarn Castle which stands above this village at the foot of Mount Snowdon. The castle is described as the most picturesque in Wales.

The Snowdon Mountain Railway starts its climb from here and this is also at the start of the Llanberis Path which walkers can take on their ascent of Snowdon.

With its mountain setting Llyn Padam has to be one of the UK's most attractive lakes. I was reliably informed that the lake can be walked around at a steady pace in three hours but I found myself in The Heights Bar, close to the lake, where one pint led to another and I never did get to start the walk.

Until the storms of winter 2020, Crib Goch, a mountain ridge near Llanberis, was officially the wettest place in Britain. Over the previous three decades the spot had averaged 4473mm annual rainfall compared with the legendary wetness of Manchester with its average of only 810mm.

Llandaff, Cardiff

Although Llandaff has a cathedral it has never been formerly recognised as a city.

Broadcasting House, Cardiff, the home of BBC Cymru Wales, is in Llandaff which became the home of 'Dr Who' from 2005 to 2012. (See Upper Boat)

Charlotte Church was born here as was Roald Dahl.

Llanddeiniolen, Gwynedd
Llanddeiniolen includes sections of the northern spurs of Snowdon.

A castell is a hill which might be artificial or natural. Llanddeiniolen Castell is natural but has been fashioned in places to take advantage of the defensive opportunities of the location. The southern side of the castell has a distinct terrace. Various sources describe this as a motte, an Iron Age fort or a medieval ringwork.

Llandeilo, Carmarthenshire
The town takes its name from Saint Teilo, there are more than 40 places dedicated to him, mostly in Britain but some in France. Llandaff and St David's Cathedrals both lay claim to his body but it is more likely he was buried in Llandeilo where the Parish Church is dedicated to him and where his baptistery stood in the churchyard until 1880. The connection with the saint was further supported by the discovery of the remains of two important Celtic crosses here. (See Salem)

Llandovery, Carmarthenshire
The Romans knew their fort not far from the modern town as Alabum.

The 13th-century Llandovery Castle is on the site where the Normans had built a castle in the previous century. In 2001 a 16-foot stainless steel statue of Llewelyn ap Gruffudd Fychan was unveiled outside the castle overlooking the place where he was executed at the order of Henry VI.

Llandrindod Wells, Powys
In 1920 the Church of Wales separated from the

Church of England and since then Archbishops of Wales have been elected in Llandrindod Wells due to its central position in the country.

Landon, as the locals call it, is self-promoted as Wales' Premier Spa Town.

In 2018 Llandrindod Wells was named the Happiest Place in Wales. The survey was undertaken by a property website and I would not for one minute suggest this accolade was a cynical attempt to flog houses in the town.
Powys Council meets at Llandrindod Wells. In 2019 Edwin Roderick was suspended as a councillor for slapping a fellow lady councillor's bottom. A character witness told a tribunal, 'It must be said that councillor Roderick is not a sophisticate.'

Llandudno, Conwy
Llandudno is the largest seaside resort in Wales.

The nation has Llandudno to blame for the fact that, following a Tory conference at the resort in 1948, a young Margaret Thatcher made the decision to take up politics.

Lewis Carroll was inspired to write parts of 'Alice's Adventures in Wonderland' while in Llandudno which explains the town's Alice Trail where visitors can meet up with the White Rabbit and other characters.

Professor Codman's Punch and Judy Show has performed in Llandudno for more than 150 years and claims to be the oldest in the country.

The cable car up the Great Orme is the longest in the UK and when you get up there you might be surprised to see more than 100 Kashmir Goats roaming freely around the headland. The goats hit the headlines when they invaded the deserted town centre during the 2020 Coronavirus lockdown. The Great Orme also boasts Britain's only cable-hauled public road tramway.

Llandwrog, Gwynedd
The first ever Sea and Mountain Rescue Team was based here and, in World War Two, RAF Llandwrog was a training airfield and later a weapons storage facility. (See Upper Llandwrog)

Llanelli, Carmarthenshire
Until 1966 the town was known as Llanelly but a public campaign resulted in the spelling going back to its Welsh form.
On a traffic roundabout near the town centre stands a rugby post with a saucepan on top, there's a similar post close to the former Sandy Water Park rugby ground which closed down to become a housing development.

Natives of Llanelli are known as Turks, this is said to be due to former tin workers wearing towels around their heads in turban-style to absorb sweat.

Cars were not provided with spare wheels until 1904 when Thomas Morris Davies and his brother Walter invented a spokeless wheel rim with an inflated tyre, this is still known as the Stepney Wheel but it was invented in Llanelli.

In 1935 Felinfoel Brewery came up with the idea of coating the interior of cans with wax to prevent the tinny taste and they then produced Britain's first canned beer.

Llanelwedd, Powys
Llanelwedd stands on the right bank of the Wye, Bulith Wells is on the opposite bank. Just about the whole world will tell you that the Royal Welsh Showgrounds is in Bulith Wells, it isn't, it's in Llanelwedd.

Llanfairpwllgwyngyllgogerychwyrndrobwlll-lantysiliogogogoch, Anglesey
Llanfairpwllgwyngyllgogerychwyrndrobwllllantysiliogogogoch has 58 characters, so long as I have spelt it correctly, making it the second-longest one-word place name in the world, the longest in Europe and it is usually known as Llanfair PG. The 58 characters are actually 51 letters because ll and ch are considered to be single letters in the Welsh Language.

The literal translation is (The) church of (Saint) Mary (of the) pool of the white hazels near the rapid whirlpool and the church of Tysillo of the red cave.

One source informs me that the long name was invented in 1869 as a publicity stunt to attract tourists by giving the railway station the longest name of any in Britain, however a record of the name has been found dated twenty years earlier than that but still not ancient.

Many people still cross from the mainland via the Britannia Bridge, take a few selfies or family photos by the station sign and then catch the next train back. The first time I came here each letter on the station sign was made from small logs, the sign is now of the standard enamel on sheet steel variety except for being much longer than the standard signs seen elsewhere.

Welsh rock band Super Furry Animals titled their first EP 'Llanfairpwllgwyngyllgogerychwyrndrobwlll-lantysiliogogogoch (In Space).'

Llangammarch Wells, Powys
Llangammarch Wells is the smallest of mid-Wales' four spa villages. (Llandrindod Wells, Bulith Wells, Llanwrtwd Wells and Llangammarch Wells.)

The hamlet from which Llangammarch grew was called Pont-rhyd-y-Fferau which means Bridge Over the Ankle-Deep Ford. The hamlet had a change of name and grew in size when mineral water was discovered here in 1732. It is claimed Llangammarch takes its name from Saint Cammarch, however it is extremely doubtful that a Saint Cammarch ever existed.

Llangollen, Denbighshire
Llangollen is world-renowned for its annual International Musical Eisteddfod.

Tourists are attracted by the Llangollen Railway and also the canal on which horse-drawn boat trips to the Horseshoe Falls can be enjoyed.

Llanneyfydd, Conwy
The river at Llanneyfydd is the Elwy which eventually runs into the Clwyd.

The local pub is the Hawk and Buckle and an online plea for any interesting facts about Llanneyfydd brought a zero response.

Llanrwst, Conwy
Llanrwst's wool trade gave way to the manufacture of clocks and harps but being less than one mile from

the edge of Snowdonia the main industry now is tourism.

In the 13th century Edward I of England built Conwy Castle and prohibited any Welshman from trading within 10 miles of Conwy. Llanrwst, being 13 miles from Conwy, took advantage of this regulation.

It is claimed that in 1947 Llanrwst Town Council made an unsuccessful application for a seat on the United Nations Security Council as an independent state but the UN has no record of this.

Llantwit Major, Vale of Glamorgan
This is a popular surfing area. Since 1983 Llantwit Major has held an annual Victorian Fair Day on the closest Saturday to 22nd June.

Llanwddyn, Powys
Llanwddyn is two miles southeast of the original Llanwddyn village which was submerged in the 1880s when the reservoir, Lake Vyrnwy, was built to provide water for Liverpool.

Llanwrtyd Wells, Powys
Llanwrtyd Wells had a population of 850 at the 2011 census leading it to claim that it is the smallest town in Britain. (See Fordwich and Maningtree)

Cambrian Woollen Mill has existed, on and off, since 1852. It tells visitors they can experience '700 years of weaving history'?

Local sporting attractions are the Bog Snorkelling Triathlon and the World Alternative Games. Unmissable events at the games include Bale of Hay Throwing and Wife Carrying.

Gigrin Farm is an official feeding centre for red kites.

Lower Brynamman
(See Brynamman)

M

Machen, Caerphilly
A local history trail can be followed around the village's coal mines and an old forge.

Machen Mountain offers views over the village.

Maerdy, Rhondda Cynon Taf
Maerdy is situated at the end of the two Rhondda valleys.

An attractive walk in Maerdy crosses a stream over the Frank Owen Bridge. A plaque on the step at the end of the bridge explains that Frank died whilst fighting in the Spanish Civil War.

Maesteg, Bridgend
Yes another former mining town that once boasted a steelworks. A large cosmetics factory has also closed down.

Australian pop diva Kylie Minogue declared that her heart will always be in Maesteg. Her mother and grandmother were born here.

Maesycoed, Rhondda Cynon Taf
Maesycoed is to the southwest of Pontypridd town centre. The Maritime Colliery was here.

Merlin's Bridge, Pembrokeshire
Merlin's Bridge is on the road to Milford Haven and anywhere boasting it's on a road to somewhere suggests there's not much happening there.

There's a chapel, a creamery and a post office. Emails and telephone calls resulted in me discovering that nobody here knows the origin of the place's name and it is extremely unlikely there was ever any local connection with King Arthur.

There are those who claim that Saint David, Patron Saint of Wales, was the son of Saint Non who was a niece of King Arthur and Saint David was born in Pembrokeshire. (See St David's)

Merthyr Cynog, Powys
The church of Saint Cynog is a place of pilgrimage. Cynog was an early Welsh martyr, the son of Prince Brychan. After his murder Cynog's relics were reputedly housed at this church. In 1188 Gerald of Wales claimed that the relics include a royal torc made from gold. (See Merthyr Tydfil)

Close to the village is the Sennybridge Army Training Centre.

Merthyr Tydfil, Merthyr Tydfil
In modern Welsh 'merthyr' means martyr but it is also similar to the Latin martyrium which is a mausoleum or church constructed over relics. Tydfil was a daughter of King Brychan with local legend claiming she was slaughtered here by pagans in the fifth century and a church was built over the place of her martyrdom. (See Merthyr Cynog)

In 1992 local GPs tested a new angina treatment, Sildenafil, on patients in Merthyr Tydfil and reported unexpected side-effect on male patients. Sildenafil is now better known by the brand name Viagra.

The Redhouse Cymru arts centre opened in 2014 in what was the Town Hall.

Statues in the town include tributes to local boxers Johnny Owen, Howard Winstone and Eddie Thomas.

Milford Haven, Pembrokeshire

Sir William Hamilton founded Milford Haven in 1793 as a centre for whaling. The first residents came from Nantucket in the USA which is why the streets follow a US-style grid pattern. Starbuck Road is named after one of the families from Nantucket and the same family is said to have provided the inspiration for Herman Melville's 'Moby Dick'. In case this has got you wondering, the Starbuck's Coffee Company comes last in this name game having taken its title from 'Moby Dick'.

This was known to be a safe port and is mentioned as such in Shakespeare's 'Cymbeline' where the Bard refers to 'blessed Milford'. In 1171 Henry II began his invasion of Ireland from here and Oliver Cromwell launched a similar invasion in 1649. Allied American troops were based at Milford Haven during World War Two.

Milford Haven is the most westerly town in Wales and the furthest from England.

The water garden, opened in 1990 by Margaret Thatcher, had previously been an outdoor swimming pool.

Milford Haven is now one of the leading Liquid Natural Gas terminals. (See Waterston)

Monkstone Beach, Pembrokeshire

Monkstone Beach, known locally as Monkstone Sands, offers safe bathing and rockpools for the children, it is rarely very busy. The beach can be reached off the coastal footpath from a parking area at Trevayne Farm, New Hedges. (See New Hedges)

Monmouth, Monmouthshire
Monmouth was the birthplace of Henry V in 1387, before it became the county town of Monmouthshire. Charles Rolls of Rolls-Royce fame was born here in 1877. In addition to his posh cars and aero engines, Rolls went on to gain everlasting fame as the first Briton to be killed in an air accident in a powered aircraft when the tail fell off his plane during an air display at Bournemouth in 1910 when he was 32-years-old. There is a statue of Charles Rolls outside the Shire Hall.

One of the largest collections of Nelson memorabilia can be found at the Monmouth Museum which, for obvious reasons, was formerly known as the Nelson Museum.

Montgomery, Powys
Montgomery is just a mile from the English border. The town has a model car museum while historical artefacts are displayed in The Old Bell Museum which, as its name suggests, was once a pub.

In 1821 John Davies was sentenced to death by hanging in Montgomery. He constantly disputed allegations of highway robbery and he prayed that, to prove his innocence, nothing would grow on his grave for one hundred years. It is claimed his grave remained grassless for at least a century, it is now grassed over but is still known as the Robber's Grave.

Morfa Nefyn, Gwynedd
The spectacular beach is attracting increasing numbers of visitors with many of the houses being

used as holiday lets. (See Porthdinllaen)

Morriston, Swansea

Although Morriston is part of Swansea and has never been a town in its own right the local football club is called Morriston Town FC.

The Tabernacle Chapel in the town centre has been described as 'the largest, grandest and most expensive chapel ever built in Wales'.

Most Welsh towns boast a male-voice choir, Morriston has two. The Morriston RFC Male Choir was founded by the rugby club in 1979. The Morriston Orpheus Choir has been around since 1935 and has recorded more than 50 albums. Concert performances take the choir on regular trips abroad.

Mumbles, Swansea

There is a Mumbles community, Mumbles district and Mumbles headland. In the Sunday Times' 2018 Best Places to Live in the UK report Mumbles was the top-listed place in Wales.

There is some dispute over how the name Mumbles came about. I think the most likely explanation is that the name originated when French sailors noticed the shape of the two islands that make up the headland and christened these Les Mamelles, meaning the breasts.

Students famously enjoyed pub crawls between the many hostelries on what was known as the Mumbles Mile. Due to numerous pub closures this is no longer the boozy challenge it once was.

N

Nasareth, Gwynedd

Named after Nazareth which becomes Nasareth in the Welsh version of the Bible, 'Y Beible'. (See Bethlehem)

Neath, Neath Port Talbot

Until quite recently Neath was a river port. Silica firebricks, as used in blast furnaces, were invented here by William Weston Young, a Quaker entrepreneur.

Nefyn, Gwynedd

If you look at a map of Wales a bit sticks out just below and to the left of Anglesey, this is the Llyn Peninsula where Nefyn can be found. If the A497 didn't end here it would run into the sea.

Fishing was once so important in this town that herring were known as Nefyn Beef.

Locals will tell you that Aimee Anne Duffy, known to the world just as Duffy, whose 'Rockferry' was the United Kindom's biggest selling album in 2008, was born here. She wasn't but she did spend much of her childhood in the town. (See Bangor)

Newbridge, Caerphilly

Newbridge and Aberdare are now separate townships but were once a single community called Abercarne.

Singer Petula Clark and her sister came to live with their grandparents in Newbridge during World War Two.

Boxer Joe Calzaghe was born in London but his first boxing experience was at the age of ten at Newbridge Amateur Boxing Club. In 2009 he became the first person to be awarded the Freedom of Caerphilly County Borough.

Stephen John Harrington, better known as Steve Strange, leader of Synth-pop band Visage, was born in Newbridge. If you watch David Bowie's 'Ashes to Ashes' video, Steve Strange is the one on the right who appears to bow to Bowie as they walk in front of the bulldozer.

Newcastle Emlyn, Carmarthenshire
Giber Ellyn, the last dragon in Wales, is said to have terrorised the castle here.

Newcastle Ellyn is a Fair-trade Town where visitors cam enjoy walks along the beautiful Teifi Valley.

Newchurch, Monmouthshire
Newchurch is a hamlet consisting of a farm, a church and a few houses.

Castell Troggy is a ruined hunting lodge standing by the Troggy Brook. In the 16th century William Camden mistakenly referred to the ruins as Striguil and this error has been repeated on maps. Striguil is a castle at Chepstow. (See Chepstow)

New Hedges, Pembrokeshire
The New Hedges Tavern used to be the Hunter's Moon.

(See Monkstone Beach)

Newport, Gwent
In 1905 escapologist Harry Houdini began his first international tour in Newport.

A tribute album by radio DJ Marc Riley and Newport singer and drummer Jon Langford, of Mekons fame, takes credit for helping to relaunch the career of Johnny Cash.

A city centre clock was removed in 2008 to make way for the Friars Walk development. The clock, which can now be seen at nearby Llanwern, splits apart each hour, on the hour, to reveal grinning devils and skeletons clutching egg-timers.

Vic Willis, who was the traffic cop in the Village People pop group, moved here with his wife after being released from custody in the US following drugs charges.

L S Lowry's weird painting of a woman with a beard was inspired when the hairy lady boarded a train he was travelling on and sat next to him all the way from Newport to Paddington.

Nolton Haven, Pembrokeshire
Nolton Haven is in the Pembrokeshire Coast National Park almost exactly halfway along St Bride's Bay. The beach is popular with horse riders so be careful where you put your feet when going for a paddle.

The village consists of just a few houses but it does have a pub. The Mariners Inn is set back from the beach and has a beer garden with sea views.

Norton, Powys
Norton is situated on the Offa's Dyke Path.

O

Oakdale, Caerphilly
The sinking of the first colliery here was started in 1907 with the second, the Waterloo Shaft, being sunk in 1911 and the model village beginning to develop shortly after to house the miners. Unusually for a Welsh village the houses were built in fields away from the mine.

York Avenue commemorates the 1920 visit by Prince Albert, Duke of York, who later became King George VI. Albert's visit came after Oakdale had been praised as 'by far the most ambitious attempt by any mining company in South Wales to provide planned housing for its workforce'.

Oakdale Business Park can be accessed via the Chartist Bridge which was opened in 2005 to commemorate the local link with the Chartist Uprising in the 19th century.

Oakford, Ceredigion
Oakford was originally called Derwen Gam but this was changed to the more anglicised name as an aid to commercial travellers.

Most visitors now come here for the holiday village with its static caravans and fishery.

Ogmore by Sea, South Glamorgan
Ogmore by Sea is a village in the community of St Brides Major. (See St Bride's Major) Due to the fast flow of the River Ogmore into its estuary bathing is not encouraged here but Hardee's Bay and Horseshoe

Bay are safe for a swim.

The church, which celebrated its 50th anniversary in 2018, started life with worshippers meeting in one of the village houses.

Old Colwyn, Conwy

Old Colwyn became a separate town from Colwyn Bay in 1974. In 1334 it was known as Coloyne and by the 17th century it had become Colwun.

At the time of writing Old Colwyn Promenade was about to reopen following work to strengthen Victorian sea defences.

Old St Mellons, Cardiff

There are 15 listed buildings in Old St Mellons including two of the four pubs. The village was a recognised stopping point on the route to London partly because it was situated in Monmouthshire which did not have to abide by the Sunday Closing Act that was applied to prevent Sunday alcohol consumption everywhere else in Wales.

At the time of writing there were plans to build 1,000 homes here as part of the Cardiff Local Development Plan.

(See St Mellons)

Onllwyn, Neath Port Talbot

A march is held each St Patrick's Day to celebrate the claim that Ireland's Patron Saint was born in Onllwyn from where he was kidnapped and taken to Ireland by raiders. (See Llanbadrig)

The Onllwyn Miners Welfare Hall was the setting

for the disco scene in the film 'Pride' based on the support a gay and lesbian group from London gave to local miners and their families during the 1984 miners' strike.

Overton, Wrexham
Also known as Overton-on-Dee, and due to become a part of Shropshire following an 1887 Boundary Commission report but the move never happened.

Yew Trees in the churchyard of St Mary the Virgin are one of the Seven Wonders of Wales.

Oxwich, Swansea
Oxwich Castle is claimed to be the oldest on the Gower Peninsula with occupancy records going back to 1459.

St Illtyd's Church overlooks Oxwich Bay. The well in the churchyard is said to be haunted by a ghost that was last seen running across the churchyard before disappearing into the depths.

Oxwich Bay is popular with visitors thanks to its attractive curve of sand.

P

Pant, Merthyr Tydfil
Pant is at the start of the Brecon Mountain Railway.

Ivor Bach who rebelled against English rule is said to be buried close to the old Pant Cad Ivor Inn.

Pant Cemetery opened in 1849 for cholera victims when the cemetery at St John's Church, Dewlaps, had no further spaces.

(See Pant, Shropshire)

Pantygog, Bridgend
The boundary between Pantygog and Pontycymer is the River Garw. (See Pontycymer) An online search for Pantygog produced photographs of attractive ladies in underwear.

Parkmill, Swansea
The West Glamorgan Girl Guides Activity Centre was once the village school while the rural crafts centre was a water-powered corn and sawmill.

An easy walk from the village takes visitors to the Parc Cwm megalithic long barrow which has been partly restored. For those who don't walk there is a free car park.

When La Charente cinema (the smallest in Wales) was dismantled it was rebuilt at the Gower Heritage Centre in Parkmill where it has now reopened. (See Gorseinon. See Barry)

Pembroke, Pembrokeshire
Pembroke Castle has water on three sides, Henry Tudor, the future Henry VII of England, was born in the castle.

Devoted Methodists are expected to sign The Pledge to abstain from all alcohol. In 1764 Methodist founding father John Wesley preached at a chapel in Main Street, ironically in 1866 the chapel became a brewery.

The Pembroke Welsh Corgi is a popular pet but it was designated a vulnerable breed in 2015. Originally bred as a herding dog, the Pembroke Welsh Corgi is likely to have been brought here from Scandinavia in the 12th century or possibly dates even further back to Flemish roots in the 10th century.

Pencoed, Bridgend
Pencoed spreads across both sides of the M4 near to junction 35. Locals will tell you the correct spelling is Pen-coed with stress on the 'coed' part of the name when spoken.

The single-board Raspberry Pi computer is produced here with the Sony Technology Centre turning out 44,000 every week.

Penparc, Ceredigion
Glacial deposits make this a source for sand.

The Battle of Crug Mawr, aka the Battle of Cardigan, is said to have taken place in 1136 on a hill known as Banc y Warren, close to the village. Although no archaeological evidence for the battle has been uncovered there, we do know the Welsh won this battle against the Normans.

Penparc, Pembrokeshire
Penparc also includes a settlement known as Square and Compass.

This is a residential area with modern housing estates and two holiday parks.

Penygraig, Rhondda Cynon Taf
The village was named after the colliery that opened here in 1857. There were several disasters here. Two miners drowned when a mine was flooded in 1875, five years later a gas explosion took the lives of 101 miners out of the 106 in the pit at the time. A further fourteen men died in an explosion in 1884.

(See Williamstown)

Ponterwyd, Ceredigion
150 red kites are fed daily at Bwlch Nant yr Arian, a centre operated by Natural Resources Wales.

As in many Welsh places the locals might try to confuse you by using their native language. Yr Hen Bont means the Old Bridge and it can be found next to the chapel.

The George Borrow Hotel takes its name from Norfolk writer George Henry Borrow who walked through Wales in the 1860s. (See Quaker's Yard)

Pontrhydfendigaid, Ceredigion
Once a place of pilgrimage, Pontrhydfendigaid is close to the Cistercian Strata Florida Abbey. (See Ysbyty Ystwyth)

Caradog Jones, the first Welshman to make it to the summit of Everest, was born here.

Pontycymer, Bridgend
In the Welsh musical comedy movie 'Very Annie Mary' Pontycymer features as the village of Ogw.

(See Pantygog)

Pontypool, Gwent
Pontypool is one of the oldest industrial towns in Wales with links back to the iron industry in the 15th century.

Pool Quay, Powys
The village takes its name from once being the highest navigable point on the River Severn where it served as the quay for Pool, now known as Welshpool. (See Welshpool)

Only just within Wales, the Offa's Dyke Path runs through the village which is across the Severn from Oswestry. (See Clun)

Port Talbot, Neath Port Talbot
Careful how you pronounce this, locals drop the first T so it sounds like 'Por Talbot'.

Several villages were combined to form a town with the name Port Talbot first being used for the docks in 1837, however it wasn't until 1921 that the town was officially known by this name.

Port Talbot is the home of the South Wales Miners' Museum, The Margam Stones Museum with its collection of early Christian stones and crosses and the Baked Bean Museum of Excellence.

The Bean Museum is owned by the former Barry Kirk who changed his name by deed poll to Captain Beany. The museum displays more than 500 bean-related items in Captain Beany's flat. Tata Steel is the largest steel works in the UK and it is here steel is manufactured for most bean cans.

Porthcawl, Bridgend
Kenfig Burrows are sand dunes to the northwest of the town where the remains of Kenfig town and Kenfig Castle were buried in 1400.

The local funfair is called Coney Beach which obviously gives you the clue that it is based on Coney Island in Brooklyn, New York.

Visitor numbers have dropped since the coal mines closed and the traditional Miners' Fortnight ended but there is a large, thriving static caravan park.

Porthdinllaen, Gwynedd
The Scottish fishing village seen in Demi Moore's movie 'Half Light' is actually Porthdinllaen. (See Onllwyn. See Llanbadrig)

The Ty Coch Inn at Porthdinllaen is listed as one of the top ten beach bars in the world and is the self-proclaimed best pub in Wales. The beach connects Porthdinllaen with Morfa Nefyn. (See Morfa Nefyn)

Prestatyn, Denbighshire
Prestatyn still attracts holidaymakers, which it has since Roman times, the remains of a fort with a bathhouse was uncovered by the nearby road from Caernarfon to Chester.

In the 2009 Christmas Special of the TV show 'The

Royle Family' the Royles visit Prestatyn to celebrate Jim and Barb's Golden Wedding and the critically-panned 'On the Buses' movie was filmed at Pontin's Prestatyn.

Major snooker championships, including the World Championship, used to stage their heats at Pontin's Holiday Camp but have since relocated to Sheffield.

Presteigne, Powys
The Welsh/English border wraps around three sides of the town resulting in Presteigne being the self-styled Gateway to Wales.

In 2004 Presteigne made international news when fun-loving mayor, Peggy Fraser-Scott, unsuccessfully attempted to enforce a curfew on the youth of her town.

Pwllheli, Gwynedd
Plaid Cymru, the Party of Wales, was founded here in 1925.
The town has two beaches.

Butlin's holiday camp Pwllheli was renamed Starcoast World in 1990 after 3,500 guests had to depart in 1989 when chalets had been wrecked by a tornado. It is is now Hafan y Mor caravan park operated by Haven Holidays.

Q

Quakers Yard, Merthyr Tydfil
A Quaker burial ground was opened here in 1665. In his book 'Wild Wales' George Borrow says: 'The rays of the descending sun gilded the Quakers' burial ground. A lovely resting place and quite in keeping with the character of the quiet Christian people who sleep within it.' (See Ponterwyd) The burial ground was very small, the Quakers did not want to draw attention to it, it is now even smaller as a road was built through it.

Quaker's Yard is part of the community of Treharris.

R

Radyr, Cardiff
Excavations in nearby Lesser Garth Cave uncovered Stone Age flints. In 1916 a 100 foot (30 m) mound in Radyr Woods revealed Iron Age pottery. Radyr Woods is now a Local Nature Reserve.

A very rare member of the daisy or aster family, Hieracium radyrense, also known as the Radyr Hawkweed, was discovered in the local quarry in 1907. In 1998 nine of the plants were spotted in a Radyr garden, it is thought only 25 of the species survive in the world.

Children's author Roald Dahl lived in Radyr in the 1920s.

'Small Worlds', an episode of 'Torchwood', was mostly filmed around Radyr Primary School.

Raglan, Monmouthshire
Two Roman roads crossed at Raglan. There has been a market here since 1354 with the manor of Raglan Court dating back to 1391. Raglan Castle is mostly 15th century and was built on the site of an Iron Age hill fort. Many of the houses in the village were constructed using stones quarried from the remains of the castle.

Raglan Castle is unusual in having six-sided towers and gatehouses rather than round or square as with most castles. It was built for its beauty not as a defence in battle.

Red Roses, Carmarthenshire
Red Roses relies on farming and tourism. You would think that with a name like this there would be a floral theme going on but the village pub, the Llwyngwair Arms closed in 2014 and reopened three years later as The Sporting Chance.

Red Wharf Bay, Anglesey
In Welsh this is Traeth Coch which means red beach and there is indeed a wide, sandy bay, ten miles of sand at low tide, in an area of Outstanding Natural Beauty.

The village is attractive and boasts three gastropubs with sea views.

Rhiwfawr, Neath Port Talbot
Most of the village was built in the 1930s on a ridge some 900 feet above sea level.

The former primary school and chapel have been converted to houses.

Rhos-on-Sea, Conwy
Dinerth hill fort is on Bryn Euryn, a hill overlooking Rhos-on-Sea.

Harold Lowe is buried in the Llandrillo yn Rhos Church graveyard. Lowe was an officer on the RMS Titanic. He fired his gun to scare off men trying to board a lifeboat before gathering several such boats together and being rescued himself.

Rhos-on-Sea had Britain's first permanent puppet theatre, the 100-seat Harlequin Puppet Theatre opened in 1958 and continues to attract visitors to performances and an exhibition of more than 1,000 marionettes.

Rhydlanfair, Conwy
Many of the houses here are holiday lets rented to people visiting nearby Betws-y-Coed.

Rhyl, Clwyd
Rhyl was a favoured childhood holiday venue for myself with my parents but doom and gloom set in when researching the modern town to discover that the most famous person reported to have come from here is Ruth Ellis, the last woman to hang for murder in Britain. (See Amersham)

The Times called this 'Britain's First Shanty Town' and an edition of 'Rough Guide' claimed 'Anything you can do in Rhyl you can do better elsewhere.'

I thought the Costa-del-Dole label might be a media exaggeration but I have seen unemployment figures in reliable sources ranging from 45% to 67% and with the Sun tabloid laying into the town in 2012 with a claim that the unemployment level was then at 80%. Whichever of these figures you believe, Rhyl had the highest unemployment rate in Britain with an estimated 25% of the 26,000 population living in long-term b&bs. In 2019 BBC News said this area of Wales had the biggest reduction in unemployment, down 20.5%. Although there were doubters claiming the drop was due to the government changing the definition of 'unemployed'. Anyone working for a minimum of one hour per week officially counting as employed.

There being so little to encourage visitors might be the explanation why a plaque was erected to commemorate a rare positive newsworthy occasion when, in 2001, Labour Deputy PM John Prescott punched someone for throwing an egg at him.
(See Kinmel Bay)

Rockfield, Monmouthshire
Just outside the village can be found Rockfield Studios.

In 1970 Dave Edmunds was the first to produce a major hit here with 'I Hear You Knocking'. Since then Hawkwind have recorded several albums at the farm, it is at Rockfield that Ace recorded 'How Long'. Number One albums have been laid down here by Oasis, Black Grape and The Boo Radleys. It is at Rockfield that Queen made their 'Sheer Heart Attack' album and Freddie Mercury completed writing 'Bohemian Rhapsody' which the rest of the band referred to as 'Freddie's Song'.

Roman Bridge Station, Conwy
This is a request stop mostly used by walkers. There is no Roman Bridge village and the actual station building is now a private house.

Railway enthusiasts come here to photograph the quirky station sign which has the Welsh name, Pont Rufeinig incorrectly spelt as Pont Rufenig.

Rosebush, Pembrokeshire
Rhos y Bwlch is Welsh for Gap Moor but the name of the village was anglicised to Rosebush.

Rosebush claims to be the first place in Wales to be supplied with piped water when the Rosebush Reservoir was built in the late 19th century.

Actor Rhys Ifans supported a community fund-raiser to keep the pub open when it was threatened with closure. Tafarn Sinc was built from timber and zinc sheets in 1876 and is the highest pub in Pembrokeshire.

Rumney, Cardiff

Rumney has a castle but is almost certainly best known for its pottery. Rumney Pottery has been run by the Giles family for more than seven generations. Visitors are welcome but are warned that pots cannot be purchased during your visit as everything is custom produced to order.

S

St Asaph, Denbighshire
St Asaph is Britain's second-smallest city in terms of both area and population. (See St David's. See Wells. See London) Although St Asaph has been considered a city for hundreds of years it did not achieve official city status until 2012.

Explorer Sir Henry Morton Stanley spent ten years of his childhood in the St Asaph workhouse. He believed this made him tougher than other explorers and is known to have exaggerated his suffering. (See Denbigh)

St Brides, Pembrokeshire
The parish church at St Brides is dedicated to St Bridget.

The 19th century mansion known as St Bride's Castle was a private home until 1923 when it became a sanatorium. In the 1990s it was converted into holiday accommodation.

St Brides Major, Vale of Glamorgan
St Brides Major's parish church is dedicated to St Bridget (See St Brides)

(See Ogmore by Sea)

St Davids, Pembrokeshire
Every pub quizzer knows that St Davids is Britain's smallest city by population but do they know that the City of London is the smallest by area. (See St

Asaph. See Wells. See City of London) St Davids first became a city in the 12th century, lost this status in 1886 and had it restored at the request of Elizabeth II in 1994.

St David, who was alleged to have lived to the ripe old age of 147 years, died in 588, possibly on 1st March which became St David's Day, and was buried in the cathedral church. The tomb, known as the Shrine of St David, is a reconstruction apart from its ruined base. The remaining bones of St David and those of a hermit, Justinian of Ramsey, were returned to the shrine having been removed by Vikings but were then removed and lost during the Reformation. (See St Non)

In the Middle Ages Pope Calixtus II made the decree that two pilgrimages to St Davids were the equivalent of one to Rome. When travel to Italy was almost impossible for most people St David's made a fortune from poor pilgrims.

St David's College awarded the first degrees in Wales. (See Aberystwyth)

St Mellons, Cardiff
The name is said to come from Saint Melaine who became Bishop of Rennes, Brittany or possibly Saint Mellonius, Bishop of Rouen. One of these bishops is thought to have been born in the area that is now the large housing estate many think of as St Mellons.

(See Old St Mellons)

St Non, Pembrokeshire
Legend has it that St David, Patron Saint of Wales, was born here during a fierce storm, to St Non,

a niece of King Arthur. (See all over the place)
As St David (Dewi Sant) was born the scene was illuminated by an unearthly glow, the storm abruptly ended and a spring of clear water sprang from the ground. The water from here was used as holy water at St David's Cathedral during the Middle Ages. (See St Davids)

The spring can still be seen on the clifftop above St Non's Bay where a stone arch covers the well which is still a place of pilgrimage.

Salem, Carmarthenshire
Salem has no car park and the road is somewhat narrow for on-street parking. The village does have a pub but if you're looking for a restaurant you'll need to travel three miles to Llandeilo. (See Llandeilo))

Saron, Carmarthenshire
This is a mining village close to Ammanford. (See Ammanford)

Saundersfoot, Pembrokeshire
Saundersfoot is on the Pembrokeshire Coast path in the Pembrokeshire Coast National Park. The village railway station is a mile from the village centre.

Saundersfoot hosts an annual cheese festival.

Sebastopol, Gwent
Sebastopol's name is a misspelling of Sevastopol, a Black Sea port that was taken during the Crimean War.

A drive through the town in 2019 revealed an area where lots of housing developments were under construction and with more second-hand car dealerships than one might reasonably expect in such a small place.

Sedbury, Gloucestershire

Included here because everyone told me the place is in Wales so this is probably where they'll look for it in the book. (See Sedbury, Gloucestershire)

Sennybridge, Powys

Probably best known for the Sennybridge Camp and Army Field Training Centre. One of the British Army's main warfare training centres.

Seven Sisters, Neath Port Talbot

The first sod for the building of the village's coal mine was cut, using a silver spade, by Isabella Bevan, a daughter of the co-owner David Bevan. He intended naming the mine after her but his own six sisters also attended the opening ceremony and with seven being a lucky number he decided to name the mine Seven Sisters. This story is disputed by some who claim that the seven sisters were all daughters of Bevan's son, Evan Evans Bevan and there's a Welsh name if ever I heard one.

The former site of the colliery is now a sheltered housing complex.

Skewen, Neath Port Talbot

To the north of Skewan are the ruins of Neath Abbey, a Cistercian monastery.

Gaynor Hopkins was born here in 1951, she is now better known as Bonnie Tyler. Eddie Izzard lived in Skewen during his childhood and it is claimed that American entrepreneur, pilot, film director and philanthropist Howard Hughes came here to visit the home of his grandparents.

Solva, Pembrokeshire
Solva is divided into Upper Solva and Lower Solva. The village and Solva Harbour are at the mouth of the River Solva on the Pembrokeshire Coast Path in the National Park.

Singer David Gray moved to Solva with his parents at the age of eight. Gray attended the local school and his parents ran the Window On Wales shop in the Main Street.

The 2014 movie of Dylan Thomas's 'Under Milkwood' was partly filmed here. (See Fishguard)

Stackpole, Pembrokeshire
The National Trust maintains the Stackpole Estate which includes two beaches and is open to the public.

Swansea, Swansea
The Welsh name for Swansea is Abertawe, Aber being an estuary and the Tawe bit because the city stands on the River Tawe. (See Ynystawe)

Goat's Hole on the Gower Peninsula is the oldest known ceremonial burial site in Western Europe. In 1823 a partial skeleton that had been dyed red was discovered in the Paviland Cave and became known as the Red Lady of Paviland. The Red Lady of Paviland turned out to be a man.

Swansea's clubbing area centres around Wind Street (pronounced as in bind or find). A 200-year-old tunnel connects Wind Street with St Mary's Street.

The Roman Bridge is not Roman, it was built in 1452

and reconstructed in 1750.

Swansea has some good restaurants but for a real local treat try the horsebox serving up shellfish on the Gower from March to October. Locals will also point you to The Big Apple. This is an ice cream kiosk at Mumbles which was originally constructed to promote cider.

T

Taff's Well, Rhondda Cynon Taf
Known to the locals as the Gate to the Valleys, Taff's Well is the home of the only thermal spring in Wales. The warm water spa can be found in Taff's Well Park.

The book and film 'The Englishman Who Went Up a Hill but Came Down a Mountain' is based on a story told to writer Christopher Monger by his grandfather who lived at Taff's Well and the hill featured in the novel is nearby Garth Hill.

Talbot Green, Rhondda Cynon Taf
The £90 million by-pass has three bridges especially constructed for dormice.

The town once had the largest Tesco Extra in Wales but this has now been overtaken by one at Fforestfach. (See Fforestfach)

Talgarreg, Ceredigion
The Glanyrafon Arms has belonged to the same family since 1954. It is the heart of the community, raises funds for local charities and even offers a monthly haircutting service.

Talsarnau, Gwynedd
The village has a pub, The Ship Aground, which should give a clue that Talsarnau stands by the water's edge. (See Ynys Gifftan)

Tangiers, Pembrokeshire
Not much here for visitors but, thanks to the name,

you can con your neighbours into thinking you are having a holiday somewhere far more exotic. Lots to do just down the road at Haverfordwest. (See Haverfordwest)

Tenby, Pembrokeshir
The D-shaped Five Arches Tower was built in the 16th century when there was a panic the Spanish Armada might be about to attack.

One of the world's most important Post-Impressionist artists, Augustus John, was born in Tenby in 1878.

Tenby attracts many tourists with its Castle Beach being voted the best in the UK in the 2019 Sunday Times list.

Thornton, Pembrokeshire
A mile from Milford Haven, Thornton has a 19th century Baptist Chapel and an Iron Age hill fort.

Tintern, Monmouthshire
The picturesque ruins of Tintern Abbey have probably graced as many jig-saw puzzles as Constable's 'Hay Wain'. On the hill to the west of the abbey stands the ruins of the Church of St Mary the Virgin. This medieval church was rebuilt in the 1860s but was left in the state in which it is now seen following a fire in 1977.

The Mason's Arms pub had a name change in 1948. After a visit from Somerset Maugham it took on the title of his novel 'The Moon and Sixpence'.

Tondu, Bridgend
Tondu stands on the River Llynfi which has famously suffered through the centuries from pollution.

Pollution began with the coal mines which poured sulphur and pyrites into the water. Additional pollution came from a paper mill at Maesteg. (See Maesteg)

112 men and boys were killed in an explosion at the colliery in 1892. 112 stones stand as a memorial to those who died.

Towyn , Conwy
Towyn is a seaside resort linked to Kinmel Bay. (See Kinmel Bay)

Treflys, Powys
Treflys is a coastal village with a church dedicated to St Michael. Many cottages here are holiday lets.

Trefor, Gwynedd
Trefor is the larger half of a community alongside Llanaelhaearn. (See Llanaelhaearn)

Granite from the Trefor Quarry is used to make curling stones which mostly go to Scotland.

Tregaron, Ceredigion
The town takes its name from Saint Caron to whom the church, where he is said to be buried, is dedicated. Caron is most probably the person known to the Romans as Carausius who declared himself Emperor of Britain and Gaul in 286. He was the self-styled Emperor of the North prior to his assassination by his finance minister Allectus.

One of Australia's best-known swagmen, Joseph Jenkins, came from Tregaron and lived here until heading south to seek his fortune at the age of 50.

Evan Shelby, frontiersman, scout, surveyor and a captain in America's French and Indian War was elected governor of the State of Franklin (now part of Eastern Tennessee) but turned down the post. Shelby was from Tregaron.

Treharris, Merthyr Tydfil
Treharris Boys and Girls Club is the oldest in the United Kingdom.

The movie 'Sunstruck', which has the alternative title 'Education of Stanley Evans', starred Harry Secombe in his final movie role and was partly filmed in Treharris.

(See Edwardsville. See Quakers Yard)

Tumble, Carmarthenshire
Tumble RFC was formed in 1897 and has won the West Wales Challenge Cup a record twelve times.

World amateur snooker champion (1963 and 1966) Gary Owen, came from Tumble.

U

Undy, Monmouthshire
I would have liked to say this village is named after something found on someone's washing line but Undy is actually an anglicisation of Gwndy which means 'white house'.

A stone coffin containing parts of the skeleton of a young woman, dating back to the 3rd or 4th century when Romans were in the area, was found here during building work in 1996. Tests have shown that the woman was right-handed. Despite a lack of grave goods she must have been from a wealthy family for them to afford such a coffin.

Upland Arms, Carmarthen
Upland Arms is the name of the hamlet but there is no pub here with this name.

The hamlet is best known for its Gwili Steam Railway.

Uplands, Swansea
Uplands has long been a Swansea nightlife centre with the likes of Sir Kingsley Amis and Dylan Thomas frequenting the Uplands Tavern, but not at the same time.

Upper Boat, Rhondda Cynon Taf
There were once three major ferry services across the River Taff and the highest ferry up the river was moored where the Upper Boat Inn is now located.

Episodes of 'Dr Who', 'Torchwood' and 'The Sarah

Jane Adventures' were filmed at the BBC Upper Boat Studios which were ten times larger than the existing studios at Llandaff. (See Llandaff).

Upper Brynamman
(See Brynamman)
Upper Chapel, Powys
The Army's Sennybridge Training Area (SENTA) is to the north of Upper Chapel. Lower Chapel is three miles to the south.

Upper Cwmbran, Torfaen
There was a brewery here until 2009.

The Square is a group of early 19th century miners' cottages.

(See Cwmbran)

Upper Killay, Swansea
The Clyne Cycle Track passes through Upper Killay which is a gateway to the Gower. Fairwood Common starts at a cattle grid to the west of the village and this is the only reference to a cattle grid in this book.

(See Killay)

Usk, Monmouthshire
The English name for the town quite obviously comes from the fact that it stands on the River Usk but in Wales the town is called Brynbuga which is said to be derived from Buga's Hill. I bet Buga came in for some uproarious banter when he popped in to the local pub!

The clock in the town square is a monument to Victoria's Golden Jubilee in 1887.

Uzmaston, Pembrokeshire
Although extensively rebuilt and restored in the late 19th century and again in the 1990s, St Ismael's Parish Church originated in 1230.

V

Valley, Anglesey

I was surprised by Valley as the area is quite flat so I could actually see no valley at all here. There is a bit of a dip that I am reliably informed was created when the Stanley Embankment, connecting Anglesey to Holy Island by rail and road, was built by Thomas Telford who dug his materials from here.

Valley is a small village but the name Valley is usually associated with the RAF station, RAF Valley, where pilots are trained to fly fast jets.

Varteg, Torfaen

In 2013 Varteg made national news when the Welsh Language Commissioner proposed the spelling of the town's name should become the Welsh Y Farteg.

Vaynor, Merthyr Tydfil

Vaynor is within the Brecon Beacons National Park.

Robert Crawshay, owner of the Cyfartha Ironworks is buried in Vaynor churchyard. (See Cyfartha)

Victoria, Newport

Victoria includes the district of Maindee with its large Asian population. Visitors flock into the area in early July for the annual Maindee Festival.

Waen, Denbighshire
A Grade II listed farmhouse in the north of the community is the subject of a letter in the Flintshire County Archives. During the Christmas period of 1812 the tenant of the farm, Robert Roberts, wrote to complain that the house was bewitched. He described poltergeist activity during which stones, coal, water and dung were thrown at the inhabitants. Roberts also claimed that on Christmas Eve spirits threw servants out of their beds.

A bridge with no apparent use, Pont Dafydc, stands in the middle of a field. It was built in 1630 over the River Clwd which was then diverted.

Waterston, Pembrokeshire
Since supplies of North Sea gas dwindled the Dragon LNG terminal, which is partly within the village of Waterston, is expected to process as much as 20 percent of the UK's gas supply. (See Milford Haven)

Waterton, Bridgend
Waterton is the home of the Bridgend Industrial Estate, Waterton Industrial Estate, the Ford Engine plant and Canadian Global Information Technology (CGI Inc). I asked for directions to 'The Park', which I'd read was an attraction, expecting to see trees and maybe a pond but was sent to an area boasting a B&Q alongside several car dealerships.

Waunfawr, Gwynedd
The local railway station has the distinct advantage of being next to the Snowdonia Park Brewpub which has won numerous CAMRA awards.

The Climbing Centre which closed recently was formerly a longwave wireless telegraph transmitting station installed by the Marconi Company to connect wireless messages between London and New York.

Welshpool, Powys
Welshpool is four miles from the border with England. It was originally called Pool but this was changed to Welshpool in 1835 due to confusion with Poole in Dorset.

The octagonal cockpit was forced to abandon its original purpose thanks to the 1849 Cruelty to Animals Act. It is now the headquarters of Welshpool Women's Institute.

(See Pool Quay)

Whitchurch, Cardiff
The Bute family attempted to establish a vineyard here in the 19th century but abandoned the project when their 1887 crop produced only 40 gallons of wine.

Whitchurch Hospital opened in 1908 with 750 patients. Known as Cardiff Mental Hospital it gained an international reputation for its research into mental health.

The national headquarters of the Presbyterian Church of Wales is housed at Whitchurch Tabernacle Church.

Whitebrook, Monmouthshire
Tucked in the Wye Valley, Whitebrook became a centre of water-powered industries from the 17th to 19th centuries. Many residential properties here are in converted mill buildings.

Wick, Vale of Glamorgan
The cliffs at Wick are part of the Glamorgan Heritage Coast. On the cliff edge at Whitmore Stairs can be seen the remains of an Iron Age hillfort.

Wick parish church is dedicated to the Apostle Saint James the Great and dates from the 12th century.

In November 2006 Wick became the first location in the UK to be switched to BT's 21CN (21st Century Network) high-speed broadband.

Williamstown, Rhondda Cynon Taf
Williamstown is a district of Penygraig. (See Penygraig)

Woodstock, Pembrokeshire
Older maps give the village the name Woodstock Slop.

A prehistoric earthwork, Woodstock Ring, shows traces of what could have been a building, indicating habitation in prehistoric times.

Wrexham, Wrexham
The Wrexham Lager Brewery was established by German immigrants in 1881. It was the first successful lager brewery in Britain.

The 18-arch Pontcysyllte Viaduct, a World Heritage Site, is the highest canal aqueduct in the world and the longest aqueduct in Great Britain.

In 1961 Rosemarie Franklin from Wrexham became the first British Miss World.

St Giles is the largest medieval church in Wales.

Local philanthropist Elihu Yales is buried here. Yale was a major benefactor of the American University that took his name. On the Yale campus is a replica of St Giles, Wrexham. The Yale replica building appears in 'Indiana Jones: Raiders of the Lost Ark'.

Wyesham, Monmouthshire
The River Wye separates Wyesham from Monmouth. The Forest of Dean starts just up the hill from Wyesham. Offa's Dyke Path and the Wye Valley Walk are close to the village.

Wyllie, Caerphilly
The colliery closed and the land where it was located is now the site of a small estate of new homes. The former miners' institute is a pub, the post office is closed and the church has been replaced by apartments.

Several of these locations begin with 'Ynys' which is Welsh for 'Island' or 'River meadow'. There are also a number of places with names starting 'Ystrad' which is a flat, wide-bottomed valley.

Y Felineli, Gwynedd
The harbour at Y Felinheli is popular with weekend sailors and includes a marina along with the expected servicing businesses for yachts.

Older maps identify this village by its English name Port Dinorwic.

Y Ffôr, Gwynedd
Y Ffôr was once known as Fourcrosses because it stood at a crossroads. The Fourcrosses Inn was a stopping place for coaches passing through the village and there are indications of occupation going back to the Stone Age.

Yerbeston, Pembrokeshire
Yerbeston Church has a quirky little tower that is partly on the roof and partly propped up on buttresses set in the end wall. At the time of writing there are plans to turn the church into a dwelling.

Ynysddu, Caerphilly
The village was founded by colliery owner John Hodder Moggridge in the early 18th century. Ynysddu is to the south of Blackwood. (See Blackwood)

Ynysforgan, Swansea
Ynysforgan is divided into two by the M4 motorway.

Prior to the construction of the motorway the village was a stretch of the main road from Swansea to Brecon, Clydach Road.

Orpheus Road most likely takes its name from the choir. (See Morriston)

The hill close to Ynysforgan is known locally as the Garth.

Ynys Gifftan, Gwynedd

Ynys Gifftan is in the community of Talsarnau. It is one of 43 islands that can be reached on foot from mainland Britain but are unconnected by bridges. Only try this at low tide.

Although now officially uninhabited, the island does have a cottage, in a state of disrepair, that was occupied until the 1960s.

Ynyshir, Rhondda Cynon Ta

Ynyshir has a history of coal mining and chapels. This could describe any one of hundreds of villages in Wales.

From 1896 to 1910 Ynyshir was the home of Lurvills Delight. This carbonated drink, invented by twins Harold and Lolo Lewis, was popular across Wales. The recipe included stinging nettles, dock leaves and juniper berry extract. Production ceased due to a lack of dock leaves but the drink was revived in 2016.

Ynyslas, Ceredigion

At the time of writing a £12 million coastal defence project is underway to protect Ynyslas and neighbouring Borth. The Ynyslas Sand Dunes are part of the Dyfi National Nature Reserve.

The Aberystwyth Beach Cricket Club played home matches here and were known as the Ynyslas Oval.

Ynysmaerdy, Rhondda Cynon Taf
Ynysmaerdy is the home of the Royal Glamorgan Hospital.

Ynystawe, Swansea
The name comes from Ynys (Island) on the river Tawe. (See Swansea)

The Bodleian Library in Oxford houses the 'Llyfr Coch' ('Red Book') which is the most complete collection of Welsh literature. 'Llyfr Coch' was complied by Hopcyn ap Tomos of Ynystawe, a memorial stone to Tomos can be seen in the park.

Ynysybwl, Rhondda Cynon Taf
Locally this village is known as The Bwl or just Bwl but nobody seems to know what Bwl means. I have explained the Ynys part of the name, in this case it would be a river meadow so maybe a ball game, 'bwl' was played in the field.

Ysbyty Ifan, Conwy
With 196 inhabitants Ysbyty Ifan is the second-smallest community in Wales after Ganllwyd. (See Ganllwyd)

There are mysterious effigies in the church which are thought to represent Rhys Fawr ap Maredudd, (1485-1510) a local nobleman who supported Henry VII at the Battle of Bosworth, Rhys's wife Lowri and his son Robert who was chaplain to Cardinal Wolsey.

Ysbyty Ystwyth, Ceredigion
Ysbyty is Welsh for 'hospital' but there was never a hospital in Ysbyty Ystwyth. The Order of the Knights of the Hospital of St John of Jerusalem built a place of rest (hospice) here for pilgrims on their way to Strata Florida Abbey. (See Pontrhydfendigaid)

Ystalyfera, Neath Port Talbot
In 1893 an iron and tinplate factory was opened in Ystalyfera which was described as 'the largest tinplate manufactury in the world' although I can find no evidence to support this claim.

Ystalyfera became newsworthy in 2017 when a landslide resulted in the forced evacuation of a row of terraced houses. One resident was fined £100 for returning to carry out structural repairs on his home without permission from the council.

Ystrad Meurig, Ceredigion
Recent excavations suggest that what was once thought to be the remains of a 12th century motte and bailey castle is in fact the earthworks of a royal hall complex of 6th to 9th century Ceredigion kings and princes.

Ystrad Mynach, Caerphilly
The pilot episode of the TV comedy series 'Porridge', 'Prisoner and Escort', included scenes filmed on location at Ystrad Mynach railway station.

Ystrad Mynach's Beech Tree Fish Bar briefly made national news in 2018 when a car demolished the front of the shop during the early evening fish and chip service. No-one was killed, three people were hospitalised and the shop-owner said he hoped to prop up the front of his store the following day.

Andy Fairweather-Low, who found fame as leader of the rock band Amen Corner, was born here.

Ystradfelite, Powys
Llywelyn Bren led a revolt against Edward II of England in 1316. He surrendered in Ystradfelite on condition that his men would be spared but he himself was executed in Cardiff two years later.

This is a popular area for walkers with spectacular waterfalls and caves. Porth yr Ogof is close to the village and has the biggest cave entrance in Wales which the River Mellte flows into. Children particularly enjoy Afon Hepste where they can walk along a footpath behind the waterfall.

Ystradgynlais, Powys
Ystradgynlais boomed with the opening of the ironworks in the 1820s, coal mining and light industries continued the financial success of the town.

Not far from the town centre are the Dan yr Ogof caves which it is claimed were once the hideout of the Welsh Wizard, Twm Siôn Cati.

Ystradowen, Vale of Glamorgan
The name of the village means 'Owen's Village' and the main building is St Owain's parish church.

Tom Jones had a home in Ystradowen until 1998.

Ystumtuen, Ceredigion
During the 18th and 19th centuries Ystumtuen was well known as a lead mining village. Silver was also mined here.

A decrease in population in the 1970s was blamed on

the high lead content in the water supply. For a time hippies re-populated the village and recently there has been an increase in the population.